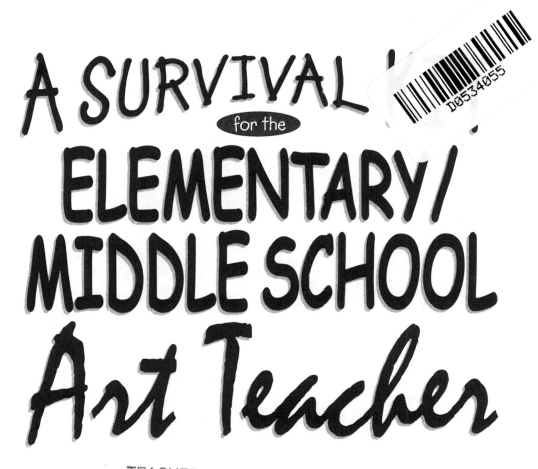

A SURVIVAL KIT for the ELEMENTARY/ MIDDLE SCHOOL Art Teacher

A SURVIVAL KIT

for the

ELEMENTARY/ MIDDLE SCHOOL

Art Teacher

HELEN D. HUME

JOSSEY-BASS
A Wiley Imprint
www.josseybass.com

Published by Jossey-Bass
A Wiley Imprint
989 Market Street, San Francisco, CA 94103-1741   www.josseybass.com

Acquisitions Editor: *Connie Kallback*
Production Editor: *Mariann Hutlak*
Composition: *Inkwell Publishing Services*

Cover Design (left to right): The cover design includes photos of student artwork, courtesy of the following teachers:

Libby Cravens, Claymont School, Parkway District, St. Louis County, Missouri

Sandra Nickeson, founder of the Earth♥Art Collective™, Guardian Angel Settlement Association, St. Louis, Missouri

Beth Goyer, Holman Middle School, Pattonville District, St. Louis County, Missouri

Pamela Olderman, apprentice teacher in Debbie McConnell's art classes at Barretts School, Parkway District, St. Louis County, Missouri

Sandra Nickeson, founder of the Earth♥Art Collective™, Guardian Angel Settlement Association, St. Louis, Missouri

Jossey-Bass books and products are available through most bookstores. To contact Jossey-Bass directly call our Customer Care Department within the U.S. at 800-956-7739, outside the U.S. at 317-572-3986 or fax 317-572-4002.

Jossey-Bass also publishes its books in a variety of electronic formats. Some content that appears in print may not be available in electronic books.

Library of Congress Cataloging-in-Publication Data

Hume, Helen D.
    A survival kit for elementary/middle school art teacher
        p. cm.
    ISBN 0-13-092574-8 (paper)
        1. Art—Study and teaching (Elementary)—United States.   2. Art—Study and teaching
    (Middle School)—United States.   3. Art—Study and teaching—Activity programs—United
    States.   I. Title.
    N362.H86 2000
707.1'2—dc21   99-054597

Printed in the United States of America

PB Printing   10 9 8

Dedication

To my sister,
artist LuWayne Duncan Younghans,
for her lifelong support and inspiration.

ACKNOWLEDGMENTS

Artists and art educators (and teachers in general) are just plain fun to be around. They like to talk, they share, they are excited about what they have chosen to do with their lives. I have been inspired during my visits to observe practice teachers by the respect and support schools give to their art programs. Dr. Ruth Brinkmann, Chairperson of the Education Department of Florissant Valley Community College, kept asking when I would write a book that our elementary and middle school teachers-in-training could use. Hopefully this Survival Kit will answer that need. Tom Lang, Chairperson of the Art Department at Webster University, was one of my professors, and in addition to teaching me, gave me the opportunity to pass on what I have learned to Webster's Apprentice Teachers and Practicum students in art. The education department at Webster University has also offered continuing support.

Artists, art teachers, and apprentice teachers who shared ideas or projects that will be found in the book are Parkway School District colleagues Carolyn Baker, Meg Classe, Jan Cutlan, Libby Cravens, Lauren Davis, Charlotte Headrick, Raizell Kalishman, Laurie Leleu, Debbie McConnell, Kathy McGinley, Beth Scott, Elizabeth Mitchell, Clare Richardson, Timothy Smith, Sue Trent, and Mary Beth Wilson. Others include Lois Beppler, Marilynne Bradley, Steve Bunton, Nancy Chrien, Elizabeth Concannon, Marcie Dairaghi, Kristina David, Dina DeMasi, Jennifer Feise, Beth Goyer, Pat Imming, Mary Ann Kerr, Theresa Long, Phyllis MacLaren, Bill Martin, Luci McMichaels, Melissa Messina, Leigh Mincks, Beth Knoedelseder, Cheryl Niehaus, Pam Olderman, Nora Olive, Diane Papageorge, Larry Peeno (Fine Arts Consultant of the Missouri Department of Elementary and Secondary Education), Maggie Peeno, Dr. Clem Pennington, Nancy Raleigh, Doris Vaughn, Cheryl Venet, Melissa Walker, Cathy Williams, Mary Jo Wilmes, Toni Wilson, Jane Windish, Ronald Young, and Diana Ziegler-Haydon. I'd especially like to express my deepest appreciation to colleagues who have been willing to read and critique portions of the book that relate to developmental characteristics: Marla Mayer, Marilyn Palmer, Dottie Metroulas, and Janet Morris.

The Saint Louis Art Museum continually inspires me as my teachers-in-training and I attend Special Events and Workshops for Teachers. Education Director Dr. Elizabeth Vallance, Educational Department members Barbara Decker Franklin, Dr. Louis Lankford, Carlene Fullerton, Kate Guerra, Jackie Lewis-Harris (now at the University of Missouri, St. Louis), Sue Hooker, and Cheryl Benjamin, and Art Museum librarian Stephanie Sigala and the library staff have been especially helpful to me throughout my teaching and writing career.

Friends, writers, teachers, artists, and colleagues whom I would especially like to thank for allowing me to talk things through are Susan Hume, Johanna Sinks, LuWayne Younghans, Jan Greenberg, Jeanne Klein, and Susan Rodriguez.

My appreciation to the following museum professionals who have assisted with permissions for inclusion in the book of artworks from their collections: Mary Sluskonis, Museum of Fine Arts, Boston; Hsiu-Ling Huang and Carrie Ann Schweiger, The Art Institute of Chicago; Robert Hesleigh, and Sylvia Inwood, Detroit Institute of the Arts; Jacklyn Burns, The J. Paul Getty Museum; Charles E. Brown, The St. Louis Mercantile Library; Stacey L. Sherman, The Nelson-Atkins Museum of Art; Barbara Goldstein, National Gallery of Art; Caroline Demaree, Philadelphia Museum of Art; Kimberly Gilhooly, Norton Simon Museum; and Pat Woods, The Saint Louis Art Museum.

This is an appropriate time to thank Sandra Hutchison, a Prentice Hall editor who first asked me to write a book for teachers based on my articles in *School Arts* and *Arts and Activities*. A special thanks to the entire production team at Prentice Hall, especially development editor Diane Turso and production editor Mariann Hutlak who can take a manuscript and turn it into something that people actually read. It is a long way from concept to conclusion, and the hand-holding and total support of editors Connie Kallback and Win Huppuch of Prentice Hall make the process mostly pleasurable. And my thanks to you, readers, who let me know that what I do is worthwhile.

We thank the following for permitting us to use their artwork.

The Art Institute of Chicago
Red Hills with Flowers, Georgia O'Keeffe; *The Bedroom,* Vincent van Gogh; *Swiss Peasant—The Blacksmith,* Ernst Ludwig Kirchner; *The Waterfall,* Henri Rousseau; *Houses at Chatou,* Maurice de Vlaminck; *The Juggler,* Marc Chagall

The Detroit Institute of Arts
The Violet Jug, Blanche Lazzelle; *Joseph Froehlich, Court Jester of Augustus the Strong,* Johann Gottlieb Kirchner; *Nine Anemones,* Emil Hansen Nolde

J. Paul Getty Museum
Irises, Vincent van Gogh

Museum of Fine Arts, Boston
Pictorial Quilt, Harriet Powers

Museum of Modern Art, New York
Model of Schroder House, Gerrit Rietveld; *Barber Shop Chord,* Stuart Davis; *Three Musicians, Fontainebleau,* Pablo Picasso; *Memory of Oceania,* Henri Matisse; *Portrait of a Young Girl, after Cranach the Younger, II,* Pablo Picasso

Artists Rights Society—Permission to use
Memory of Oceania, Henri Matisse; *Portrait of a Young Girl, after Cranach the Younger, II,* Pablo Picasso

The St. Louis Mercantile Library at the University of Missouri, St. Louis
Arctic Tern, John James Audubon

National Gallery of Art
Arctic Hare, John James Audubon; *The Equatorial Jungle,* Henri Rousseau; *The Cornell Farm,* Edward Hicks; *The City from Greenwich Village,* John Sloan; *Beasts of the Sea,* Henri Matisse; *Lion,* Peter Paul Rubens; *The Harvest,* Vincent van Gogh; *Cutout of Animals,* American 19th Century; *Peaceable Kingdom,* Edward Hicks

The Nelson-Atkins Museum of Art
Olive Orchard, Vincent van Gogh; *Pew Group,* Aaron Wood; *Second Phase Chief's Blanket; Navajo Aquamanile; Pueblo Tesuque, No. 2,* George Bellows; *Edge of Town,* Charles Ephraim Burchfield; *Jane Avril,* Henri de Toulouse Lautrec; *Serape Blanket; Apple Blossoms,* Georgia O'Keeffe; *House Post,* Northwestern Coastal Indians; *Sarah Bernhardt as "La Samaritaine,"* Alphonse Mucha

Norton Simon Museum
Exotic Landscape, Henri Rousseau

Philadelphia Museum of Art
Jug, Attributed Thomas J. Davies Pottery; *Chilly Observation,* Charles S. Raleigh

The Saint Louis Art Museum
Red and Blue Armchair, Gerrit Rietveld; *Side Table,* Gerrit Rietveld; *Bone Coffins; Black and White Head,* Roy Lichtenstein; *Sulphurous Evening;* Charles Ephraim Burchfield; *Composition of Red and White,* Piet Mondrian; *Ballet Dancers in the Wings,* Edgar Degas; *Scholars and Waterfall,* Yang Shanshen; *Old Badger in Misty Bamboo,* Okoku Konnshima; *Side Chair,* Carlo Bugatti; *Pitchy Patchy Costume,* Millicent Matthie; *Chanter,* Emmi Whitehorse; *Storage Jar,* Pre-Columbian; *Mask,* Middle Sepik, Iatmul People; *Headpiece,* Bella Coola People

ABOUT THE AUTHOR

This is art educator/author Helen Hume's fifth teacher resource book. Her previous four books are *The Art Teacher's Book of Lists; American Art Appreciation Activities Kit: Ready-to-Use Lessons, Slides and Projects for Grades 7-12; Art History & Appreciation Activities Kit: Ready-to-Use Lessons, Slides and Projects for Secondary Students;* and *Survival Kit for the Secondary School Art Teacher* (all published by Prentice Hall or its subsidiaries).

She has taught art for over thirty years from elementary through graduate school, including courses in Advanced Placement Art History, Photography, Crafts, Sculpture, Advertising Art, Painting, Drawing, and Ceramics in public schools in the Parkway School District in St. Louis County, Missouri, and in private International Schools in Antwerp, Belgium (where she established the art program) and Sao José Dos Campos, Brazil. She studied painting for three years at Het Vrij Atelier in Antwerp, Belgium and has graduate and undergraduate degrees from Webster University.

Mrs. Hume taught Education and Art for Children methods courses for elementary teachers for many years at Florissant Valley Community College and currently supervises art education and practicum students in art for Webster University, St. Louis, Missouri. She has done presentations at National Art Education Association State and National Conventions, as well as to art educators at the Saint Louis Art Museum.

A painter/printmaker/photographer, she has had one-person exhibits and participates in juried group exhibitions and has served on the Board of Governors and Presidents' Council of the St. Louis Artists' Guild.

ABOUT THIS BOOK

A Survival Kit for the Elementary/Middle School Art Teacher is for beginning art teachers, classroom teachers, and seasoned art educators who might be looking for a new approach to a tried-and-true lesson. The projects can be used at most levels because a complete-in-one lesson might, with modifications, serve as an introductory project for more advanced students. The information in this book comes from my years of teaching at all levels of instruction, National Art Education conferences, and shared (and borrowed) teaching ideas from friends in the field of art. In the past few years I have been privileged to observe apprentice teachers in classrooms at all levels and in many different districts, and am thrilled at the innovative ways art teachers present "standard" information, and their solutions to classroom management. It is no wonder art education is alive and well—it is as much fun as ever, and offers strength to any school's educational philosophy.

I remember hearing a fairly new teacher remark about promoting her art program, getting favorite projects funded, getting support from parents and colleagues, and learning classroom organizational skills. She said, "They didn't teach you how to do that in art school." This book responds to some of those concerns. It is a collection of many tidbits of information to be shared with fellow art teachers. While the book's *organization* is content-centered, it is also strongly student-centered. The lessons are based on the curriculum of art: the elements and principles of design. New skills and techniques are introduced, and most of the lessons can easily incorporate the tenets of Discipline-Based Art Education including production, art history, art criticism, and aesthetics. Each of the lessons enhances the student's *individual* self-expression and problem-solving ability.

Multicultural connections are the basis of many of the projects. As the world becomes smaller through television, the Internet, and other technological advances, the recognition of diversity of the population becomes far more important in teaching art. Some schools are selecting schoolwide themes dealing with diversity to be taught throughout the year. Interdisciplinary connections are also incorporated into many of the projects in the book. Research has shown that students who participate in the arts also perform better in other disciplines such as Math, Social Studies, Science, and Language Arts. Encouraging students to perform or to solve visual arts problems assists them in finding solutions to other problems more easily. Some middle schools use team teaching techniques, with art, music, and unified studies teachers all teaching the same unit to students from their unique perspectives.

The book is divided into two parts:

- Part I contains information about managing the art program that includes handouts on developmental characteristics of students as they apply to art. Another section in Part I has ideas for incorporating art history and appreciation into art and classroom projects. Some of the tips for the teacher in this section are about safety practices, special needs students, photographing student work, matting work, bulletin boards, writing lesson plans, sample lesson plans, grant writing, and advice for the substitute teacher.

- Part II of the book is divided into 9 units on various techniques such as projects using paper, drawing materials, ceramics, three-dimensional materials, architecture, painting, and new technology. Although directions for each project are on the "student" pages, the teacher will have to tell them to younger children, but can hand them out to older students to follow on their own. Everything in this book is reproducible and copyright free.

A special feature of this *Survival Kit* is the more than 50 museum photos—both black and white *and* color—that will greatly enhance your art classroom!

Primarily the book is about students—what they like, helping them feel good about their art, channeling their natural artistic development, and encouraging art as a life-long interest. Whether students like to "do" it or would rather be "appreciators" of other people's art, the "doing" it is especially important in the development of elementary and middle school students. You can allow students to become informed, to make "mistakes," and then find out that using their mistakes is sometimes the best thing that can happen to a work of art. They can learn to like, accept, and value what they and others do.

HELEN D. HUME

CONTENTS

Part I   THE ART PROGRAM

SECTION 1
MANAGING THE ART PROGRAM   3

SECTION 2

MAKING ART HISTORY AND APPRECIATION FUN   55

Part II   THE ART CURRICULUM

Unit 1
EXPLORING THE ELEMENTS AND PRINCIPLES OF DESIGN   81

Contents   *xvii*

UNIT 2

PAPER 129

UNIT 3

DRAWING WITH PENCIL, PASTELS, CRAYONS, MARKERS   165

UNIT 4

PAINTING   203

Contents

UNIT 5

PRINTMAKING   249

Contents

UNIT 6

THREE-DIMENSIONAL DESIGN 277

UNIT 7

CERAMICS 329

Unit 8

ARCHITECTURE, THE BUILT ENVIRONMENT 363

Unit 9

TECHNOLOGY: COMPUTERS, PHOTOGRAPHY, VIDEO 401

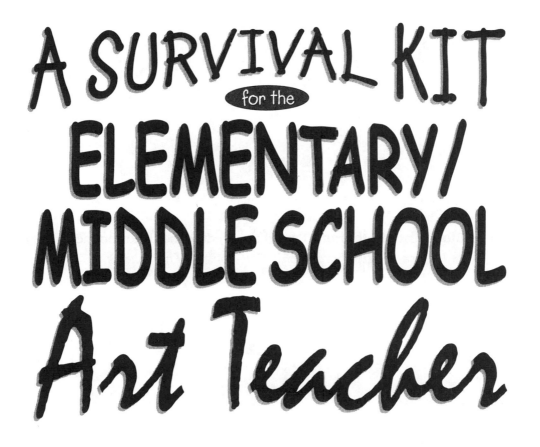

A SURVIVAL KIT for the ELEMENTARY/ MIDDLE SCHOOL Art Teacher

Part I

The Art Program

Section 1

Managing the Art Program

WHY WE TEACH ART

In all our "teacher-talk" about our various purposes for giving art instruction, we know why students so often look forward to their art classes. It is a change and it is fun! It is a time when there is no right or wrong answer, it is impossible to fail, nothing to memorize, your ideas are welcome, almost any solution you devise is acceptable, and you might have an opportunity to socialize with friends.

Art did not become a formal discipline until the late 1800s, and even today art is sometimes considered a "frill." Fortunately for students, most states now require a specific minimum weekly period of art instruction, and even those schools that do not have an art specialist comply by giving weekly art lessons.

Whole-Brain Development Recent research has shown that students who participate in the arts (visual arts, music, drama) perform better in other fields of study. This whole-brain development helps students better develop higher-order thinking skills (HOTS) and problem-solving ability. Students can be *challenged* to come up with creative solutions. It is amazing how inventive students can be when they are allowed freedom within a given project. (This has been labeled a "freefall" approach to teaching versus the "cookbook" approach that often results in all work looking the same.)

Teaching Cooperative Learning Art classes offer the opportunity to create visible evidence of a cooperative (collaborative) art project. In today's culture, learning to work effectively with others is an important skill that is taught throughout the curriculum. When students learn to discuss their ideas, compromise, take turn being "leaders," and appreciate (or at least accept) the contributions of others, they are being helped in their personal development.

Teaching Responsibility Art offers frequent opportunities for each student to take personal and classroom responsibility. When students store their work, get out and put away supplies and equipment for a table, or help the teacher hang a display, they are developing a sense of self-responsibility. If you establish a set routine at the beginning of the year, that includes arriving in class prepared to learn, then you are helping students learn time management.

Teaching Art Appreciation Not all students will feel they can draw competently, and a child may eventually perceive that a classmate draws with more skill than he or she has. Teaching students about various kinds of art and different cultures helps them to appreciate that art does not have to be "pretty" to be valued. Aesthetic conversations about art and artists let them realize that their original ideas have value, and that there are many ways to be artists besides drawing well. Even if "doing" art is not a total visual success for everyone, all students can learn to appreciate art.

Character Development   Art is such a personal thing! If a student feels you do not approve of what he or she has made, it is almost as if you have said, "My, what an ugly face you have." This does not mean that you should never criticize children's art nor that your expectations needn't be high, but simply that students are highly sensitive about their work, and your expectations and suggestions should be phrased carefully. Let them know that you expect their best efforts, and don't hesitate to send them back to develop something further. Try to avoid simply telling a student the work is good. Instead, try for a specific remark, such as "You really made an effort to fill the page," or "I notice that you varied the thickness of your lines." *Ask* them how they think they might improve or complete a composition. If you want to show them how to do something, or you have an idea that might improve their work, draw it on another sheet of paper, or even put tracing paper on top of their work to show them, then wad it up and throw it away. When you draw on a student's work, you are virtually telling them they can't do it so well as you do. I also have misgivings about showing an artwork "sample" you have made when you introduce a project, as students then try to do what they know will be pleasing to you.

Recently I saw a child throw away a work of art that he had worked on carefully all hour. It was as if he were saying "tell me to get it back out and that it is beautiful." My personal opinion is that students should understand from the beginning that they are not allowed to throw away artwork. I tell them that if they don't want their artwork, I certainly do. I also feel students should be expected to manage with just one piece of paper. At a certain age, their expectations are so high that they rarely meet them, and some students keep "starting over," and never get anything finished. Perseverance is important in character development, and art is a wonderful place to reinforce it.

WHAT WE TEACH

Elements and Principles of Design   The Curriculum of Art may be taught in many different ways, but in Western culture it is based on the elements and principles of design. We help students notice differences in shapes and forms, lines, colors, differences in light and dark (values), texture, balance, variety, symmetry, space, and so on through an early introduction to art history, aesthetics, appreciation, and production. Materials become more sophisticated as students learn techniques in ceramics, drawing, painting, computer graphics, and sculpture. Increasingly complex concepts are added, allowing students to build on prior skills and knowledge.

As in other disciplines, National Art Standards have been developed by groups of art educators. State organizations have also been involved in determining what students should know and be able to do at specific ages. Many states are now doing statewide art testing, and those who teach art should become aware of what students are expected to learn in each grade level. Art experiences should revolve around these standards.

National Visual Arts Standards   What students should "know and be able to do in the visual arts Grades K–4, 5–8, and 9–12" has been defined as follows:

1. Understanding and applying media, techniques, and processes.

2. Using knowledge of structures and functions.

3. Choosing and evaluating a range of subject matter, symbols, and ideas.

4. Understanding the visual arts in relation to history and cultures.

5. Reflecting upon and assessing the characteristics and merits of their work and the work of others.

6. Making connections between visual arts and other disciplines.*

DBAE (Discipline-Based Art Education)   Contemporary Art Education is based on the four components of a modern discipline-based art lesson. They may not all be present or used in equal proportions in every lesson, but good curriculum design suggests their use. Art educators are now aware that while doing art (*art production*) is still very important in the development of elementary students, lesson plans should also include the study of art from the past and from other cultures (*art history*), talking about the student's own work and that of others (*criticism/analysis*), and discussing standards of beauty (*aesthetics*).

ART PRODUCTION   Many art educators feel that at the elementary level, the actual process of creating is of crucial importance to students' development. Art-making encourages individual expression and creative problem solving, as well as introducing tools, skills, and techniques that students may use throughout their lives. They can learn to develop personal ideas that will make their own work unique. The materials and techniques vary, but these lessons remain standard because they teach children important things about themselves and their surroundings. A contemporary curriculum may include interdisciplinary and multicultural projects, enhancing all subjects, but these should not exclude the simple process of creating art.

ART HISTORY   The rich heritage of the past can serve as inspiration for today's students. As they learn about artworks, they may be gradually introduced to more complex concepts. Even the youngest students can talk about art through analyzing the elements and principles. Concepts that can be introduced as students advance are: the style used, themes, the artist's name, the time period, date, media, techniques, and the culture from which the artwork came (the who, what, where, when, and why of an art piece). They can learn to recognize the work of individual, representative artists. Students will recognize cultural differences in art, symbolism, and learn about outside influences on art such as literature, patronage, religion, government, and technology.

ART CRITICISM/ANALYSIS   Students need to learn to talk about their own work and that of others. This can be done through art-appreciation activities, games, or through individual and classroom analysis of their own artwork. They learn to compare and contrast images. The process of criticism does not differ vastly from that of the study of Art History. It is based on a description of what is *seen*—the content or subject matter, elements, and principles of design used by the artist, the medium, and the artist's style; *analysis*—why something is unique, what its special qualities are; *interpretation*—what was the message, the artist's intent; and *judgment*—based on the point of view of the critic, and the value and significance of the work (not simply "I like it").

AESTHETIC AWARENESS   Aesthetics, sometimes called *the art of the beautiful,* is considered the Philosophy of Art. In some cultures there is not even a concept that functional, well-designed, useful objects could be considered "art," yet they are aesthetically pleasing. Forms that might be con-

*These standards are taken from a National Art Education Publication, NAEA News, of Spring 1994, Copyright 1994 by the NATIONAL ART EDUCATION ASSOCIATION. Reprinted with permission.

sidered "ugly" to one culture or "unoriginal" to another are perfect for their time or place. Aesthetic discussions seldom lead to actual answers, but may lead to greater awareness that the *idea* rather than the beauty of the artwork may be important. Getting students to define what art is, to ask "why," to talk and even argue about it helps them become more aware of why they make some of their own choices.

Personal Expression   Children draw from the time they can hold a pencil. Through art education, they become more aware of how to depict themselves and their surroundings in more realistic ways, until ultimately they are able to develop a personal style of expression that might be realistic or totally unrealistic. If art education stops at a particular age (for example, fifth grade), often the inability to draw beyond the level of a fifth grader persists as an adult.

Traditional and Nontraditional Techniques   In some cultures, learning to duplicate something as nearly as possible is a technique that is recommended to continue a stylistic tradition. In China, copying the work of an old master is considered a compliment to the master and the tradition. Traditional techniques are also passed down through families, with the young ones learning from their elders. In African carvings and bronzes, for example, stylistic traditions have continued for hundreds of years, and identify a particular region or cultural group.

In Western artistic culture, we tend to stress "breaking the rules" as a way of getting individualistic expression, but students first need an awareness of the "rules" (elements and principles of art) in order to be able to depart from them.

TOPICS WE TEACH

Units   Rather than a random approach to teaching the curriculum, develop units such as a multicultural approach to masks, creating books at all levels (maybe for Library Week), or a unit emphasizing one of the elements or principles of design. Occasionally doing an all-school project such as paper crafts of a particular culture (such as Mexico, Poland, or Germany) gives a cohesiveness to your program that saves it from being just one random project after another.

The following is a list of unit suggestions:

- *animals:* bears, lions, giraffes, zebras, cats, dogs, cows, horses
- *birds:* cranes, parrots, songbirds, geese, ducks, chickens
- *careers in art:* industrial designer, advertising, clothing designer, architect, illustrator
- *circus:* animals, acrobats, clowns, big top, Ferris wheel, merry-go-round
- *dinosaurs:* environment, appearance
- *ecology and environment:* undersea, space, land, tropics, tundra
- *endangered species:* walk through the tropics
- *future:* transportation, clothing, food, roads, buildings, underwater cities, outer space
- *home furnishings:* chairs, patterned rugs, vases
- *insects:* butterflies, ladybugs, spiders, centipedes
- *interdisciplinary subjects:* science and art, music and art, math and art, social studies and art
- *manufacturing:* assembly line, factories, chimneys, machinery

- *multicultural activities:* Native American, Egyptian, European, Hispanic, Asian, African
- *nature:* flowers, leaves, trees, water, clouds, hills, mountains
- *people:* (self, family, community) playing games or ball, eating, standing, sitting, celebrating
- *reptiles:* alligators, frogs, snakes, crocodiles, turtles
- *transportation:* skates, bicycles, cars, trucks, trains, helicopters, planes, rockets, boats
- *weather:* seasons of the year (clothing for various seasons), changes in nature or atmosphere
- *what people celebrate:* holidays, birthdays, vacations, graduations, weddings, dinner out, parties
- *what people do:* doctors, nurses, servers, actors, teachers, cooks, bus drivers
- *what people feel (emotions):* anger, love, sadness
- *what people use:* cars, shoes, TVs, airplanes, computers, helicopters, transistors, cameras
- *what people wear:* hats, shoes, sunglasses, uniforms, masks, hair styles, ties
- *where people live:* cities, countryside, community
- *where people work:* firehouse, McDonald's, shoe store, grocery store, theater, studio

Middle School Teaming   Many school districts include the visual arts in team teaching. Some have an "arts elective" that might include Music, Art, Dance, and Drama. At the middle school level, for example, Rockwood School District in St. Louis County combines Unified Studies, Music, and Art.

Multicultural Connections   An awareness of the diversity of the student population gives art teachers an opportunity to foster sensitivity in students. When you are teaching something "in the manner of . . . " (a culture), allow students to tell you what they know. Take the opportunity to teach some aspect of the lives of a culture or ethnic group that goes beyond just the artwork. It is important not to trivialize other cultures by simply copying something they have done, but to discuss the *reason* behind their artwork. Why they made masks, for example, or what part the masks played (and perhaps still play) in that culture.

Interdisciplinary Connections   Art teachers are well aware that they teach many things besides art; that while art does have its own curriculum, this curriculum often can be effectively combined with subject matter from other sources. Interdisciplinary teaching with art is important, but it must get beyond map-making. Art projects enhance other subjects, but mustn't take away from the doing and appreciation of art, particularly at the elementary level.

Interdisciplinary learning is beneficial to the classroom teacher, the student, and the art teacher. As the art teacher, you can help the students (and their teachers) with projects that serve both subjects well. Effective art specialists at the elementary level make an effort to become aware of what students are studying in their regular classes. Take home social studies books during the summer and talk with the classroom teachers to find out when they will be studying particular units. If you are a classroom teacher who will teach art, try some creative approaches to integrating art in your regular lessons. This eliminates some of the necessity of explaining to students how something is structured.

An example would be a unit on dinosaurs for students who are studying them in class. A natural art outcome is for them to create dinosaurs in clay. If fourth graders are studying Egyptians, then this is a wonderful opportunity to do artwork based on the Egyptian culture.

When students measure something, they are using knowledge gained in math. When they write a poem about an artwork, their language arts training is used. If students can make a work of art in the manner of people of a certain country, then it is both an art project and a social studies project. The following list offers suggestions for several interdisciplinary connections:

Foreign language:

- learning about cultures throughout the world through their art
- learning about artists
- learning about typical cultural art forms
- learning foreign art terms

Language arts:

- listening
- writing books
- mythology and art
- puppetry
- reading
- speaking
- writing a poem about your artwork
- writing and illustrating a story

Math:

- ratios: enlarging numerically
- enlarging/reducing using a grid
- figures using only triangles, squares, circles
- geometric forms
- 3-D forms with something else added
- geometric shapes—cut and lay back
- golden section (geometric work of Renaissance artists)
- buildings using squares and circles
- learning to use the compass
- tessellations, M.C. Escher
- making books—measuring and cutting
- making designs using only angles
- measuring (using a ruler)
- numbers as design elements
- perspective
- computer graphics

Music:

- dancing to music
- drawing dancers
- drawing to music
- drawing musical instruments
- drawing orchestras

Nature:

- birds
- clouds
- flowers
- landscape
- leaves
- trees

Science:

- animals
- bugs and insects
- dinosaurs
- flowers
- human form
- jungle plants
- reptiles: frogs, lizards, snakes
- universe
- space
- time
- rocks
- land forms
- oceanographic study
- weather—clouds, tornadoes, sunsets

Social Studies:

- self, family, city, state, country
- global
- presidents
- geography (people and customs)
- costumes

Celebrations   Art has a curriculum, just as any other discipline, and a sensitive teacher can find many activities within that curriculum that do not involve teaching about the holidays of one segment of the population. There is no lack of themes for students. Formerly, art educators and classroom teachers took advantage of monthly celebrations in the school year for creating artworks. In the diversity of today's classroom, however, much less emphasis is being put on specific religious-based holidays because these are not celebrated by everyone, and may leave some children on the "outside." The following list gives something appropriate for each month that is not oriented to a particular religious celebration; instead, the themes are based on seasons of the year.

Themes Based on Seasons of the Year

September
Labor Day
first day of Autumn
Citizenship Day
back-to-school clothes

summer vacation
first day of school
children at play
grandparents' day

October
Fire Prevention Week
Columbus Day
National School Bus Safety Week
leaves
people in costume (carnival)

fall flowers and weeds
United Nations Day
circus
scarecrows
Daylight Savings time ends

November
election day
National Native American Heritage Week
Veterans' Day

bare trees
harvest celebrations
family gatherings, food

December
first day of Winter
winter vacation
celebrations around the world:
  Hanukkah, Ramadan, Christmas, Kwanzaa

packages
gingerbread houses
winter clothes
nutcrackers

January
National Book Month
New Year's Day
animals in winter: wolves,
  polar bears, deer, rabbits
winter landscapes
winter sports: hockey, volleyball, ice skating

Super Bowl
National Popcorn Day
snow-covered houses
sledding
Dr. Martin Luther King's Birthday

February
Groundhog Day
people in costume (carnival)
masks

Black History Month
Presidents' Day
Chinese New Year

March
Youth Art Month
first day of Spring
National Nutrition Month

kites
birds flying north

April

April Fool's Day
opening of baseball season
rain
flowers
baby animals
butterflies

baby birds
National Arbor Day
blooming trees
Earth Day
National Library Week
Secretaries Day

May

May Day
Cinco de Mayo
Memorial Day
Holocaust Remembrance Day
flowers

trees with leaves
summer sports: swimming,
 bike riding, baseball
zoo

June

International Volunteers Week
National Fishing Week
Flag Day
first day of Summer
summer activities

"unbirthdays"
 (for summer birthdays)
amusement park
landscape
water sports: swimming, water skiing
summer solstice

In addition, here are general themes you can use for art projects:

- I am helping to rake leaves
- my family
- my family at a restaurant
- my house
- the zoo
- carousel with various animals
- birds in the forest
- playing ball
- me at my desk
- playing a game with a friend
- my closet
- in the bathroom
- cereal boxes in the grocery store

- we are building a treehouse
- we are jumping rope
- we are playing a circle game
- the parade is going by
- everyone faces front in an elevator
- going up the escalator
- my friend and I at a shopping mall
- planting a garden
- helping my family prepare a meal
- room with a view
- the surface of Mars
- a candy factory
- me in my winter clothes

Career-Based Lessons   In addition to basing projects on the curriculum of art, you can help students become more aware of careers in art. Select projects that help them *be* clothing designers, commercial artists, book illustrators, cartoonists, architects, sign makers, card designers, sculptors, painters, scientific illustrators, craftspersons, puppeteers, and industrial designers.

HOW WE TEACH

Personal Relationships   Research has shown that friendliness, caring, tolerance, and consistency are important attributes for teacher–student relationships. If you are relaxed and calm, and students know you love teaching them, they will be sensitive to this. If you are not in control, they will also sense this. Knowing students' names and using them demonstrates your respect for them. Interaction with the students helps to keep their attention, and allows them to know that you value their input. Be a good listener. After you have presented a lesson, ask individuals in the class what the "steps" will be, or ask if they have an idea they would like to share related to the project. This helps to keep them involved, and allows you to clarify any misunderstanding. Afterward ask the students what they learned (if you write this on posterboard as they talk, the answers can be displayed with the artwork).

Suggestions for Maintaining Discipline   Avoid behavior problems by having a set routine. While it takes a little time for everyone to understand the routine, this will save you trouble in the long run. When you are presenting a lesson, don't begin until every student is quiet. If someone is disruptive while you are talking, simply pause and stare at the offender, waiting until the interruption ends, allowing peer pressure to help you with discipline. The other students want to get on with it, and they will shush the offender. The occasional fake smile at that student when he or she notices you waiting is as effective as having to discipline severely.

It is often easy to pick up clues when a student is having a bad day, and sometimes a little extra attention may be something you can easily do to make it better. It is to be expected that some children will not fit into the mold, and that it is simply not possible to give them as much attention as they would like to have from you.

Allow students to help make the class rules, which might be based on respect for each other, respect for materials, respect for ideas, etc. Post these in the room, and remind students that these were their choices. Your expectations for student behavior become apparent early on, but students can quickly become manipulative if they sense a lack of certainty.

Motivating Students Depending on the age of the students, motivation for a specific project can be accomplished in many ways. Students often love to do art that relates to personal experience. Helping them recall their experiences by writing or talking about them can be a great way to start an art project. Reading stories, showing pictures in a book, discussing a particular artist, playing art history games, showing videos, or talking about an artist while showing slides are all valid ways to inspire students.

Sometimes you may dress like an artist, or encourage students to do a tableau based on a famous painting. Students might even draw themselves as part of a famous painting.

Creating an Anticipatory Set This term simply refers to helping students notice as soon as they come into the room that something special will be happening. You might have materials in the center of each table, or set up a new still-life. A riddle written on the board, posters on display, a special illustration on a video monitor, even music playing will announce that something is different.

Younger children can be made more aware of how to draw a circle game by having them actually play a circle game. Or they might be made more aware of the proportions of the human form if they are led through a body-awareness exercise. Have them watch a classmate pretend to kick a ball or run. You may prefer to have younger students sit on the floor close to you if you have something to show them from a book or wish to have a discussion. Involve students in the lesson. Ask them questions, find out what they know. When students have art only one hour a week, they have difficulty remembering what they were doing the previous week, so they may need reminders of the objectives of the lesson. If it means that you cannot always present a full lesson within the prescribed amount of time, then allow each class to contain a skill-building lesson that can stand alone, yet lead toward a finished artwork. The quality will usually be higher, and results will be individualized as they have more time to think things through.

Making Lesson Plans If you have taken the trouble to develop a complete lesson plan, you will increase both your and the children's satisfaction. Naturally you will deviate or come up with better ideas as you present the lesson, but the plan will help you. Define your primary objective (main concept) for the lesson, and develop a presentation that will help you reach that objective. You may have secondary objectives that are also important, or accommodations for special students in your class that are important to think out in advance. The generic lesson plan described here may give you some ideas. Most good teachers develop at least one new project per class per year, while some of their "old standbys" get better every year as they work out the kinks. Sometimes it takes two years to gather illustrative materials and develop a new plan.

Writing on the Board Students can quickly be trained to look at the board each day when they arrive in class to see what preparations they need to make for the day's learning. You might include the title of the lesson, the goals students are expected to achieve, and any new vocabulary words. You might even have a riddle or two about the lesson (for the age groups that can read). Magnetic clips that attach to chalkboards are often used by teachers to support paper they are using for demonstrations.

Allowing for Individuality   Personally I find nothing more boring than presenting an art lesson to students that has a predictable outcome. If the students have followed the directions (and perhaps copied patterns), then the teacher knows in advance what the finished project will look like, and every student's work will look like everyone else's. Involve students in learning. Students may want to help in selecting the medium you use for a given project (offer a choice of cut paper or tempera, for example). Remember to give the students the chance to surprise you!

TIPS ON WRITING ART LESSON PLANS

Writing lesson plans is one of the realities of teaching art. Some districts use standard forms, while others leave it entirely up to the teacher's judgment. Most are based on a format such as the Madeline Hunter model, the Clinical Theory of Instruction, or Mastery Teaching. A fully developed lesson plan might take several pages, but a short one-page lesson will serve as a reminder to the teacher of information to be covered. Most lesson plans include the general headings listed here.

1. *Unit goals (themes).* These usually cover several individual lessons.

2. *Title of individual lesson (concept, problem).*

3. *Instructional objectives.* These relate to individual lessons, and should include at least some of the following: knowledge and skills to be learned, art history, aesthetics, art production, art criticism. An instructional objective normally contains:
   - a *subject* (**example:** the student [learner] will . . .)
   - a *verb* (**verbs frequently used:** analyze, apply, arrange, compare, construct, contrast, create, define, demonstrate, depict, describe, develop, discover, discuss, draw, emphasize, experiment, explain, express, identify, illustrate, interpret, judge, list, manipulate, produce, recognize, select, show, solve, use, utilize, verbalize, work)
   - *conditions* (**example:** using pastels [allotted time, supplies to be used, technique])
   - *standards of quality* (**examples:** overlap at least four objects; include five colors)

4. *Instructional model* (based on Madeline Hunter).
   - anticipatory set: questions, posters, photos, slides, quotations on board, riddles
   - statement of objectives and evaluation criteria: stated or written on the board; unit vocabulary: discussed, written on board, handout for journals; art history/aesthetic discussions
   - provide input (strategy, procedure, directions, or motivation)
   - demonstration/skill training, modeling
   - check for understanding
   - art production: guided practice/active learning strategies
   - independent practice (students apply what they have just learned)
   - closure

5. *Other possible additions to a lesson plan.*
   - modifications for students with special needs (gifted, students with disabilities and different learning styles)
   - national or state *key skills/core competencies*
   - application to real-life world (career, patron, consumer)
   - extensions (further applications of the project)
   - interdisciplinary connections (music, math, language arts, social studies, science)
   - safety considerations

6. *Evaluation standards.*
   - criticism: The student will discuss his/her own work or that of others through description, analysis, interpretation, judgment.
   - evaluation criteria: These should relate to the objectives. (Older students might help evaluate their own work according to criteria.)

7. *Closure.*

Art Lesson Plan

Title_____ Unit_____ Grade level(s)___
Medium_____ Suggested time_____

Instructional Objectives:

Elements of Design (circle one or more): line, color, shape, space, texture, value

---

Principles of Design (circle one or more): repetition, balance, emphasis, contrast, unity

---

Materials and Equipment

Vocabulary

Art Production (the format of this lesson plan is based on the Madeline Hunter model)

1. anticipatory set
2. state objectives
3. input: art history, instructions

4. demonstration, modeling behavior
5. check for understanding
6. guided practice

7. independent practice
8. closure

Art History/Resources (film, books, posters)

Aesthetic Questions: could be asked during input, guided, or independent practice

Art Criticism/Analysis Questions: could be during closure

Evaluation Criteria (should relate to objectives)

Modifications/Special Notes/Drawing

ASSESSMENT

Art specialists have always assessed student work through a variety of methods, but these have not been standardized, as they may become in the future. Art assessment historically has varied widely depending upon the ages of the students and the requirements of a school district. In some elementary schools, primary students are seldom graded, while students in upper elementary and middle schools frequently receive letter grades. Other schools expect written evaluations for each child. Assessment of a project or activity may be as simple as looking to see if the student has met the lesson's objective. At the present not all states require statewide testing in art, but with National and State standards currently being formulated by art teachers, testing may well become the norm.

Authentic Assessment   It is suggested that the art teacher can offer authentic assessment (real evidence of real learning) by building assessment methods into the lesson or a unit. Art teacher Cheryl Venet (Visual Arts Coordinator for the Columbia, Missouri Schools) recently termed this *embedded* assessment. This is currently done in classrooms across the nation, reflecting the relationship between lesson plan objectives and evaluation strategies. Students should be told what they are expected to learn, and instruction given with that in mind. The evaluation is then based on how well the students met the objectives. The assessment should be manageable and appropriate for the age group.

Portfolios   Keeping a portfolio is a tradition in art that begins at a relatively young age. As students get older, work kept in the portfolio is more selective. Portfolios can include records of the creative process by including preliminary sketches, providing a way for teacher, parent, and student to evaluate continued growth. Personal discussion with students about their portfolios is ideal, but if this is not feasible, students can do a written self-evaluation, about which they think is their best work and why. Or a written comparison could be made between work done early in the year and later work.

Standardized Art Tests   A national trend is underway in which students are being assessed in all subjects, including the visual arts. In tests given in 1997 to a national sample of eighth-grade students (as reported in *NAEA News,* February 1999), the students were tested in three areas:

- *Responding:* Students analyze, describe, and interpret works of art.
- *Creating:* Students generate original art, perhaps around an assigned theme.
- *Performance:* (1) Students recreated existing works of art. (2) Students created works of visual art with various media. (3) Students wrote an evaluation of their own work. (4) Students were given an opportunity to place artworks in historical and cultural contexts.

Written Work, Journals/Sketchbooks, Self-Assessment   Student journals (three-ring looseleaf binders are excellent) give students the opportunity to react to art through writing. The journal could include a daily log, free writing, sketches, and critiques of their own art and that of others. A standard reflection page could be photocopied for students to occasionally turn in, containing questions about their own work based on the following:

- the medium (tempera, watercolor, pencil)
- category (painting, print, weaving, collage)
- descriptions of elements such as texture, line, shape, color; or principles such as repetition, emphasis, contrast, symmetry
- subject or what you were thinking of as you created it

Active Watching   When showing *The Agony and The Ecstasy,* Lois Beppler of Fort Zumwalt School District has a worksheet for students to fill out as they are watching. The students are aware that they will be tested later. The test consists of ten questions taken directly from the worksheets, so if the students have been doing their work, the questions should easily be answered.

Classroom Critiques/Discussions   Discussions about their own work and that of others is another way of finding out about students' perceptions of art. When talking about art, students often use terms such as line, or shape, or symmetry. They may place an artwork within a specific culture or recognize the work of an individual artist.

Rubric/Scoring Guide   Teachers might have written standards of achievement for each project that allow for individual differences. Scoring Guides vary depending on the weight given various components. They might include:

- ability to follow instructions
- preparation/preliminary work
- class participation, cooperation
- design, craftsmanship, attention to detail
- creativity/originality/quality/imagination/individuality/expression
- effort, learning, and progress
- use of higher-order thinking skills and problem-solving ability
- attitude, respect for materials, time management

Interviews   Students and teachers talk about completed work and work-in-progress. Students could also share their ideas with each other in cooperative learning groups.

WHO WE TEACH

Remember that *all* children are equally deserving of your attention—those to whom art comes easily, those to whom nothing comes easily, and those in the middle who do not give you trouble but who also deserve their share of your attention. Too often the students who are compliant (often girls) do not receive as much of our time as they are entitled. Observe your interactions with students from time-to-time to be sure you are being fair to all.

Students with Disabilities   Many of these students are mainstreamed (placed in the least restrictive environment) or are participants in inclusion, where they attend a special resource classroom part of the day, and are included in special classes such as art, physical education, and music. The handout later in this section gives some ideas for adaptations in art for students with disabilities.

Students with Unusual Behavior Problems   For some students, negative attention will serve just as well as positive attention. You can help these students control themselves by intervention techniques. Give this student more classroom tasks and responsibilities. Let him or her be a special helper to get out and put away supplies. Have a table or place where a student who is disturbing others can be moved for a time to work alone. If necessary, get eye-level with this child and clearly state what you would like for him or her to do, then ask for your request to be repeated back to you. Sometimes you just have to back off, busying yourself nearby and getting back to it later. One of the hardest things is to remind yourself that *all* students are equally entitled to their share of your time. If the student is severely behaviorally disordered, work closely with the classroom teacher to keep art a pleasant learning experience for *everyone*.

Gifted Students   Students who are gifted in art usually love to draw at an early age. They show unusual perseverance in completing a project, and will often put in far greater detail than most, and sometimes take an idea far beyond the basic premise. Keeping this type of child content is seldom difficult because they naturally tend to work harder and longer at most open-ended assignments. However, they may become more easily bored if they have completed a simple task before the rest of the class. They are usually willing to try something that is unique, and frequently show extraordinary originality. Encourage this student to draw in a personal sketchbook, or to make a drawing of a still-life that you have set up elsewhere in the room. Art teacher Janet Morris, formerly of the Hazelwood School District, St. Louis County, Missouri, always has small extensions of a project (such as allowing the student to do a version of the project on smaller pieces of paper) after his or her work is satisfactorily completed and the student has time to spare.These small examples can be mounted and displayed as a group. A few school systems are offering special classes that feature problem-solving and skill development for artistically gifted students. The students often have been nominated by the art staff, parents, and classroom teachers. Other ways of identifying gifted students are through interviews, portfolios, and intelligence and creativity tests.

WHERE WE TEACH

While the ideal is a separate art classroom, many specialists teach in the regular classroom from an art cart, while others, who travel from school to school, teach out of the trunk of a car. Almost two thirds of art taught in elementary schools is taught by the classroom teacher. Wherever or however you teach, you may find something here that will be useful to you in organizing your situation.

The Art Classroom   Some teachers are fortunate enough to have a special Art Room that by its very nature can be an exciting place to enter. It has been my great privilege recently to visit many schools in various districts, and I am consistently overwhelmed with the creative solutions art teachers have come up with to make their Art Rooms more flexible and student friendly.

Most elementary and middle school art classrooms contain historical reproductions, art timelines, a color wheel, posters with the elements and principles of art, and rules of respect. In addition, bulletin boards might feature one artist or artwork done by all grade levels that month.

From a Cart   You will need a home base, which realistically will probably be a storage closet. Ideally it will contain a sink, your desk and chair, and a file cabinet. Sturdy shelving for supplies, and storing plastic crates and works-in-progress will make it easier to keep your cart up-to-date. Obviously communication with the classroom teachers is vital. Keep them informed in writing about what you will be doing each week so students are prepared for your arrival (smocks, pencils, scissors, etc.). If your school has stairs or outside classrooms and a "cart" is not feasible, put supplies in tote trays and use student power to help you get things from one classroom to another (being aware of school and state policy about whether students are allowed to assist in moving heavy items). Work out a schedule with the principal that allows travel time between classes and gives you time to download or reload the cart.

In general, your students' artwork will be stored and displayed in or near their classrooms. Try to have a tagboard portfolio for each student's artwork stored in the classroom. The teacher might be willing to set up a special table where students can earn the privilege of continuing to work on an art project.

Your cart should be stocked with standard supplies of crayons, oil pastels, markers, glue, and construction paper, all of which can give students a satisfactory art experience. Just because you are limited in where you can work does not mean you need to avoid large or three-dimensional work altogether. Carry two or three buckets to fill with water if hands will need to be washed, and leave plastic bags or boxes with the teacher if work must dry on newspaper or plastic outside in the hall before being gathered up. Works-in-progress can be placed in a general portfolio to be continued on your next visit. It is essential that you keep a close eye on the clock to facilitate moving from one room to the other.

From a Car Trunk   Obviously your trunk is never quite so clean as you would like it to be, but a dedicated teacher can learn to live with almost anything. An audiovisual-style cart that will fit into your car sideways will allow you to put the materials you need directly on the cart for wheeling into a school. A wheeled luggage cart allows you to stack boxes and materials (holding supplies in place with "bungee cords") to get them to and from the car. Stacking see-through lidded storage boxes would also make your life easier. If you have to make more than one trip, use "kid power" whenever it is available.

THOUGHTS ON TEACHING ART

Saving Time   Getting students in and out of class and to work immediately in an orderly fashion makes the art experience more pleasant for everyone. Students will live up to your expectations if you start teaching your routine at the beginning of the year and stick with it. To avoid confusion at the beginning and end of the hour, you may train students to use certain pathways to enter and exit, and to approach and leave the sink or drying rack.

Displaying Student Work and Art Reproductions   Have plastic-covered bulletin boards made that are approximately the width of all your cabinet doors. Theresa Long of Eureka High School in St. Louis County, Missouri, had these display boards permanently attached to metal cabinets with screws. Use pushpins to easily hang examples of artwork or reproductions all around your room.

Making Seating Charts   For many years I did not believe in teachers placing students according to seating charts, but after experimenting with them and seeing them used in a variety of situations, I see that the teacher-prepared seating chart results in more productive classes. Arranging to have students of various abilities and genders at each work table seems to cause everyone to work at a higher level of achievement. Self-adhesive notes with each student's name on them can be put on a chart and easily rearranged as you get to know the students better. From time to time move a few students who would benefit from working with a different group of people.

Have tables identified by color or number so you can get the attention of a group of students easily. Some teachers suspend triangular or rectangular matboard forms from the ceiling directly above the tables, so that the identification can easily be seen.

Protecting Clothing   When doing messy projects, save yourself time and trouble by having students arrive at the art class wearing their own smocks and bringing their own pencils. Each student should have a smock (a large T-shirt or an adult short-sleeved shirt worn backwards—if the collar is cut off, and elastic sewn at the neck, even the youngest student can put it on easily). It should be clearly identified on the outside of the *back* with the student's name in permanent marker (this helps you, a parent helper, or a substitute with names). (**Note:** When smocks are shared, you run the risk of passing lice from one student to another.) Another alternative is to have a form prepared to put in teachers' boxes to advise what you want the students to bring to the class that particular lesson. For older students, work aprons kept in the art room are easy for them to put on when they are needed. Emergency cover-ups for really messy work can be as simple as a plastic trash bag with slits cut for the neck and arms.

Classroom Organization   Keep supplies organized. Use small trays for the center of each table that contain sufficient pencils, markers, crayons, rulers, and scissors for each student at the table. Table monitors can be responsible for keeping pencils sharpened and checking supplies at the end of each hour. Or have classroom sets of supplies such as brushes, rulers, erasers, crayons, etc., arranged on counters in coffee cans, cut-off bottoms of plastic gallon milk jugs, or small baskets. Storage is usually a problem in an art room, so having supplies well organized is always attractive and makes your life easier. Have a box for unused portions of construction paper.

Portfolios   If you do not have a drawer for each class in which artwork-in-progress may be kept, make large portfolios of folded 24 × 48-inch tagboard and label them with the teacher's name for each of your classes. Work can be kept in individual student portfolios (made of folded and stapled 18 × 24-inch tagboard) either in the art room or in the classroom, until it is ready to be taken home or displayed. This allows you to see the progress a student has made, and you are easily able to select work for displays and exhibitions. This reinforces the value that you and students should place on their artwork. If you do not have room for individual portfolios, perhaps the classroom teachers will encourage students to keep their artwork in portfolios within their regular classroom.

Student Notebooks   Many middle schools purchase pre-punched copy paper and clear plastic-fronted three-ring binders for their art students that are normally kept in the room. Students are requested to date and keep their thumbnail sketches, journals about art, notes, homework, and small works-in-progress in their notebooks. The students' first project can be a drawing for the front of their notebook.

Artwork Storage   Work-in-progress is often wet and messy, and must go on a drying rack, the hall floor, or a corner of the room until it dries. When it is dry enough to handle, the two-dimensional work can be stored in a class drawer or a class portfolio. Three-dimensional work can be placed in trash bags and identified with the teacher's name. When work is complete, of course, you get it out onto available walls and counters around the school or in the library for display. If absolutely necessary to send it home, keep a list of pieces you may want to have brought back for an art exhibit. Teacher Janet Morris suggests reserving at least three to five examples from each student project, keeping a record of what projects were kept from each student. She suggests a dot by the grade in the gradebook and a tally in an exhibit column to make this relatively painless.

Supply Storage   Art supplies can be part of the decor of the room and contribute to the exciting atmosphere we all try to create. Tops and insides of open-storage shelves can contain stacks of colored paper and rows of tempera paint arranged to look like the colors of the spectrum. Corners or tops of cabinets could be filled with the makings of a good still-life such as nonfunctioning musical instruments, plants, stuffed animals, pottery, old chairs, antique containers, and boxes of fabric and yarn. Realistically, most people have a too-small supply closet that can quickly become a disaster if it isn't organized from time to time. Storage for student work-in-progress is a necessity. Most teachers have table or class folders (often kept in different color construction paper for each table for ease of identification). Sometimes one might be allowed to keep clay in a furnace room, or seldom-used equipment in a closet some distance from your room. You can never have too many shelves in a storage closet or cabinet. Household organizers and storage boxes will help you keep things under control.

Equipment Management   The budget for art is never large enough, and it is important to take care of equipment in order to keep from constantly replacing it. Simple supplies such as scissors and erasers are frequently borrowed and not returned. Spread new scissors out and spray-paint the handles for easy identification. Shiny things have a way of vanishing, and by making the scissors ugly, you tend to keep them longer. If erasers keep disappearing, put them into an interesting container and post the number of erasers on the front of the container. Or give out two erasers per table and collect them at the end of the hour. Foster pride in students that they still have x number of erasers. Make wooden boxes for long rulers, and $2 \times 6 \times 8$-inch wood platforms with holes in them for individual brush or ink pen storage. A number on each hole that corresponds with the number of the student in your gradebook lets you know at a glance who still has not cleaned and put his or her brush away. This same system works with scissors. Or, in order to keep from replacing scissors every year, many teachers keep a specific number (15, for example) in each of two small cans. Student monitors are given the responsibility for counting these each time at the end of the hour. Cutting knives can be kept blade-down in a Styrofoam block, but it is recommended that these be mostly kept in a cabinet.

Clean-up   Most art rooms have a single sink. If at all possible, avoid having young students wash their brushes or hands at the sink. Several teachers whom I've observed have enough inexpensive wash cloths (watch for sales) for every student, which they keep in an open-sided plastic crate. When these are kept damp and rinsed from time to time, they are good for cleaning hands and tables. Machine-washing weekly is sufficient.

Rinse sponges in a bucket of water, then *you* squeeze out the water and distribute sponges at the end of the hour for table clean-up. If you do not have a sink, a series of buckets may be used for hand-washing if necessary. If it is a desperate situation, you can take all of the students to the bathroom to wash their hands. Plasticine clay is more easily cleaned off hands by using dry paper towels.

Dismissal   Giving students ample warning about the end of the period helps. A clean-up bell that can be rung by a student five minutes before the end of the hour gets their attention. If a reward (such as being first to line up) is given to the table that is finished first, with everything clean, all the students seem to help each other. Assigning different table monitors each week to get supplies and put them away is helpful. Some teachers devise and post the duty schedule before the year begins in order to be fair to all. If sweeping is necessary, a different table can be given that duty each week. Another teacher tells students she will slowly count to ten to allow students time to get their work put away and their tables clean.

Rewarding Good Behavior   Simply put, "You can catch more flies with honey than with vinegar." Disciplinary measures need to be taken at times, but catching students being *good* is far more effective than catching them being bad. Rewards can be as simple as giving a student a task of responsibility ("Will you be my monitor to pick up the artwork today?") or assigning table monitors for the week or a line leader for the day. You can make small certificate slips that you personally sign and hand out to individuals or to an entire class. Melissa Messina of Pond Elementary School in St. Louis County has made a plain "artist's palette" on white paper for each class and laminated it. If a class is well-behaved, one student is allowed to color in one of the colors on the palette. For a particularly good month, you can offer food (a lollipop or popcorn party—a handful of popcorn on a piece of paper in front of each student). If they are absorbed in work, drop a jellybean into a jar (they love the sound). This will eventually result in sharing the jellybeans when the jar is full. Allow the students to listen to music if they are especially cooperative (simply turn on a radio or tape if they are working especially well).

Noise Control   The philosophy of allowing talk during art lessons varies from school to school. Many feel that students have too little time during the school day for socialization, and art class offers a more relaxed atmosphere that fosters social development. It is very easy for students to go beyond quiet productive time to the chaos we have all had to deal with. Most teachers try for a minimum of ten minutes of quiet time during "creative thinking" sessions. Some allow talking privileges to be earned by good behavior. Students can be taught to become silent immediately if you get their attention by an arranged signal. Some teachers simply turn off an overhead light; another claps twice and waits for the students to clap twice in response.

Mary Ann Kerr of the Jackson Park Elementary School in University City, Missouri solved the problem of noisy stools that were much too tippy by cutting a one-inch x in the side of a tennis ball to place on each leg of a stool. The stools glided easily and quietly.

New Art Materials   Manufacturers of art materials are constantly coming up with innovations. Your students will usually become excited when you bring in something new. If a product (such as the nonbreaking, self-supporting acrylic mirror) comes onto the market, but is relatively expensive, start by buying just a few a year until you have enough for your class. Vendors attend state and national conventions and have some of the finest art educators in the country demonstrating how to use new materials. Even young students can be told that they are using very special materials, and that care must be used in putting them back in the box to help make them last. If they mistreat new boxes of materials, then these should be put away and the old ones brought back out.

Recycling   Art teachers are natural scavengers. They use things from nature, and were into recycling long before it became fashionable. Notes sent home to parents will result in marvelous things being sent in to the classes. Of course, you must be prepared to store all the goodies you get, or use them quickly. Have boxes labeled that will form a storage system.

Some states have equipment and supplies available for teachers to buy simply by visiting the warehouses in the capital. Some towns have organized recycling centers for teachers, where for a slight fee, outthrows from factories—such as foam sheeting, film canisters, paper ends, newsprint roll centers, fabric, centers from fabric bolts, carpet tubes, etc.—are available for teachers. If your town doesn't have one of these centers, get together a group of teachers (or parents) and organize one! Let local manufacturers and merchants know that you are always in the market for quality junk.

THOSE WITH WHOM WE TEACH: STAFF RELATIONSHIPS

The Art Specialist as a Resource Person   Some classroom teachers lack confidence about their abilities to teach art because they themselves "never could draw a straight line." Others have happily learned that art can serve as a motivating force in other disciplines. There is nothing more exciting than walking into a school that is an "art school." *Every* classroom has student artwork hanging inside and outside each room in addition to the "art" displays. If the school does not have a resident art specialist, most districts have an art supervisor who visits the school regularly. These art specialists are willing to serve as "idea" people for other teachers. Sometimes a few minutes of conversation will assist a classroom teacher to devise a dynamic idea for a project in another discipline. It is important to eat lunch with the classroom teachers, visiting their classrooms, being interested in what they teach also. Try not to isolate yourself with the excuse that you have work to do.

At the elementary level the classroom teacher normally will accompany students to a special art room, or help students get ready for an art lesson in their own room. Smocks might be kept in the students' classroom, for example. If you have other things for them to bring to the art class besides a sharpened pencil, you can place notes in teachers' boxes weekly. Notes sent to all the teachers may help them to devise a project using artwork done in the artroom from time to time. For example, all my classes made handmade paper, and each grade level did something different and exciting with the paper.

The classroom teacher may be pleased to receive student artwork to display within or just outside the classroom, or to keep artwork within individual student portfolios.

PARENT AND COMMUNITY RELATIONS

At the elementary level, parents *are* the community. They are very interested in their children's success, and artwork is a visible means of showing what is happening at school. Chances to display student work occur through changing displays in the school itself, occasional displays in the school library or at a local library, and a larger district exhibition (often at a recreational complex or shopping mall). One reason for keeping a separate classroom folder for each teacher is to allow you to accumulate work from each class as the year goes on, and have it prepared for display to avoid the last-minute problem of matting 60 to 200 works of art. Even primary students can be taught to center their work and glue it onto a construction paper background, signing their names on the lower left or right with their room number below it (for ease of sorting the work). Presentation is simply considered one of the skills students are expected to learn.

Parent Volunteers   Although many families have two working parents, it is still possible for these parents to volunteer to give occasional help. When you are involved in a large schoolwide project—such as paper making, marbling, or mural-making—send home a request asking parents to schedule just one hour of work; you will find fathers, mothers, and grandparents who are willing to help. Make an appeal early in the year for several parents who are willing to give two or more hours per week on a regularly scheduled morning. They can help by cutting paper, matting artwork for display, arranging bulletin boards, taking down one display and helping to hang another, or simply providing another pair of hands to do something that needs doing. If you have a parent who works with wood, that person may be willing to help you make display boards, scissors and brush holders, boxes for storage, etc. Parents are also willing to accompany you on a field trip or assist at an open house. You may have a parent who is a photographer who will come in and take photos of work-in-progress for publicity or simply record the students at work to be shown along with the artwork.

Parent volunteers can form a cadre of "Picture Persons," who come in on a regular basis to show posters or slides and talk with the students about a specific painter or culture. They do not have to know a great deal about art to do this, but will be a wonderful resource to complement your program. One of our superintendents made time to be the picture person for his son's fourth-grade class.

Field trips require volunteer adults to accompany a class. A field trip needn't involve a bus, but might be a visit in the neighborhood to a park, grocery store, or old home for students to draw from life. Ideally you would be able to take older students to a museum or art gallery at least once a year.

Newsletter   Art is important in student lives! Let families know what you are doing and why. Include in a newsletter information about museum exhibitions in your town or a nearby state, art classes available in the community for students, jokes, cartoons, examples of student artwork, quotes about art, art-related crossword puzzles and games, and recipes for art materials. You might feature information about one artist in each newsletter (students could do the research). Inform families about projects and goals for each specific level. Art news can be included in a Principal's newsletter, sent home with students, or posted on a web site.

An example of modern communications with parents is demonstrated by the Meramec School in Clayton, Missouri, which sends a weekly letter to each parent for the appropriate level. The art teacher, Maggie Peeno, simply enters in her classroom computer what is happening with each grade level that week. This information is automatically incorporated into the weekly newsletter for parents of that grade level, along with news about other classes and schoolwide information.

Displaying Student Work Outside the Art Room   One way to let all students see that their work is valued is to display the work of every student, not selecting just a few of the "best." Put artwork in your room, outside your room, outside their classroom, and inside and outside the office. Displays in community, school district, and state art exhibitions all offer opportunities to allow your students' work to be shown. One general guideline is that the further away from the art room, the higher the quality of the work should be. If the artwork is arranged with the more eye-catching compositions on the outsides and near the middle, even average work takes on importance. It is also very effective to make a placard to place with a group of similar projects to explain what was learned (ask the students, they will tell you). Any time a student has work on display outside the school, have a form note ready to inform the family when and where it can be seen.

Labels   To have work instantly ready for display, it is worthwhile to make labels (not stick-on) on the computer for each class so that work is labeled the minute it is done. Type names in columns on one page, listing on three lines the student's name, the teacher's name, and the grade level. Have several pages printed, then cut these into label size on the paper-cutter, putting a complete set in a paper clip, and keeping them in an envelope with the teacher's name. Each hour have a student helper spread these out on your desk next to the stapler, and the students can staple their labels in the lower right-hand corner before turning in their work.

Signing Work   Of course, before beginning, students still will put names in pencil on the back of their work (small in a corner, so the back of the paper could be used if necessary). If you want students to sign their work on the front, show them how they can inconspicuously print or sign their names next to a subject (such as an arm or leg of a figure), without detracting from the composition.

PUBLIC RELATIONS

Publicity   Newspapers and television stations are always looking for publicity about something good happening in the schools. If you are doing something that is special (a mural, outside display, a monumental work of art, an unusual technique, sponsoring a visiting artist), contact your local newspaper or TV station. Sometimes the newspaper will send out a photographer, and the tele-vision station will send a crew to film it. More often you will find that if you take black-and-white photos and send in pertinent information to the newspaper, eventually the photo will find its way into print. Call them first to find out what size they might use, or if color prints would be usable.

Student Recognition   Have a place near the office (a bulletin board or easel) where you can feature an "Art Student(s) of the Week (Month/Year)." This is fairly easy to accomplish, by fea-turing one or more pieces of work along with the student's name. The name could go in the school newsletter, and the student can be presented with a fancy certificate. Involve parents in helping you select one picture a year to be beautifully framed to add to a "Principal's Collection" for the office. Another way for students to have their work recognized is to select a line drawing to reproduce for the school newsletter, or to allow students to design covers for a school telephone directory. Student work could also be selected for posting on a school web site.

Writing About Art for Publication   Sometimes you and your students have done a proj-ect with an unusual and exciting result that might be surprising even to you. Share it with your fel-low art teachers. Art publications such as *School Arts* and *Arts and Activities* welcome articles with photographs, and your students will be thrilled to see their artwork in a magazine.

State and National Conventions   Consider doing a presentation at a district, local, state, or national convention for art teachers. Successful interdisciplinary projects can be presented at state teachers' conventions or at conventions for other disciplines. You will get as much out of these as you give as you become acquainted with teachers whose experiences differ from yours.

Competitions   You will find yourself besieged with ideas for competitions for your stu-dents' work, or "art exchanges." Some art educators are vehemently opposed to these competitions because students can be so disappointed if they don't win. If you pick and choose, however, some of these are very well organized and worthwhile for the students. Manufacturers offer supplies, cash prizes for your school, or recognition for individual students. Be wary of those that want the stu-dents to use cartoon characters that are not their own. If the competition fits into the curriculum and the students can learn something from it, probably no harm is done. If you are sending work away that may not be returned, it is now possible to make a color copy of it at a copy shop so the student will still have it. Although prizes are not awarded, consider submitting your students' work for displays at your state capital during Youth Art Month.

Getting Funding for Special Projects   While it is sometimes difficult to get funding for ordinary daily needs, become resourceful in obtaining funding for extraordinary projects. Included among these might be hosting a resident guest artist for two weeks; a field trip to the museum; a special, expensive piece of equipment such as a kiln; purchase of display boards for student work; or a trip for the art teacher to the National Art Education Convention or to a summer workshop for teachers.

Most states have some type of distribution of funds, often administered through the local school district. You will have occasions when you are encouraged to write a Grant Application for funding. As one who has written grant applications many times (not always successfully), and reviewed other teachers' grant applications, I have the following suggestions:

- Read the rules carefully, checking and double checking. You don't want to have it rejected for a technicality.

- Answer all the questions in detail, yet keep your application brief. Try to use a conversational method of presenting it rather than using educational jargon. Let the *person* writing the application show through.

- Make sure of the amount needed and list it in detail.

- Have more than one colleague look over the application for readability before submitting it.

- Make every effort to obtain funding from several resources. Evidence that you have approached various sources (P.T.O., Principal, District Coordinator) is persuasive that you are serious about getting this project funded. Sometimes you may have a small amount from each source, but it adds up to an impressive total. You may even offer to pay some portion of the amount yourself (meals, for example).

- Begin your appeal for funding to your principal and district coordinator early in the year before the funds have been granted to other people.

- When funding is granted, express your appreciation in writing to the granting agency.

- Consider a partnership with a nearby university. Sometimes grants are given to two collaborating groups.

- Approach a local or national business about sponsorship of your art program. A number of corporations take pride in their support of young people and education in general. Sometimes the employees themselves are willing to take something on as part of a public service.

- Don't give up. If it isn't granted one year, at least you have a head start on the next year's application.

An excellent booklet published by the National Art Education Foundation is *Grant Applications in Art Education,* which is published each year and sent to members.

WHAT CHILDREN SHOULD KNOW AND BE ABLE TO DO

Teaching the curriculum of art is an ongoing (sequential) process. The elements and principles of design, which are the basic building blocks of art, are introduced in Kindergarten and reinforced and expanded upon as the student grows older. Ideally the student will learn about a number of artists, styles, and cultures throughout the elementary years. Some districts have a curriculum that suggests specific artists and elements to be emphasized in a given year in order to give students throughout the district a consistent education.

Skill-building is also an ongoing process. Students should have experience *every* year in creating from clay, painting, sculpture, drawing, and printmaking. The Japanese National Art Curriculum places special emphasis on printmaking each year, and the expertise of the students demonstrates their familiarity with the technique. In-depth experience in a medium fosters creative exploration. These grade-level characteristics are written as a result of many teachers sharing their experiences of appropriate experiences for each grade.

The Kindergarten Child

Characteristics of Kindergarteners

- able to verbalize needs
- quite self-centered
- unable to sustain any activity for terribly long
- leave out things that are not important
- feel no need to make colors relate to reality
- do not work particularly well in groups
- have little sense of scale—they are the center of the universe in their art

What Kindergarteners Can Do with Materials

Art equipment. learn to take care of brushes and put them back in proper containers

Clay. manipulate to form a ball; make a coil; flatten; squeeze; make a pinch or coil pot

Drawing and painting materials. learn to use large markers, crayons, large and small brushes, Payons®

Paper. cut; glue; tear; bend; fold; curl; pleat; fringe; fold in half and match edges

Print. make stamp designs with fingers; potato designs; Styrofoam meat trays

Scissors. use to cut curved or straight lines

Sculpture. create sculpture from found objects

Kindergarteners' Understanding of Concepts

- Identify and draw differences in line: thick, thin, zigzag, curved, straight, interrupted.
- Recognize and draw geometric and free-form shapes.
- Identify and use light and dark colors.
- Identify red, yellow, blue, green, violet, and orange, but not whether they are primary or secondary.
- Make large shapes by combining geometric and free-form shapes.
- Create pattern by repetition of designs.
- Perceive things that are alike and different.
- Learn about and use art tools in a safe, responsible manner.
- Recognize differences in art media after introduction and use of various media.
- Talk about their own art and that of other artists.

- Communicate ideas that are personally important.
- Are aware of houses, buildings.
- Are able to talk about design on clothing.

Suggestions for Teaching Kindergarteners

1. Allow kindergarten students to experiment with materials.
2. Let them draw about personal experiences and themselves.
3. Give skills and media lessons step-by-step.
4. Allow each student to make an individual portion of an all-class project.

Kindergarten Interdisciplinary Connections

Language Arts: develop left-to-right hand-and-eye movement; sequence thoughts; use puppetry; use journals with writing and drawing

Mathematics: identify shapes; make patterns; measure; counting concepts

Science: classify living and nonliving; differences; seasonal change; weather; plants; habitats; animals (wild and domestic); measure volume

Social Studies: learn about self, home, family, relatives, neighbors, community, holidays, and safety

The First-Grade Child

Characteristics of First Graders

- have difficulty with more than one idea at a time
- more aware of the people around them, and can work with others in a group
- can draw a complete figure, but exaggerate the more important parts
- love lessons that are full of activity and fun; imaginative stories, fantasy, plays, games, and dances
- can work enthusiastically and be absorbed in creating art
- show satisfaction with artwork and desire approval of the teacher and classmates
- interested in mechanical devices and moving parts
- draw what they know, not what they see
- have a great range of maturity that results in wide differences among ability to listen, comprehend, and follow directions

What First Graders Can Do with Materials

Brush. learn to make controlled strokes with the brush

Clay. make pinch pots or form a piece of "pinched out" sculpture from clay; make simple coil pots and apply glazes; simple slab construction

Equipment. use safe practices with art tools

Markers. use markers effectively (not scribbling)

Paint. mix primary colors to make secondary colors; can make colors lighter or darker; fingerpaint; watercolor; understand and use crayon resist

Paper. fold; glue; fringe; pleat; tear (with difficulty); cut

Weaving. weave paper in a simple pattern

First Graders' Understanding of Concepts

- Recognize and describe the use of line in historical artworks.
- Appreciate rhythm in a work of art such as van Gogh's *Starry Night*.
- Understand that form and function go together (a clay pot must be strong).
- Know that artists have designed clothing, buildings, and furniture.
- See the difference between two-dimensional and three-dimensional work.
- Discuss subject matter in art; understand differences in still-life, portrait, landscape, seasons.
- Understand careers: police officer, doctor, minister, fire fighter, barber.

- Understand how to show space (with reminders): overlapping, figures smaller in background.
- Recognize texture and pattern in clothing or in nature, and describe it.

Suggestions for Teaching First Graders

1. Teach students one step at a time.
2. Encourage them to talk about their own work and that of others.
3. Introduce the vocabulary of line, rhythm, shape, space.
4. Have them identify line and shape in the room or on their clothing.
5. Ask them to bring something from home or wear something that is decorated with line or shape.
6. Teach them to thread a large-eye needle, tie a knot, and do simple stitchery.

First-Grade Interdisciplinary Connections

Language Arts: follow oral directions; work in sequential steps; make rhyming words; categorize objects; draw picture stories; understand care of materials

Math: understand patterns, sets, geometric shapes, rhythmic curves; compare lengths; picture graphs; symmetry; problem solving; corners and sides

Science: grasp size relationships; changes in nature (moon, plantlife, wind, clouds, light, animals, seasons); light and shadows; mechanical devices

Social Studies: understand extended family; community helpers (barber, police officer, grocer, fire fighter); earn and spend money; symbols such as traffic signs; U.S. symbols (flag, Liberty Bell, eagle)

The Second-Grade Child

Characteristics of Second Graders

- welcome responsibility—the chance to show they know how to do something
- observe more details in their surroundings (buildings, people, clothing)
- love nature (animals), imaginary creatures, fantasy
- extremely self-confident; willing to tackle anything
- fascinated about how things work: castles, boats, machinery
- open to new experiences: field trips, TV, books, movies, new clothes
- love games, stories, dances, plays

What Second Graders Can Do with Materials

General. able to construct sculpture from found objects; create realistic forms such as animals

Brush. wash brushes; mix colors with the brush

Clay. create sculptures, pinch pots; apply glazes

Equipment. understand the need for safe practices; assist in getting out and putting away

Paint. mix tempera paint

Paper. use joining methods; curling; bending; scoring; folding; attaching

Second Graders' Understanding of Concepts

- Become more aware of size relationships in comparing objects and in regard to themselves.
- Become more aware that things are designed by artists (cars, clothes, kitchen items, furniture, buildings).
- Become aware of themes in artworks from various cultures.
- Are able to add texture that resembles real texture; for example, hair.
- Understand that personal selections, such as clothing, reflect personal expression.
- Understand that line can be used to make something appear three-dimensional.
- Understand positive and negative shapes (may be best done with cut-paper).
- Describe how atmosphere can be shown by color differences.
- Observe design (pattern, balance) in natural organisms such as butterflies, insects, and in art.
- Recognize differences in art media.

Suggestions for Teaching Second Graders

1. Introduce unfamiliar art forms and materials.

2. Stress cooperation, sharing, and responsibility.

3. Teach value differences, mixing tints and shades of color, using transparent and opaque colors.

4. Talk about jobs that artists have—let them *be* designers.

5. Allow them to combine found materials in sculpture.

6. Allow them to write a play and act in it, or create puppets for a puppet show.

7. Show them fantasy art in history and allow them to encourage fantasy paintings and sculpture.

8. Caution them about not using *symbols*—suns with rays, stick figures, pointy mountains, "balloon" trees.

Second-Grade Interdisciplinary Connections

Language Arts: create and illustrate a sequence story; write a book; learn to observe details; make "literary" paper-bag puppets

Mathematics: recognize pattern; temperature; measure length and area; symmetry

Science: geographic environments; animals in their habitat; seasonal changes; geology; human growth

Social Studies: neighborhoods; style variations between Western and Asian landscapes; traffic signs; changes in shelter, transportation, clothing from earlier times

The Third-Grade Child

Characteristics of Third Graders

- enthusiastic, open to new experiences and using new materials
- anxious to please their peers, careful not to do anything too different from what the other students are doing
- tend to separate themselves by gender outside the classroom, but work well in mixed group projects
- interested in learning to draw realistically, frustrated at times when they are not able to
- appreciate that fantasy exists in the imagination, and may be used in artwork
- enjoy art museum visits and learning about the role of artists in society

What Third Graders Can Do with Materials

General. distribute, collect materials; clean tables; take general responsibility

Brushes. wash brushes; mix colors with the brush

Clay. create sculptures, pinch pots; apply glazes

Paint. mix tempera; understand crayon resist; use and take care of watercolors

Ink. stamping with vegetables; potato prints; fingerprinting or brayer prints; monoprints

Paper. cut well with scissors; use joining methods; curl; bend; score; fold; attach

Crayons. color firmly for scratch-art

Ink. collagraph printmaking; stamping

Metal foil tooling. emboss and stipple

Papier mâché. cover balloons; facial mask forms

Third Graders' Understanding of Concepts

- Use overlapping shapes, variation in lines, textures, colors, and sizes.
- Comprehend foreground, middleground, and background, and show these in several ways.
- Discriminate between warm and cool colors; identify how artists have used colors for expression.
- Define symmetrical, asymmetrical, and radial balance.
- Identify columns, beams, domes, and arches, and analyze how a building is constructed.

- Develop personal use of color and other elements effectively in two-dimensional work.
- Become aware of articulation of parts of the human figure.

Suggestions for Teaching Third Graders

1. Allow them to create a nonobjective work of art through the introduction of historical artworks.

2. Teach them to *see*—teach contour drawing of a hand and the human form (blind contour drawing may be a little beyond them).

3. Discuss proportions of the human form; have them draw their classmates as models.

4. State objectives when beginning, then help them evaluate halfway through whether they are meeting the objectives in their own work.

5. Talk about *how* things work (buildings, machinery, transportation)—the *why* of form and function.

6. Have them draw flowers, trees, animals, and plants either from life or reference photos. (There are many ways to make a mountain!)

Third-Grade Interdisciplinary Connections

Language Arts: write sentences about artwork; create a story and illustrate it

Mathematics: map-making; geometric forms; symmetry; multiplication; division

Science: solar system; electricity; magnetism; environment; energy (light); rocks, classify animals, reptiles, birds, amphibians, mammals, simple machines (inclined plane, balance)

Social Studies: communities (differences due to location and weather); ancient and foreign cultures; multicultural similarities and differences (any art project should relate to the history of the culture that worked in the same manner)

The Fourth-Grade Child

Characteristics of Fourth Graders

- are developing a sense of humor; love comics and cartoon characters
- can develop feelings of inferiority about their lack of ability to draw what they see
- compare their work to that of peers
- open to viewing different art styles and do not yet judge if something is "good" or "bad"

What Fourth Graders Can Do with Materials

Brushes. successfully mix paint; care for watercolors; wash brushes and clean up

Clay. ceramic coiling; pinch pots; clay animals; portrait and figure sculpture; apply glazes

Paint. mix colors to make tints and shades; watercolor wash and resists

Ink. brayer printing; glue-line print; collagraph; monoprint on plastic sheet; pen and ink

Paper. cut skillfully with scissors; score; curl; fold origami shapes

Yarn. weaving; decorative stitchery

Sculpture materials. handle plaster-gauze well; do additive sculpture; papier mâché

Fourth Graders' Understanding of Concepts

- Comprehend color scheme based on color wheel: warm/cool, contrasting, mood, "grayed" colors.
- Develop a more realistically proportioned human figure; movement will be shown
- Become aware how artists depict animals and the human figure through looking at art.
- Can identify different media, subject matter, and art forms such as sculpture, tempera, watercolor, prints, portraits, landscapes.
- Comprehend that form follows function in design, and can point out or bring in specific examples.
- Understand that many artists express themselves and their cultural identities through their artwork.
- Recognize architecture from various climates and cultures of the world based on the construction materials used, including their own regional architecture.

Suggestions for Teaching Fourth Graders

1. Show various styles of art, and discuss aesthetics issues: "Could something ugly be art?" "Should the artist care whether other people appreciate what he or she is doing?" "Why might mountains look different depending on which culture paints them?"

2. Avoid having them copy, as many already lack confidence in their ability to draw. Remind them to avoid *symbols* such as "balloon" trees, happy faces, and rainbows.

3. Introduce still-life to foster the decision-making process, emphasizing unity, variety, emphasis.

4. Introduce proportions of the face; do self-portraits; draw fellow students; discuss body proportions; learn to really look.

5. Encourage exploration of color schemes through an open-ended landscape assignment.

6. Introduce sculpture in-the-round.

Fourth-Grade Interdisciplinary Connections

Language Arts: research skills related to artists; book-making

Mathematics: estimating fractions; shapes (trapezoids, parallelograms, pentagons, hexagons, octagons); money; measuring length; computer drawings; calendar; metric system

Science: ecology; constellations; weather forecast; space travel; light and color; body systems; machinery

Social Studies: American culture; state history (pioneers); regions of the world (tundra, rain forests, deserts); map-making; Native American cultures

The Fifth-Grade Child

Characteristics of Fifth Graders

- love *being* designers—doing an actual assignment to design clothing, furniture, a house, etc.

- eager to help; enthused about art; take responsibility; are helpful to classmates; work well in groups; open-minded to creative problem-solving

- interested in learning new tools and techniques; capable of working with almost any material

- some lose confidence in their artistic ability because their drawings are not "real" enough or think their classmates' projects are better

- boys and girls tend to stay separate, with different interests, hobbies, activities

- able to concentrate for much longer periods of time

- giftedness in art becomes apparent at this age when children who love art will devote long hours to it

What Fifth Graders Can Do with Materials

General. charcoal; pastels; pencil; colored pencil

Equipment. use scissors; lino tools; cutting knives

Clay. clay tiles; boxes; slab or coil construction; portion of a mural

Paint. tempera; watercolor; acrylic; Payons®

Ink and markers. ink wash; control of line; markers used with style and control

Paper. folding; scoring; cutting with scissors; controlled tearing

Fabric decoration. batik; printing; tie-dye; stitchery; appliqué

Sculpture materials. assemblage of found materials; papier mâché and plaster-gauze; ceramic sculpture; cardboard

Fifth Graders' Understanding of Concepts

- Learn that sculptors are sometimes commissioned to do monumental artwork for public places.

- Respect that sculptural materials must be used appropriately, or the sculpture may disintegrate.

- Recognize the influence of geographic and climatic conditions on building materials used in private homes and public buildings.

- Recognize differences in artworks from a variety of cultures.

- Recognize the artist's intention in using ideas and using color to create mood.

- Identify symbols, natural images, and objects used to create artworks.

- Understand and use several different ways of showing depth (overlapping differences in color and size, rudimentary perspective).

- Discriminate that light, distance, relative size, and motion affect the appearance of an object.

Suggestions for Teaching Fifth Graders

1. Let *them* point out strengths and weaknesses in their artwork and changes that might improve it.

2. Introduce many different styles of art and discuss whether something has to be "real" to express the artist's idea.

3. Assign research projects about artists.

4. Enlist them to assist in hanging artwork, organizing materials, any of the art room chores.

5. Review concepts of realism, abstraction, positive and negative space, light and shadow, texture.

6. Introduce one- and two-point perspective.

7. Do group study, reporting, and projects.

Fifth-Grade Interdisciplinary Connections

Language Arts: advertising; group work on research of famous Americans

Mathematics: decimals; fractions; angles; Roman numerals; computer drawings; length (metric and feet)

Science: machinery (turbines, water power, pulley); habitats; human functions; astrology; flight; environmental preservation; use of microscope; classification; nutrition

Social Studies: American history; cultural symbols; environment; geography

The Sixth-Grade Student

Characteristics of Sixth Graders

- know everything, or think they do, but are still quite open to new experiences
- interested in learning about artists, why their work looks the way it does, what contemporary artists are doing; have begun to form a real opinion on certain kinds of art and artists
- experience dramatic mood swings because of physical and emotional changes; seek peer approval
- have a short attention span at times
- display a preadolescent interest in music, language, videos, movies, television
- often prefer being by themselves, independent of adults
- respond positively, and are proud to see their work on display

What Sixth Graders Can Do with Materials

Drawing media. charcoal; pencil; pastel; oil pastel, applying tip side firmly or softly

Clay. sculpture bust; boxes; slab or coil construction

Paint. mix colors in all paint media; blend colors; modeling; group mural; self-portrait

Ink. control ink wash; line drawings

Paper. sculpture; three-dimensional forms; origami folds

Fabric decoration. batik; printing; tie-dye; stitchery; appliqué

Sculpture materials. assemblage; papier mâché; cardboard; cut paper

Sixth Graders' Understanding of Concepts

- Understand one- and two-point perspective concepts; want to learn how to show depth.
- Open to learning new, difficult technical skills in drawing, painting, print-making, and sculpture.
- Judge works by formalism (elements and principles of art), emotionalism (the viewer's emotional reaction to the art), and realism (the belief that the best art closely resembles reality).
- Understand the elements and principles of art, and identify their use in their own artwork and that of others.
- Identify functions of architecture for worship, burial, and public and private use.

Suggestions for Teaching Sixth Graders

1. Base as many projects as you can on *self* (self-portrait, human form).
2. Help develop abstract thinking through giving several different three-dimensional projects.
3. Assign a research project for them to learn about the life of an artist and present it to the class.
4. Conduct aesthetic discussions about nonrealistic works of art and varying cultural standards.
5. Take them outside the classroom to draw houses, buildings, people, cars, playground equipment.
6. Help them progress sufficiently in their art skills so they will want to continue learning, rather than concluding that because they may not draw realistically, they are not "artists."
7. Find out what they know and understand about art and artists; have ongoing discussions about the influence of society on the type of art that is created and the place of the artist in society.
8. Interest them in art from other cultures and trying their hand at similar projects.
9. Introduce them to making posters—teaching the use of balance, space, and emphasis.
10. Motivate through encouraging fantasy art or depicting imaginative experiences; they are very interested in Surrealism.
11. Make hand-made books to be used for journals.

Sixth-Grade Interdisciplinary Connections

Language Arts: research and report on an artist's life; keep an art journal; write poetry related to artworks; learn about literature from other cultures; follow oral directions

Mathematics: measuring; geometric figures; scale drawing; ratios and proportions; fractions; area; volume; perimeter

Science: weather; geology; climate; natural resources; magnetism; nuclear energy; human organisms; genes and chromosomes; substance abuse; aviation; space exploration

Social Studies: ancient world; current events; environmental concerns; animal rights; their country's heritage

The Seventh-Grade Student

Characteristics of Seventh Graders

- more aware of physical appearance than previously; suddenly interested in the opposite sex
- would like to be treated like an adult, yet often revert to childish solutions and behavior
- want to be individuals, yet very sensitive to peer pressure and want to identify with a group
- interested in exciting experiences

What Seventh Graders Can Do with Materials

General. capable of handling materials and equipment with skill

Equipment. lino-cutting tools; X-acto® knives

Clay. slab and coil building; sculpture; pinch pots

Paint. understand mixing color to make tints, shades, "grayed" colors

Ink and markers. hatching; cross-hatching; sketching; ink wash; controlled directional use of markers

Paper. handmade paper; origami; paper sculpture

Fibers. stitchery; weaving; woven yarn basketry; batik; fabric collage

Sculpture materials. able to use files; sandpaper

Seventh Graders' Understanding of Concepts

- Transform personal experiences into art forms.
- Recognize that different cultures have styles in artwork that reflect people's values and beliefs.
- Compare and contrast two artworks by artistic style, media, and art processes.
- Do research on something if it is of interest to them.
- Record reality in landscapes, cityscapes, and portraiture.
- Aware of how color, line, shape, and composition affect a composition.
- Interest in learning about architecture; recognize different cultural influences and location on the style of buildings.

Suggestions for Teaching Seventh Graders

1. Encourage them to take photographs or use the video camcorder to record their world.

2. Encourage computer-graphics experimentation.

3. Assign small groups to research the life of an artist to share with the class.

4. Spend more time talking about what artists might have been thinking, why they work the way they do, what effect society has on the appearance of art.

5. Give assignments that are open-ended enough to allow the students to show unique interpretations.

6. Occasionally allow students to select the appropriate media to express themselves.

7. Discuss appearance: about how people look, why people wear what they do, hair styles.

Seventh-Grade Interdisciplinary Connections

Language Arts: dictionary and encyclopedia; be an "art critic" for a newspaper; group discussions and presentations; listening skills; speaking in front of the class

Mathematics: volume, area, perimeter; shape and space; segments and lines; parallel and perpendicular lines; circumference of a circle; angles; square roots; percents; fractions

Science: human body systems; genetics; ecosystems and community; animals and their habitats; reptiles; flowers; trees and shrubs

Social Studies: world geography; inventions; Renaissance art; political organizations; mythology; religious architecture; maps

The Eighth-Grade Student

Characteristics of Eighth Graders

- highly self-conscious and interested in personal appearance; aware of how others see them

- raging hormones; volatile personalities, trying various roles from week to week

- helpful; interested in service projects and environmental concerns

- inquisitive and interested in complex ideas; want to relate education to their real lives

- interested in personal lives of entertainers, sports stars, TV personalities

- sensitive about artistic ability; take criticism of their artwork personally

- interested in working with others on a joint project

What Eighth Graders Can Do with Materials

General. physically work with most artistic materials, simply differing in degree of skill

Crafts. work skillfully with crafts such as jewelry, weaving, stitchery, and batik

Technology. apply elements and principles of design to photography and the use of a video camcorder

Clay. capable of skilled work with coil and slab building; pinch pots and sculpture

Paint. mix paint; modeling; show depth; represent something realistically

Eighth Graders' Understanding of Concepts

- Want to know why things are taught and the application to real life.

- Can continue to learn about careers related to the visual arts.

- Use perspective, diminishing size, and color to show depth.

- Use materials and techniques to depict moods, ideas, feelings.

- Apply design elements to creating objects and materials for living.

- Identify artwork from different cultures and time periods by specific common characteristics.

- Think abstractly; can grasp double meanings, morality, and symbolism in artwork.

Suggestions for Teaching Eighth Graders

1. Encourage writing about their own art through keeping a sketchbook/journal.

2. Help them improve skills in a variety of media, introducing new ways of using the same materials.

3. Give them "real" assignments when possible: posters, designing jewelry, fabrics, murals.

4. Assign open-ended topics that allow them to express moods such as happiness or sadness.

5. Help them develop aesthetic judgment and discuss how they apply it to daily life (as consumers and connoisseurs of art).

6. Continue to introduce and discuss historical artworks from a variety of cultures.

7. Relate the history of American art to their studies of American history and literature.

8. Personalize some projects, encouraging them to use their own faces, names, or initials as design elements.

9. Encourage them to work in groups on a large project such as a mural, or reports on artists, or even several working together as collaborative artists.

Eighth-Grade Interdisciplinary Connections

Fine Arts: creating and painting scenery; painting to music; relating the music and visual arts of a specific time period

Language Arts: American literary heritage; communication and research skills; illustrating a short story; using encyclopedia and dictionary; oral presentations; using the library

Mathematics: problem solving; English/metric conversions; perpendicular and parallel lines; area, volume, shape and space; fractions; percents

Science: astronomy; energy; weather; oceanography; land forms; volcanoes; earthquakes; geology; fossils; mapping; population

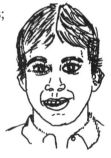

Social Studies: American history to 1900; economic organization; research skills; political organizations

TIPS ON SAFETY

General Suggestions   For the students' protection and your own, always instruct students in the safe use of tools and materials, beginning in Kindergarten and reinforcing each year. It is crucial that you take responsibility for making the environment in your art classroom safe for yourself and your students. Students under the age of 12 are particularly vulnerable to substances in art that might not affect older students. Be certain your materials have an AP (approved product) or CP (certified product) seal that is given by the Art and Craft Materials Institute. Check old materials for this seal, and throw them away if they do not have it. It is also advised that you use materials that state on the label "Conforms to ASTM D-4236." Some art materials also come with Material Safety Data Sheets (MSDS).

Working with Clay   For a healthy environment, your kiln should be in a separate room or at least separated by a screen. If this is simply not possible, consider using self-hardening clay; or, rather than using glazes, paint the fired clay. Have students wipe the tables with damp sponges after working with clay and dry them. Ideally, have your floor mopped nightly to avoid dust in the air.

Care of Cutting Tools   Give frequent instructions on safe practices with scissors and such cutting tools as lino-tools, snips, or cutting knives. Tools such as cutting knives or lino-tools should be kept in a cabinet, counted before distribution, and again at the end of class. Be aware of age-appropriate use of certain tools. Sharp cutting knives and lino-cutters are wonderful tools, but should not be used by anyone younger than fourth or fifth grade (and then only with very specific safety instructions). Have students use bench hooks when doing lino-cuts, and instruct them to always keep the knife facing forward, while keeping the other hand *behind* the knife. For curved cuts, show students how to revolve the material rather than the cutter.

Equipment
- If you must use extension cords, they should be three-pronged and rated for the appropriate wattage for the purpose. Make every effort to run them around the side of the room or even up and over the top of a door rather than across a floor. If necessary, tape them down on the floor.
- Staple guns should be off-limits to students. Students cannot resist trying to see if they work.
- Have electrical equipment (kiln, electric drill) checked on a regular basis for proper operation.
- Make sure your fire extinguisher is routinely inspected and/or replaced.
- Have a sturdy ladder and stepstool and use them rather than climbing on stools, chairs, or tables.
- Make sure the guard on your paper cutter is always in place. If you allow older students to help you cut paper on the paper cutter, give them careful instructions on its use, and always be in the room while they are working.

Recommended Materials
- CP or AP pencils, watercolors, tempera, acrylic, oil sticks, crayons, chalks, and colored pencils
- CP or AP water-based inks instead of oil-based inks
- CP or AP pastes for papier mâché, or CP or AP cellulose papier mâché
- CP or AP clear acrylic emulsion can be used to fix drawings
- CP or AP lead-free glazes for ceramics
- mineral spirits instead of turpentine or kerosene
- water-based markers; nonscented instead of permanent or scented markers
- glue sticks or white glue instead of rubber cement
- shellac containing denatured alcohol
- food or vegetable dyes (onion skins, tea) in place of procion dyes
- wet, premixed talc-free clays

A fine book called *Safety in the Artroom by* Charles A. Qualley is published by Davis Publications, Inc., Worcester, Massachusetts, and will assist you in creating a safe environment.

TIPS ON ADAPTATIONS IN ART FOR THE STUDENT WITH DISABILITIES

Today's art teachers try to accommodate different learning styles by using a variety of methods such as demonstrating, writing on the board, talking about art, and hands-on work. For the student with physical and mental disabilities, other methods of learning can be utilized that will make their art experience easier and more successful.

General Suggestions Be aware of the goals on the student's Individual Education Plan (IEP) in order to help that student achieve personal goals. It might be a more important goal for the student to learn socialization, to complete a task, or to develop fine-motor ability than to make a fine work of art.

Some students might be able to concentrate better by being allowed to work somewhat apart from other students, while others benefit from being right in the middle of a group of students.

A different medium might be easier for certain students (oil pastels instead of tempera paint, for example).

Assign a different student each month to be a buddy for a student with a disability (to help get supplies and make sure the student understands). This is good for both students.

The Student with Visual Disabilities
- Use tactile materials such as clay, wire, fingerpaint, cardboard pieces, Popsicle sticks, or other three-dimensional materials that allow the student to feel the texture.
- Place supplies within a frame taped on the table. (This could be no bigger than a roll of masking tape, or could be a taped-down box lid.)
- Tape screenwire to a piece of cardboard as a drawing board. (The student can feel a waxy surface left by drawing with crayon on screenwire.)
- Outline a design in wax crayon, or with a glue gun; a visually disabled student can then draw or paint within it. White glue outlines done in advance can serve the same purpose.
- Add sand to paint so the student can feel what has been painted. Or the student can "paint" on cardboard with tiny balls of softened plasticine clay.
- If the student cannot see at all, speak when you approach. Also let the student know when you are leaving. Have the student touch your hands while you are demonstrating.

The Student with Hearing Disabilities
- Make sure the student understands the assignment.
- Touch the student's arm to get his or her attention. It may be necessary to draw or write what the assignment is about.

The Student with Motor Disabilities
- Cutting may be a problem, and several types of special scissors are available. *Squizzers,* snip loop scissors, and spring-action scissors spring open after being squeezed. Some children's scissors have four finger holes so a "guiding hand" can be used to help the student cut.
- A student might find it easier to tear paper rather than cut it. Or someone else could hold the paper between both hands while the student cuts from the bottom toward the top.
- Tape paper to the table to hold it in place.
- Tempera paint is now available in large refillable markers.
- For a student who has difficulty gripping a crayon, place the crayon inside a foam curler or tape it on the hand.

The Student with Behavioral Disabilities This student often does well with three-dimensional materials or those that offer resistance (such as lino-cuts or carving). This student usually thrives on being given responsibilities and being a helper. Especially to this student, offer praise freely for a task well done.

The Student with Developmental Disabilities Select projects that are appropriate for the ability of this student. If necessary, substitute a different medium or goal.

Overteach! Allow the student to complete one stage before beginning another. For many students, each task should be explained in separate steps. Explain repeatedly if necessary.

TIPS ON PHOTOGRAPHING ARTWORK

Materials and Equipment

- 35 mm camera
- tripod
- photo floodlights, 3200 K.
- foamboard background
  covered with black paper or felt
- close-up or macro-lens or close up rings
  (to photograph small artwork or pictures
  from books)
- slides: *indoors*—Ektachrome 160 ISO
  for Tungsten Lighting;
  outdoors—Ektachrome 100 or 200 ISO

- gray card
- cable release
- stands for the photo floods
- pushpins
- film: 35mm print film for color prints:
  (Kodacolor, Fujicolor, Agfacolor)—
  use blue 80 B filter if filming indoors
- black-and-white prints:
  125 (Plus-X) or 400 (Tri-X) ISO

General Reminders

1. Place the artwork on an easel or flat on a table so it is vertical and at camera level (tilted artwork will look distorted).
2. Work closely enough to the artwork that it fills the frame of the viewfinder, eliminating distracting borders (even if you lose a small amount of the artwork).
3. If you place the artwork on a black background, you will not have distracting edges if the artwork is not the same proportion as the camera lens. Or make two pieces of L-shaped black construction paper or matboard that you can adjust to conceal the edges.
4. Hold the gray card directly in front of the artwork, walk forward and fill the lens with the gray card, then "take a reading." Step back to make the exposure at that reading.
5. The lower the film ISO number, the finer the grain will be. The higher the aperture (smaller lens openings), the greater depth of field (and therefore sharpness) you will have.
6. "Bracket" exposures. To bracket, make an exact exposure according to the gray card. Then overexpose one or two stops and underexpose one or two stops. If taking many photos, it may cost less to take the pictures a second time if necessary than to bracket.
7. If you must expose at slower than 1/60th of a second, use a tripod and a cable release (or delayed timer) to avoid camera shake.

Indoors with Flash If using an automatic camera with a flash, stand approximately 6 feet back and use the telephoto function to frame properly.

Outdoors Do this on a calm day in a spot that is sheltered from the sun. A cloudy bright day is ideal. Use a gray card to take a reading.

Indoors with Photo Floods

1. Take the photographs some distance from windows, with no overhead lights.
2. Position photo floods on standards at a 45-degree angle, approximately 3 feet in front of the artwork and between the camera and the artwork.
3. Make sure there is no glare. If you see it in the viewfinder, it will show in the photograph. If this occurs, you may have to move the photo floods to a 90-degree angle to the artwork.

To Make Slides from a Book

1. Place the book on a table, away from windows. Turn off overhead lights.
2. Position a photo flood on each side of the book and 12 to 16 inches from the surface. Use a weight to hold the book open and flat. (It may be necessary to place something under one side of the book to hold it level.) Use two L-shaped pieces of black matboard to surround the picture.
3. Hold the camera horizontally, looking straight down at the picture. (Copy stands are available in most libraries for this purpose.) If it is a very small picture, use a macro lens or close-up rings to get it in focus. Take a reading on the gray card. Adjust the lights to eliminate glare on the pictures, as it will show in the slide.

TIPS ON CREATING ART BULLETIN BOARDS

Compare a bulletin board to a billboard or poster. The viewer only has a few seconds to get the impact and the message. If it is too busy, it simply cannot be absorbed. As in any composition, plan ahead and have a main element that catches the eye. A few large words and a main element draw in the viewer. The supporting information may be smaller If you only have small items to use, group them together on one sheet of background paper. Try to have larger elements at the bottom in order to keep the composition from looking as if it will fall over.

Materials

- posters, postcards
- roll paper in a variety of colors
- cloth
- pushpins or staple gun
- magazine reproductions
- construction paper, fadeless paper
- corrugated borders (if desired)

Hints

- When you take down a display, place letters and other elements into a tagboard portfolio to keep them flat for reuse.
- Cut paper into 4 × 6-inch pieces and cut out the letters by hand. Or request that your school purchase a letter-cutting machine.
- For easy hanging and reuse of frequently used handcut letters, mount them on strips of paper and laminate.
- For titles, use questions such as: Who is this artist? Did you know? Can you imagine? Can you explain?
- Cut geometric and freeform shapes from construction or fadeless paper to place behind artwork.
- Cut silhouettes of people, buildings, animals, trees, flowers, etc., to emphasize the message.
- Vary the color scheme when you put up a new display.

Suggested Themes

- *Historical Artist(s) of the Month.* Select an artist from history to feature each month, including the artist's name, reproductions, and biographical information. These themes could be assigned to groups of older students. Student work based on that artist's technique could be added nearby.
- *Student Artist(s) of the Month.* Feature the work of one or more students, posting the student's name, and matting artwork to give it importance.
- *Design concepts.* Feature one element or principle of art, using large letters and various examples:
  Color   Positive/negative space
  Line   Balance: formal and informal symmetry
- *Seasons.* Display artists' interpretations of Summer, Fall, Winter, and Spring.
- *Nature.* Show different interpretations of the same subject by artists from different time periods or cultures (mountains, animals, landscapes, seascapes, cityscapes).
- *Portraiture.* Show unique approaches to portraiture by several different artists.
- *Crafts.* Display photos of crafts such as basketry, ceramics, jewelry, masks, weaving. Or feature the work in several media by artisans of one culture.
- *Architecture.* Put pictures of local buildings or famous buildings. Identify individual elements of a building such as columns, different roof styles, door or window styles, differing cultural styles.
- *Cultures.* Display examples of artwork by such cultures as Native American, Asian, Inuit, African-American, Indian, African, Cajun, Mexican, Hispanic. Make a comparison between the traditional art of one culture and a contemporary artist who is inspired by his or her cultural background.
- *Ancient and modern cultures.* Include Egyptian, Greek, Cave art, German Expressionism, Cubism, Abstract Expressionism, Impressionism.
- *Book illustrations and illustrators*

TIPS ON MATTING STUDENT WORK

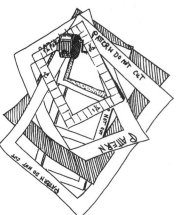

Placing a mat on student work enhances and gives it importance. These suggestions are for simple, relatively easy-to-make mats, *not* archival matting. It is important to teach presentation and mounting skills to students from the earliest years. They can learn that mats must be kept clean and that artwork must be centered.

Materials

posterboard	metal ruler
construction paper	pencil
masking tape	markers
matboard	utility or craft knife

Personalize Purchased Mats   These are available for bulk purchase in white, black, or colors.

1. Use a metal ruler and wide-nib marker to draw a line in a color related to the artwork around the outer and inner edges of a purchased white mat.
2. Have students mount their pictures in a purchased mat or on construction paper and "continue" the composition onto the mat by drawing on the mat.
3. Double-mount work by using a purchased white mat and cut a colored piece of construction paper that will show 1/4 inch on the inside and 1/4 inch on the outside of the mat. Or simply place the matted picture on construction paper.

Things to Keep in Mind

- Colored work is effective with a mat in a related color, even if it is just a single line drawn with a marker on a white mat, or a double-mounted artwork.
- Neutral media—such as pencil, charcoal, and ink—look better mounted on neutral mats (gray, black, brown).
- The mat should be the same size on at least three sides (the bottom may be slightly wider if you wish). The mat should be 2 to 3 inches wide on all sides.
- Display several small unmatted works together on a single large sheet of construction paper to set them apart.

The Easy Way   Make posterboard patterns with a variety of opening sizes for older students to trace around. Hang the patterns on a nail and use marker on both sides to identify sizes. They should be told to always mark on the back of the mat to keep the front clean. Several construction paper mats can be cut at a time on the paper cutter. Mark the inside dimensions, then loosely fold them in half, cutting first one direction, then the other.

Cutting a Mat

1. If the paper or matboard used for matting is not the appropriate size, cut the outside dimension of the mat on a paper cutter.
2. Measure the artwork and make the mat opening 1/2 inch smaller in both height and width.
3. On the *back* of the mat, hold a long ruler diagonally from corner to corner and make a small X in the center.
4. From the center of the mat, mark the size of the opening on all four sides of the back. Either measure in from the edges and draw a straight line or use a T-square to mark where you will cut.
5. Hold a metal ruler steady and, starting at a corner, cut along the edge several times, making sure to cut all the way to the corner so the inside will fall out.
6. After cutting the mat, place masking tape on the *back* edges of the artwork, allowing the tape to extend over the edge. Turn it over and center the mat above the front of the artwork before placing it firmly down.
7. Turn both artwork and mat over and firmly press down the edges of the tape.

TIPS FOR THE SUBSTITUTE ART TEACHER

1. Introduce yourself to the teachers in classrooms on either side of yours so they will be aware a substitute is in the room.
2. Ask the teacher to note on the seating chart if any of the students need extra TLC (tender loving care), any children who need medications and when, and if any student has other special needs.

Be Aware of General School Rules

1. Some school districts prefer that no student go to the bathroom unescorted.
2. You may wish to have students sign out, writing the time and destination if for any reason they must leave the room. When they return, they will write the return time beside the time they left. Because students know their regular teacher will see this, they are less likely to want to make unnecessary trips.

Always Read the Teacher's Instructions Carefully
You are expected to teach and help students with their lessons, and to carry out the plans left by the regular classroom teacher. Students appreciate being allowed to get on with their work.

1. Get off to the right start. Time spent setting the tone at the beginning will save time in the end.
2. Stand outside the door and greet students as they arrive.
3. Let them know your name (also write it on the board) and let them know if you are an art educator.
4. Begin class on time, in a calm, no-nonsense manner.
5. Take attendance, make announcements, etc.

How to Get the Students Over "the Substitute" Mentality

1. Be firm, yet friendly.
2. Never embarrass a student or accuse a student of doing something wrong.
3. Show a sense of humor.
4. Be interested in what the students are doing.
5. Circulate around the room rather than sitting at the desk.

Your Responsibilities

1. In the event of an emergency (fire, earthquake, or tornado drills), keep your students in line and take the attendance booklet with you.
2. Never leave the class unattended. If help is needed, send a student for a nurse or administrator.
3. Never use corporal punishment or try to physically restrain a student. Use your voice.
4. Never send a student to the nurse unescorted.

Be Prepared If the Teacher Did Not Leave Instructions

1. Have several appropriate one-day lessons prepared in your "bag of tricks." These can include:
   - drawing with fine-line marker (flowers, vegetables, shoes, art supplies)
   - cut-and-paste collage
2. You might have some photocopied one-page puzzles or art word games for the student who has completed the work.

Tips from Experienced Substitutes

1. Keep careful track of the time. At the end of class, make sure students have cleaned their work spaces and classroom work areas.
2. Allow enough time for clean-up so the teacher will want to have you return.
3. Expect older students to remain in their seats until the bell has rung.
4. Younger students are probably expected to line up by the door to be collected by the classroom teacher.

SECTION 2

MAKING ART HISTORY AND APPRECIATION FUN

Those of us who teach art know that we should include art history, aesthetics, and criticism/analysis as part of any production lesson, but too often these are omitted for lack of time. You undoubtedly have tried-and-true lessons that are always successful and that students enjoy. Consider how you can vary a lesson by showing an artwork that is related to the subject or technique that you are teaching. This section presents some activities that could be used to introduce or end a lesson, some sponge activities, and a few art history/appreciation lessons.

Some schools recommend the introduction of new artists and cultures at each grade level to encourage students to build on what they already know. It is all too easy to rely on favorite periods, such as the Impressionists, and cultures, such as Egyptian, when the whole range of art history and the whole world of art would be of interest to students. At the end of this section is a list of some artists and their subjects that might be helpful. As we move into statewide testing, students at the elementary or middle-school levels might be expected to know something about many of these artists and periods.

In teaching art history, make an effort to incorporate information about the family life of the artist. Tell a story about what this artist was like when he or she was growing up. Take advantage of some of the wonderful children's books about various artists, and teach students to find information about artists on the Internet. Although the artwork is still the important part of an artist's life, nevertheless, students enjoy finding out about the human side, and what that artist might have been like as a young person. This is also an opportunity to talk about what *life* was like when the artist was growing up, and how art might have been affected by religious customs, patronage, government, literature, and other outside influences.

Vary the study of art history and art appreciation by using print or postcard reproductions, slides, videos, books and posters, color photocopies, works from the Internet, and occasionally inviting a *real* artist to visit your school. Images that can be accessed and printed out in color on the computer are generally very good. Excellent resources are also available through museum shops or art resource vendors. If you have time, you can make your own slides from books (see "Tips on Photographing Artwork" in Section 1).

Most museums make a sincere effort to make their works readily accessible to teachers through slide kits, videos, the Internet, posters, and, in some cases, a museum display in a suitcase, all of which can be checked out by teachers.

We need to remember that game-playing can enhance learning. If we can engage students in learning through a variety of methods, then it goes beyond game-playing. We are trying to get students to use higher-order thinking skills by getting them to be active participants in learning. *Bloom's Taxonomy of Educational Objectives*, which follows, is as applicable to teaching art as any other discipline:

1. *knowledge:* recall of facts
2. *comprehension:* participating in a discussion
3. *application:* applying abstract information in practical situations
4. *analysis:* separating an entity into its parts
5. *synthesis:* creating a new whole from many parts, as in developing a complex work of art
6. *evaluation:* making judgments based on criteria*

USING ART REPRODUCTIONS

A collection of prints can be built up over a period of time. I recommend you laminate any that you purchase, or buy sets already laminated. They will last longer if you can punch a hole in the corners and hang them with pushpins. Change displays frequently to keep students interested. Build your personal collection of art reproductions by cutting up your art magazines, holiday cards, or having color photocopies made, as well as purchasing postcards, small posters, and reproductions.

Portrait Gallery   Post only examples of portraits and place a number over each one. Ask students to note their opinion of which portrait is:

- the person who looks the most unhappy
- the person who looks the richest
- the person with whom they would most like to have a conversation
- the one who might be the best teacher
- the one they'd most like as a relative
- the person they would like to marry

Token Response   Make appropriate construction paper tokens for each student to place by the painting:

- that cost the most money (*green rectangles*)
- that you (the curator) would buy for your museum if you had unlimited funds (*white building shape*)
- that you think took the longest to make (*clock face*)
- that is your favorite (*heart*)
- that you like the least (*hand with down-turned thumb*)

Draw an Artwork from a Description   Have one student be the *describer* of a work of art in a reproduction. This student is the only one who will actually see what the artwork looks like. The other students must draw a picture (on photocopy paper) based on a verbal description. Ten questions can be asked of the describer that must be answered "yes" or "no."

---

*Bloom, Benjamin S. *Taxonomy of Educational Objectives: The Classifications of Educational Goals* (New York: Longmans, 1984)

Scavenger Hunt   Post a variety of reproductions in the hall. Give students a list of things they should search for that are in the particular reproductions you have posted. They could work with a partner or in teams. Include a blank for the name of the artwork, the name of the artist, and the year it was created. If you have art textbooks, this game could be played individually, with each student using an individual text. Because this project will take advance planning, it is an ideal one to request a volunteer to organize. The following is a sample list:

Scavenger Hunt Item	Title of Artwork	Name of Artist	Year
someone wearing a sailor hat			
a specific animal (dog, bear, bird)			
landscape			
a bridge			
a painting by Vincent van Gogh			
a mountain			
a lady in a hat			
a night scene			
a house			
a bright red area			
a sunflower			

Compare and Contrast   Divide students into small groups to examine and compare two art reproductions from a specific culture, such as early Native American, contemporary Native American, Hispanic, Asian, African, or African-American. Several versions of art playing cards contain such reproductions. The students should be looking for similarities and differences between several artworks. The results of these discussions could be shared with the class.

Bulletin Board   For art history displays throughout the entire school year, select one bulletin board that will be strictly decorated by *students*. Divide students into groups, each group to take responsibility for one artist or culture. Make a calendar for the year so students will be able to plan ahead. The board could include posters, postcards, color or black-and-white photocopies of the artist's work, a biography of the artist, an explanation of the medium that was generally used, a description of what life was like during the artist's lifetime, an art timeline that shows when the artwork was created, and even the students' personal interpretations of that artist's work.

Be a Painting   Relieve the mid-term doldrums by having students "become" a painting or an artist. We are familiar with how some artists looked, and a famous artwork or style of painting is easily recognized. Have reproductions and books around the room that would allow students to get ideas for how they could dress. Bring in a few large frames and plan to take photographs of your student as they "frame" themselves dressed as a painting or an artist. This could be combined with a writing and research exercise about the artist's life.

A variation on this was developed by Beth Knoedelseder, a Ladue, Missouri third-grade teacher, whose students each dressed for a *royal* portrait snapshot (with a crown, scepter, and fancy clothes—they all wore the same thing). The individual portraits were made into a class album, with an individual's best qualities (as suggested by classmates) listed below the student's portrait and name.

Gallery Curators   Select a stack of art reproductions or postcards at random and form students into groups of three or four people. They will pretend they are the curators of a museum and need to arrange an exhibition of the artwork that their museum owns. They must plan how the artworks will be exhibited in galleries. Instructions can vary as follow:

1. The "Curators" divide the artwork in half and give a logical name to the two halves. (*Note to the teacher:* Do not suggest a name. Allow the students to do this, and hope that they go for something more sophisticated than man/woman!)

2. The "Curators" now should divide the artwork in half again, perhaps starting over and rearranging entirely. Again they should give names to their groupings.

3. If time allows, have each member of the group be responsible for arranging the work around the "gallery," considering how one work goes with the one next to it because of color, subject, or culture.

4. The "Curators" could create an actual "gallery grouping" of postcards within a plexiglass frame for exhibition. These could be changed from time to time.

5. "If one of these paintings has to be de-accessed (sold because you need the money for something you like better), which would you choose?"

6. "If you could purchase only one painting for the museum of which you are curator, which would you choose?"

7. "If you could purchase one for your personal collection, which one would you choose?"

ART ACTIVITIES WITH POSTCARDS

Purchase individual art reproduction postcards, postcard books, or sets of artists' notecards from museum shops or art resource catalogues. Or cut reproductions from art magazines, mount them on index cards or cardstock, and laminate. Have your students or their families send you art postcards when they travel. There are many ways for students to use them in art games, and your collection can quickly grow.

Postcard books are available from the following publishers.

Alfred A. Knopf, Inc., 201 East Fifth Street, New York, NY 10022

Fawcett Columbine, Pavilion Books Ltd., 196 Shaftesbury Avenue, London England WC2H8JL

Pomegranate Artbooks, Box 808022, Petaluma, CA 94975

Running Press Book Publishers, 115 East 23rd Street, New York, NY 10010

Postcard sets are available from Parent Child Press, P.O. Box 675, Hollidaysburg, PA 16648.

Write information on the back of the card, including the name of the artist, title of the artwork, the medium used, its dimensions, and the year it was created. It is recommended you laminate the postcards and have expectations that they will be carefully handled. For your convenience, have labeled game folders with pockets for a variety of activities for individuals or groups. The games you select can be greatly simplified or made more complex, depending on the ages you teach.

Sorting and Matching

- Find four paintings done by one artist.
- Sort into various categories: portraits, abstractions, realism, families, animals.
- Match art reproductions that you think were made in the same time period.
- Find art reproductions that you think were made in the same society (examples: Native American, Asian, Hispanic, Italian, Colonial America).
- Sort reproductions by the century in which you think they were made.
- Match titles and artists to artwork.
- Match artists' names to the artists' work.
- Play "Concentration." Turn cards face down and find matching pairs.
- Arrange the work from what you think is the oldest to what you think is the most recent.
- Identify which paintings were done in oil, which in watercolor, which were prints, etc.

Edges, Lines, and Colors   Have enough postcards of artwork available for each student to have a different reproduction. Have students:

1. Write about the edges. Are they soft, blended, hard, fuzzy?
2. Write down colors using descriptive words—such as *lime* green, *lemon* yellow, *soft red*, *hot* pink—so you will remember the exact colors.
3. Write about the quality of the lines. Are they thick, thin, curved, straight?

OPTION 1 Collect the postcards and distribute (or display) reproductions of sculpture or masks from any culture. Have students draw the sculpture, based on their written descriptions of colors, lines, and edges.

OPTION 2 Put a list similar to this on the board: landscape, portrait, seascape, cityscape, animals. Have students turn in their postcards and select a subject from the board that is *different* from their postcard. The assignment is to make an artwork from the list using the *descriptions* they wrote about edges, colors, and lines in their postcard.

Extend a Postcard   Have students bring in a postcard from home and paste it anyplace on a piece of 12 X 18-inch white paper. Show them how to match the colors in the postcard as closely as possible by mixing paint. "Extend" the card to the edges of the paper. They may have to add more buildings, trees, or people. They might also draw themselves somewhere in this scene.

Expand a Postcard   Cut a postcard vertically in several sections—then *expand* it. Lay the sections on a piece of paper, spacing out the pieces before gluing. Use colored pencils or paints to fill in the spaces between and extend the picture to the edges of the paper.

Postcard Puzzles   Photocopy the postcard before cutting it and paste the photocopy on the outside of the envelope in which the puzzle will be stored. Also write the names of the artist and artwork on the envelope. Use an art knife to carefully cut the postcard into puzzle pieces. The number of pieces will depend on the age group that will use it. If you wish a larger puzzle, dry-mount an art reproduction on posterboard and cut it out.

PURCHASED EDUCATIONAL GAMES

Special games and learning aids are available through museum shops or vendors. Other useful resources are posters, books, sets of reproductions, timelines, videos, interactive video, and the Internet.

Art Bits® Card game

Artery®

Artifacts®

Art Memo Game®

Art Rummy®

Artdeck® Mexican Artists Playing Cards

Artdeck® African Artifacts Playing Cards

Artdeck®, 52 paintings on a deck of
   playing cards

Artpack®

Double-Deck Illusions Cards®

Impressionist Memo Game®

Izzi 2® Game

National Gallery of Art Lotto Game®

National Gallery of Art Rummy Game®

Nature in Art Quiz®, National Gallery of Art,
   Washington, DC

Where Art Thou?®

Question Arte®

Token Response®

Women Artists Teaching Board®

Art Game Vendors

Crizmac, P.O. Box 65928, Crizmac, AZ 85728-5928

Crystal Productions, Box 2159, Glenview, IL 60025

Sax Visual Art Resources, P.O. Box 510710, New Berlin, WI 53151

Word Games   Popular games such as Bingo, Password®, crossword puzzles, Old Maid, and Trivial Pursuit® can all be adapted as art games. Challenge a group of students to make up an art game, complete with game board and rules. If your classes are younger and have not yet learned about many artists, you can still adapt very simple games.

Jumbles   Take the names of a *group* of approximately ten artists—such as American artists, female artists, Impressionists, landscape painters, or Pop artists—and write a set of names on a large piece of paper, with the letters scrambled. You could have several of these prepared to use at either the beginning or end the of a period. Form teams of two students each. The first team finished wins. Other categories for scrambled letters would be art media and famous art museums.

Mix and Match   Based on artists or concepts with which you know students are familiar, write the names of famous artists and their most famous artworks or styles in two nonmatching columns. Students can draw a line from the artist to the title.

TALKING ABOUT ART: A GALLERY EXPERIENCE

A Real Museum Visit The following are questions students might answer when looking at an artwork in a museum:

What information is given on the label?

- Who created this work of art?

- What is it? (sculpture, painting, conceptual art)

- When was it made?

- What medium was used?

- When did the museum acquire this? (Usually the accession number will be something like 3:1999, which usually means it was the third work of art acquired in 1999.)

- Was this donated to the museum, or did it say Museum Purchase? Who gave it to the museum?

*Describe the artwork (**analysis**)*

- What are the dominant colors?

- What is a recognizable subject?

- What is in the background?

*What do you think the artist was trying to say? (**interpretation**)*

*How do you feel about the artwork? (**judgment**)*

- What emotion does this artwork make you feel?

- Would you purchase this artwork if money was not an issue? Why or why not?

Conversation Starters

What are some objects you see in this artwork?

What are some objects from nature?

Could you create a story from what you see in the picture?

What shapes are repeated (circles, squares, etc.)?

What title would you give this picture?

What do you think the artist is telling you in this picture?

What technique do you think is used?

Do you know anything about the artist?

Do you think a museum might like to purchase this picture? Why?

Why do you think this artwork was created?

What kinds of things belong in a museum?

Why would people sometimes steal artwork from a museum?

What kind of music does this picture make you remember?

GALLERY WALK

Ideally this could be done in a museum, but since students rarely are able to go to a museum, make a "Gallery" in your room or in the hall by hanging posters at intervals all the way around. Before beginning this activity, it would be helpful for you to stand in front of one painting and demonstrate a short analysis for the students.

In talking about artwork, effective criticism generally follows this order:

- *Description:* stating exactly what is seen; recognition of elements; medium; subject
- *Analysis:* formal evaluation of the elements and principles used; personal style of the artist
- *Interpretation:* what you think the artist might have meant; what it means to you; what influence the artist's environment might have had on the work
- *Judgment/evaluation:* originality; craftsmanship; how the artwork causes you to react; comparison of its quality with similar works of the same or another historical period; artistic and aesthetic merit

Divide the class into groups of three or four. Assign a number to each group and put numbers above each reproduction equal to the number of groups. Ask each group to station itself in front of the painting with "its" number. Give several index cards to each group and let the students take turns being the "recorder" for their group (*optional*). Give the group a few minutes to talk about things they notice about the artwork (such as color, line, subject, repetition, emphasis, etc.). When you say "Walk," the group moves on to the next painting until it has visited several. If the situation is comfortable enough, ask students to sit in front of the last artwork they analyzed and share what their group observed in that painting. Tell the students that each one must say something about the painting, so they have to decide who will talk about what. Then ask students from other groups that analyzed the same painting if they saw something that wasn't mentioned.

AESTHETICS

Aesthetics, the "philosophy" of art, is sometimes called "the art of the beautiful." Consider how the idea of "beauty" changes over a relatively short time period. As an example, talk with students about how hair styles, shoes, or even the shapes of pants' legs have been transformed over the years. As they examine those things created by artists, help students identify such principles of fine design as proportion, exaggeration, function, form, simplicity, classicism. Aesthetic questions rarely have specific answers because of the changing tastes of society, but they do get students to talk about preferences, which can lead to some interesting discussions.

When leading discussions, try not to ask your questions in such a way that you will get just a "yes" or "no" answer. Follow up answers with "Why do you think that?" or "Is there someone else here who agrees (or disagrees) with that answer?"

Here are a few sample aesthetic questions:

Can something ugly be art? Give me an example.

Can something such as a *manufactured* T-shirt be considered art? Why?

Which automobile do you think has the best design? Why?

If you exactly copy something from a magazine, could you feel that you have created an original artwork? Why or why not?

Is one work of art better than another if it costs more?

Why do you think one artist becomes famous and another one does not?

Do we have to know what the artist was thinking to appreciate the art? If not, why not?

Can you think of something that might improve the design of this work of art?

WRITING ABOUT ART

To get students in the habit of writing reflectively about art, you could have them keep a journal in which they would write for a few minutes each time they come in the classroom. You might ask them to write about a color that you have put in a prominent position or about a painting.

Writing Projects   These activities can be based on an artwork posted in the room.

- Write a letter to an artist. Ask questions about the artwork.
- Describe an abstract work of art in writing.
- Look at a photograph or painting and write about the "sounds" you hear in the background.
- Give a title to an artwork. Write why you would call it this.
- Write a conversation between characters seen in a work of art. For example, what are Rodin's *Burghers of Calais* talking about as they are led off in chains?
- Write a press release for a newspaper about the work of an artist whose show just opened.

Writing Poetry About Art   Students love to write poetry, but getting started is always difficult. I find that the *diamante* (so-called because of its shape) is a good icebreaker. I tape several posters in front of the class, then have students write a diamante poem about a poster. When I ask for volunteers to read their poetry, most are eager to do so, and the other students try to guess which poster was written about. This is particularly effective with Impressionists' work.

Students should know that many poets have written about works of art that have moved them, and that artists sometimes like to write about their own art.

DIAMANTE #1

One-word descriptive equivalent	Woman
Action phrase	smiling mysteriously
Simile	as if to keep her secrets forever
Summation (one word)	Mona

DIAMANTE #2

One noun	Sky
Two adjectives	dark, starry
Three verbs (-ing words)	swirling, shining, moving
[*Examples:* running, skipping, eating]	town, cypresses, mountains, valleys
Two nouns (1st subject); two nouns	glowing, concealing, revealing
(2nd subject)	Night
Three verbs (-ing words)	
One noun	

CINQUAIN #1

This five-line poem uses the following form:

Line 1: Noun	Television
Line 2: Two adjectives describing the noun	Bright, loud
Line 3: Three verbs showing the action of the noun	Teaching, entertaining, boring
Line 4: Four-word sentence telling about the noun	We watch too much
Line 5: Repeat the noun, or use a synonym for the noun	Television

CINQUAIN #2 This second example of a cinquain does not rhyme. It allows a pattern of five lines containing 22 syllables.

Line 1: Two syllables	Dinner
Line 2: Four syllables	Whole Family
Line 3: Six syllables	Cooking, talking, eating
Line 4: Eight syllables	Someone has to clean up the mess
Line 5: Two syllables	Daily

BIO-POEM This is a short biography telling about the life of someone.

Line 1: First name	Vincent
Line 2: Four traits	volatile, impulsive, compulsive, eccentric
Line 3: Related to	his friends, painters all
Line 4: Cares deeply about	sunlight, moonlight, color, motion
Line 5: Who feels	love, pain
Line 6: Who needs	friends, money, respect
Line 7: Who gives	everything for his friends
Line 8: Who fears	being alone
Line 9: Who would like to see	his work respected by
Line 10: Resident of	France, the world

LIMERICK A limerick is an amusing verse of three long lines that rhyme and two short lines that rhyme. The following example is from *More Limericks* by Cosmo Monkhouse:

Line 1: There was a young lady from Niger

Line 2: Who smiled as she rode on a tiger

Line 3: They came back from the ride

Line 4: With the lady inside

Line 5: And the smile on the face of the tiger

FREE VERSE Unless this is an English lesson that also incorporates art, I find that sometimes free verse is easier for students than trying to make a rhyming poem because it does not have a structure or rules. Students usually ask, "How long does it have to be?" Even though this is not a sonnet, I tell them that it has to be at least 14 lines, just to get them to work beyond the minimum. Suggest that they look at an abstract work of art by such artists as Mark Rothko, Jackson Pollock, and Helen Frankenthaler and write a poem about it.

HAIKU Haiku is a three-line poem consisting of 17 syllables. Two examples are given here. (These are particularly effective on accordion-folded books.)

Line 1: 5 syllables	The Mockingbird sings
Line 2: 7 syllables	A melody so soothing
Line 3: 5 syllables	Her voice sweet and clear.

> *Melissa Walker*, student at Florissant Valley Community College, St. Louis, Missouri

Butterflies swimming
Through the misty morning air
With gossamer wings.

> *Melissa Walker*, student at Florissant Valley Community College, St. Louis, Missouri

ACROSTIC This type of research format is a nonthreatening way for students to learn about artists, as shown in this example about Claude Monet. Proper sentence structure and punctuation are not required.

Contributed the name "Impressionism"
Lived outside of Paris
Afflicted with cataracts
Understood the color wheel
Died in 1926
Exhibited many paintings

Michel was his youngest son
Outdoor was where he liked to paint
Nature was his subject
Entranced by light
The moment was what he sought

> *Melissa Walker*, student at Florissant Valley Community College, St. Louis, Missouri

PROJECT 1
WRITE & ILLUSTRATE A MYTH

FOR THE TEACHER Most Westerners know something about Greek and Roman mythology because it was frequently a subject in familiar paintings and sculpture. Also of interest are myths from Africa, the Far East, India, and the Middle East. In their mythology the Egyptians, for example, used the bodies of humans and such animal heads as a cow, hyena, falcon, or ram, or their most famous hybrid, the Sphinx, which had the head of a Pharaoh and the body of a lion. Animals were depicted by combining features from many different living creatures. In Greek Mythology some such mythical creatures were the *chimera* (a fire-breathing she-monster that had a lion's head, a goat's body, and a serpent's tail), or the *satyr* (rear half was goat and the front half was human). The *minotaur* was half man and half horse, a *harpy* was a human female-headed winged bird, and a *mermaid* was half human female and half fish). In Chinese mythology, the *dragon* was a serpent with the head of a camel, horns of a deer, eyes of a demon, ears of a cow, neck of a snake, belly of a frog, scales of a carp, claws of an eagle, and the paws of a tiger!

Drawn from *Sleep and Death Lifting the Body of Sarpedon*, c. 515 BC, Euphronius (painter), Euxitheos (potter), Metropolitan Museum of Art

Vocabulary
myth	hybrid
watercolor crayons	contemporary

Preparation Read several myths from different cultures, and talk about natural phenomena such as thunder and lightning, the waning and waxing of the moon, magnetism, wind, floods, the tides, rain, love, death, childbirth, planting and harvesting crops, snow, the seasons, etc.

Alternative Projects
MAKE A GOOD-LUCK SYMBOL Have students soften plasticine clay in their hands while you are reading a myth to them. Ask students to make a "symbol" for good luck (to assure that the crop will come in next year). Some symbols that have been used by other cultures are "the evil eye" (seen on the U.S. dollar bill), *Venus* (female figures), the *Figa* (a thumb held between the first two fingers of a closed fist [Brazilian]), the *Ankh* (Egyptian), and the *Tiki* (New Zealand).

Stonehenge, c. 2000 BC, Salisbury Plain, Wiltshire, England

Interdisciplinary Connections
SOCIAL STUDIES AND SCIENCE

CIRCLES AND STANDING STONES Introduce ancient circles and standing stones as found in England, France, and North America. Have students find out how the people of ancient times identified special dates such as the Equinox.

CALENDAR Ask them what they know about the modern calendar, how it was determined, what a year consists of, and even study calendars of different cultures.

Multicultural Connections

STORYTELLING Have students select a particular culture that interests them. They could work in groups to research and make a synopsis of a story or myth that came from the culture they selected (*suggestions:* Africa, Northwest Coast Native Americans, Chinese, Greek and Roman). These stories could be written, acted out, or drawn.

Stone Calendar, 1450–1500, Museum of Archaeology, Mexico City, Mexico

PROJECT 1   WRITE & ILLUSTRATE A MYTH

Materials

newsprint
white drawing paper
Payons® or watercolor crayons
water
brushes

Directions   Your job is to create a modern myth. Imagine in ancient times what a mystery it must have been that the sun came up in the East each morning and went down in the West each evening. Cultures all over the world have created stories (myths) that explain this and other natural phenomena. Some of these stories were written down, but many were passed from generation to generation through storytelling.

When the Greeks illustrated myths on vases, and the Romans created myths, they dressed the characters in the same types of clothing everyone wore in those days. Your characters (animal, human, or half animal/half human) can be dressed in jeans, T-shirts, and athletic shoes or other contemporary clothing.

1. Decide what natural occurrence you want to explain. It could be a volcanic eruption, an earthquake or tornado, or something to do with the Earth's rotation such as the movement of the stars at night. Although you may already understand why something occurs, pretend that you do not and invent an explanation.

2. Make up a story of how the phenomenon *might* have occurred. Maybe some mythical creature or a mysterious person caused it. Come up with several explanations that seem reasonable to you (remember, you are ignorant of real science). Write a myth to read to the class. Select some part of it that seems especially interesting to you, and on a sheet of newsprint, draw your character.

3. Draw what your imaginary character (human, animal, or a combination of human and animal) might look like. Now think about motivation. Some mythological characters were warlike, or exceedingly strong, or very jealous. Why does this character behave the way it does? In the lore of Northwest Coast Native Americans, for example, "Raven" was responsible for many things that happened, and he was very mischievous.

4. Fold a piece of drawing paper in half the short way. Open it. On the left side, carefully copy the myth you have written. On the right side, use watercolor crayons to illustrate your myth. Payons® are drawn with as if they were crayons. You can outline, fill in, and use combinations of color. After your drawing is complete, use a brush to add water to the drawings—and it will look like a watercolor painting. If you want more detail, you can draw into the wet painting with the watercolor crayon.

PROJECT 2
GEOMETRY AND RENAISSANCE ART

FOR THE TEACHER Renaissance artists were searching in science and mathematics for the secrets of the universe. This was the time of alchemy, the beginning of medical practice and exploration of the world. Buildings were constructed using geometric forms such as the rectangle, triangle, and circle, and artists such as Leonardo da Vinci felt that even the human form could be analyzed through geometry. Artists of the Renaissance composed their paintings using geometric perspective that allowed them to measure and create the illusion of depth. A formula was developed for the perfect shape for painting called "the golden rectangle" or "golden section." They also composed figures within rectangular, triangular, or circular shapes. Some of their paintings were religious, while others were based on classical mythology.

Drawn from *The School of Athens*, Raphael de Sanzio, Vatican

Vocabulary

figure/ground	color	line
shape	value	unity
wash	contour	structure
perspective		

Preparation Show students slides or reproductions of Renaissance paintings. Help them to locate the inner construction of the painting, by having them trace geometric designs with a pointer or their fingers. If you have enough reproductions, students could use tracing paper to lay on top of the reproductions and actually use the same geometry they find in a particular picture for their own composition. Examples would be Leonardo da Vinci's *Madonna of the Rocks*, Sandro Botticelli's *Adoration of the Magi*, Raphael's *School of Athens*, and Pietro Perugino's *Delivery of the Keys to Saint Peter*.

Alternative Project

TONDO PAINTINGS On large paper, trace around a circle, such as a stool, and have students compose an artwork within a different format. Suggest they "pour" whatever they are drawing to fit within the circle. Artists of the Renaissance used these "Tondo" (round) paintings to contain mostly religious paintings, but your students could draw themselves and their pets, or animals from the zoo within these circles.

Interdisciplinary Connection

MATH Golden rectangle. Have students make a "golden rectangle," which is roughly in proportion of 8 to 13. Using a compass and ruler, draw two lines of equal length at right angles to each other (AB, BC). Extend a line half the length of AB, creating BD. With D at the center, use a compass to make an arc CE, intersecting line AB at point E. To make a rectangle, draw a line from E parallel to BC and from C parallel to BE. These meet at point F, forming rectangle BCFE.

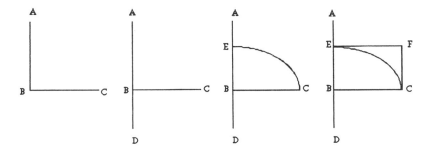

PROJECT 2 GEOMETRY AND RENAISSANCE ART

© 2000 by John Wiley & Sons, Inc.

STUDENT PAGE

Materials

pencils
rulers
compasses
white drawing paper
tissue paper
polymer medium or thinned white glue
ink or permanent black marker

Drawn from *The Last Supper*, 1495–1498,
Leonardo da Vinci,
Santa Maria delle Grazie, Milan

Directions You will not be copying a Renaissance composition, but looking at it carefully to find where the artist used *hidden* geometric forms. For example, three figures might be organized within a triangle or a group of people gathered within a circle. Use your finger to see if you can identify triangles, circles, and rectangles.

1. When you have located these forms (there may be more than one in a painting), use a pencil and a ruler or compass to draw similar lines on a piece of white drawing paper. Remember to use the space well, making your triangles or rectangles large enough that you won't have empty space.

2. Consider a subject for *your* geometric composition. It could be a group of friends sitting together, a still-life composition of various objects, trees grouped together, or even animals arranged within the geometric composition.

3. Select a color scheme of approximately five cool or warm colors of tissue paper for the background. Simply tear the tissue paper *or* cut it into geometric shapes and apply it to the white background paper, arranging all the paper before applying the polymer medium.

4. Brush a small area of polymer medium on the white paper, then put the tissue paper in place. Brush polymer on top of the tissue immediately after you apply it to the paper, and it will give a shiny finish. The colors may run some and the paper will be wrinkled, but this is not a problem. Keep applying tissue until the white drawing paper is covered. It should dry overnight. You should still be able to see the pencil-drawn geometric figures through the paper.

5. Now is the time to draw your own geometric composition on the background. Draw this either with permanent black marker or with black ink. Remember that you will keep the geometry "hidden," just as Renaissance artists did.

PROJECT 3
IN THE MANNER OF . . .
ARTISTIC INTERPRETATION

FOR THE TEACHER   Although artists were not generally known by name until the Renaissance, styles of art are typical of many other times and cultures. Because photography is a relatively new arrival on the art scene, the traditional way of recording how someone looked was the portrait. Portraits of royalty were painted at court and taken (often by the painter/diplomat) to another court to facilitate marriages. Families often had miniatures painted to have a memento of a loved one. Kings, Queens, diplomats, church leaders, and wealthy patrons were frequently the subjects of portraits. Self-portraits are valued by today's students and their families because it is the artist's view of himself or herself at that moment in time, and therefore is special.

Vocabulary

portrait	miniature
sitter	value
foreground	subject
middle ground	background

Preparation   Discuss the proportions of the face with students before they begin their self-portraits. Mirrors are helpful to have, but depending on the age of the students, some teachers feel students can't get on with the business of drawing because of their fascination with their own faces. Students could work from a school photo of themselves, because this project is not about getting a likeness, but about transformation based on portraits from a variety of artists. Although each student will have a unique picture—even if all of them were done in *one* style, such as that of Henri Matisse or Leonardo da Vinci—it still might be better to have reproductions of at least five artists, just to give variety to the group of portraits.

Select the medium based on the size of the portrait the student will make. Colored pencil is labor intensive, so the size probably should be small; if tempera is chosen, the picture can be considerably larger.

Alternative Projects

LINE DRAWING IN AN ARTIST'S STYLE   Make simple line-drawing photocopies on $8\frac{1}{2} \times 11$-inch paper of a familiar subject (rooster, cat, dog, pig, hand, baseball and bat, horse, cow, car, house, flower, person). For each class you teach, have a different subject. Assign each student to interpret the subject in the manner of a famous artist whose style is recognizable and distinctive.

PUT YOUR FACE RIGHT HERE   Students could paint a reproduction of any famous work of art, substituting their own faces in place of those in the actual painting (they could work from a school photo if necessary). Japan-born artist Yasumasa Morimura paints massive historical portraits in which his face is substituted for *all* the characters in a painting.

Drawn from *George Washington,* 1796, Gilbert Stuart, Saint Louis Art Museum

CARNIVAL BACKDROP PAINTINGS This project was done at a Missouri State Art Educators meeting. Several groups of artists working together enlarged a famous painting (without bothering to paint the faces) onto cardboard using acrylic paint. For a more permanent base, use foamboard or plywood (assuming you have someplace to store them until the next year). Each enlargement had one or more faces that were cut out with utility knives, leaving empty ovals. If you do this on plywood, use an electric keyhole saw. Photos were then taken of the reproductions, with different groups of people standing behind with their faces showing through the ovals. Suggested paintings are *The Mona Lisa, American Gothic,* and *Syndics of the Draper's Guild.* This would be an ideal project for a schoolwide Art Fair.

PROJECT 3   IN THE MANNER OF . . . ARTISTIC INTERPRETATION

STUDENT PAGE

Materials

drawing paper
pencil
mirror or school photo
tempera, pastel, colored pencil, or acrylic paint

Directions   In this project, you will paint yourself in the manner of a famous portrait painter. You may need to find clues as to how to "dress" by looking at portraits created by the artist you have chosen.

A portrait was usually painted to tell the viewer something about the sitter. Women often were painted with an animal (the dog was a symbol of faithfulness). Children sometimes were shown holding a toy or sitting with a pet. Men might be painted seated at a desk, with a book in their laps, and other items that told something about their professions. Sometimes people were painted wearing a uniform. Most portraits were painted indoors, although a window might be behind the subject that showed a boat in a harbor or a prosperous farm.

1. Do pencil drawings of yourself, paying careful attention to differences in value (areas of light and dark). Select a portrait reproduction that appeals to you. A number of artists became famous because of their method of applying color (Seurat), or their style (Matisse, Rembrandt, or Modigliani).

2. Look at the costumes that are worn by the person in the portrait or the shape of the face. Some artists exaggerated features, making very long faces such as those painted by Amedeo Modigliani, or very fat faces such as those of Fernando Botero. Some artists painted their sitters wearing fancy clothing, jewelry, or a hat.

3. Draw yourself in the manner of the artist whose work you are *quoting*. You may choose to dress yourself in the same type of clothing worn by that artist's normal subjects.

4. After you have drawn yourself, this can be colored by using tempera or acrylic paint. Think about what will be in the background. You can put yourself in front of a window or draw a painting on a wall, such as the one in *Whistler's Mother*. If you want the background to be plain, you can make one side of the painting quite dark and the other light.

Madonna of the Magnificat, c. 1483, Sandro Botticelli, Uffizi Gallery, Florence

Artists and Their Subjects

Here is a partial list of several cultures and artists whose work is well known. The descriptions of their work are *greatly* simplified, as almost all artists have done more than one particular subject or medium, but these are particularly suitable as a base for a lesson or unit.

Cultures

Aboriginal Australian
African
African-American
Asian: Chinese, Japanese, Korean, Laotian, Tibetan
Egyptian
European
Greek
Hispanic: Mexican, Caribbean, South American, Spanish
Indian Moghul
Native American: Northwestern, Plains, Southwestern, Eastern, Southern, Woodlands, Desert, Coastal
New Zealand: English and Maori cultures

Time Periods and "Schools" of Art

Prehistoric (cave paintings)
Medieval
Renaissance
Baroque
Romantic
Realistic
Impressionism
Cubism
Fauvism
Expressionism
Modernism
Surrealism
Abstraction
Pop Art
Naive

Drawn from *American Gothic*, 1930, Grant Wood, The Art Institute of Chicago

Animals

Audubon, John James. wildlife and birds
Beardsley, Aubrey. art nouveau black-and-white illustrations
Butterfield, Deborah. sculptured horses
Durer, Albrecht. animal studies
Eakins, Thomas. studies of horses
Hicks, Edward. Realism; combinations of animals and people
Rousseau, Henri. animals; jungle scenes

Architects

Gehry, Frank, Guggenheim Museum, Bilbao, Spain
Graves, Michael. Post-modernist; color on buildings
Wright, Frank Lloyd. "prairie school" architect
Sullivan, Louis B. architect; modernist architecture

Cities

Canaletto, Antonio. paintings of Venice
DeChirico, Giorgio. cityscapes with a fantasy theme
Demuth, Charles. the rushing of a fire engine through wet city streets
Estes, Richard. photorealist paintings
Grooms, Red. distorted, humorous views including people, firetrucks, cars, etc.
Hopper, Edward. realistic scenes of the city at night; children at play
Marin, John. watercolor cityscapes; harbors; landscapes; abstract
O'Keeffe, Georgia. scenes of New York
Sheeler, Charles. Precisionist paintings of factories, cities, machinery
Stella, Joseph. Futuristic scenes of the city
Utrillo, Maurice. Post-impressionist cityscapes

The Solomon R. Guggenheim Museum, 1957–1959, New York, Frank Lloyd Wright

David, 1501–1504, Michelangelo

Expressionism

deKooning, Willem. paintings usually of women, or a woman on a bicycle

Klee, Paul. subject matter such as fish, people, interesting colors, grids

Kokoshka, Oskar. portraits; often strong hands

Marc, Franz. blue horses; nature

Munch, Edvard. people; sad paintings; dancers; *The Scream*

Pollock, Jackson. layers of dripped paint filling large canvases

Families

Cassatt, Mary. Impressionist; mostly mothers and children

Tanner, Henry O. tender moments among different generations

Drawn from Poster Design . . . Whitney Exhibition, 1974, Jacob Lawrence, Terry Dintenfass, Inc., New York City

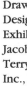

Flowers

Nolde, Emil. bold, brilliantly colored abstract flowers

O'Keeffe, Georgia. giant flowers include tiny details, yet fill and spill over the picture plane

van Gogh, Vincent. sunflowers; irises

Impressionism

Cezanne, Paul. scenery; mountains

Manet, Edouard. portraits; people in nature

Monet, Claude. atmospheric landscapes; buildings; trees; lilies; watergarden

Renoir, Pierre Auguste. cafe scenes; people

Seurat, Georges. Pointillism; landscapes with people

Landscapes

Cezanne, Paul. Impressionistic; patches of color

Constable, John. English romantic landscape; atmospheric skies

Currier, N. & Ives, J.M. scenes of country life in America

Gauguin, Paul. bright colors; Polynesian scenes

Grooms, Red. collage; bright patches of color

Monet, Claude. Impressionistic landscapes; waterlilies; garden scenes

O'Keeffe, Georgia. flowers; hills; landscapes; bones; cityscapes

Reynolds, Joshua. realistic landscapes

Rousseau, Henri. jungle landscapes; animals; hidden figures

van Gogh, Vincent. swirling brushstrokes; gardens; flowers; people

Whistler, James Abbott McNeill. romantic landscapes; portraits

Wood, Grant. idealized countryside landscapes; farms; small towns

Drawing after *Fought Cight Cockfight*, Nancy Graves, 1984, Saint Louis Art Museum

Letters and Shapes

Davis, Stuart. words; collage-like shapes combined with words

Johns, Jasper. hatching in different colors; targets; American flag; maps with letters

Lichtenstein, Roy. black outlining; dots; cartoon style; word balloons (as in comics)

Matisse, Henri. patterned clothing; reclining figures; flowers; cut-outs; simple shapes

Rivers, Larry. French words in background

Warhol, Andy. silkscreen or Campbell® soup cans; Coke® bottles (multiples)

Narrative (Storytelling)

Bearden, Romare. collage; prints; scenes of African-American life

Benton, Thomas Hart. muralist; people at work

Hicks, Edward. realism; combinations of animals and people

Lawrence, Jacob. people; historical African-American references

Pippin, Horace. African-American; fantasy; historical African American stories

Remington, Frederic. his stories of the Wild West bring history alive

Ringgold, Faith. quilts; African-American; historical references

Rubens, Peter Paul. painter of grand narratives; mythological or religious

West, Benjamin. American History scenes

Native American (Contemporary)

Gorman, R.C. simple scenes of Native Americans in traditional dress

Martinez, Maria. black pottery

Scholder, Fritz. bright colors; simple shapes

Whitehorse, Emmi. traditional symbolism

Acoma, c. 1910

Nature

Audubon, John James. birds and animals

Non-objective

Frankenthaler, Helen. stained shapes from poured paint

Mondrian, Piet. red, blue, yellow, straight-line geometric paintings

Picasso, Pablo. Cubism; blue period

Pollock, Jackson. poured paint; swirling lines

Stella, Frank. geometric shapes in bands of color

People (Groups)

Bearden, Romare. collages with photographs of people; prints

Bingham, George Caleb. realistic scenes of Missouri politicians; river boatmen

Botticelli, Sandro. religious and mythological paintings of large groups of people

Brueghel, Pieter. landscapes, usually including numbers of peasants

Dubuffet, Jean. patterned, abstract figures using red, white, blue, and black

Dyck, Anthony van. portraits of wealthy patrons and royalty

Gauguin, Paul. scenes of Brittany and Tahiti; people in costume; unrealistic colors

Haring, Keith. simple outlines of generic figures filling space randomly

Hicks, Edward. groups of people and animals used in landscape; narratives; *Peaceable Kingdom*

Leger, Fernand. black outlines of faces; hand with sausage-like fingers

Moses, Anna Mary (Grandma). scenes of country life filled with people at work and play

Pippin, Horace. African-American; narrative

Ringgold, Faith. African-American; quilts; historical references

Seurat, Georges. *Sunday Afternoon on the Island of Grande Jatte*

Toulouse-Lautrec, Henri de. outlining; simple colors

Photographers

Adams, Ansel. master of black-and-white landscapes

Brady, Matthew. Civil War

Lange, Dorothea. documented the Great Depression and migration

Parks, Gordon. African-American photographer of life in America

Sherman, Cindy. disguised self-portraits

Weston, Edward. sharp photos of dunes, green peppers, people

Drawn from *Eight Water Glasses Under Fluorescent Light*, Janet Fish, 1974, Private collection, New York City

Portraits

Arcimboldo, Giuseppi. fruit or vegetables in place of a face

Botero, Fernando. characters are all exaggeratedly fat

Catlin, George. showed Native Americans in early history of U.S.

Close, Chuck. super-realist faces painted using a squared grid

da Vinci, Leonardo. traditional portraits; *Mona Lisa*

Durer, Albrecht. self-portrait with long hair

Giacometti, Alberto. sculptor; elongated figures

Grooms, Red. cartoon-like collage portraits

Hals, Franz. Dutch Baroque group portraits and genre portraits

Kahlo, Frida. self-portraits with monkeys and jungle plants

Lange, Dorothea. Depression-era photographic portraits

Lichtenstein, Roy. individuals and groups in cartoon-like manner

Marisol (Escobar). wooden people sculptures; realistic and caricatured faces

Matisse, Henri. patterned backgrounds; unusual colors; Fauvism

Modigliani, Amedeo. elongated faces

Neel, Alice. insightful realistic portraits

Picasso, Pablo. Cubistic and realistic portraits

Rembrandt van Rijn. dark background; old-fashioned clothing

Renoir, Pierre Auguste. Impressionist; soft-edged portraits of girls, women; some landscapes

Reynolds, Joshua. family portraits

Rouault, Georges. heavily impasto Expressionistic paintings

Sargent, John Singer. portraits; watercolors

Stuart, Gilbert. colonial American portraits; *George Washington*

Toulouse-Lautrec, Henri de. lithographs and drawings of Parisian nightlife

van Gogh, Vincent. swirling vigorous brushstrokes; outlining

Velazquez, Diego. portraits of royalty; history; *Las Meninas*

Vermeer, Jan. portraits; Dutch genre

Whistler, James Abbott McNeill. atmospheric paintings and portraits; *Whistler's Mother*

Drawn after *The Quilting Bee*, 1950, Anna Mary (Grandma) Moses, Private collection

"Primitives" (Naive Painters)

Moses, Anna Mary (Grandma). nostalgic scenes of sugaring, quilting, farm life

Rousseau, Henri. this customs agent drew his jungles from the Paris Botanical Garden and his house plants

Printmaking

Albers, Josef. prints used square-within-a-square motif; relationships of colors

Bearden, Romare. African-American genre scenes; photography and collage in prints

Cassatt, Mary. studies of families, friends

Close, Chuck. head studies in various print media

Davis, Stuart. abstract cityscapes and other subjects combined with words

Degas, Edgar. monotypes; ballet dancers; horses

Dine, Jim. ordinary tools such as brushes; his bathrobe

Francis, Sam. specialized in abstract spatter-prints around the edges

Graves, Nancy. sometimes contain images from mythology, nature, and art history

Grooms, Red. a sense of humor is in every cartoon-like collage-style print

Hockney, David. people in their Southern California environment

Indiana, Robert. his original *LOVE* has been much parodied with other "letter messages"

Johns, Jasper. symbols such as flags, targets; lines used to make patterns

Kunioshi, Yasuo. modernist painter

Lichtenstein, Roy. Benday dot or stripe patterns used in cartoon-like scenes; sometimes "quotations" based on work of Surrealists and German Expressionists

Nevelson, Louise. this sculptor's prints strongly resemble her box-like sculptures

Oldenburg, Claes. a sculptor whose work takes an object meant for one use and transforms it to another use

Picasso, Pablo. black-and-white bullfight prints; Cubist work in color

Rauschenberg, Robert. "combines" letters, photographs, and unlikely objects

Trova, Ernest. human form moving through space, often machine-like; the *Falling Man* series

Ukiyo-e. Japanese prints of Geisha and actors

Printer's Marks, 1205

Warhol, Andy. Pop Art used famous people, Coke® bottles, Campbell® soup cans, and an electric chair in his photo-silkscreens

Religion

Michelangelo. painter, *Sistine Chapel*; sculptor, *David*

Raphael. painter for the Popes; *School of Athens*

Rembrandt. Northern Baroque painter/printmaker; mostly portraits and religious scenes

van Eyck, Jan. Flemish painter of altarpieces

Seascapes

Homer, Winslow. romantic landscapes, cityscapes, seascapes

Turner, Joseph Mallord William. romantic seascapes; atmospheric landscapes; swirling clouds

Sculpture

Brancusi, Constantin. simplified portrait shapes (heads); rough-hewn sculpture and bases

Butterfield, Deborah. sculptured life-size horses

Calder, Alexander. creator of mobiles and stabiles

Christo. environmental transformations; wrapping huge buildings; *Running Fence*

Cornell, Joseph. box assemblage/collages of items including art reproductions

Giacometti, Alberto. elongated figural sculpture

Goldsworthy, Andy. environmental sculptor

Graves, Nancy. natural materials cast in bronze and enameled

Marisol (Escobar). wooden sculpture/assemblages

Michelangelo. human figures; *Moses*; *Medici Tomb*

Moore, Henry. human figures, often seated; families

Nevelson, Louise. assemblages of wood, plastic, driftwood

Oldenburg, Claes. soft sculpture; giant badminton birds; folding knife

Pfaff, Judy. colorful assemblages of plastic

Stella, Frank. abstract, patterned metal shapes organized as 3-dimensional design to hang on wall

Still Life

Braque, Georges. Cubistic; tables with still-life

Fish, Janet. contemporary watercolorist; tabletop still-lifes

Flack, Audrey. hyper-realistic still-lifes

Harnett, William. *trompe l'oeil* painter

Picasso, Pablo. Cubism

Surrealism/Fantasy

Arcimboldo. faces composed of fruit, fish, flowers

Chagall, Marc. fantasy art; his self-portrait had seven fingers on one hand; scenes of his native Russia included upside-down houses, cows flying

Dali, Salvador. landscapes with watches and other strange shapes in background

DeChirico, Giorgio. lonely cities; people "lost"

Duchamp, Marcel. "found" objects as sculpture

Magritte, René. blue sky and clouds, with floating black derby hat and pipe

Miro, Joan. Surrealist, his work still was based on reality

Other Famous Artists

Banister, Edward. African-American; simple scenes of family life

Bierstadt, Albert. landscapes of the great West

Escher, M.C. visual mystery and the use of Tessellations in his (mostly) black-and-white work

Hiroshige, Ando. Japanese printmaker

Hokusai, Katsushika. Japanese printmaker

Mondrian, Piet. rectangular shapes; basic colors of white, black, red, blue, and yellow

Rauschenberg, Robert. collage; photo transfers; sculptural assemblage

Wyeth, Andrew. American painter of people and landscapes in Pennsylvania

Wyeth, Jamie. portraiture; farm animals

Wyeth, N.C. illustrator/painter

Drawn from *Flying Dragon*, 1975, Alexander Calder, The Art Institute of Chicago

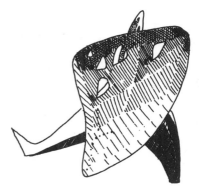

Drawn after *Still-Life Violin and Music*, 1988, William Michael Harnett, The Metropolitan Museum of Art, New York City

Part II

The Art Curriculum

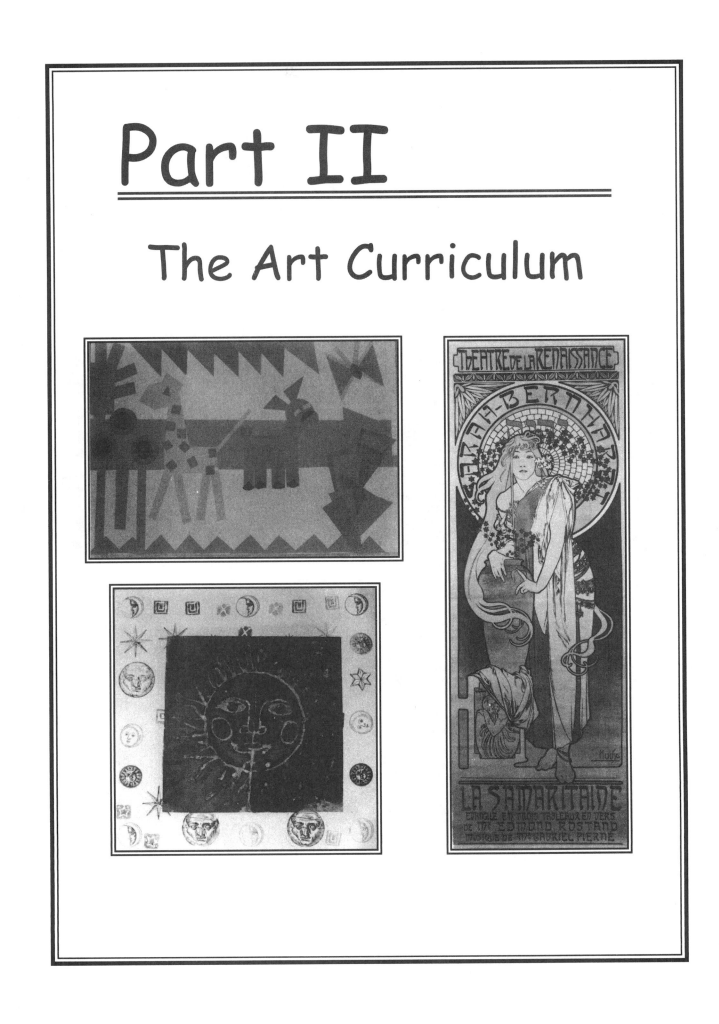

UNIT 1

EXPLORING THE ELEMENTS AND PRINCIPLES OF DESIGN

Art educators of today talk about the elements and principles of design as if artists had *always* based their work on them. These formal terms used to describe art have come into use in the relatively recent past. One element may simply appear to be more dominant in a specific work of art, and that is the premise of the projects in this section. In actuality, every artwork uses a combination of *elements* organized through the use of the *principles* of design.

In some cultures the traditional method of working has changed very little over the centuries. Designs were passed down through family members or from artist-to-artist in a system of apprenticeship, or through copying existing artworks. Work done by contemporary artists in some cultures look as if they might have been done hundreds of years ago. For example, anthropologist and African specialist Jackie Lewis Harris of the University of Missouri, St. Louis, says, "Time is not relevant to the study of African Art." Artists instinctively understood how to use color, space, texture, line, and form to create works of art that would be beautiful in their culture, even though these might appear "strange" to people from another culture who lack understanding of the tradition.

Methods of working, materials, and subject matter evolve, and it is often not possible to go back and create artwork in the old manner because the methods and the craftsmanship training have been lost. Then again, new materials and techniques have opened methods of working that could not have been dreamed of in the past. Creative artists and art educators are constantly experimenting with materials. Art educators also were probably the original recyclers!

Today's art educator has many approaches to teaching art in addition to basing projects on the elements and principles of design. We can base a study unit on subject matter such as portraiture, landscape, animals or flowers in art, or on a specific culture. In addition to teaching students how to "do" art, we also teach them how to analyze it, to know something about the history of the technique, and to evaluate it according to accepted standards of beauty. We teach problem-solving and skill-building as a matter of course. In addition to the "traditional" art forms that formerly were taught—such as sculpture, fine crafts, architecture, drawing, and painting—we now include photography and cinema, industrial design, and illustration. Art educators are often team members who are working on schoolwide educational goals or themes. Interdisciplinary teaching of a unit can benefit understanding of both subjects being taught.

Art educators must never lose sight of the simple joy that producing a work of art gives to most children. It gives children another way to express themselves, and awakens a wonder in them that no other discipline can.

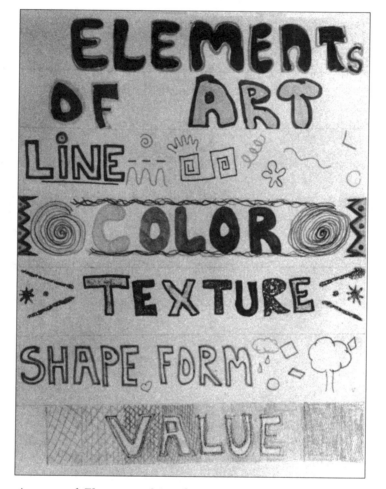

A personal *Elements of Art* chart can introduce students to the curriculum of art. (Created by student Karen Gammon.)

LINE

Line is the first mark made by a child and is present in most works of art. We see it as we look at the branches of a tree, a plowed field, a road going off into the distance, or the horizon. It is used to describe emotion or thought. The character of a work can be determined by how thick or thin, close together, or far apart the lines are. Movement and direction, energy, and restfulness can be depicted through the use of line, which is often used to lead the eye to the main subject in a work of art.

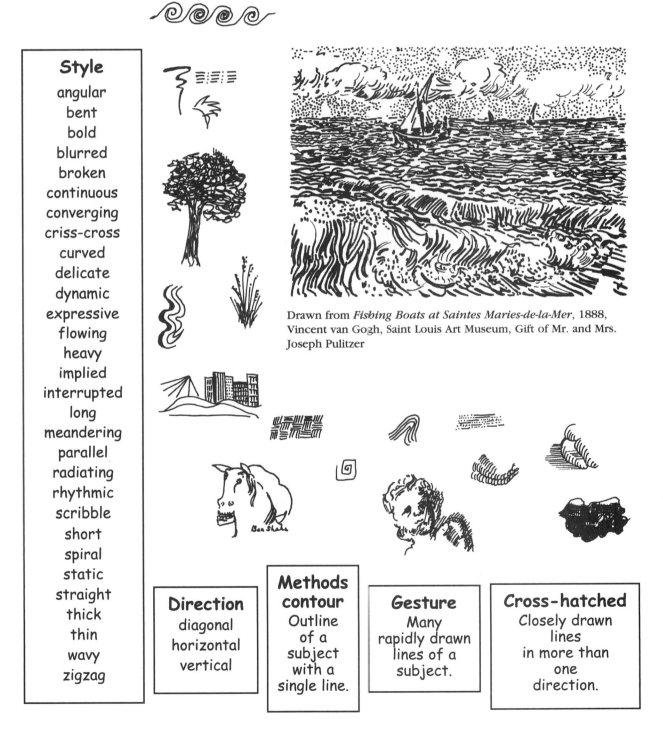

Style
angular
bent
bold
blurred
broken
continuous
converging
criss-cross
curved
delicate
dynamic
expressive
flowing
heavy
implied
interrupted
long
meandering
parallel
radiating
rhythmic
scribble
short
spiral
static
straight
thick
thin
wavy
zigzag

Drawn from *Fishing Boats at Saintes Maries-de-la-Mer*, 1888, Vincent van Gogh, Saint Louis Art Museum, Gift of Mr. and Mrs. Joseph Pulitzer

Direction
diagonal
horizontal
vertical

Methods
contour
Outline
of a
subject
with a
single line.

Gesture
Many
rapidly drawn
lines of a
subject.

Cross-hatched
Closely drawn
lines
in more than
one
direction.

PROJECT 1–1
THREE PEOPLE

FOR THE TEACHER   This project asks students to draw three large figures standing side by side or overlapping, with portions of the figures touching the edges of the paper. Either the figures or the negative background space around and between the figures will be filled with varieties of patterns using line.

Contour (outline) drawing is often one of the first introductions for students to draw what they see, and most of them enjoy posing for each other. They learn by beginning with simple line figures in early grades, progressing to more richly detailed drawings as their skills progress. Show them artwork by a number of artists to demonstrate the many ways that artists interpret the figure.

Suggested Historical References

Jean Dubuffet

Alberto Giacometti

Max Beckmann

Henri Matisse

Fernand Leger

Fernando Botero

Ben Shahn

Keith Haring

Vocabulary

figure/ground

contour

pattern

line

negative space

overlapping

Preparation   Discuss the proportions of the human figure. Have the students stand and, using both hands, feel their own faces, necks, shoulders, elbows, waists, hips, knees, and ankles. Have them place a flat hand on their face, then on their foot to see the relative size of the hand; to notice where their hands and elbows are in relation to their waists when they hang straight at their sides. Either on a chalkboard or on a piece of paper taped to a board, demonstrate blind-contour drawing while one of your students poses for you.

Explain that the figures should be large enough to "bump" the edges of the paper or even go off the paper. Depending on the arrangement of your classroom, you can either have one student pose for everyone or have four drawing groups with students taking turns posing. Each pose should last approximately 10 minutes. Remind students to try to get the entire figure on the page, with a little space both above the head and below the feet. Because students often make the head too large or too small, suggest they use approximately one third of the page for the head and shoulders, one third for the chest to the upper thighs, and the lower third for the legs and feet.

PROJECT 1–1   THREE PEOPLE

Materials

18 × 24-inch drawing paper

pencil

masking tape

black marker

Directions   This project involves drawing three figures on the same piece of paper. They should be figures standing side by side or one slightly in front of or behind another (overlapping). Plan ahead so you can get the three entire figures on the paper. They should be large enough that the paper is almost filled with the three figures.

1. Use masking tape to attach the drawing paper to your table.

2. Do the first figure drawing in the middle of the paper. Look at the model as you draw, and try not to lift your pencil from the paper. Draw slowly, and pretend the pencil is touching the outline of the model as you move it. Allow the pencil to show all the bends and details you see.

3. Draw the second figure on the paper next to the first figure. These figures can be side by side, in front of, or behind each other.

4. Draw a third figure on the paper. They will overlap now because your composition is crowded.

5. Outline the outer edges of the figures in black marker.

6. Divide the background space out to the edges with a few lines. Within the shapes formed by these lines, draw patterns such as lines, dots, circles, squares, triangles, or checkerboards. Or use the pattern to fill in only the figures.

COLOR

If colors were not so important to children, their clothing would be neutral; their toys, bland; and their paintings, subdued. Instead, most children wear brightly colored clothing and they paint with bright pure color. They haven't yet learned about "blue Monday," "green with envy," or "he had a yellow streak down his back." "Black for mourning" (in Western Culture) and "white for the bride" are still traditions, but the lines are becoming blurred on these color preferences also. The symbolism of color is more important to adults, and while the color symbolism used in Renaissance paintings would have been understood during that time, it is now mostly obscured. Young children are also far less concerned with "realism" in color.

Color Terms:

bright	dull	warm	cool
light	dark	grayed	intense
strong	weak	tranquil	disquieting
loud	quiet	stimulating	calming

Definitions:

Hue. the undiluted color in its purest intensity
Value. lightness and darkness of the hue
Tint. hue plus white
Shade. hue plus black
Intensity. brightness or dullness of a color
Neutral colors. white, black, gray, tan
Primary colors in pigment. red, blue, yellow
Primary colors in the light spectrum. magenta, cyan, yellow
Cool colors. (blue, violet, green) appear to recede
Warm colors. (red, yellow, orange) appear to advance

Drawn from *La Desserte Rouge*, 1908, Henri Matisse, The Hermitage, St. Petersburg, Russia

Color Wheel

Color schemes based on the color wheel

Primary Colors
Red, Yellow, Blue

Secondary Colors
Orange, Green, Violet

Intermediate Colors
Red-orange, Red-violet, Blue-violet, Yellow-green, Blue-green

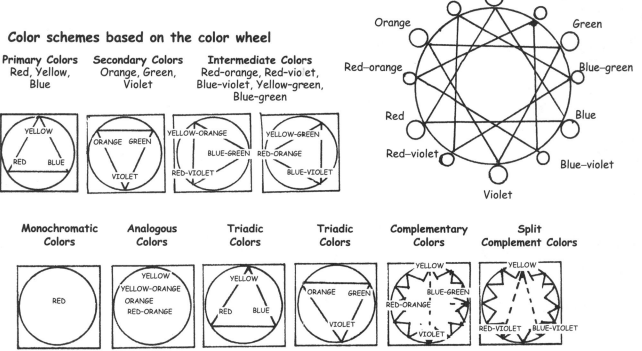

PROJECT 1-2
PERSONAL RAINBOW COLOR WHEEL

FOR THE TEACHER Personal experience in mixing three primary colors to produce a complete color wheel is a wonderful introduction to painting. Although pre-mixed tempera is a staple of the art classroom, students understand how color is achieved when they mix their own colors. Each composition will be different from others as students mix their own colors and use their own shapes. Ellsworth Kelley's work in colors of the spectrum may help them to realize that simple colors and shapes are beautiful.

Vocabulary

hue

primary

secondary

complementary

template

tertiary

Preparation This project will probably take two sessions, but is worth the effort. Use 3 × 6-inch pieces of tagboard (old file folders or 3 × 5-inch unlined index cards would also work). Discuss real and abstract shapes with students and ask them to draw a *simple* shape (if these are too complex, the cutting out gets tedious). Show them an example of a real color wheel and talk about the colors of the spectrum. Remind students that colors need to be mixed well to avoid streaking, and that they need to cover the surface but not build up the paint too thickly. Remind students to save the negative shapes from the cards to use later in a collage.

Adaptations for Younger Children: Primary and Secondary Colors
Give each student a 3 × 3-inch card. Have them draw a shape and then use scissors to cut it out. Distribute 3 × 3-inch squares of red, yellow, and blue paper to each student. They should trace around their shape with pencil, then cut out those shapes and glue them on the corners of a (roughly) 5-inch triangle they have drawn on white paper with marker. Then distribute orange, green, and violet paper. Have the children draw a second triangle on top of the first, and appropriately glue the secondary colors in place on the other triangle. Hopefully they will notice that they have made a circle (wheel). (See the color wheel on the Color Handout.)

Alternative Project
RAINBOW WAVE: MOVING FIGURE Have students make a tagboard template of a figure or shape. Beginning at one side or corner of a piece of white drawing paper, they draw the entire figure, then partially trace around this 12 times, overlapping (part of the design will be hidden when it is painted). It can go across the page in a curved line, or smaller repetitions of the same shape can cause it to diminish in size. Have students lightly write what the colors will be in the 12 shapes to assist in placing the paint in the appropriate areas. These should be painted in the order of the spectrum to avoid wasting paint.

GROUP PROJECT COLOR WHEELS To speed up this process, students can work in groups of three to mix and paint four colors on cards for everyone in the group. To save paint, each of the three people would select one primary color and make variations on it. Have students be sure their names are written on the backs of the cards.

Interdisciplinary Connections

SCIENCE

COLOR IN LIGHT: COLOR IN PIGMENT This is a good opportunity to teach differences in colors seen in light versus colors in pigments. Also discuss prisms, rainbows, and the spectrum of light.

Student Karen Gammon's color wheel serves the purpose of teaching the complexity of color mixing and painting.

Student Jennifer Watson's color wheel fish has eyes of the complementary color.

PROJECT 1–2 PERSONAL RAINBOW COLOR WHEEL

STUDENT PAGE

Materials

tagboard cut into 3 × 6-inch rectangles
18 × 18-inch black construction paper
red, blue, and yellow tempera paint
newspaper
pencils
brushes
paper palettes (doubled slick sheets from a magazine)
rubber bands
scissors

Directions

1. Write your name on the back of all 12 cards. You will be mixing all 12 colors from the three primary colors. Paint three tagboard pieces using only undiluted red, yellow, and blue. As you finish painting, place your wet pieces on a sheet of newspaper.

2. To mix secondary and tertiary colors, select two primary colors.

    ● **Red and Yellow:** Mix to make orange. Add more red to make red–orange and more yellow to make yellow–orange.

    ● **Red and Blue:** Mix to make violet. Add more blue to make blue–violet and more red to make red–violet.

    ● **Blue and Yellow:** Mix to make green. Add more blue to make blue-green and more yellow to make yellow–green.

3. Draw a shape on a 3 × 6-inch tagboard rectangle and cut it out. The shape could be something simple such as lightning bolt, arrow, crayon, tree, car, animal, your initials—but you must use the full 6-inch length. Avoid doing ordinary shapes such as a triangle or star.

4. Arrange the 12 shapes on a black background arranging red, yellow, and blue in a triangle, then make a second triangle with orange, green, and violet. Insert the tertiary colors. Do this in a perfect circle, leaving a border on all four sides *before* gluing the shapes in place. You may have to overlap near the center. Make sure you have the colors in the order of the spectrum.

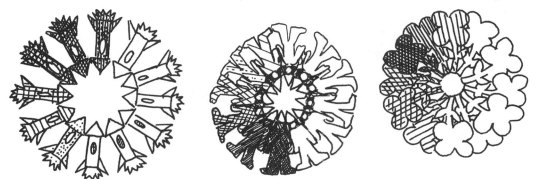

PROJECT 1–3
COSTUMES AND COLORS

FOR THE TEACHER This project introduces students to experiments in watercolor. It is also a cross-cultural lesson because you may have several students who have a hat or costume from a different culture (for example, Western dress or an Asian robe). Even if the costume is large, drawing a classmate in costume, or even a hat, gives the idea that this is something special. This is also a lesson in value, as students will be forced to notice that some areas are vastly lighter than others. Teach students to squint through their eyelashes to see differences that might not otherwise be apparent to them.

Vocabulary
hue

complement

value

dilute

glaze

Preparation Ideally the lesson would take two days, with the first day used simply to introduce students to the potential of watercolor. Demonstrate how to soften watercolor cakes by adding a few drops of water to each cake in advance. Show students how to mix sufficient color in the lid of the box to paint an area. Have two water containers for each table—one for clean water and one for dirty water—and explain how to clean brushes. Students should have a paper towel in hand to wipe brushes, and test their colors on newsprint before applying them to the white paper. At the end of the period, require the students to show you (or a helper) their clean watercolor boxes and brushes before they close the boxes.

Alternative Projects
SPLIT COMPLEMENT A split complement color scheme could be used with three colors, selecting one hue, then using the other two hues that are on both sides of the true complement (for example, red, yellow–green, blue–green.

COLOR STILL-LIFE This project would also work very well with a still-life of vegetables, key chains, toys, or objects found around the art room (such as glue, scissors, tape).

Multicultural Connections
SOCIAL STUDIES
ANCESTORS' COSTUMES If real costumes are not available, have students research what clothing used to look like in the country of their ancestors. If they do not know that country, have them "adopt" one. Have them observe how clothing has changed, even in the last ten years. Ask them why they think this might be. Talk about how clothing or costumes sometimes identify the occupation of the wearer.

LANGUAGE ARTS
INTERVIEW Students could interview anyone older, either a family member or a neighbor, to find stories of what life was like when that person was young.

PROJECT 1-3   COSTUMES AND COLORS

STUDENT PAGE

Materials

2 strips of 3 × 18-inch white
    paper per student

18 × 24-inch watercolor paper
    or white drawing paper

pencils

watercolors

water containers

newspaper

brushes

paper towels

Directions

1. Fold the long strip of paper in half and in half twice again to make eight rectangles. Write your name on the back of the paper. If you have time, try either of these experiments in a different hue.

   GRAYED COLORS Beginning at one end, paint one undiluted primary or secondary color. In the second square, add a tiny amount of the complementary color. Color choices could be red/green; yellow/violet; blue/orange. Continue adding a tiny amount until you have the pure color of the complement at the other end of the strip. This helps you learn to control the amount of complementary color needed to "gray" a hue.

   MONOCHROMATIC COLOR SCHEME. Begin with the most intense color of the pure hue on one end. On the next three squares, gradually add water until the hue is almost white on the fourth square. On the next four squares add another color to the pure hue, noticing all the changes you can make, yet still having a one-color painting.

2. Use pencil to lightly draw the model in costume. This can be a full-figure painting or just the face, hat, and shoulders. Look carefully, noticing where the lightest areas (highlights) are, the darkest areas, and the middle areas.

3. When you paint, you are not concerned about realistic colors—you are simply looking at *value*. Paint the figure, using *only* the two complementary colors that you have used for experimenting (you may leave some areas white). If you feel a color is too dark, you can quickly dilute it with water and use a paper towel to blot up some of the excess.

4. When you have finished, step back and look at your painting from a distance. If you feel you need more contrast, you can add more paint to some areas to make them darker. Watercolor is transparent and can be overpainted (glazed) many times.

Examples

All red	4 red, 1 green	3 red, 2 green	2 red, 2 green	2 green, 2 red	3 green, 2 red	4 green, 2 red	All green

All red	3 red, 1 water	2 red 2 water	Pink water	red, yellow	red, blue	red, brown	red, violet

VALUE

Value describes variations of a hue, ranging from the lightest to the darkest. An example of value that does not involve color would be a newspaper photograph that has black and white areas, and a range of grays in between. A monochromatic composition would incorporate different values of the same hue, while a composition with a variety of colors would still have some dark values and some light values. Value can even be shown in a one-color object, such as sculpture, through differences in depth and texture. Any artwork utilizes value to lend emphasis, contrast, or balance to the composition.

Drawn from *Guernica*, 1937, Pablo Picasso, Prado, Madrid

Definitions

Aerial perspective. change in value indicating distance

Chiaroscuro. light and dark areas in a composition

Contrasting values. differences in dark and light

Gray scale. tones ranging from lightest to darkest

Monochromatic. different values and variations of one hue

Shade. black added to a pure hue

Tint. the pure hue with white added

Tonal gradient. subtle changes in value

Value scale. a means of showing differences in value

Ways to Show Differences in Value

Blending. making soft transitions from light to dark

Cross-hatching. intersecting sets of parallel lines

Gradation. a gradual darkening from light to dark

Hatching. making parallel lines close together or far apart

Stippling. making dots to create light and dark areas

Shading (modeling). showing roundness by darkening edges

Value Scale

Techniques that show differences in value using only one color

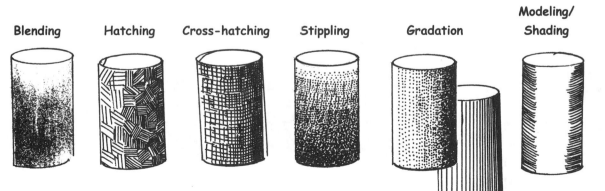

| Blending | Hatching | Cross-hatching | Stippling | Gradation | Modeling/Shading |

PROJECT 1–4
THE OLD HOUSE

FOR THE TEACHER   This project teaches students to apply color using different values of only one hue. Although brushes are used to mix color, "painting" is done using the edge of a piece of cardboard. Architectural details are stamped by holding the cardboard vertically. (This project was developed by Cheryl Niehaus of the Pattonville School District, St. Louis County, Missouri, and is used with her permission.)

Vocabulary

value

intensity

plane

texture

siding

gutter

Preparation   Talk with students about some of the materials used in building houses. Ask them about patterns that are seen. How would they use paint to show differences in boards or shingles on a roof? Ask them to think about the textures on the exteriors of their own homes, for example, or show them paintings of homes by Charles Burchfield. Burchfield often painted rather gloomy-looking houses, showing them in evening light. Point out areas of light and dark values that cause some areas of a house to appear shadowed or on a different plane than others. Encourage students to use a color different from that of their neighbor. Red, violet, or turquoise could be as effective as black. Make black-and-white photocopies of enough simple homes from architectural books or magazines that each student can select a design. Students' photos of their own homes could also be photocopied. This needn't be an entire house, but could be only a section such as an entryway.

Adaptations for Younger Students   Talk with students about their homes: the colors of the outside; how many windows are on the front; how many stories tall their home is; if there is a front porch, trees, flowers, or even toys in the front yard. Try to get them beyond the stereotype "house drawing" with the square façade, triangle roof, and smoke coming out the chimney.

Interdisciplinary Connections
LANGUAGE ARTS
DESCRIBE YOUR OWN HOME Have students write a description of their own home from the moment they walk up the front steps. Have them talk about the exterior, interior flooring, color of the walls or carpets, describe pictures, colors of furnishings, wallpaper patterns, what is on tables. They can especially describe their own rooms so that people would recognize their room from the description of it. Students could even describe their closets!

MATH

MEASURE YOUR ROOM AND FIND THE AREA Students can use a yardstick or tape to measure their own rooms. Have them use graph paper to make a floor plan of their rooms, including bed, dresser, closet, chairs, or anything else that takes up floor space. They could then use these dimensions to compute the room's area.

Sulphurous Evening, 1922–1929, Charles Ephraim Burchfield, watercolor on paper, 23³/₈ × 25⁵/₁₆ inches, Eliza McMillan Fund, Saint Louis Art Museum

PROJECT 1–4   THE OLD HOUSE

STUDENT PAGE

Materials

watercolors

brushes

photos or photocopies of houses

corrugated cardboard and
    matboard pieces, 1 to 3″ wide
    by 3″ long

watercolor or white drawing paper

pencil

Drawn from *House by the Railroad*, 1925, Edward
Hopper, Museum of Modern Art, New York City

Directions   Look at the photocopy of a house. The differences between light
and dark are called *value*. Although the picture from which you are working is in
black and white, you will use only one color (*hue*) and make it as light or dark as you
want by how you control the color *intensity*. Notice how one side of the house is
darker than another, or how the windows may have light and dark areas in them.
What kind of siding do you see? What do the shingles look like? Is there a gutter?
Porch? Steps? Grass?

1. Using a pencil, draw the picture *lightly* on the paper. It isn't necessary to
   use a ruler, though if you want to straighten lines after drawing by using a
   ruler, you may do so. Use the entire page. This house should not just "float"
   in the middle of the page, but have a sidewalk, shrubbery, and trees. After it
   is drawn, think about where you will put the darkest and the lightest values.

2. You will use a brush to mix different values of a color in the lid of the paintbox to make the lightest and darkest areas. Then you will dip a piece of
   cardboard into the mixed paint and use the cardboard to spread the paint.
   The width and thickness of your cardboard will affect how the paint looks.
   You might use a 1-inch piece of cardboard to make bricks or shingles, and a
   wider piece for windows.

3. Another way to use the corrugated cardboard is to hold it straight up and
   down, and dip the edge into the paint. Then use the edge to *stamp* designs
   such as bricks, siding, or shingles onto the picture.

4. Evaluate your painting to see if you have some very light areas and some
   very dark areas. You can go back and make some areas darker if you think it
   will improve your composition.

SPACE

Space is the area that surrounds a form or that form occupies. Artists consciously use space, organizing their work through techniques that make the painting appear to project outward to the viewer, or almost appear to draw the viewer inward. Renaissance artists organized their artwork with geometric forms such as rectangles, triangles, and circles, or used formal perspective. Artists sometimes add drama in compositions through the use of open space, or by organizing the work within a frame or box such as a window. Sculptors consider the space that surrounds and is within the sculpture as an important element of the design.

Definitions

Actual space. the space that can be measured
Aerial perspective. areas farther away are lighter
Linear perspective. a geometric means of organizing space
Vanishing point. lines meet on the horizon at this point
Foreground. the area closest to the viewer
Middle-ground. the area between the foreground and background
Background. the area farthest away
Figure–ground relationship. figure (form) is distinct from the ground
Foreshortening. the illusion that the form projects outward
Projecting form. an object actually projects outward
Gradient. gradual change in value indicating distance
Negative space. the area surrounding a form
Picture plane. the flat space defined by height and width
Positive shapes. forms that are drawn or constructed
Shallow. no actual depth or illusion of depth
Three-dimensional. the object has height, width, and depth
Two-dimensional. the object has height and width

Drawn from *Vaudeville*, 1951, Jacob Lawrence, The Hirshhorn Museum and Sculpture Garden, Washington, DC

How the Illusion of Space is Done in Art

Aerial perspective (gradation). objects in the distance become lighter
Linear perspective. vanishing point(s) show accurate size changes
Size changes. objects in the distance become smaller
Detail. objects in the distance have less detail
Overlapping. objects in front are closer
Vertical location. objects higher in a painting are farther away
Value differences. sky and ground (or water) nearer the horizon are lighter

Size Changes	Overlapping	Gradation/Detail	Vertical Location	Linear Perspective

PROJECT 1-5
COLLAGE CITYSCAPE

FOR THE TEACHER   Many artists have used the city as their subject, including Georgia O'Keeffe, Joseph Stella, Richard Estes, Edward Hopper, Maurice Utrillo, Grant Wood, Robert Henri, and other members of the Ashcan school. Introduce your students to the work of one or more of these painters and talk about how some of these were night scenes, some day scenes. Discuss how artists create an illusion of space by making distant shapes smaller and with less detail (aerial perspective), and the closest items much larger. They overlap shapes and create much more detail in the shapes closest to the viewer.

Vocabulary

space

depth

aerial perspective

cityscape

foreground

middle-ground

background

architect

Preparation   Pick up travel brochures or make photocopies of a variety of buildings to lead into a discussion about different buildings in your town or in a big city in your state. Ask students to close their eyes and make a picture in their minds of tall buildings and what might be on top of such a building. This project may take two sessions. Try to have all the buildings glued on the paper in the first session; the details will be added in the next session.

Adaptations for Younger Students   This project could be much simpler by using pre-cut shapes of construction paper in three sizes. After gluing only a few "building" shapes (smallest near the top, medium near the middle, and largest near the bottom), students could then draw details (people, trees, clouds) on the buildings with marker. This would be a good project for talking about shapes such as squares, rectangles, triangles, and circles, as students use these shapes to construct their buildings. Younger children can still understand the concept of space and how things farther away look smaller.

Alternative Project
PAINT A CITYSCAPE   Instead of collage, this same project could be done as a painting project. Caution students to make the closest objects the darkest in color; the farthest away, the lightest. They could first draw their buildings in pencil before applying paint.

Interdisciplinary Connections
SOCIAL STUDIES
EVOLUTION OF A CITY   Discuss with the students how a city evolves, asking them what the most important factor would be in a place where people want to live (drinking water). Discuss how a city grows; why some cities remain the same size or even die, while others become huge; or why

some that have more than enough drinking water fail to grow. Talk about human needs when a city grows: why people feel a need for work, law and order, adequate food, religion, the arts, recreation.

MAPPING Students could do a map of their town, or at least of their own neighborhood. They could study an aerial map of the county and try to locate their own homes.

LANGUAGE ARTS

THE OLD TOWN Have your students interview an older person who lives in their town and write what the town was like during the childhood of that person. Then have the students compare it with their own lives and what they do. Students can write about experiences in parks, movie theaters, malls, restaurants, ice rinks, or swimming pools.

MATH

COMPUTER CITYSCAPE USING GEOMETRIC SHAPES Students could do a cityscape on a computer, using the functions to make buildings of geometric shapes. Challenge the students to incorporate every geometric shape they know by name into their buildings.

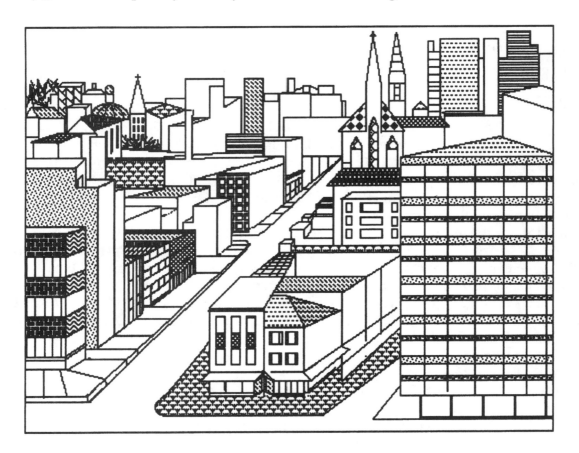

PROJECT 1–5 COLLAGE CITYSCAPE

STUDENT PAGE

Materials

colored corrugated cardboard

12 × 18-inch construction paper

scraps of construction paper

rulers

scissors

white glue

Directions   You will be making a picture of a city and creating the illusion of space by cutting out building shapes and putting details on them with construction paper. Although many buildings look like tall boxes, think about how architects shape the tops to make them different. The roofs of buildings have spires, flagpoles, elevators, air conditioners, domes, signs, and decorative trim. Architects vary the shapes of the windows, add balconies, and sometimes even put elevators on the outsides of the buildings.

You will make your buildings in three different sizes to be background (the smallest), middle-ground (medium size), and foreground (the largest).

1. Begin first with the background (the area farthest away). Cut out a variety of *small* construction paper shapes to use as the background buildings. The buildings farthest away usually appear lightest in color. Glue these across the paper, near the upper third. Don't be concerned with details such as windows or doors.

2. Next make medium-sized shapes for the middle-ground and glue these near the middle of the paper (one or two of these could be corrugated paper if you wish). These may slightly overlap the buildings near the top.

3. Make the largest shapes of construction or corrugated paper (the lines can go in either direction) and glue them to about two inches from the bottom, leaving room for cars. You will have some blank spaces, and your buildings will not have details on them yet. To fill up empty spaces, cut out some shapes from different colors of green paper to represent the tops of trees between buildings.

4. Cut out details to complete the buildings in the foreground and middle-ground. You can glue on windows, doors, people in front of the buildings, cars, street signs, signs on top of buildings, balconies, and decorative details such as strips of paper to represent stone or brick. When you think you are finished, stand back at a distance and look to see if there is anything else you need to add to make the cityscape more interesting.

SHAPE/FORM

Shape has two dimensions: height and width; whereas form has three dimensions: height, width, and depth. Shape may be enclosed by a line, but some shapes with indistinct edges are defined by their inner structure (such as a cloud). Geometric shapes appear stronger than the free-form or biomorphic shapes. Artists such as Matisse and Toulouse-Lautrec recognized the drama that can be created by allowing shape to be the dominant element in a composition.

Shape

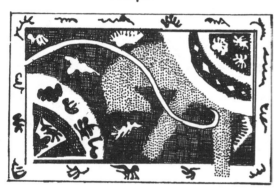

Drawn from *The Horse, the Equestrienne and the Clown*, 1947, Henri Matisse, National Gallery of Art, Washington DC

Form

Drawn from *Baboon and You Vallauris*, 1951, Pablo Picasso, Museum of Modern Art, New York City

Definitions

Abstract. shapes that may be based on reality
Amorphous. lacking definite form (clouds)
Geometric shapes. triangles, rectangles, Squares, parallelograms, circles, ovals
Free-form. shapes are irregular and asymmetrical (oil spills)
Mass. shape in three dimensions such as sculpture
Natural shapes or forms. rocks, clouds, water
Organic/biomorphic shapes. living organisms such as animals, fish, flowers
Positive shape. the main form of a composition
Negative shapes. the area surrounding the main form

Abstract	Amorphous	Geometric	Organic	Natural	Positive/ Negative

  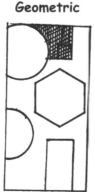   

PROJECT 1-6
GEOMETRIC CUT-OUT ANIMALS

FOR THE TEACHER   This assignment is for students to make a cut-paper collage using geometric shapes. They can make humans or animals, or a combination of humans and animals. Picasso often used collage (a French word that means "to glue"), and was one of the first artists to use a form of art called *Cubism*, making decorative patterns. Although he worked with *abstract* shapes, it is always possible to recognize the forms in his paintings.

Preparation   Try to find a reproduction of some of Pablo Picasso's work, such as his *Three Musicians* from the Museum of Modern Art. It will help students to understand abstraction (taking something real and reducing it to shapes, yet still with enough realism to be recognizable). You can see the instruments, the three musicians, some musical notes, and (if you look closely) a dog that is behind the musicians.

Save scrap paper, cutting it on the paper cutter. Place an assortment of strips, triangles, squares, and odd shapes at each table.

Vocabulary

Cubism

abstract

form

shape

contrast

negative shape

extinct

Adaptations for Younger Students   Allow younger children to recognize relationships among geometric shapes. Let students make other geometric shapes from pre-cut *squares* of different sizes. They can cut diagonally across a square to make two triangles; two different-sized rectangles from a square; cut a circle from a square; make diamonds or a trapezoid. These shapes could then be assembled and glued on construction paper to make imaginary *creatures*. Students love using paper punches to make decorative circles. Ask them to give their animals special names.

Alternative Project

PAPER CUT-OUT COLLAGES: NATURAL FORMS Students could make cut-paper designs based on *natural* forms of sea life, plants, or humans such as those of Henry Matisse. This could be done with construction paper or hand-painted paper such as Matisse used. Have students paint full sheets of paper a day in advance by using sponge brushes and watered-down tempera. Remind students to keep their "negative shapes," as these can also be incorporated into the final composition that will be pasted on white paper.

Interdisciplinary Connection

SCIENCE

EXTINCT ANIMALS Help students become aware of what is happening to many life forms that are close to extinction. Discuss the effect of humans on the balance of nature. Should wolves and bears be reintroduced where they once roamed wild? Should deer be "harvested" when their numbers become so great that they starve? Assign students to research and debate conservation efforts.

Three Musicians, Fontainebleau, 1921, Pablo Picasso, oil on canvas, 6′ 7″ × 7′ 3³/₄″, Museum of Modern Art, New York City, Mrs. Simon Guggenheim Fund. Photograph © 1999 The Museum of Modern Art, New York

PROJECT 1–6   GEOMETRIC CUT-OUT ANIMALS

STUDENT PAGE

Materials

paper punches

scissors

newsprint

pencils

black construction paper

white glue

assorted construction paper shapes

Directions   Think about animals you know or have seen. Some of you have pets; you may have seen wild animals on television; and you may have seen animals at the zoo or circus. You may be aware of animals that used to exist, such as dinosaurs or mastodons. In this project you could make either *real* animals or *extinct* animals. Because you will be using *only* geometric shapes, your composition will be *abstract*. You started with a real animal, so you don't want it to be too abstract—otherwise people won't know what it is!

1. Select an assortment of colored paper. This project allows you to experiment with a variety of *geometric* shapes. Neatly cut a large assortment of geometric shapes, then move them around until you are able to make an animal. If you wish, you may have several different or human shapes.

2. Consider the *original* environment in which this animal would be found. Would it be in a tropical jungle? the desert? underwater? on a mountain? in the zoo? in a tree? in a barnyard? in a forest? in a cave? underground? on the snowcaps of the Arctic or Antarctic?

3. When your animal is complete, cut shapes other than geometric shapes to make plants, barns, or other objects that might be found near the animal. Think about whether this animal is shy and might even be hiding behind plants, or if its babies are sometimes hidden behind rocks.

4. Sign your name carefully by letting it "follow" one of the shapes, such as right next to a leaf. It is important not to let your name be so big that it becomes more important than your drawing.

TEXTURE

Texture in an artwork can be *real* or *implied;* you can actually feel it or it may only be an illusion. Some artists, such as Vincent van Gogh, reveled in a *real* textural emphasis in their paintings, while others, such as Pablo Picasso, often used pattern in a painting to *imply* texture. Sculptors use texture effectively by varying smooth and rough areas to call attention to one surface or another. Pattern differs from texture in that it is deliberately repetitive, two-dimensional, and is used for decorative purposes. Texture and pattern are terms sometimes used interchangeably.

Actual texture

rough
smooth
slick
bumpy
velvety
jagged
prickly
grainy
soft
wiry
pebbly

Pattern

brick
ogee
triangle
shell
square
diamond
bands
mottled
scallops
plaid
checkerboard
octagon
waves
scale

Drawn from *Jirling the Hunter*, 1989, George Mung Mung (Jampin), National Gallery of Victoria, Melbourne, Australia

Texture

Wood   Fur   Grass   Tree   Rock   Leaf

Pattern

Brick   Ogee   Triangle   Shell   Diamond   Octagon   Scale

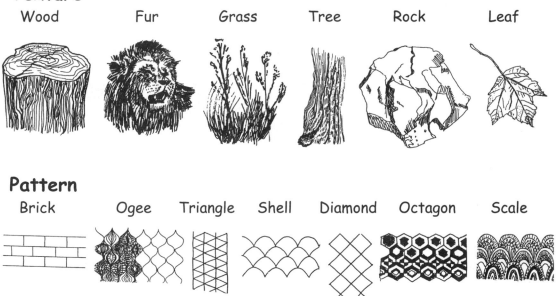

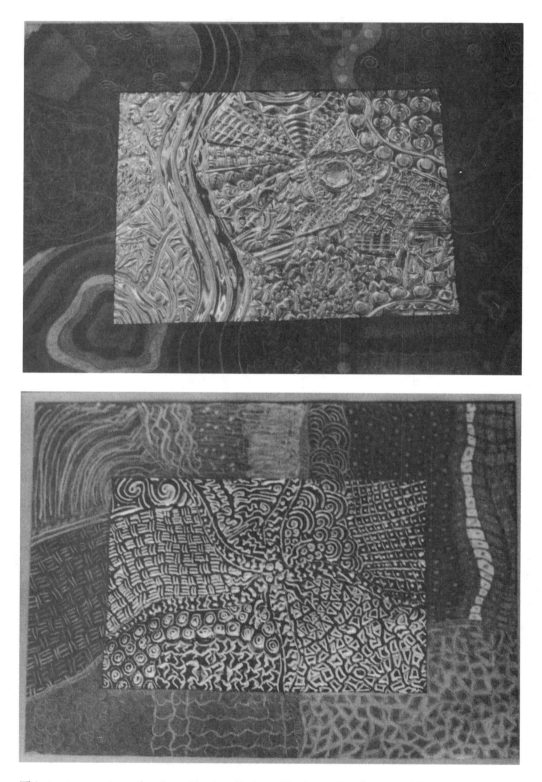

This texture project, developed by Jan Cutlan of Parkway Northeast Middle School, St. Louis County, Missouri, helps students explore texture first on foil, "carrying" the design to the dark mat using either metallic marker or Prismacolor® pencil.

PROJECT 1–7
MEXICAN SUN

FOR THE TEACHER The circle has been a popular shape throughout the history of Mexico. This project is based on the suns and moons that continue today as popular motifs in Mexican folk art. They have been interpreted in a variety of materials including beadwork, stone, copper relief, papier mâché, embroidery, and paper.

Vocabulary

texture

implied texture

pattern

ogee

scale

shell

motif

Preparation
Discuss actual texture with students. Have them use descriptive terms such as smooth, soft, rough, bumpy. Then ask the students how they could make something *appear* to have texture, yet be smooth to the touch. Show examples by artists—such as Pablo Picasso, Georges Rouault, and Frank Stella—who have depicted texture in their artwork. Talk about what a pattern is, and ask students about some of the various patterns with which they are familiar, such as squares, polka dots, checkerboard, zigzags, circles, and stripes. Demonstrate some other methods of organizing pattern, such as the shell, scale, triangle, and ogee. You may also want to mention that sometimes pattern is more effective when a *plain* area allows a place to "rest the eye."

Adaptations for Younger Students
This lesson could easily be adapted as a stitchery project for younger students. Using brightly colored burlap, have them stitch a circle using yarn, drawing eyes, nose, and mouth with fabric marker. These designs could be very simple. To help young students thread their own yarn needles, show them how to fold a small (1/2 × 1-inch) piece of paper in half lengthwise, then place the end of the yarn inside the paper and push the paper with the yarn inside through the eye of the needle.

Alternative Project
PAPER BATIK SUNS Art teacher Libby Cravens of the Claymont School in St. Louis County, Missouri developed this wonderful paper batik suns project. The students draw a sun on rice paper and outline it in white wax. They then immerse it in yellow or orange dye. When dried, some areas are then painted with watercolor. After drying, the wax is ironed out between sheets of newsprint. When mounted, stamped images of suns are placed around the border. Some stamps can be home-made, while others can be purchased as a set. These are beautiful enough to frame!

Interdisciplinary Connection

MATH

COMPASSES AND PROTRACTORS Use this opportunity to teach about the use of a compass and the measurement of a circle. Students could learn to use a protractor to create triangles using specific angles. All of the decorative elements could use straight lines, as if these were made of actual beads.

These Mexican beaded sun masks were made on wooden carved forms. Collection of Mr. and Mrs. David Hume, St. Louis, Missouri

PROJECT 1–7 MEXICAN SUN

Materials

colored pencils

drawing paper

compasses

pencils

Directions   Going back many
centuries, the circle has been used as a *motif*
in Mexican art. Even in modern Mexico, suns
and moons with faces and other designs on them
can be found in a variety of materials such as copper, beadwork, stitchery, and ceramics.

1. Draw several sun-face designs on drawing paper with pencil. When you find
   a design you like, prepare to enlarge it. Draw at least an 8-inch circle.

2. In addition to a mouth, nose, and eyes, think about other pictures you might
   draw to decorate within the circle. These can be symbols of animals, plants,
   flowers, clouds, or other designs based on Mexican motifs. Draw these in
   pencil, then use colored pencil to fill in the shapes.

3. When the space is filled with various symbols, use colored pencil to fill in
   the circle. Try not to leave white space showing. When finished, make a
   design—such as sunburst lines or triangles—around the outside.

4. To complete this assignment, write about some of the personal symbols you
   used and where you got your ideas.

REPETITION

Repetition is the use of color, line, or shape in more than one place in a composition. Repetition such as that seen in a checkerboard or wallpaper pattern can be boring unless relieved by some variation in color, or emphasis is given to one area. *Pattern* is created by the repetition of the elements of design, and can be used to give an *implied* texture to a composition. *Rhythm* can be established in a composition through the repeated or alternate use of an element or motif in much the same way it exists in music.

Definitions

Pattern. the systematic use of line or motif

Random pattern. groups of similar motifs arranged randomly

Rhythm. the use of pattern to create movement

Tessellation. the interlocking of shapes in an overall pattern

Drawn from *Against the Enamel of a Background Rhythmic with Beats and Angles, Tones and Colors, Portrait of M. Felix Fénéon in 1890*, 1890, Paul Signac, Museum of Modern Art, New York City

Rhythm   **Tessellation**   **Repetition**   **Random Pattern**

PROJECT 1–8
ABORIGINAL "DREAMINGS"

FOR THE TEACHER   The paintings of the Aboriginal people of Australia represent day-to-day happenings such as hunting for food or sitting around the fireside with friends. Many of their paintings represent the "Dreamtime," the time before man came, when the Earth was inhabited by ancestral beings that were part human, but resembled plants and animals. Sometimes in Aboriginal drawings, the actual animal is shown; but in paintings by Aborigines from the desert regions, only the *movement* of these animals is represented through symbols, lines, and dots. The paintings traditionally are painted in earth colors such as brown, gold, white, red, and black; however, contemporary aboriginal painters often use acrylic paint, sometimes in soft colors. They continue to represent the things of nature such as flowers, shrubbery, water, rocks, and trees. Almost everything is seen from an aerial view, and every painting tells a story, though it may be known only to the artist because many of the symbols have several meanings.

Preparation   It would be useful to be able to show reproductions of Aboriginal paintings so students can see the limited palette. A library book about Australia should contain more information. The writing project listed under Language Arts would be a good introduction to the actual art project, as it would cause students to think about details. Australia is a large country, and just as Native Americans from different parts of the United States developed different art forms depending on the materials available, so have these differences occurred in various Aboriginal groups. The Western Coast Aborigines, for example, rely more on straight lines and geometric designs. They mount their finished paintings at the top and bottom on sticks.

Wild Banana by J. Paige represents two women seated on either side of a bush plum where they dig for witchetty grubs. The seated women (horseshoe shapes) have digging sticks and bowls beside them. Collection of Susan Hume and John Baker

Alternative Project

BARK PAINTINGS Cured, flattened sheets of eucalyptus bark are used as "paper" by the artists of Arnhem Land. Painting is done with red and yellow ochres, white kaolin clay, and black manganese or charcoal. You can substitute kraft paper for eucalyptus bark, using tempera as a base, and a marking pen for the designs. These drawings are highly decorative, with stripes, dots, diamonds, cross-hatching, and patterns used to decorate thin "supernatural" dancing figures and animals. X-ray paintings (that show the bone structure) of animals and humans are also common. Find reproductions of Aboriginal art or show a filmstrip so students can see examples of this unique art.

Interdisciplinary Connection

LANGUAGE ARTS

WRITE A WALKABOUT Students can do a *written* description of a walk in their own yard or neighborhood. Ask them to describe in detail the things they see: the colors of trees, animals, smells. They may prefer to base this on a visit to a nearby park, or someplace they have gone on vacation. Explain that you want them to write very detailed accounts of what they have encountered on their "walkabout."

Bone Coffins, 1989, eucalyptus wood painted with natural clays, Northern Territory, Central Arnhem Land Region, Ramingining, Australia. Artists are Australian Aborigines Ray Munyal, Jimmy Moduk, Charlie Djurritjini, Mick Daypurr'yun, Ken Minyipirriwuy, Bob Ropani. Museum Shop Fund, Saint Louis Art Museum.

PROJECT 1–8   ABORIGINAL "DREAMINGS"

STUDENT PAGE

Materials

9 × 12-inch construction paper: brown,
    ochre, black, reddish-brown

chalk

acrylic or tempera paint: brown, ochre,
    white, sienna, black

brushes

pencils

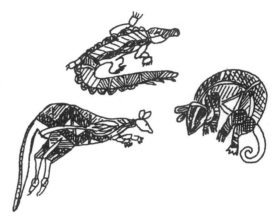

Directions
An Aboriginal "dreaming" is a painted story. It will include things from nature such as bushes, trees and flowers; stars; constellations; the Milky Way; animals; birds; waterfowl; centipedes; snakes; fish; witchetty grubs; beetles; lizards; kangaroos; wallabies; and koala bears. It will probably only include a few of these, as your story would not likely involve them all at once. The stories tell about journeys and what was seen along the way.

Because the Aborigines usually paint things seen from above, or sometimes only the tracks left by creatures, they used symbols that might mean one of several different things. You are going to paint a "dreaming" based on animals and places you know.

1. Select a color of paper as your background. Close your eyes and think for a moment about a dream time. Imagine yourself as a bird, because you will mostly be looking straight down, seeing things from a "bird's-eye view." You might have animals in your dreaming, or this may be a journey you will make by yourself or with a friend. You need to remember some of the things you see, such as trees, bushes, water, or bugs. You could include animals that *might* have been there at one time, that you haven't seen.

2. Use your finger to trace your imaginary journey on the paper. Think about where you stopped to rest. Did you have a friend with you? Did you encounter any animals in your travels? What about trees and bushes? Where did you see water? After you have made the journey with your finger, use a piece of chalk to make a very light line that will serve as a guide for applying paint.

3. Create a pattern by making dots on one of your chalk lines in one color. Use a pencil eraser dipped in color to stamp the dots. Or use the wooden end of a brush to dip in paint and then place the dot on the paper. Select another color and place the dots next to the first line. Leave some areas unpainted, and fill in a few areas with solid colors outlined with dots. Use enough variety in color and value to make it a beautiful design.

4. Some of the Aboriginal people tie their paintings to sticks at the top and bottom of a composition with pieces of string. This would be a nice way to finish and display the dreamings.

Aboriginal Symbols

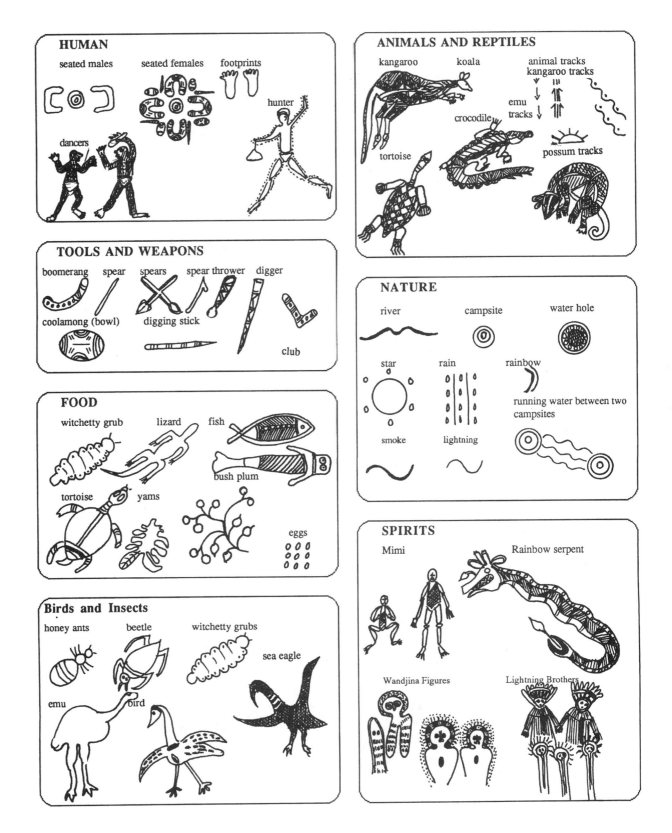

HUMAN
- seated males
- seated females
- footprints
- hunter
- dancers

TOOLS AND WEAPONS
- boomerang
- spear
- spears
- spear thrower
- digger
- coolamong (bowl)
- digging stick
- club

FOOD
- witchetty grub
- lizard
- fish
- bush plum
- tortoise
- yams
- eggs

Birds and Insects
- honey ants
- beetle
- witchetty grubs
- sea eagle
- emu
- bird

ANIMALS AND REPTILES
- kangaroo
- koala
- animal tracks
- kangaroo tracks
- emu tracks
- crocodile
- possum tracks
- tortoise

NATURE
- river
- campsite
- water hole
- star
- rain
- rainbow
- running water between two campsites
- smoke
- lightning

SPIRITS
- Mimi
- Rainbow serpent
- Wandjina Figures
- Lightning Brothers

Balance

Balance is the equilibrium of the forms used in a composition, and is achieved by giving equal weight on both sides of a composition. Formal (symmetrical) balance often results in a static composition, while informal (asymmetrical) balance is somewhat livelier. The upper and lower halves of a composition should also be considered when thinking of balance, with weight somewhat heavier on the lower half of an artwork to keep it from appearing to fall forward.

Definitions

Formal (symmetrical) balance. if the composition were folded in half, both halves would be equal

Informal (asymmetrical) balance. one side dominates, but balance is still achieved

Quadrilateral symmetry. four quarters of the composition are similar

Radial symmetry. similar elements radiate from a central point

Drawn from *Femme de Tahiti* or *Sur la Plage*, 1891, Paul Gauguin, Musée d'Orsay, Paris

Radial Balance

Drawn from *Stone Calendar*, 1450–1500, Museo Nationale, Mexico City, Mexico

Formal Balance (Symmetrical)   **Informal Balance (Asymmetrical)**

Drawn from *Around the Fish,* 1926, Paul Klee, Museum of Modern Art, New York City

Drawn from *Todi Ragini,* 1630, Central India, Museum of Fine Arts, Boston

Krishna approaching the tryst dressed as Radha, Rajasthani, Bundi, c. 1760, Private Collection

PROJECT 1–9
"SELL YOUR PRODUCT" POSTER

FOR THE TEACHER   A poster has the same basic components whether it is done on a computer or on a large placard. Ask students what they think a poster is used for, why they might see posters around school or in town. The idea is to get information across with an eye-catching design that will cause the viewer to come in closer to get necessary information. Students should be accustomed to seeing posters at video shops or the movies. Review different ways of achieving balance.

Preparation   Show children examples of posters. Henri de Toulouse-Lautrec, Alfonse Mucha, Aubrey Beardsley, and others frequently made posters, but other less-known artists were the backbone of the industry. Decide before beginning what medium you prefer the students to use. This project could be effective using poster paint, cut-paper images combined with cut-paper lettering, or marker. Any of these could be used alone or in combination with the others. If you have access to a computer and would like to have the students do their lettering on it, this is certainly the simplest way to do the lettering portion of this project. To enlarge computer lettering, it can be copied on an overhead transparency and projected onto the posterboard.

Interdisciplinary Connection
SOCIAL STUDIES

ANALYZE MARKETING STRATEGIES   Help students become aware of marketing strategies. Ask them which boxes of cereal they first notice when they go into a store. Ask if there are certain colors that seem to be used more often than others. Discuss advertising on television, and whether the actual product they got based on that advertising lived up to their expectations. Talk about billboards, advertising on the Internet, telephone soliciting, and ads in a newspaper.

Sarah Bernhardt as "La Samaritaine," 1897, Alphonse Mucha, lithographic poster, $67^{1}/_{2} \times 23^{1}/_{2}$ inches, The Nelson–Atkins Museum of Art, Kansas City, Missouri

Jane Avril, 1893, Henri de Toulouse-Lautrec, lithographic poster, $50^{3}/_{8} \times 36$ inches, The Nelson–Atkins Museum of Art, Kansas City, Missouri (Purchase: Nelson Trust)

PROJECT 1–9 "SELL YOUR PRODUCT" POSTER

Materials

posterboard	fadeless paper
rulers	newsprint
poster paint	markers
scissors	brushes
glue	pencils

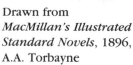

Drawn from
*MacMillan's Illustrated
Standard Novels*, 1896,
A.A. Torbayne

Peter Handke

Directions   This project is an advertisement for a product that bears your name. It might be a brand of toothpaste, a car, a video game, a doll, a cereal, or an action figure. The main element in your poster will probably be a large drawing of the product itself. The large lettering (your name) could be on top of the product, with smaller information off to one side.

1. Select a product to advertise and decide whether you will use your first name or your last name. Draw several small rectangles on newsprint to make thumbnail sketches. Each sketch should take no more than a minute or two. Try different ways to arrange your product and your name, remembering that the poster needs to appear *balanced*. Things to remember:

- Have one big image. It might be a drawing of your product and your name.

- Decide whether you want the drawing to use *symmetrical* or *asymmetrical balance*.

- A composition will look unbalanced if all the "heavy" stuff is at the top.

- Most posters are vertical for better visual impact.

- Lightly draw the letters in pencil before adding color, or do your lettering on a computer.

- Leave margins around the outside.

- Some empty space is important and calls attention to your message.

- Too much empty background space can be broken up with a curved, diagonal, or vertical line, perhaps using different colors on either sides of the line.

- Make a border if you feel you have too much empty space.

- Keep the message simple enough to be read in a few seconds.

- Letters should be in a straight line.

- Avoid light colors for lettering, as they cannot be seen from a distance.

- Avoid using mixed colors for lettering. Letters are more effective if they are all the same color.

PROJECT 1-9 *(Continued)*

2. When you have decided how you will arrange the poster, use a pencil to *lightly* draw lines (that will later be erased) for your lettering. Count the number of letters and measure the space available, as then you will know how large the letters can be. Try to have only a few words.

3. Decide on the main image, which will be your product. Will your name also be seen on the product? Make it large and colorful enough to be interesting. It could be made with cut-paper or marker. Remember, neatness counts.

4. Prop the poster against the wall and walk back to look at it from a distance. Do the letters show well? Does the poster look top-heavy, as if it would fall over? How could you fix that? Would outlining some of the images with a dark marker make it show up better from a distance?

Drawn from *Harper's*, New York

Emphasis

The principle of emphasis is used to focus attention in a composition. It may be an isolated form, or the largest, brightest, or darkest area. Attention can be drawn to the focal point by convergence of lines (as in da Vinci's *Last Supper*); isolation that sets one part apart from the others; textural interest; or contrast between light and shade. The theory of domination–subordination is that one portion of a composition is the major focal point, with subordinate areas being complementary to it. In general, a composition is more interesting if the area of emphasis is not in the center, but rather placed to the left or right.

Definitions

Center of interest. the area of main interest; usually *not* in the center

Converging lines. lines may be used to direct attention to the focal point

Contrast. the center-of-interest is indicated by being lighter or darker

Dominant. the major element of a composition

Subordinate. elements that repeat or complement the dominant form

Focal point. the first thing the eye sees when viewing an artwork

Isolation. one form is set apart from others

Rule-of-thirds. an imaginary tic-tac-toe grid, with the main subject placed at an intersection

Drawn from *Classic Landscape*, 1931, Charles Sheeler Collection of Mr. and Mrs. Barney Ebsworth, Saint Louis Art Museum

Contrast	Focal point	Dominant/Subordinate	Isolation

PROJECT 1–10
MAKING THE SMALL MONUMENTAL

FOR THE TEACHER   Artists such as Georgia O'Keeffe understood how to make a small object dominate a landscape and appear larger-than-life. Using natural articles such as shells, flowers or bones, she placed them in the foreground and made them *monumental*, dominating the composition.

Vocabulary

emphasis

balance

unity

center-of-interest

Preparation
First discuss the concept of *monumental*. Then have students list things that are smaller than a hand. Write these on the board as they are named; examples are: shells, a mouse, a model car, a ladybug, a penny, flower, baseball, jacks, Legos®, Cheerios®, a shoelace, a wishbone, keys, etc. Also talk about what might be found in an imaginary landscape. It could include mountains, rivers, etc., just like any landscape, but it might also be on the moon, in the ocean, on a space station, or in an all-yellow garden.

Oil pastels are messy, so have the students wear smocks and push their sleeves above their elbows. They could use a "cover sheet" (piece of 8½ × 11-inch paper) on which to rest the hand to prevent smearing a completed area while they work on another part. If crayons are used instead of pastels, have the students color firmly, then paint over the crayons with ink or black tempera to emphasize the colors.

Alternative Projects
THE WHOLE ROOM AND YOUR HANDS Instead of using an object, students could use drawings of their own hands as the "objects" in the drawing. They could then draw the portion of the room that they see behind their hands. The background could be selected by simply moving the hand around until satisfied with the view behind it. Scale can then be seen in relation to the hand.

Red Hills with Flowers, 1937, Georgia O'Keeffe, 50.8 × 63.5 cm, Art Institute of Chicago. Bequest of Hortense Henry Prosser

PROJECT 1–10   MAKING THE SMALL MONUMENTAL

Materials

12 × 18-inch drawing paper

pastels, chalk, oil pastels, or crayons

small objects: shells, flowers, bones, model cars

Drawn from *Red Hills with Flowers,* 1937, Georgia O'Keeffe, The Art Institute of Chicago.

Directions   Before beginning, think about the one subject that you will *empha-size*. This will be the largest object in an imaginary landscape, perhaps the one that appears closest. Use your *finger* to trace a tic-tac-toe grid on the entire paper. Sometimes artists place their "center-of-interest" not in the center of the page, but rather on one of the intersections made by this division—which is sometimes called the "rule of thirds."

1. Use pencil to draw a 1-inch border all the way around the paper to keep from smearing pastels on your desk. Decide what your object will be and draw it on an "intersection." Make the object at least as large as your open hand.

2. Decide what would really be a strange location for your object to be in. Try to think of an "environment" that is *not* normal for your subject. Have you ever heard the expression "a fish out of water"?

3. After completing the pencil drawing, you will use pastels to color the whole page. Oil pastels are similar to crayon, but a little messier. They are most beautiful when they are colored firmly. You can add one color on top of another, and even scratch designs through top layers to show those underneath.

4. Except for the one real object, this is an imaginary drawing. Consider using unrealistic colors. Trees don't always have to have brown trunks and green leaves, and skies don't always have to be blue. You might even choose to use a "color scheme" based on analogous or complementary colors. When you are finished, trim the edges on the paper cutter or place the drawing behind a mat.

Contrast

The design principle of contrast is used to bring a work of art to life. In essence, contrast and variety in composition refer to differences that separate one form from another. This is usually accomplished by contrasts in intensity of hue, the use of complementary colors, or changes in value. "Op" (Optical) artists, such as Josef Albers, Bridget Riley, and Victor Vasarely, used the principle of simultaneous contrast in their compositions. They took advantage of the tendency for the eye to see forms as darker or lighter, or larger or smaller, depending upon the background used.

Definitions

Simultaneous contrast. optical illusions caused by size, intensity, and placement of colors
Variety. similar to contrast in that it deals with differences

Types of Contrast

figure/ground
bright/dark
large/small
rough/smooth
patterned/plain
monumental/intimate
warm/cool
soft edges/hard edges
subdued/intense
abstract/realistic
defined/loose
symmetrical/asymmetrical
wide/narrow
thick/thin
bold/delicate
old/young

Drawn from *In the Car*, 1963, Roy Lichtenstein, Scottish National Gallery of Modern Art, Edinburgh

Figure/Ground

Bold/Delicate

Soft Edges/Hard Edges

Abstract/Realistic

Bas-Relief
Paper Sculpture

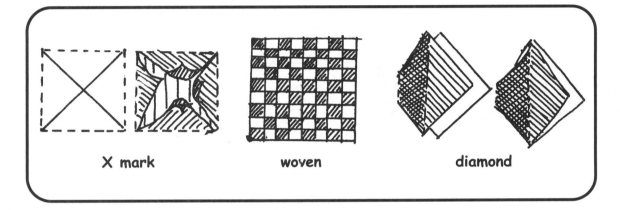

X mark   woven   diamond

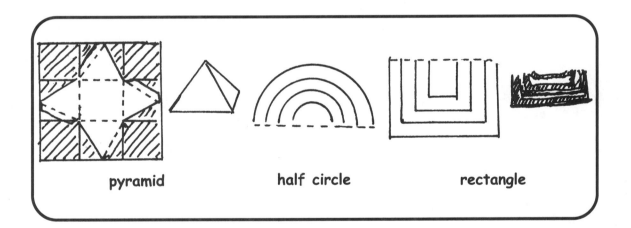

pyramid   half circle   rectangle

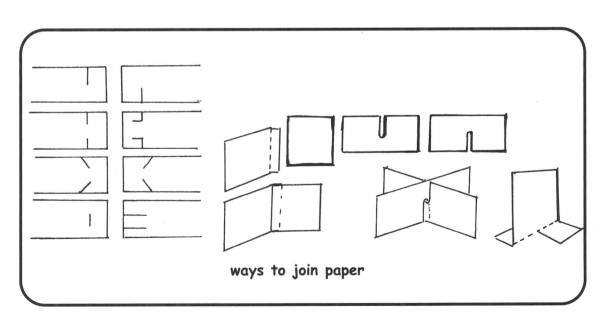

ways to join paper

Bas-Relief Paper Sculpture *(Continued)*

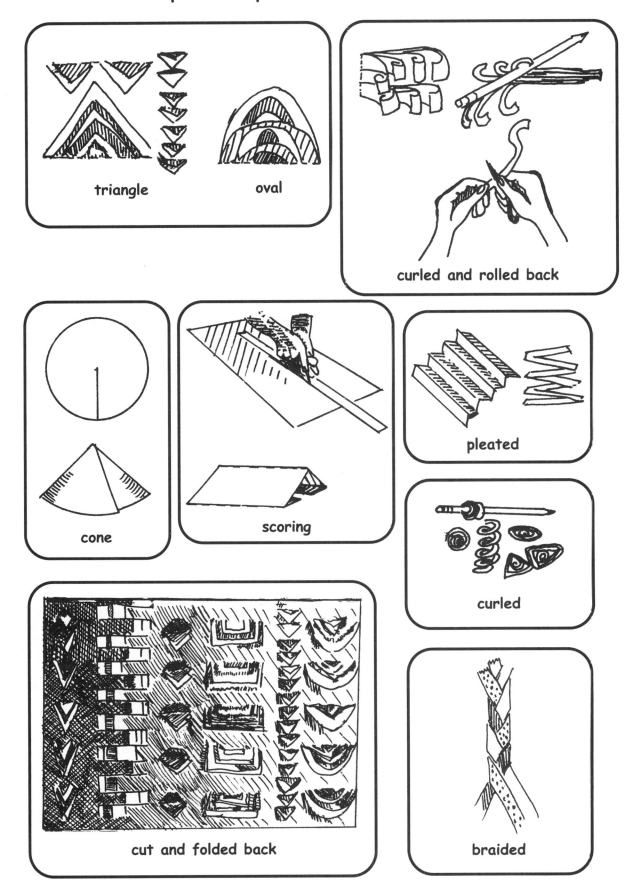

triangle

oval

curled and rolled back

cone

scoring

pleated

curled

cut and folded back

braided

PROJECT 1–11
BLACK AND WHITE MAKE IT RIGHT

FOR THE TEACHER This project is to cut and fold strongly-contrasting paper using a variety of methods. Although it could be done with any complementary colors, it is especially effective in black and white. Two different methods of making these cut-paper compositions are described. For either of these compositions to be effective, the amount of white and black visible should be almost equal. The two methods could be combined into a final project.

Vocabulary

contrast

form

variety

shapes

low-relief

sculpture

balance

Preparation Demonstrate various methods of making cuts and folding paper. I find that simply making a 1/2-inch grid on the back of the paper helps to make a neat composition, but this is not always appropriate for younger age levels. Older students might benefit from practicing attached cuts on 1/2-inch graph paper. Show students how to use a ruler and point of scissors to score paper in order to make it fold easily.

Interdisciplinary Connection
MATH
MEASURE, CUT, FOLD BACK This project is a natural for teaching students to measure accurately with a ruler to make a grid, to use a compass to make half circles, and to try a variety of geometric shapes. After students have done the project, allow each student to select one geometric shape and interpret only that shape on an 8-inch square of black paper. Have students plan out the entire pattern in advance and draw their designs with pencils on the back of the paper before cutting. Tell them neatness counts. Mount these on white paper and display together.

Multicultural Connection
PAPER-CUTS AROUND THE WORLD Paper-cuts based on nature have been traditional in countries around the world. *Scherenschnitte* (usually on black paper) comes from Germany; *Wycinanki* (brightly colored birds and flowers), from Poland; *Day of the Dead paper cutting* (white thin paper), from Mexico; and traditional *Chinese paper-cuts* (usually on red shiny paper). Information on paper-cutting traditions is available in many library books.

PROJECT 1–11   BLACK AND WHITE MAKE IT RIGHT

STUDENT PAGE

Materials

12 × 12-inch construction
   paper: black and white

1/2-inch graph paper

newsprint

scissors

ruler

glue sticks

Directions   This project is a "sampler" of the low-relief sculpture that can be done with paper. You do not actually have to design the entire piece of paper at once, but still need to consider balance and variety as well as contrast. Ideally there will be as much white showing as there is black. Experiment with different types of cuts.

1. To help make cuts neatly, draw a grid on the back of the paper using a pencil and a ruler. You will make cuts from the back, loosely folding part of the paper along a line and cutting with scissors. If you use the tip of your scissors to "score," the lines will be easier to fold.

2. *Attached cuts*. Various cuts can be made by cutting on a fold. Make triangles, half circles, squares, diamonds, or simple slits. Remember to leave one side of the cut attached to the paper and score with the point of the scissors before folding it back. Repeat some of your cuts to make the composition interesting.

3. *Sculptured paper*. Another method is to work with loose squares and strips of paper, folding, curling, weaving, or pleating each piece before pasting one end onto a contrasting background. If you have many different pieces of paper treated this way, move them around to find the best composition before gluing them.

4. Stand back and look at your work to see if you have almost equal parts of top paper and background paper showing. Would you want to add *one* piece of a different color somewhere just to make your composition exciting? It could be very interesting.

Unity

Unity is the combination of the elements of art using the principles of design. It is the consideration of the complete composition, adding color here, simplifying an area there, considering balance, variety, and emphasis. As artists work, they sort through options, making changes that create an overall harmony. They can create an exaggeration, the push–pull, or visual tension that creates a bond between forms. Placing a form near an edge of the picture plane is one way to create such tension. The use of symmetry is another way to achieve unity or stability. Repetition of form or the regular placement of motifs can create a stillness. Asymmetry leads to a livelier organization that can still be harmonious, as the eye is led through the composition.

Definitions

Coherence. all parts coming together in harmony
Dominance/subordination. one main element, others complementary to it
Harmony. combining elements of art to create a restful composition
Dissonance. abrupt changes, apparent disunity
Symmetry. balancing elements equally
Asymmetry. unequal balance of form
Proportion. proportion may be normal or exaggerated

Methods of achieving unity

balance of weight
circular or triangular composition
clustering small objects together
creating a variety of forms
having one major center-of-interest
limiting the variety of shapes, colors, or lines
order—isolate important details to emphasize the dominant form
organizing elements through geometry
overlapping objects or figures
radiation—having everything else radiate from a central point
simplifying the color scheme
surrounding the dominant form with space
using convergent lines to direct attention

Drawn from *Woman in Purple Coat*, 1937, Henri Matisse, The Museum of Fine Arts, Houston

Asymmetry	Symmetry	Dissonance	Harmony	Triangular Composition

PROJECT 1–12
"LEAF" IT TO ME

FOR THE TEACHER   This project challenges students to consider the entire picture plane. Have students on the lookout for the "happy accident" that gives a beautiful effect. Students need to consider value, form, and space while having one dominant element. This could be the largest leaf or the brightest area.

Vocabulary

picture plane

unity

value

space

color

repetition

dominance/subordination

Preparation   In the fall it is simply a tradition to do a "leaf project." It is a good time to take students outside to gather fresh leaves (although you could always simply bring in a sackful of fresh leaves if time does not allow the gathering process). Remind students to bring in several different kinds of *thin* leaves. Discuss value, repetition, dominance/subordination, and color schemes. Charlotte Headrick, of the Parkway School District, St. Louis County, Missouri, who developed this project, says that for young students she allows them only to use a yellow background, while older students understand that very light washes of other colors are also effective backgrounds.

Talk with students about various options for finishing the project, such as spatter effects with dark colors, or with thinned white tempera when the painting has dried but before the leaves have been removed. Caution students against overworking the paper, as it quickly becomes soggy and muddy-looking. This project lends itself especially well to a critique.

PROJECT 1–12 "LEAF" IT TO ME

STUDENT PAGE

Materials

thin fresh leaves (a variety of sizes and shapes)

watercolors (large sets with more variety are nice)

12 × 12-inch watercolor paper or white construction paper

large brushes

water

newspapers

Thin leaves were selected and placed vein-side up on paper with a still-wet light-colored background. The leaves were then painted around with a variety of colors of light, medium, and dark values. They were left in place to dry overnight.

Directions   This project could be done with several different types of leaves or several sizes of the same variety of leaf. The leaves should be thin (maple, for example) and freshly picked. Pinch off the stems for best results.

1. Paint the entire paper with yellow paint diluted with water. Don't let the paper dry; keep adding water to it. While it is still wet, lay the upper side of your largest leaf into the still-wet area. The underside (vein-side) of the leaf is facing up.

2. Using one dark, one light, and one medium color for each leaf, paint around each leaf with a dabbing technique. The colors will run together and some will creep underneath the leaf, which will act as a stencil. (Don't use brown or black because these colors deaden the painting.) Continue to work color all over the paper, leaving some areas light and making some dark. The leaves will remain in place until the paper is completely dry (the next day). When you are satisfied, put this painting on the drying rack and begin another one.

3. If your painting has turned out well, leave it alone. However, if you think the painting is weak and needs some help, there are several ways to change this composition once the painting process is complete.

   - while it is wet and the leaves are still in place:

     Would it be improved by adding more dark color somewhere?

     What would happen if you were to "charge" the brush with a dark color and hit it against your forefinger, splattering small dark spots all over the painting?

     More light? What about using white tempera to do the spattering?

   - after it has dried:

     Select your best leaves from one composition and cut them out, pasting them onto another composition.

     Cut out around the leaves and put them all on a dark background.

     Use a fine-line black marker to carefully draw around the leaves and some of the other shapes made by the watercolor.

UNIT 2

PAPER

It is safe to say that the most commonly used universal art material is paper! It comes in a vast array of colors, textures, and sizes, and is adaptable for use with most media. Because of its relative low cost and wide availability, it is the backbone of most elementary art programs.

Historically, the use of paper dates back to the Egyptians, who used the stalks of the papyrus plant to make a form of paper. Ancient scrolls date back to approximately 2200 B.C. The Chinese invented paper as we know it in approximately A.D. 105. Today, varieties of paper such as *papyrus*, *amate* paper made in Mexico from the inner bark of special trees, rice or *mulberry* paper made in Asian countries, and *tapa* "cloth" made in the Pacific islands are familiar to us. These papers have been made from cloth, bark, papyrus plants, rice, or almost any organic material.

Although a paper project can be as messy as any material, it can also be the most accessible, easily stored and cleaned up, so it is particularly suited to interdisciplinary lessons or projects that can be worked on for several periods. Cut paper is particularly appropriate for teaching a multicultural lesson, as there are regional paper (or cloth) design traditions in almost every culture throughout the world.

While the more exotic papers are generally too expensive for classroom use, effective programs recycle paper grocery bags, wallpaper samples, newspapers and magazines, along with the paper "staples" of the classroom: newsprint, construction, drawing, and kraft papers. Copy paper and tagboard file folders may be recycled. Most teachers expect students to be frugal with paper through recycling and use of a scrap paper box. They remind students that the negative shapes are often as interesting as the positive shapes in a collage. More expensive papers such as fadeless paper, colored corrugated board, bond, and watercolor paper are generally reserved for special projects.

PAPER TREATMENTS

accordion-fold	coat with oil	cut holes
batik	chlorine bleach	cut, then bend
bend	combine all kinds	collage
braid	crumple	dip and dye
burn the edges	curl	emboss

cut and expand	make mosaics	sew
fingerpaint	make pop-ups	shape
fold and dye	punch holes	snip
fold, then iron	do a resist	stencil
gesso	roll	tear
make a fan	papier mâché	tie-dye
make flowers	pleat	twist
make greeting cards	print on it	wad
make kites	quill	watercolor
make masks	quilt	transform
make mobiles	score	weave
		wet and drape

This red Chinese paper cutting continues a 2,000-year tradition of working in paper.

The Polish paper-cut involves brightly colored layers of animals and flowers.

Paper Manipulation

EYES

NOSES AND EARS

MOUTHS

SPECIAL EFFECTS

HAIR

HATS

PROJECT 2–1
PORTRAIT HEADS IN PAPER

FOR THE TEACHER   This project allows students to use their imaginations and problem-solving skills, while learning to manipulate paper. They are also challenged to perceive and create value differences and variety using a one-color material.

Vocabulary

value

scoring

accordion-fold

curling

form

variety

portrait

Preparation   Show students portraits by such people as Amedeo Modigliani, Fernando Botero, Frederick Remington, and Red Grooms to demonstrate different ways that artists perceive the human face. Show students how to score paper to control folds, and demonstrate various techniques such as curling strips around a pencil, cutting spirals, curling on the edge of scissors, and fringing. (Refer to handout on Bas-Relief Paper Sculpture in Unit 1.) They can also be shown how to make the crown of a hat to fit within a brim.

A walk around the room to look at other people's solutions to a problem may help students arrive at a new approach. These "gallery walks" can help every student work at a higher level. Assure them that through the ages, artists have been inspired by the work of their fellow artists, and that the originator of the idea should be honored to have inspired someone else.

Alternative Projects

TORN-PAPER FACE COLLAGE   Tearing paper for a flat (2-D) collage offers another method of working that students may not have tried. Encourage them to make the pieces small enough to have a variety of shades.

BAS-RELIEF PORTRAITS   Teacher Mary Ann Kerr (of the University City schools in St. Louis County, Missouri) uses multicultural packs of paper to allow students to consider differences in skin tones and hair styles as they make self-portraits. The faces are glued on flat paper for ease of display, with low-relief features and hair glued on. Portraits also incorporate three-dimensional objects such as buttons, buckles, or balls made of plastic tape. Hair is made of crinkled paper filler from a crafts shop or fringed and curled paper of an appropriate color.

Interdisciplinary Connections
LANGUAGE ARTS

GIVE IT A LIFE   Students can make up an adventure story or biography about their portrait head. They can give it a name, write about where it lives, what kind of work it does, what its favorite quotation is, and something else about its lifestyle.

SOCIAL STUDIES

REAL PEOPLE PORTRAITS These paper faces could be based on real people from the past or present, such as colonial leaders, presidents, royalty, world leaders, famous inventors. Hats and collars might give clues to a personality even though it will be difficult to have a likeness. The face could be displayed next to a research paper about this particular person.

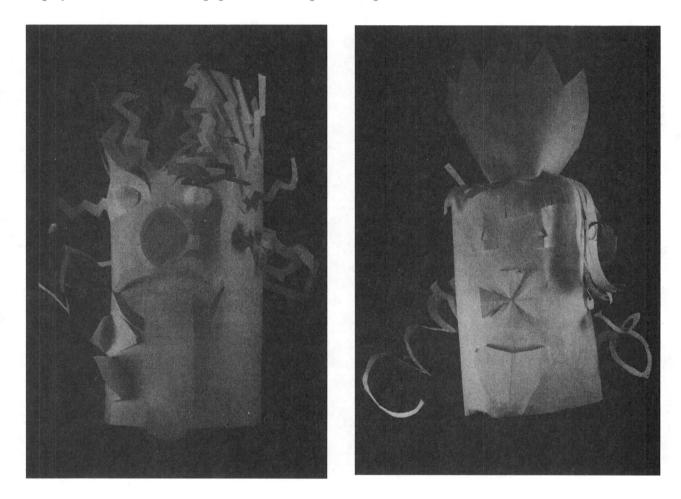

PROJECT 2–1   PORTRAIT HEADS IN PAPER

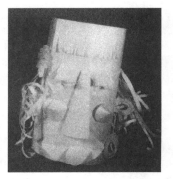

Materials

12 × 18-inch white drawing paper
scissors
glue
paper clips

Directions   In this project you are challenged to
make a portrait of an individual. It might resemble a real person, but also might be a
"character" such as a cowboy, police officer, old man or woman, or a clown.

1. Before beginning the actual head, use one piece of paper to experiment
    with various things you can do with paper. Some of these experiments will
    probably become part of the portrait head. You can curl it, accordion-fold it,
    braid it, make tiny cuts to make fringe, or make spiral circles or squares that
    will droop. You can make geometric shapes such as cones, triangles, or
    cubes as part of the head.

2. Decide whether your portrait is to be male or female. Use a paper clip to
    hold the two ends together so you can mark where to locate the eyes
    (halfway down the head), nose, and mouth for your portrait head. Paste the
    features onto the flat paper.

3. Join the two ends of the paper together with glue. Although the rounded
    form could be smaller at the bottom than the top, it needs to be large
    enough on the bottom to support itself.

4. Think how to complete your character portrait. Could you add a collar? a
    hat? lots of hair? cheeks? Make the face interesting by adding eyelashes, eye-
    brows, or, possibly, a mustache. Be thinking about how to make hair—
    whether to have it fringed or curled. Remember that you are using only one
    color of paper, so you need shadows to make it more interesting to look at.

5. When you are almost done, group all the portrait heads together and discuss
    which ones seem to show the most differences in value. Perhaps you will
    want to talk about your idea and ask if anyone else has a suggestion about
    improving it with slight changes.

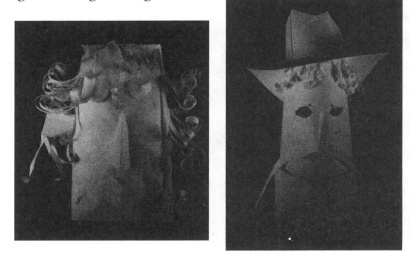

PROJECT 2-2
HANDMADE PAPER

FOR THE TEACHER   Paper was invented by the Chinese almost 2,000 years ago, and is being made by much the same method today. Cultures around, the world independently developed paper-like materials using various plants. Give students the exciting opportunity to make their own paper for later use in writing or art projects. These instructions are for simple 5 × 7-inch sheets of paper. Students can also *cast* paper into molds (plastic packaging is interesting), or can *pour* slurry onto screens through cookie cutters to make animals, hearts, or other designs.

Vocabulary

slurry	pulp
couche (pronounced koosch)	wire screening
cotton linters	mold and deckle
watermark	sizing
post	pour
cast	vat

Preparation   This project is appropriate for students from kindergarten through adulthood. Depending on the ages of your students and how many will be involved in papermaking at one time, this is a good time to involve parent volunteers to *grind* paper to *make* paper and to come in and help. Send a note asking for parent or grandparent volunteers, and you will be amazed at the response. Set up a schedule so you can have helpers in each class. In a two-and-a-half-week period, for example, my 650 elementary students made approximately 5,000 sheets of paper that were used for a variety of projects in their art and regular classrooms! This can also be done on a much smaller scale, of course, having only a few students at a time create paper.

While students can be involved in tearing paper into small pieces (approximately 1 x 1 inches) to be ground in a blender, I do not recommend having young students do the actual grinding. It is easiest to send students home with a bag of pieces and request parents to grind the scraps in a blender or ask them to come in and do it at school. The procedure for grinding is as follows: add *only a few* pieces to a blender full of water. Grind for approximately ten seconds, then pour the *slurry* (the material that floats in water to make paper) through a sieve, and place the *pulp* in a plastic container. Cotton *linters* may be purchased at an art supply store or through an art catalogue (white blotters also work). These can be combined with old dress patterns, construction paper, scrap paper of all kinds (check with your local print shop), or old tests (children love to use them in this manner).

Cellulose plants—such as boiled iris leaves (first cut into half-inch pieces), dried ginkgo leaves, or dried rose or chrysanthemum petals—can be incorporated in the slurry. A *watermark* can be made by using wire to form initials and placing it on the screen before dipping in the vat.

Cover your tables with plastic and fill one or more dish tubs with slurry. Student tables should have several individual setups that include a mold/deckle combination, five to six white felts; small sponges, and a bowl to put excess slurry into (this can be recycled and added to a vat to create *mystery* slurry). If you do not have a drying rack, use old window screens separated by sponges for drying the paper. Although deckles are not absolutely necessary, they make nice neat *deckled* edges. However, I have seen 10 × 12-inch unmounted pieces of metal screenwire used for dipping and rug samples or cut-up blankets used in place of felt to absorb water. This will give irregularly shaped pieces, but they can be combined, placed in molds (cast), or used with the irregular edges.

Interdisciplinary Connections

LANGUAGE ARTS

RECIPES, POEMS, STORIES ABOUT PAPER Depending on the age of your students, they may write prose, poetry, a "recipe" for making paper, a story, or make an individual or classroom book. To write on paper it is best to first *size* it with diluted white glue, polymer medium, or spray starch. However, it can be written on with marker without sizing first.

SCIENCE

PAPER IN THE EGYPTIAN AND CHINESE STYLES This could involve research into plants that are used in paper making. Students might like to look at fiber lengths through a microscope, or to make papyrus by flattening the fibers in a plant that has stalks. Even in Egypt they make imitation papyrus with cornstalks. The Chinese made paper by boiling vegetable fibers with lye (a tablespoon of lye to a quart of water works).

SOCIAL STUDIES

TIMELINE: DEVELOPMENT OF PAPER Have students research the use of paper in various cultures. While they may take books for granted, ask students to find out when writing on paper actually began, and when the printing press was invented. This could include making a timeline about the invention of paper.

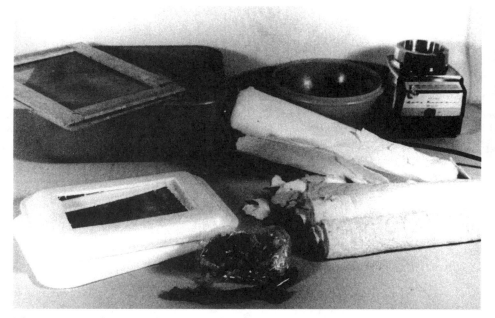

These paper-making supplies include butcher foam or wooden deckle frames, a tub of slurry, rolled white felts, embroidery thread, and boiled iris leaves.

PROJECT 2–2   HANDMADE PAPER

Materials

molds (wire stapled to wood battens or taped to plastic meat trays)

deckles (a piece the same size as the mold but with an empty rectangular opening)

cotton linters (one sheet makes approximately 75 to 100 sheets of 5 X 7-inch paper)

old window screens of any kind

dish pans (vats)

iron (*optional*)

shallow trays

2 boards of the same general size as the paper

white felt (cut-up blankets, rug samples, or sheets could be used)

paper (*National Geographic*, dress patterns, construction paper, scrap paper, old tests, etc.)

embroidery hoops (filled with hosiery or wire) to make round or oval paper

sieves

sponges

blender

metal screenwire

duct tape

Procedure: Dip, Shake, Couche!

1. Stir the vat with your hand to evenly distribute the slurry. Add a handful of slurry to a vat when the paper seems thin. Hold the mold and deckle sideways and slide it down the side of the vat. At the bottom, turn the mold and deckle horizontally and lift it straight up.

2. Hold the deckle over the vat to drain the water, and shake it forward and backward, then side to side (this helps the fibers to interlock). Use a finger to take off any excess slurry from the edge of the deckle.

3. Remove the top deckle and lay the mold paper-side-down on top of a felt. Use a small sponge to press all over the screen (this step is called couching), which will transfer the paper from the screen and onto the felt. Place a piece of felt on top of this, go back to the vat, and go through the process again. An alternating stack of paper and felts is called a *post*. It will be quite wet. You can use a rolling pin (inside a tray) to roll out excess water, or you can place the paper between two boards inside a tray and stand on it to remove excess water. (Note to teacher: Very young students don't weigh enough to get out sufficient water.)

4. Use the *pads* of the fingers to gently remove the paper from the felt. Lift it and place it on a screen to dry. To identify your own paper, encircle it with a piece of yarn and place your name within the circle. Individual sheets will dry overnight, or the water may be ironed out by placing the paper between sheets of newsprint, changing the paper and ironing it until dry. You can decorate your paper before removing excess water by adding embroidery thread, flower petals, or thin strips of contrasting paper.

5. Dried paper can be drawn or written on by using a size made of thinned white glue or sprayed with spray starch. It can be used as part of a collage and combined with materials from magazines. Think about making an imaginary landscape collage using pieces of your handmade paper.

A. Students are dipping paper-making screens into vats filled with different types of paper slurry.

B. This student is transferring his paper onto the felt.

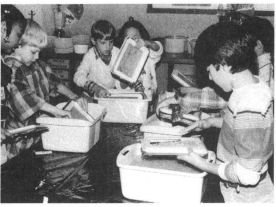

C. Students are couching their paper onto the felts that are rolled up beside them. When each felt is filled, excess water is squeezed out of all of them at one time by placing them between two boards (inside a tray to contain the water) and stepping on the board.

D. The slurry table with five different slurries in the trays.

E. Examples of handmade paper show bits and pieces of dress patterns, tests, and construction paper. The paper at the upper right had a string dipped in slurry and laid on top of a screen before it was couched.

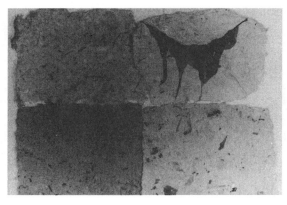

PROJECT 2–3 MARBLEIZED PAPER

FOR THE TEACHER Marbleizing is another craft that is related to making books. It originated in Japan in the eighth century and was brought (probably by sea) to Persia and Turkey. It was widely used in Europe to decorate the endpapers of books. Students love doing marbleizing, and you can make it as simple or as complex as you wish.

Vocabulary

marbleizing

endpapers

size

carragheenan

rakes

combs

size

Preparation Cover tables with paper or plastic, and have students wear smocks. The project can be done "professionally" with carragheenan (available from art supply stores). Dissolve approximately 1 tablespoon per gallon of water—blend 1 teaspoon in a blender with six cups of water. This solution is best prepared 24 hours prior to using. Dilute acrylic paint in water (the amount varies because of the chemical makeup of the paints). Use a brush to drop the color on the size in the tray to see how it works (it should not make huge circles, and it should not sink directly to the bottom). Always try this the day before introducing the project. For some reason the size works better when it has been used before. The size can be used for several days, then it begins to smell (it is made from dried seaweed, an organic matter). Cleanup is easily accomplished and the table kept in order by placing an open sheet of newspaper for scrap paper next to the tray and changing it each hour.

Students can dry their marbleized paper on newspaper. If the excess size "puddles," use toilet paper or paper towels to sop up excess water.

An alternative is to make this a one-day project at the sink, using liquid starch and a purchased comb with a handle and only a few teeth.

Alternative Projects

MARBLEIZE WITH PASTELS A form of marbleizing can be done by using a knife to scrape pastels onto water, and stirring with the handle end of a brush to make a pattern. Drop a piece of paper onto the surface and lift off. These will be pale, but lovely.

MARBLEIZING ON LIQUID STARCH Undiluted liquid starch can be used to support diluted acrylic paint. All other directions are the same.

TRADITIONAL MARBLEIZING WITH OIL ON WATER Oil paint diluted with mineral spirits will float on water that has been slightly thickened with gelatin.

Uses for Marbleized Paper

- Cut up marbleized paper and use it to decorate the fronts of note cards.
- Use for beautiful covers or endpapers for handmade books.
- Make small gift sacks.
- Do a lino-cut print on it.
- Cover juice cans for pencil holders. Use for other desk accessories.
- Make a small memo book.
- Have students find animals within the lines using fine-line black markers to emphasize the patterns.

Handmade combs and rakes are used for making patterns on the surface of the paper.

PROJECT 2–3   MARBLEIZED PAPER

Materials

carragheenan (size)

thinned acrylic paints

baby-food jars to hold different colors
   of paints

cookie sheets

brushes

broomstraws

drinking straws

rakes: make by inserting pins into a
   piece of cardboard at 1-inch intervals (I used corsage pins in 1/2-inch
   square X 12-inch long balsa wood)

combs: (make by inserting pins at 1/4-
   inch intervals)

trays (tote trays or photo-developing trays)

cookie sheets

plastic gallon milk jugs

vinegar in a spray bottle (or alum, *optional*)

sponges

paper cut smaller than the trays (construction paper absorbs the colors well)

newspaper, cut into half sheets and 2-inch strips

The flowers in this marbleized paper
were made by putting a drop of oil on
the surface to make the hole, then
using a straw to pull paint out of or
into the hole. The centers were made
by adding a drop of paint from a drinking straw.

Directions   Marbleizing paper means to make it have beautiful designs in it
that resemble real marble. It has been used to decorate the endpapers in books for
almost 1,000 years.

1.   Put your name on the back of the paper. Prepare your paper to print by
     lightly spraying the front with vinegar, then use a sponge to spread the vine-
     gar. A solution of alum can be used in place of vinegar.

2.   Before adding fresh paint, clean the size in the tray by holding a 2 X 12-inch
     strip of newspaper straight up and down by the ends and pulling it across
     the surface. Throw away the newspaper.

3.   Make designs on the surface by dropping several colors of paint from a
     brush onto the surface. Three to five colors would be the most you would
     need. Here is a list of possible designs:

     ● *pebbles.* Make splashes by simply dropping paint onto the surface.

- *feather pattern.* Drag the *rake* the length of the tray, then back again.

- *comb feather pattern.* First make the feather pattern, then use the comb in the same manner.

- *standard pattern.* Use the *rake*, then the *comb* to go the length of the tray and back; then go crossways and back with the *rake* and the *comb* on the paint surface.

- *stars.* Dip a broomstraw in eye-makeup remover (or another oil). Touch it on the surface and pull into or away from the hole made by the oil to make points.

- *circle within a circle.* Use an oil-dipped broomstraw to make a hole. Then dip a drinking straw into another color of paint, hold your finger on the end to hold a drop of paint in the straw, and drop the paint into the center of the hole. This can be repeated with a third color.

4. Place the paper onto the prepared surface. To avoid white bubbles in the center, hold it by opposite corners and place the center of the paper down first, then allow the ends to drop. Place a cookie sheet at the end of the tray, and lift the marbleized sheet face-up onto the cookie sheet, allowing extra liquid carragheenan to drip off. Carry the cookie sheet to the sink and gently pour water over the surface to remove excess liquid. Place the marbleized paper on newspaper to dry.

COLLAGE

Cut-and-paste . . . collage . . . it can be wonderful and it can be terrible! It's wonderful to build confidence in young people who are uncertain of their skills in art, or who have difficulty drawing what they see. It's wonderful for artists who are trying to come up with an abstract or nonrealistic composition, or who want to express an idea but don't quite know how to start. It's terrible, however, when students are simply given magazines and allowed to cut out too many images and paste them on a piece of paper. These all tend to look exactly alike and are so crowded that everything is seen—and nothing is seen.

Collage (which comes from the French word *coller;* meaning "to glue") is the reason art teachers never throw anything away. It is for this that you save scraps of paper, yarn, marbleized paper, wrapping paper, and ribbon. Collage can be made entirely from one material, such as construction paper, or from combinations of a variety of materials, such as cut paper, wood, cloth, handmade paper, wallpaper samples, or torn-up handpainted paper. Just remember that it needs to be taken beyond cut-and-paste. Composition and unity, emphasis, and variety are principles of art that are incorporated into every lesson. Young people might find it easier if they try to make an abstraction of something realistic.

Examples of the work of many artists can be shown to inspire students in collage. Young people are very interested in Surrealism, another French word, that means "above reality." The Surrealists—such as René Magritte, Man Ray, Max Ernst and Salvador Dali—use unlikely objects in landscapes (such as Magritte's sky full of open umbrellas or Dali's melting watch-dotted landscapes)   Pablo Picasso and Georges Braque popularized collage with their early twentieth-century Cubist collages using words from newspapers and materials such as oilcloth. Henri Matisse, when he could no longer paint, began a second career with his cut-and-pasted handpainted paper shapes based on life-forms from nature. *Montages* were created from combinations of photographs by Bauhaus artist and teacher László Moholy-Nagy.

Beasts of the Sea, 1950, Henri Matisse, collage on canvas/paper collage on canvas, 116³/₈ × 60⁵/₈ inches, National Gallery of Art, Washington DC, Ailsa Mellon Bruce Fund. Matisse's paper-cuttings are universally recognized collages, bringing the art of paper-cutting to the mainstream of art.

PROJECT 2–4
FLOWER GARDEN

FOR THE TEACHER   Unlike construction paper and other papers that are a solid color throughout, the colors on brightly colored fadeless paper are applied onto a white surface. By tearing shapes from fadeless paper toward yourself from the back, the white paper underneath is allowed to show around the edges of the torn shape. This project is based on a flower garden, but would be equally appropriate for something like an undersea scene of fish and water plants, or birds in a jungle. If fadeless paper is not available, students can handpaint watercolors onto heavy paper, allowing the paper to dry before tearing it.

Vocabulary
negative and positive shapes

grain

fadeless

variety

repetition

foreground

middle-ground

background

Preparation   Demonstrate for students how to tear the paper to allow the maximum white edge to show, and caution them against throwing any paper away (because it is relatively expensive and even the smallest piece that they don't need might be used by a neighbor to make a composition more interesting). Explain how they can use the grain of paper to tear straight when they are tearing stems. Cut some of the paper into squares of various sizes to make tearing easier.

Alternative Project
CITYSCAPE TORN-PAPER COLLAGE A "cityscape" collage of buildings, with their many forms and shapes, can easily be torn and pasted from fadeless paper for an effect similar to the flower garden. Remind students of foreground, middle-ground, and background.

Fadeless paper was torn to leave a white edge showing.

The same technique was used to make this cityscape.

PROJECT 2–4   FLOWER GARDEN

Materials

9 × 12-inch white drawing paper

fadeless paper (cut into various shapes)

glue

Directions   Think about what a flower garden looks like. There are usually flowers of many different colors, sizes, and shapes. Some are tall and round, some grow on bushes, some are short and tiny. Some are buds, and some just seem to be tall stems because the blossoms have fallen off. Leaves are of all different shapes and colors of green and yellow.

1. Draw some shapes on the back of the fadeless paper and carefully tear out only small areas at a time. If you take your time, you have almost as much control as if you were using scissors. Tearing *toward yourself* from the back allows white edges to show—and when the shapes are pasted on paper, they will have white outlines. It doesn't matter if you make "mistakes" because you will find a use for extra pieces of paper.

2. Make several shapes of approximately the same size and color to represent one variety of flower. Use more than one shade of green for leaves, make tall skinny stems, and fat or thin leaves.

3. Place the tallest flowers with the longest stems in the background, medium height in the middle-ground and small flowers in the foreground (nearest the bottom). Flowers in the middle-ground and foreground may have to be glued on top of stems already in place. Remember that every flower needs a stem. At the bottom you may want to make some skinny blades of grass.

4. Look at the scraps of paper from which you tore your flowers. These "holes" are negative shapes. Sometimes the negative shapes can also be used by tearing around the edges of the "hole" to make a thin shape for decorating. See how you can "embellish" your flowers with the addition of centers and leaves.

5. When you are done, put your artwork down and move about ten feet from it to see if it needs anything more.

PROJECT 2–5
WAXED COLLAGE

FOR THE TEACHER   Early precursors of Pop Art, such as British artist Richard Hamilton, used magazine cut-outs in collage. Pop artists from the 1950s and 1960s, such as Andy Warhol, Roy Lichtenstein, Robert Rauschenberg, and Tom Wesselman, used popular subjects in advertising and comic art as subjects. Letters, Coke® bottles, soup cans, and household appliances were all used as subjects.

Vocabulary

space	repetition
variety	scale
emphasis	center-of-interest

Preparation   To make a successful magazine cut-out collage, explain that most collages involve too many images, making a confusing composition. Suggest instead that students think of a theme—such as a landscape, seascape, or cityscape—and use the varied colors they find rather than relying too much on letters and people. A one-color scheme created with variations of one color torn from a magazine can result in many different shades of one hue. Patterns and letters of one color can unify and emphasize a subject. Combining the magazine cut-outs with colored paper may help students simplify their collages.

A slightly heavier support such as tablet backing or matboard is suggested. Keep the size relatively small, as the whole process is simpler when smaller.

Melt paraffin in a coffee can set in a pan of boiling water, using a candy thermometer. If you have an electric skillet or electric crockpot that will enable you to control the temperature, so much the better. (CAUTION: This must only be done by an adult—or with adult supervision for older students.) A temperature of 200 degrees is adequate for this project. **Safety note: Paraffin can ignite spontaneously at approximately 350 degrees, so take care to control the temperature. If it starts to smoke, the temperature is too high.** You will need the hot paraffin for only one or two days. Keep it in a central place that is covered to protect the table. Sacrifice several brushes, softening them in the paraffin and saving them for paraffin projects next year. Try the wax process yourself first—it is fun and will help you explain it better to the students.

Alternative Project
MAGAZINE COLLAGE/PHOTOCOPY/PASTEL

Colleague Tim Smith has his students make collages of magazine pictures, then these are photocopied and the photocopy is colored with colored pencils. Students then select a small area of the photocopied collage and make a very large pastel composition that appears almost abstract.

Memory of Oceania, Nice, 1952–1953, Henri Matisse, gouache and crayon on cut-and-pasted paper over canvas, 9′4″ × 9′4⁷/₈″, The Museum of Modern Art, New York City, Mrs. Simon Guggenheim Fund, Photograph © 1999 The Museum of Modern Art, New York. © 2000 Succession H. Matisse, Paris/Artists Rights Society (ARS), New York

PROJECT 2–5 WAXED COLLAGE

STUDENT PAGE

Materials

magazines

fadeless paper

scissors

glue sticks

8 × 10-inch cardboard (tablet backing works)

paraffin

electric skillet, hot plate, or crockpot

candy thermometer

hair dryer

1-inch brushes (use only a few)

string

tape

This collage of fadeless paper and magazine cut-outs is mounted on chipboard and has three coats of wax, which give it a luster.

Directions   When going through magazines looking for pictures that you can use in your collage, work in a *color scheme*. Cut out pictures mostly in one color that you can combine to give *emphasis* to your main subject (center of interest). This main subject might be a person, animal, tree, group of letters, an apple, or a car. Sometimes you can use two things that are very different from each other to make a humorous combination.

1. Carefully trim your magazine cut-outs and move them around on the cardboard until you find a pleasing combination of colors. You will probably combine these with colored paper to fill in empty spaces. Think about your main subject or *center-of-interest* (it doesn't always have to be placed in the center), and carefully choose other cut-outs that don't detract from it. Glue these down flat with a glue stick. Make sure no corners are sticking up.

2. Coat the surface with melted paraffin with a brush. *Go one direction*, repeatedly dipping the brush in the paraffin; do not go back over the same area. Apply a second coat, going the *opposite* direction. A third coat applied in the original direction will completely cover the paper, hide the cut edges, and give the collage an opaque appearance (you can see still through it, but everything is slightly hazy looking).

3. Although you may prefer the rough surface, you can use a hair dryer to smooth the surface somewhat. Hold it about two inches above the surface until an area has become shiny and molten, then move on to the next area. The surface will look opaque, but as it cools, the white surface will become clear again.

4. On the back of the piece of cardboard, tape a 4-inch piece of string to hang the collage after the wax has been applied. The front will scratch easily, so you will want to handle it carefully when it is finished.

PROJECT 2-6
WEARING BLANKETS

FOR THE TEACHER This woven-paper project is based on the woolen wearing blankets that were the Navajo and Pueblo equivalent of modern students' jackets. Early Navajo blankets and woven dresses were simple horizontal-stripe designs of red and blue, or gray, black and white. By the mid-1800s more colors were introduced, and subtle variations within the black areas were achieved by alternating thin black stripes of another dark color such as dark green, blue green, or dark violet. Geometric designs were placed on the stripes or background. The weavings were sometimes called chiefs' blankets because they were expensive and were owned primarily by wealthier people. The blankets are quite large and heavy, approximately 4-1/2 feet wide by 6-1/2 feet long. From approximately 1650 to 1875 (the First Phase), the blankets were meant only for wearing; but from 1875 to 1895 (the Second Phase), the yarns used were heavier, and the weavings were often created for use as rugs (sometimes called pound blankets because they were sold by the pound). A Third Phase evolved as blankets and rugs were created for outside sales through trading posts. Pictorial blankets, using dyes that sometimes faded, were made from the late 1890s onward.

Vocabulary

warp (vertical "strings")

weft (crosswise weaving)

tapestry

Preparation
Bring in pictures of Native Americans wearing traditional dress such as their wearing blankets or woven dresses. Although the Navajos do not have chieftains, chiefs from other tribes proudly wore these status symbols. Compare the purchase of a Navajo blanket to the students' selection of shoes or clothing because of its particular name brand. Photocopy rug designs from books and post around the room so students can become aware of subtle design differences.

Make diamond-shaped tagboard templates and crosses (all arms equal) that students can use to make "appliqués" for their stripes. Have several different sizes so they can make layers of colors.

Adaptations for Primary Grades
Allow the younger children to weave the simple First Phase striped blankets of black, white, and gray paper, or use only red and blue together. Select a piece of 12 X 18-inch gray, black, or white construction paper. Have 1/2- and 1-inch strips cut of gray, black, and white. The students will weave with a simple in–out (tabby) weave using the two colors that are different from the background.

Alternative Projects

YARN WEAVING ON CARDBOARD Make or purchase a 9 X 13-inch cardboard loom. Have students use string for the warp, and decide in advance the pattern they will use before beginning to weave yarn from the bottom to the top. Have them use traditional colors and patterns.

ALL-CLASS WOVEN WEARING BLANKET Make an all-class tapestry on a large loom by using canvas stretchers or 2 X 2-inch boards to make a frame. Drive nails in each end 1/4 to 3/4 inches apart, and use string as the warp (vertical) threads. Beginning at the bottom, allow students who wish to participate to take turns weaving on the loom. Remove from the loom and hang on a stick. Make fringe at the bottom with more yarn.

Interdisciplinary Connections

LANGUAGE ARTS

FAMILY TRADITION Write about something that was taught you by a family member, not part of formal education, but just something you learned as part of growing up, such as cooking or gardening. Navajos learned how to weave simply by being around it when other family members wove.

MATH

GRAPH-PAPER BLANKET Using graph paper, make a rectangle, then work out a horizontal design, including diamonds and plus signs (crosses).

COMPUTER GRAPHICS BLANKET Create three blankets from one basic pattern using a computer graphics program. Make a grid on the screen. Locate the center of the blanket first, then work from there to make an overall design. Make and print a First Phase blanket of simple horizontal stripes of different widths. Change that design by adding diamonds or crosses on the stripes to make a Second Phase blanket. Make a Third Phase blanket using pictorial elements such as horses, flowers, birds, trains, cars, recreational vehicles.

SOCIAL STUDIES

IMPACT OF RAILROADS ON NATIVE AMERICAN ART Research how the opening of the railroad affected artwork done by Native American peoples.

Second Phase Chief's Blanket, 1855–1865, cochineal-dyed and natural wools, $52^{1}/_{4} \times 70^{7}/_{8}$ inches, The Nelson–Atkins Museum of Art, Kansas City, Missouri (Purchase: Nelson Trust)

Serape Blanket, American Indian (Navajo), 1865–1870, wool, $52^{1}/_{4} \times 69^{3}/_{4}$ inches, The Nelson–Atkins Museum of Art, Kansas City, Missouri (Purchase: Nelson Trust)

5. Using the same color scheme, use cardboard templates (patterns) to make three-layered diamonds that will be glued on top of the stripes. The diamonds sometimes had "steps" because of the way they were woven. The diamonds in the center of the blanket will be complete, and the diamonds on the sides will be cut in half vertically. (When the blankets were worn, the half diamonds met in the front of the blanket wearer to form a whole diamond.) Glue these decorations in place. Finish the "blanket" by putting several "strings" of paper hanging from each corner.

Transitional Chief's Blanket/c. 1890s

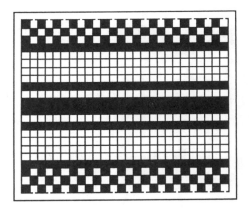

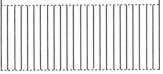

Transitional Chief's Blanket/Rug, c. 1890

PROJECT 2–6   WEARING BLANKETS

STUDENT PAGE

Materials

12 × 18- or 18 × 24-inch construction paper
scissors
rulers
white glue or glue sticks
tagboard templates

Directions   You will be weaving paper in the same way Navajo and Pueblo Native Americans wove their woolen wearing blankets. The blankets were woven horizontally, with the stripes going around the person. Few colors were used, but because they were pure and bright, they are as beautiful today as when they were created.

1. Before you begin weaving, plan a pattern that will make your stripes interesting. Some stripes will be wide bands and some will be narrow. The stripes on both top and bottom and in the middle are often combined, and may have several different widths. The center stripes are usually much more elaborate than the other bands, perhaps containing diamonds or crosses.

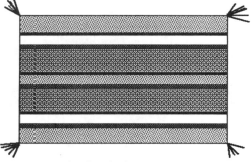

Chief's Blanket, c. 1870

2. Decide what the background color of your rug will be (usually black, gray, or red). Select strips of paper 1/2- to 1-inch wide that have been cut on the paper cutter in three to four other colors (gray, white, black, dark blue, dark violet, dark green).

3. Carefully fold the large piece of construction paper in half lengthwise (like a hot-dog bun). Lightly mark a line 1 inch from the top edge. Use a ruler to draw lines 1/2- or 1-inch wide along the fold. Cut to the line that is 1 inch from the top. Open the paper.

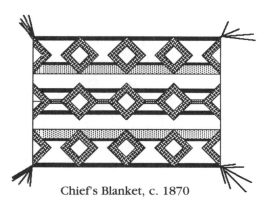

Chief's Blanket, c. 1870

4. Plan ahead for the pattern so the bottom and top stripes are alike. The middle stripes can be wider. After you have woven the entire "blanket," use a glue stick to glue the stripes to the sides to hold them in place.

PROJECT 2-7 STORY QUILT

FOR THE TEACHER Appliqué and other old quilting techniques were brought to the United States by slaves from Senegal, Ghana, Nigeria, and Angola, and were an influence on quilting in the American South. The Fon people of Benin, Africa have a tradition of appliquéd quilts or banners. These quilt blocks were often joined by multicolored, pieced narrow strips of cloth that were reminiscent of Kenté cloth (traditionally woven in Africa for kings). Harriet Powers (1837–1911) was a famous African-American quilter who has inspired other artists with her appliqué in the manner of African artists. Your students might like to know that some African-American quilters purposely included a "mistake" in the quilt because they felt that only God could make something perfect. Contemporary artist Faith Ringgold continues in the tradition of the story quilt with her painted and sewn quilts. Her work is represented in many museum collections.

Vocabulary

unity

variety

balance

emphasis

Preparation

Your students will enjoy making a portion of a class quilt that tells a story. A quilt might have a single subject such as all birds, fish, pigs, or human forms; or each block might be different in order to tell a story. Involve students in making the decision whether to have a specific theme for the story quilt. They may prefer to tell a personal story. This is a good opportunity to use up scrap construction paper. A photograph of the mounted story quilt could be taken and photocopied so each student would have a souvenir of this special artwork.

Alternative Project

MUSLIN QUILT Small squares (6 x 6 inches) of muslin could be created by each student using fabric markers, crayons, paints, or pastels.

Interdisciplinary Connections

LANGUAGE ARTS

WRITE THE STORY OF YOUR QUILT BLOCK After students have created their individual blocks, have them write a story about the event they have depicted. These may be quite detailed and be compiled into a classroom book. When the "quilt" is displayed on the wall, have the students tell their story to the class, or invite parents for a special evening.

MATH

"MATH PROBLEMS" QUILT Depending on the ages of the children, each individual square could contain cut-out objects and a number telling how many objects there are. Because these numbers and objects will be relatively small, use few background colors, allowing variety in size and style.

TRADITIONAL GEOMETRIC BLOCKS On 8 X 8-inch construction paper squares, have students assemble triangles and squares of various sizes to make a block. Four identical 8-inch squares glued together on 18 X 18-inch paper (leaving a 1-inch border all around) forms yet another type of pattern.

SCIENCE

"CREATURES AND THEIR ENVIRONMENTS" QUILT BLOCKS Select an environment and have students research living creatures within that environment. A patch could include a creature and its surroundings, perhaps including a predator. Students could make several smaller "quilts" using such environments as the ocean, African forest, tropical rain forest, or veldt.

"FAVORITE FOOD" QUILT Sandra Nickeson's students of the Guardian Angel Settlement (in St. Louis, Missouri) made a quilt in which each square had one item of food, such as pizza, an ice cream cone, a tomato, a green pepper, and so on.

SOCIAL STUDIES

"MY STATE" QUILT BLOCKS Each student could select a location in his or her own state (or city) that people come to visit. They could base their picture on information from the state's tourism bureau about the park, monument, building, harbor, historic event.

CULTURAL QUILT BLOCKS An entire class quilt could be made that represents one particular culture such as Native American, Asian, Egyptian, Hawaiian, Inuit, Hispanic, Pennsylvania "Dutch," or Scandinavian, using motifs that are unique to that civilization. For example, South American *arpilleras* are handmade folk art appliqué fabric blocks that tell a story of every-day life of the people of the Andes.

"TRANSPORTATION" QUILT BLOCKS Research the evolution of transportation from ancient times. Each square could include something different, such as carts, trains, planes, automobiles, horse-drawn carriages, bicycles, boats, submarines, helicopters, balloons, blimps, in-line skates, etc.

PROJECT 2–7   STORY QUILT

STUDENT PAGE

Materials

pencils
10 X 10-inch squares of construction paper
12 X 12-inch squares of construction paper
fine-line black markers
scissors
white glue

Directions   In this project you will be telling a true story about yourself.
Picture one of the following scenes: my favorite sports activity, at the zoo, my family,
my home, my bicycle, train ride, on the school bus.

1. Before you cut out paper, think about yourself in this picture. You will be
   fairly big, and other objects and people may be smaller. Draw your cut-outs
   on the back of the paper. After you have cut them out, turn the paper over
   so pencil marks won't show. This will reverse the image.

2. Before gluing, arrange all the pieces and get the teacher's approval.
   Background pieces have to be glued on first, then details added later.

3. After everything is glued in place, you will do "embroidery." Because this is
   paper, you won't actually sew this, but by carefully making short black lines
   (about 1/4 inch) around the edge of each piece and onto the background,
   you can make it look like you sewed this piece onto its block.

4. When all the individual "blocks" are finished, they can be assembled into a
   quilt on the wall by mounting all the blocks on a piece of paper 1 inch larger all around than the block itself. Use the same background color for everyone in the class. "Stitches" can also be drawn on the background blocks.

This story quilt by third graders at Barretts School, St. Louis
County, Missouri, was created by students of apprentice-
teacher Pamela Olderman in Debbie McConnell's classes. It
was created with cloth, with forms outlined with permanent
black marker to make it look as if it were sewn. The use of
Native American myths provided unity.

MAKING BOOKS

Books written on scrolls or clay tablets date back several thousand years. The book as we know it today dates back to Roman times when wax-on-wood tablets were bound together to form a *Codex* (a bound book with separate pages). The Emperor Charlemagne (768–814), who was illiterate, was known as one of the great patrons of the written word, because of the monasteries built under his patronage where monks might copy scripture and classical books by hand. By the fifteenth century, a book was still considered to be something very rare. The beautifully illuminated manuscripts owned by wealthy patrons of that time are especially appreciated today for both their calligraphy and decorations.

It wasn't until Johan Gutenberg (c. 1400–1468) invented the movable-type printing press in the fifteenth century that books became widely available. Prior to that, printed books including both text and illustration were carved (backwards, of course) from a single wood block.

The book projects in this section are adaptable to many formats and uses, and are especially adaptable to interdisciplinary lessons.

PROJECT 2–8
POP-UP GREETING CARDS

FOR THE TEACHER   Skill building is an important part of making books. Students need to start small, such as cutting and folding to make a pop-up card so they understand the process before making a folded book with pop-ups. Experiments that allow for mistakes and innovations will give each student an individual approach to his or her work. A basic thing to emphasize is that no paper is to be removed from the cuts. The cuts are made, then the paper folded inward or outward to balance. No paper is actually removed.

Vocabulary

scroll

binding

scoring

accordion-fold

pop-out

Preparation   Pre-cut 4 × 6- and 7 × 10-inch pieces of paper for students to use freely to experiment. Practice several of these procedures yourself first. Several fine books are available on making pop-up books and pop-up cards.

PROJECT 2–8   POP-UP GREETING CARDS

STUDENT PAGE

Materials

4 × 6-inch white construction or drawing paper

7 × 10-inch pieces of white paper

scissors

rulers

Directions   To make a pop-up card, try out ideas by making several cut and folded small pieces of paper that look like sculpture. Each person can end up with an entirely different looking project, simply through experimenting for awhile.

1. Experiment cutting folded paper as illustrated in the Pop-ups Handout. Fold a piece of 4 × 6-inch paper in half (the short way).

    a. *straight cut.* Make a partial cut into the fold. Fold the paper back in asymmetrical triangles.

    b. *two straight cuts.* Fold these cuts inward. When you open the card, you will find you have made a chair or stair step. You can glue a design, such as a butterfly, on the front of this. Or draw the back of the chair and cut out the front legs.

    c. *stair steps.* Use a ruler to score a line 1 inch in from the open edge. Measure and make single cuts toward the line. Then alternately fold them in and out. To make stair steps, make a diagonal fold line and cut to it.

    d. *curved cuts.* Make two curved cuts. Fold inward, then fold the sides of the paper to meet in the center. You will now have more places where you can cut.

    e. *two cuts.* Make a second cut from the fold and score the paper between the two cuts, which will allow you to make beautiful folds.

    f. *spiral cut.* Cut a circle. Beginning at the outside, make a continuous cut around the outside toward the center; this creates a spiral when one end is grasped. Glue one end of this to the left side of the card and the other end to the right side. When it is opened, the spiral naturally opens.

2. Fold a 7 × 10-inch piece of construction paper in half (the short way) for the outer part of the card. For the inside pop-out, fold a second piece of 5 × 7-inch piece of paper in half. First make tabs to glue onto the card by using the tips of scissors to score 1/2 inch in from the edges. Fold these back for gluing. From the center fold, make a cut. Fold the design inward.

3. Glue the tabs to the pages halfway in so the folded insert does not extend past the outer edges of the card. It is important that this will "pop" when the card is opened and closed. If you have holes in the pop-out, within the card, you could also make cut-outs that would show when the card is opened.

Pop-ups

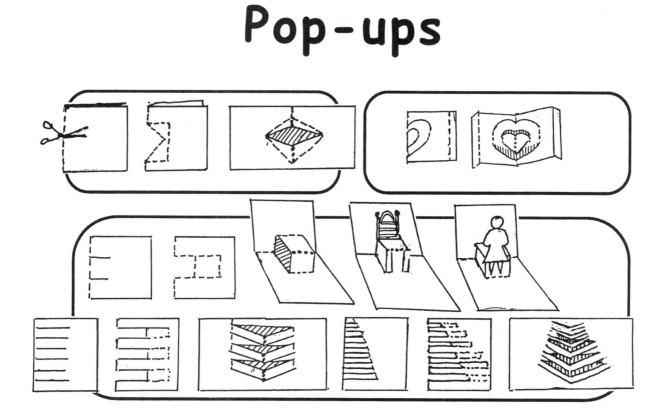

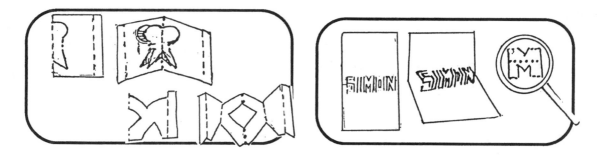

Cut	_____
Valley fold	- - - - -
Mountain fold	. . . .

PROJECT 2–9
THE ART BOOK,
AN ACCORDION-FOLDED POP-UP

FOR THE TEACHER   While beautiful paper may be purchased and used for making books, this project is based on individually-prepared brightly colored papers that make it a visual delight. Although there may be very little writing, Dr. Clem Pennington, who presented this project on bookmaking at a National Art Education Convention, said "A book is not a book if it does not have *some* sort of writing in it." Even a single quotation on the endpaper of a book gives it meaning.

Vocabulary

mountain and valley folds

haiku and diamante (poems)

accordion-folds

pop-ups

Preparation   Have students experiment with several different decorating methods to prepare paper for this. I found it was a natural tie-in to printmaking, as students are already printing with brayers, and ink is available. The accordion-folded book can be done with plain pieces of paper, but the beautiful colors that can be made with inks encourage unique solutions for each student. The tagboard templates used for folding (start with a valley fold at the center) allow students to make proper, even folds.

Interdisciplinary Connections
LANGUAGE ARTS
HAIKU, ALPHABET, OR POETRY BOOK   The accordion-folded book is especially appropriate for haiku, poetry, or a story. Each student could do a decoration for one page to make an alphabet book, and these decorations (or pop-outs) could be glued on a page.

QUOTATION OR STORY   A favorite quotation could be printed on the inside of the front cover, or one word might be written on each page.

SCIENCE
A NATURE BOOK   Have students select one science-related subject (botany, cell structure, astronomy, reptiles, flowers, butterflies) to create an entire book. Facts (one per page) could be handwritten or done on a computer.

FOREIGN LANGUAGE
STORY BOOK IN A FOREIGN LANGUAGE   Teacher Vicki Howard's Spanish students (of St. Williams Catholic School, St. Louis County, Missouri) made and illustrated charming story books.

A and B. Student Barbara McDonald's accordion-fold *Dinosaur* book includes pop-ups.

This travel book by student Heidi Wilson makes effective use of collage and pop-ups.

Vicky Howard's eighth-grade Spanish students at St. William Catholic School adapted the book format for Spanish translations.

PROJECT 2–9   THE ART BOOK, AN ACCORDION-FOLDED POP-UP

STUDENT PAGE

Materials

5 × 5-inch tagboard templates	paper punch
railroad board or corrugated cardboard cut 5-1/2 × 5-1/2 inches (for covers)	Pritt® or Ross® paste (often used for papier mâché)
brayers	brushes
water-soluble printing ink or tempera paint	white glue
plastic or glass slabs for rolling out ink	rulers
scissors	ribbon
18 × 24-inch drawing or watercolor paper	black, silver, or gold markers

Options for Preparing Paper in Advance

- Use fingers to cover the paper thinly with paste and distribute pigment on it. Paint could be spattered by hitting the pigment-loaded brush on a finger.

- Tempera, watercolor, or acrylic all mix well with the paste. If the tempera/paste becomes too thick, make a monoprint by placing a clean piece of paper on top and pressing all over.

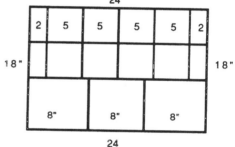

- Paper may be done on both sides if the book is to be displayed accordion-fashion with the covers not actually connected or on one side only if the covers will be connected at the back.

- Make circles by keeping one end of the inked brayer in place while swinging the other end around.

- Use ink straight from the tube (rolled out on glass).

- Use a brayer to roll ink in a plaid pattern or use thin layers of color on top of each other, allowing underneath colors to show through.

- Ink a brayer, then use a pencil to make designs on it before applying the ink to paper.

- Use a brush to paint ink onto the paper, or thin the ink and spatter-paint with a brush.

- Print lino-cuts, potatoes, or various found items to stamp designs all over the paper.

- Use fingers and hands to apply designs with ink or tempera.

- Designs can be emphasized later by going over them with black, silver, or gold marker.

Directions

1. Make the two covers of the book by rubbing glue on the back of each 5-1/2 × 5-1/2-inch piece of cardboard and placing the glue side on the middle of an 8 × 8-inch piece of decorated paper. Turn this over and trim diagonally across the corners. Smear glue on each tab and fold it inward. These edges will soon be covered by one of the accordion folds of the book.

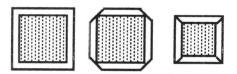

2. To display the book wide open, put a piece of ribbon across each cover with the ends hanging loose. To have a closed book, put the ribbon across both pieces as shown.

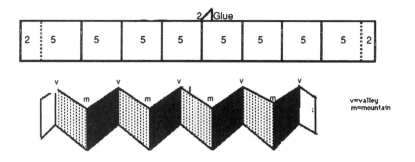

3. Lay the ends of one 5 × 24-inch piece of paper on top of another and glue together overlapping 1 inch at the center (you will trim the ends later). Use the 5-inch tagboard template and begin with a valley (inward) fold at the center. This will have both ends of the accordion folds facing the correct direction to paste on the ends of the book, covering the back edges. Fold backward and forward until you get to the end. Trim the last folds to 1 inch. Paste these on the two covers.

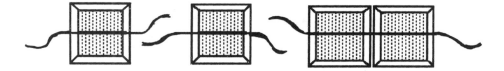

4. Paste a plain or decorated 5 × 5-inch piece of paper on the inside of each cover. The title and author's name or a saying could be written here. Think about a theme for the book. Look at the colors you have chosen and the designs that are made. It could have a theme such as: ocean, geometric shapes, numerals, a favorite saying, a car moving along, family memories.

5. Holes may be cut in the accordion folds (such as a circle or irregular shape) going all the way through it. Pop-out inserts may be placed in some of the pages (using the extra 8 × 8-inch piece). Use extra paper to make pop-up shapes between the pages.

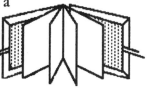

PROJECT 2–10
THE SHAPED BOOK

FOR THE TEACHER   This is an interdisciplinary project that allows the student to write and relate the shape of the book to the story. Discuss what is inside a book. (The first page will have a title, date of publication, and name of the author.) Students may want to make a *dummy* (small model on plain paper) of the book to decide what will go on each page.

Preparation   The basic-shaped book is always sewn or stapled at the fold before cutting, whether it is on the side or on top. The other three outside edges are cut at the same time. The cover may be slightly larger. Depending on the surface of the paper that is used, a story may be written directly onto the paper, or perhaps created on the computer and cut and pasted onto the pages. Other methods of folding books are shown below.

Adaptations for Younger Students
ONE-FOLD BOOK   Pages simply folded in half allow young students to write and illustrate a story about something, such as the planting, growing, and harvesting of a seed.

DICTATED STORY   Even the youngest children can create a story by dictating it to a willing parent or older student mentor (borrow some volunteers from upper grades for this purpose). Young students are capable of cutting out and pasting features on a creature or windows on a "house" book. Show young students how to easily thread a yarn needle by laying the end of a strand of yarn inside a 1/2 X 1-inch folded piece of paper, then threading the paper through the needle's eye and pulling it through to the other side.

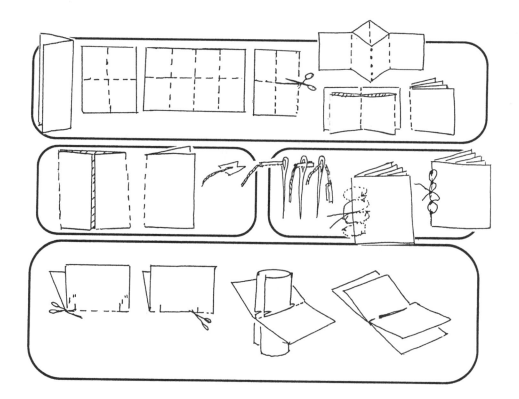

PROJECT 2–10   THE SHAPED BOOK

Materials

construction paper
awl or pushpins
drawing paper or
   photocopy paper
yarn needles
tagboard or 3 × 5-inch
   cards for templates

ruler
stapler
string
paper punch
paper clips

Directions   Consider the subject of your story before you decide what the shape of the book will be. You could write about your home, yourself, a place you like to visit, a sports day, a pet, or a favorite wild animal. The book could be round (a soccer ball?), shaped like a house, elephant, butterfly, and so on.

1. Carefully fold the paper in half, then in fourths, matching up the edges. Crease the inside paper first one way, then another, so the folds are sharp. When the edges are cut, this will give you an 8-page book. Hold the pages together with a paper clip. Fold a cover paper (construction paper) of the same size in half and paper clip the inner pages to the cover. Make a *template* for the shape of your book from a piece of tagboard or a 3 × 5 inch card, leaving one side straight. If you want to make a large book, make a tagboard pattern for the pages and cover, and simply fold your paper in half.

2. To sew a *signature* (a section of a book) together, use a ruler to measure between the top and bottom of the book at the crease to find the center. Mark the center, then mark the crease on either side of the center at 3/4- to 1-inch intervals. You can use an awl (sharp-pointed tool) or pushpin to poke holes through all the sections of the paper at one time.

3. Start sewing the paper from the outside of the center hole, leaving 3 inches of the thread hanging loose (you will tie it later). Sew first toward the top, then come back and sew the other direction (skipping the middle hole), ending again at the center, where you will tie a knot.

4. When the sewing is finished, draw around the outside of the template on the cover and cut through all the layers of paper at once. If the paper is too thick, cut through half of the book, then do the other half. Decorate the outside of the book with cut-paper decorations or designs. The book should be able to be displayed by standing partially open, so you can also decorate the back.

UNIT 3

DRAWING WITH PENCIL, PASTELS, CRAYONS, MARKERS

DRAWING

Two-dimensional design is the backbone of "making art" in school, and could be the reason so many students decide early on that they are "no good in art—they can't draw a straight line." Certainly we know that drawing is the foundation of art, but what is important for art teachers is to help students understand that there are many kinds of drawing and many kinds of drawing instruments. Some students, for example, "draw" better with scissors than they do with a pencil, crayon, marker, etc. Students become aware at a very young age that their work does not look like what they *think* they are drawing. Some simply quit trying, because true representation is important to them. Students *can* be taught to draw. Remind them that just as musicians or sports figures practice, so can they improve their artistic skills with practice.

Perseverance is a word that usually doesn't occur when we think of art, but encouraging students to persevere, to do the hard thing, and to not keep starting over again is best for the student. Many teachers find it important to limit students to one sheet of paper and to discourage the use of erasers. If something is truly "ruined," then the student can turn over the paper and work on the back of it (another good reason for printing the name small in one corner). When teaching art in the elementary school, time constraints seldom allow us to have students do much pencil drawing prior to beginning a project. Show students drawings by such artists as Leonardo da Vinci and Amedeo Modigliani where they can actually see lines repeatedly drawn as artists have tried for the "right" line. Tell them to *use* their mistakes!

Many teachers have students do a preliminary chalk drawing prior to painting or working in color or marker or, if time allows, students can make thumbnail sketches and then a proper sketch on a piece of newsprint, transferring it to drawing paper later.

PROJECT 3–1
THE BESTIARY; ANIMAL DRAWINGS

FOR THE TEACHER   Some of the earliest evidence we have of humanity is through the drawings of animals on cave walls. Creatures that share the Earth with us have always been fascinating to artists, and many famous paintings include animals. Artists whose wildlife and domesticated animal artwork would be of interest to students are John James Audubon, Edward Hicks, Frederick Remington, Martin Johnson Heade, Winslow Homer, John Singer Sargent, Rubens and Rembrandt Peale, and many contemporary artists.

Vocabulary

unity

value

balance

render

species

bestiary

environment

habitat

Preparation   Students should find reference material to differentiate among animal groups. Ideally this could be a library assignment where each student does library research about a different group of animals. If you do not have time for students to do such research, make photocopies from *National Geographic*, encyclopedias, and science books.

Send a note to parents and other teachers asking for leftover light-colored latex paint (or use gesso). (The color is not important.) Have students prepare more than one piece of paper for later use. Because this project will be done in pencil or colored pencil, it can be ongoing. (If you use colored pencils, have students use hand-held sharpeners on them or the pencils will quickly be ground down.)

Adaptations for Younger Students   Either use smaller pieces of paper if you use colored pencil, or use marker with larger paper. The underlying texture of the latex paint will show through.

Alternative Project

MYTHICAL CREATURES Students may make *one* imaginary creature by combining parts from many different animals, and attributing special personality quirks to their own animal. Historical antecedents for these would be the *Sphinx* (head of a pharaoh, body of a lion); the *Chimera* (lion's head, goat's body, serpent's tail); the *unicorn* (body and head of a horse with a single horn, hind legs of a stag, tail of a lion); the *dragon* (in the Chinese tradition, it has the head of a camel, horns of a deer, eyes of a demon, ears of a cow, neck of a snake, belly of a frog, scales of a carp, claws of an eagle, and paws of a tiger); and the *griffin* (head and wings of an eagle and the body, hind legs, and tail of a lion).

Interdisciplinary Connections
LANGUAGE ARTS
ANIMAL JOURNAL Students write an ongoing journal about their animals, listing characteristics of the animal and its environment.

ANIMAL PERSONALITY STORY Students write a fictional story about one animal of its species. They are certainly familiar with such stories as *Bambi, One Hundred and One Dalmatians, Clifford*, and *Curious George*. Older students might relate to *Call of the Wild*.

SCIENCE
ANIMAL BEHAVIOR Students can investigate poisonous species and coloration, migration, amphibians, reproductive systems, endangered species, evolution of species, habitat, eating habits, metamorphosis, hibernation, regeneration, grouping behavior, specific groups. The animal names in the handout, *Animals*, are simply a sample listing of species.

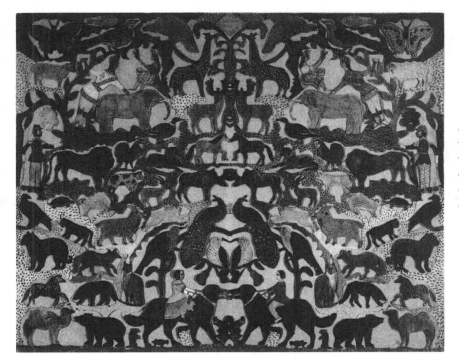

Cutout of Animals, second quarter 19th century, cut paper and watercolor, 18³/₄ × 23³/₄ inches, Gift of Edgar William and Bernice Chyrsler Garbisch, National Gallery of Art, Washington, DC

Lion, c. 1614, Peter Paul Rubens, black and yellow chalk heightened with white, 9¹⁵/₁₆ × 11¹/₈ inches, National Gallery of Art, Washington DC, Ailsa Mellon Bruce Fund

Animals

Bears
Black
Brown
Grizzly
Panda
Polar

Cats (a sample)
Angora
Burmese
Calico
Siamese
Tabby

Elk
Fox
Giraffe
Hyena
Kangaroo
Koala
Leopard
Lion
Manatee
Moose
Rabbit
Gazelle
Hippopotamus
Ox
Panda
Platypus
Porcupine
Possum
Reindeer
Rhinoceros
Skunk
Wolf
Zebra

Iguana
Lizard
Python
Galapagos tortoise
Sea turtle

Rhinos
Black
Indian
Java
Square-lipped
Sumatra

Birds
Albatross
Canada goose
Chicken
Duck
Egret
Emu
Flamingo
Frigate bird
Heron
Kiwi
Macaw
Mallard
Ostrich
Parrot
Puffin
Rhea
Robin
Secretary bird
Stork
Swallow
Swan
Toucan
Turkey
Woodpecker
Wren

Dogs (a sample)
Beagle
Bulldog
Dalmatian
Great Dane
Greyhound
Schnauzer
Setter
Spaniel
Terrier

Fish
Blowfish
Dolphin
Flying fish
Jellyfish
Shark

Stingray
Swordfish

Insects
Butterfly
Fly
Ladybug
Mosquito
Spider

Primate Family
Ape
Chimpanzee
Gibbon
Gorilla
Macaque
Orangutan
Squirrel monkey

Snakes
Black
Cobra
Copperhead
Coral
Rattlesnake
Sidewinder

Whales
Blue bowhead
Humpback
Right
Sperm

Wild Cats
Bobcat
Cheetah
Jaguar
Leopard
Lion
Lynx
Mountain lion
Ocelot
Wildcat

Birds of Prey
Condor
Eagle
Falcon
Owl
Red-tailed hawk
Vulture

Mammals
Antelope
Badger
Beaver
Squirrel
Deer
Bighorn sheep
Bison
Camel

Penguins
Crested
Emperor
King
Yellow eyed

Reptiles
Alligator
Crocodile
Frog

Wild Dogs
Coyote
Dingo
Fox
Gray wolf
Red fox

Animals *(Continued)*

OTHER CLASSIFICATIONS OF ANIMALS

Creatures with Shells
Armadillo
Crab
Lobster
Snail
Turtle

Domesticated Animals
Cat
Chicken
Cow
Dog
Goat
Horse
Pig
Sheep
Turkey

Animals with Tusks
Elephant
Narwhal
Walrus
Wild boar

Poisonous Animals
Lizard
Scorpion
Snake
Spider
Toad

Flightless Birds
Cormorant
Ostrich

Africa
Aardvark
Antelope
Ass
Baboon
Cape buffalo
Cheetah
Dikdik
Elephant
Gazelle
Gerenuk
Giraffe
Gorilla
Hartebeest
Hippopotamus
Hyena
Impala
Jackal
Leopard

Mongoose
Monkey
Oryx
Ostrich
Panther
Porcupine
Rhinoceros
Vulture
Warthog
Water buffalo
Weasel
Wildebeest (gnu)
Zebra

Lion

Animals of Australia
Duck-billed platypus
Echidna
Fairy penguin
Kangaroo

Koala
Wallaby
Wombat

Creatures of North America
American bald eagle
Bear
Beaver
Buffalo
Deer
Elk
Jackrabbit
Moose
Muskrat
Whooping crane
Wildcat

Water Creatures
Dolphin
Killer whale
Manatee
Manta ray
Octopus
Otter
Porpoise
Sea elephant
Sea lion
Shark
Whale

Galapagos Islands
Blue-footed booby
Flightless cormorant
Galapagos tortoise
Land iguana
Lava lizards
Marine iguana
Sally Lightfoot crab

This group of African animals is brightly painted on 3 X 3-inch pieces of Masonite. Collection of the author.

PROJECT 3–1 THE BESTIARY; ANIMAL DRAWINGS

STUDENT PAGE

Materials

newsprint

drawing paper

latex house paint (any light color)

utility brushes

colored pencil

pencil sharpeners

Directions   A bestiary (pronounced "beestiary") is a Medieval term that describes the appearance and habits of real or imaginary animals. Your bestiary will be based on a group of related animals grouped and overlapped on a single sheet of paper.

1. Coat a piece of drawing paper with latex house paint, applying it first one direction; then, after it has dried slightly, applying a coat the other direction. Or put it on haphazardly if you prefer. The texture that you create will make your drawings more interesting.

2. Research a species of insect, mammal, or reptile. Use at least three varieties to make a composition. First draw the creature on a piece of newsprint. Then scribble over the back of the drawing and transfer it to the latex-coated drawing paper. The sizes may vary. They will overlap one another.

3. When you have transferred several outline drawings to your paper, use colored pencil to "render" the animals (draw them realistically). Spaces between them may be left uncolored, or you may make them relate to one another through letting one color blend into another. You could add plants or water behind the animals.

4. Walk away from your artwork and look at it from a distance. The colors should be bright enough and the animals large enough that each animal is distinctly recognizable. When it is all finished, you could write in each name with a fine-line marker or affix a computer-made label listing each species by name.

PROJECT 3–2
SIGNING ALPHABET;
DRAWING THE HAND

FOR THE TEACHER   While visiting a childrens' museum recently, I saw a signing alphabet posted on the wall and realized that it would be a wonderful project for students. This project first involves helping students to draw their hands as they see them, then doing a drawing of their own hand signing one letter of the alphabet. Teaching students to "draw what they *see* rather than what they know" is a method developed by Betty Edwards and described in her book *Drawing on the Right Side of the Brain*. It is exciting for you, the teacher, to realize that you have helped students make the breakthrough and have helped them to look. The final drawing of each letter could be assembled into a class poster or book.

Vocabulary

contour drawing

emphasis

Preparation   Demonstrate blind contour drawing on the board by looking at your own hand as you draw. Students will enjoy how terrible it is, but then are willing to try it themselves. Make photocopies of the signing alphabet. (See the Handout.) Cut it up into groups of four and distribute it, making sure the entire alphabet is covered. Have each student make drawings of their hands showing four different letters of the alphabet. These can be cut out later and assembled on one sheet of paper. Their best drawing can be transferred to the posterboard for drawing with marker. If uniformity of lettering is important, make an alphabet from the computer and allow students to trace these letters onto their final drawings.

   Art Teacher Marilynne Bradley formerly with the Webster Groves School District, St. Louis County, Missouri, posted signing-alphabet paintings on the ceiling of her room. Consider it!

Drawn from *Study of Ten Hands*, Anonymous (Dutch or German), National Gallery of Canada, Ottawa

PROJECT 3–2   SIGNING ALPHABET; DRAWING THE HAND

Materials

9 × 12-inch drawing paper

9 × 9-inch posterboard

tracing paper

masking tape

pencil

scissors

colored pencils, markers, or tempera paints

glue

Drawn from student's work in
Debbie McConnell's classes, Barretts
School, St. Louis County, Missouri

Directions

PRELIMINARY DRAWING

1. Tape a piece of newsprint to the table. Find an interesting position for your hand. Now do a drawing of your hand. Put your name and the date on the paper.

BLIND CONTOUR DRAWING

2. This time you *will not look at your paper at all* while you are trying to draw exactly what you see, and *you may not lift your pencil off the paper.* Put your pencil to the paper as if it were touching the outside of your hand. Now, without naming parts of the hand, slowly move the pencil along the paper as if it were touching the skin. When you get to wrinkles, allow the pencil to go inward and back out.

MODIFIED CONTOUR DRAWING

3. Again, tape your paper to the table. You will do a modified contour drawing, which will allow you to look at the hand while you are drawing it. Practice doing this, and you will see continued improvement.

4. You will have four drawings to make of your hand "signing" a letter. (See Handout, *Signing Alphabet.*) Work slowly and carefully, remembering to draw what you see, *not* what you know. When you have completed the four drawings in pencil, go over the pencil with marker. You may cut these out and mount them on a separate sheet of paper.

5. Select your best drawing and trace it. Go over the back of the tracing paper with pencil, then transfer this drawing to a square of posterboard. Use marker or paint to carefully color the drawing of the hand and the letter it represents.

Signing Alphabet

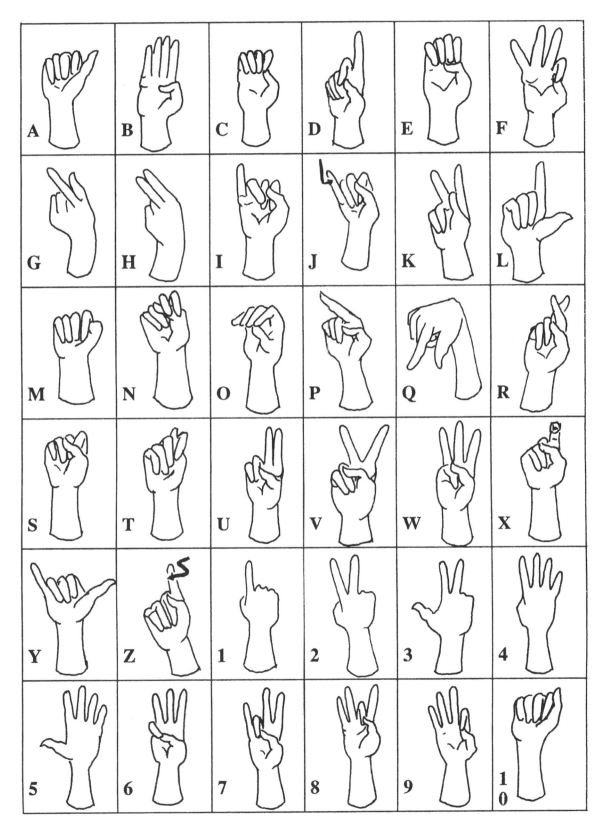

PASTELS AND CRAYONS

Pastels and chalks come in a variety of sizes and shapes. They are made of ground pigment held together with a binder and pressed into stick shape. Oil pastels are slightly different from regular pastels, as the binder is oil. They are similar to crayon, but are softer and lend themselves well to blending, almost resembling oil paint.

Regular pastels are usually applied using the darkest colors first, then putting the lightest values on top. They are often applied with most of the strokes going one direction. To get shading, complementary colors are built one on top of another. Pastels smear easily, so often they are fixed. **CAUTION: Make sure any fixative you use bears a CP or AP Nontoxic certificate from the Creative Materials Institute. If it does not bear this label, you, personally, should spray artwork outside or after class.**

Artists whose pastel work is especially well-known are Mary Cassatt and Edgar Degas.

PROJECT 3-3
STILL-LIFE

FOR THE TEACHER The still-life communicates information about the culture in which it was done. Dutch still-lifes, by such artists as Pieter Claesz Heda, had paintings filled with items that symbolized the fleetingness of life such as a broken glass, a half-eaten loaf of bread, or a clock. William Harnett and John Peto were American painters who specialized in *trompe l'oeil* (fool the eye) still-life paintings. Contemporary American painters Audrey Flack and Janet Fish continue the tradition of realistic still-lifes, and photographer Sandy Skoglund creates sculptural still-lifes that she then photographs. Impressionists such as Paul Cezanne and Henri Matisse specialized in interior paintings of flowers and the table set for a meal.

Vocabulary

still-life

trompe l'oeil

intensity

artistic license

viewfinder

depth

overlapping

Preparation Have students collect objects for a huge still-life. This could include mechanical objects, a bicycle, toys, cloth, rope, a hat, skull, rubberized face masks, ladders, a window frame, buckets, stools, etc. The still-life should be arranged, then left untouched until the drawings are finished. If you prefer, you can make individual still-lifes around the room for several students to use.

Make viewfinders in proportion to the paper that will be used. Individual slide mounts make ideal viewfinders. Tell students that looking through a viewfinder is similar to taking a photograph, isolating one subject with a single well-composed view. Demonstrate to students that the viewfinder should always be held the same distance from the eye when looking through it, and show them how to place objects on their paper in the same location as they find them in their viewfinder.

PROJECT 3–3   STILL-LIFE

Materials

viewfinders (paper or slide mounts)

drawing paper

white chalk

tissues

oil pastels

fluorescent markers

pencils

Directions

1. Use the viewfinder as if it were the viewfinder of a camera. You will isolate a particular section of what you see to make a pleasing composition. Remember to hold your arm at the same distance from your body whenever you look through the viewfinder.

2. Notice where an object is in relation to the top, sides, or bottom of the viewfinder. Then, using chalk, draw it in exactly the same place on your drawing paper (you can use the tissue to correct the chalk line if necessary). When you are satisfied that your chalk drawing has sufficiently filled the paper, you are ready to begin applying oil pastels.

3. Do not concern yourself with making true colors. In fact this composition might be more interesting if you were to use, for example, only five colors. Apply color firmly, but allow some paper to show through the crayon.

4. When you have applied sufficient oil pastels, go over them with contrasting colors of fluorescent marker. This is similar to crayon resist with ink, but the markers give an entirely different effect.

PROJECT 3–4 PUEBLO

FOR THE TEACHER This project, based on pueblo architecture of Southwestern Native Americans, was recently introduced to her classes by Mary Ann Kerr of the University City School District in St. Louis County, Missouri. Appropriate as part of an ongoing unit about Southwestern Native Americans, this project could be based on a George Bellows painting of adobe buildings.

Vocabulary

value

hue

shape

adobe

pueblo

Pueblo Tesuque, No. 2, 1917, George Bellows, oil on canvas, mounted on Masonite, $35^5/_{16} \times 44^1/_4$ inches, The Nelson–Atkins Museum of Art, Kansas City, Missouri (Gift of Mr. and Mrs. C. Humbert Tinsman)

Preparation

Discuss regional architecture, and how climate and available building materials often determine how people live. Some early Southwestern cultures built stone dwellings into the sides of mountains, under a gentle overhang. Another favorite building material was adobe (sun-dried earth-and-straw bricks, "plastered" on the outside with Earth). One such thriving, growing pueblo community is Taos, New Mexico. Box-like buildings are placed together, sometimes one on top of another, sometimes next to another, each story set back so they look like stair steps. Upper floors are sometimes reached by ladders. Traditional pueblo crafts—such as carving, pottery, and weaving—continue to be practiced, and passed from generation to generation. Students could make a stencil and they could trade with a partner.

Alternative Project

PUEBLO BOXES This project made by local school children, was seen on the Acoma trading post in New Mexico. Boxes of all sizes and shapes (most approximately 9 × 12 inches) were covered with brown kraft paper. Windows, doors, and vigas (poles that support the roof) were painted on. Most of the doors were turquoise or green. The boxes were then stacked and joined together. Another version of their pueblo was a group of smaller boxes (approximately 3 × 4 inches) constructed of brown cardboard. Matchsticks or twigs were used for vigas. Stepladders were constructed from twigs and twine.

This pueblo was stenciled by a student of Mary Ann Kerr of Jackson Park Elementary School, University City, Missouri. The student used soft colors, accented with turquoise and brown.

PROJECT 3–4 PUEBLO

Materials

12 × 18-inch drawing paper

4 × 12-inch drawing paper strips for stencils

pastels in "Southwestern colors"

tissues

scissors

Directions   Your stencil strips will resemble the top of adobe buildings of the American Southwest. These squarish buildings were developed by Native Americans to take advantage of available building materials, and have been widely copied in other architecture of the Southwest. They are coated with mud on the outside; and because of the thick walls, are cool inside. Ladders are used to go from one level to the next. Pastel colors that would be best to use are Earth colors of tan, brown, reddish brown, pink, and deep yellow.

1. To make stencils for the pueblos, draw rectangular shapes (the tops of pueblos) along the top edges of 4 × 12-inch drawing paper. Draw a few small square windows. Cut along your drawn edges.

2. Solidly apply one pastel color to the upper edge of a stencil. Place the stencil near the upper third of a large piece of paper. Use a tissue to lightly smear the pastel upwards from the edge of the stencil onto the drawing paper.

3. Apply a different pastel color to stencil and move the stencil slightly lower on the paper. For a third layer of pueblos, cut your stencil (or trade with a classmate) to form other adobe shapes.

4. The ovens used for baking bread outdoors were rounded beehive shapes, and might be appropriate in front of the buildings. Use the end of pastel sticks to draw windows, doors, ladders between floors, and people. Traditional colors for trim are dark brown, turquoise, or yellow.

Taos Pueblo, Taos, New Mexico

PROJECT 3–5
THE WILD BEASTS (THE FAUVES)

FOR THE TEACHER   They were called the "wild beasts" (direct translation for French word *fauves*). These were European artists whose use of color was just too strange for people accustomed to the soft colors of the Salon and even the Impressionists. Those included with the group, whose work was mostly exhibited between 1905 and 1907, were André Derain, Paul Signac, Albert Marquet, Georges Rouault, Raoul Dufy, Georges Braque, Henri Matisse, Maurice Vlaminck, and Kees van Dongen. Their work emerged from Impressionism and was similar to German Expressionism, but was primarily concerned with vividly contrasting, pure intensity, and nonrealistic colors. Rarely was anything painted in its actual color.

Vocabulary

Fauve

nonrealistic

contrast

hue

Alternative Project

EXPRESSIONISTIC GROUP MURALS Because the roofing paper comes in rolls, it would be appropriate for group oil-pastel projects based on the work of the Fauves. Cut a piece long enough for three or four students to work on at one time (3 X 5-feet would be good). Whatever the subject, simply stress that the colors should be *unrealistic* (**examples:** red leaves instead of green leaves, or a blue horse instead of a brown one).

PROJECT 3–5   THE WILD BEASTS (THE FAUVES)

Materials

roofing paper (available at home building-supply stores)

tissues

chalk

white glue

oil pastels

Procedure   The reason the work of the Fauves (wild beasts), 1905–1907, was so shocking to the French people of the early twentieth century was that all the colors they used were so *unexpected*. Water was red rather than blue–green; horses were blue; a face had a green stripe down the middle (a painting of Henri Matisse's wife). Even though your subject matter may not be extraordinary, make sure that your use of color is bizarre (strange)! Sometimes the Fauves outlined everything in black. Working on black paper will give you that same effect.

Suggested subjects: animals among the trees; people in costume at a carnival; a bridge over the water; buildings reflected in the water; red trees and blue horses.

1. Use chalk to draw a picture on the roofing paper. Holding a bottle of glue upright, make a bead of glue along the chalk line. Allow this to dry overnight.

2. When the glue is dry on your design, color strongly, using pure, bright colors in unexpected ways. Really think about a color for a face rather than using actual skin tones. What if you made it blue or light purple or orange? What if you put a green stripe right down the middle of the face?

3. When you have finished drawing, use a tissue to wipe excess pastel from the glue lines so the black will show.

Drawn from *Houses at Chatou*, c. 1905–1906, Maurice de Vlaminck, The Art Institute of Chicago

PROJECT 3–6
HIDDEN BIRDS

FOR THE TEACHER John James Audubon (1785–1851) is one of many illustrators who drew birds and animals. Audubon (for whom the Audubon Society is named) made it his life's quest to record every bird in North America. He did large, detailed paintings, frequently traveling for months at a time. His paintings were reproduced in *Audubon's Birds of America, The Elephant Folio*. In it, birds were depicted in their natural habitat of swamp, tree, reeds, grasses, nests, water, or the seashore.

Vocabulary

sgraffito

scientific print

Arctic Tern, 1835, John James Audubon, St. Louis Mercantile Library at the University of Missouri, St. Louis.

Preparation *Audubon's Birds of America* paintings are the inspiration for this project. Depicting birds accurately and with sufficient detail is important, so unless you can take students to a zoo, you may have to rely on small black-and-white photocopies. A miniature of *The Audubon Society Baby Elephant Folio of Audubon's Birds of America* is inexpensively available in most museum shops. (Color is unimportant in this project.) Try to have a variety of photos so that no two drawings are the same. Encourage the students to draw the birds accurately; then encourage them to use wildly unrealistic colors in their drawings.

Interdisciplinary Connections
SCIENCE
SPECIES IN DANGER This project is a natural for students to investigate what has been done to rescue bird species in danger of extinction (such as the Whooping Crane) or to analyze flight. Students might even be able to participate in the Audubon Society's annual backyard bird count.

SOCIAL STUDIES
ARTISTS AND PIONEERS Students could investigate the opening of the West, and the part that explorers, surveyors and naturalists (such as Audubon) played in luring adventurous people to move Westward. Or students could do biographies of some of these famous explorers and pioneers.

These bird drawings by students of Carolyn Baker of Shenandoah Valley School in St. Louis County were brightly colored with crayon. They were then coated with India ink mixed with a small amount of liquid detergent. When dry, the ink was scratched using a ruler and nail.

PROJECT 3–6   HIDDEN BIRDS

Materials

9 × 12-inch paper

photocopies of various birds

crayons

India ink mixed with liquid detergent

rulers

2-inch finishing nails

Directions   John James Audubon was a famous illustrator who made a painted record of all the birds and animals of North America. Your job is to illustrate an actual bird.

1. Work from a photocopy or photo of a bird. Draw the size as accurately as possible, and be careful with details such as the legs, wings, beak. Place the bird in an environment such as a jungle, water, seashore, or forest.

2. Now that the bird has been accurately drawn, use your imagination to color it brightly. The bird can be in very bright colors. Background items such as trees and leaves can be done in blues, yellows, turquoise, light green, and dark green. Put paper underneath the edges as you color to protect the table. Color intensely, not allowing the paper to show through.

3. Before doing this step, make sure your name is on the back of the paper. Brush India ink mixed with detergent (to keep it from "crawling") on top of the entire composition. Allow this to dry overnight.

4. Use a ruler and a nail to scratch straight vertical lines through the ink from the top to the bottom of the paper. These lines should be approximately 1/16th inch apart. The more carefully this is done, the better the result will be. The brightly colored bird will shine through the black "cage." These lines may be done diagonally, but the use of the ruler is important because the straight lines contrast nicely with the curves of the bird.

PROJECT 3–7
I SAW A SHIP COME SAILING IN

FOR THE TEACHER Painters such as Winslow Homer, J.M.W. Turner, and John Marin found ships and boats a fascinating subject. Students may have photos of boats, or might enjoy finding pictures of various kinds of boats in books. Some suggestions are Viking sailing ships; schooners; whalers; ironclads; the *Amistad*; pirate ships; modern yachts; warships; cruise ships; river gambling boats; Chinese junks; *Nina, Pinta,* and *Santa Maria;* freighters; warships, etc.

Vocabulary

foreground	middle-ground
background	space
hatching	

Preparation
While it takes time for the students to prepare their paper for this project, the results are worth it. They end up with two pictures: the transfer print (black and colored lines on white) and the etched print (white and colored lines on black). Demonstrate how to cross-hatch and to get more detail in a composition through the use of line. Discuss how to make a ship composition more interesting with details that might be found in a harbor. Caution against putting a sun in the corner simply to fill space, but instead, show them how horizontal lines can be used to make clouds. A ballpoint pen is perfect for this project because you can see where you have retraced the design.

Alternative Project
This technique is suitable for almost any subject that has a lot of detail. It would be perfect for drawing insects, butterflies, flowers, or trees in great detail.

Interdisciplinary Connections
SOCIAL STUDIES

FLAT WORLD SOCIETY Have students research the importance of sea voyages in the opening of the world. Discuss the lives of famous explorers.

The construction paper "plate" was coated with chalk, then light-colored crayon, finally dark-colored crayon. When the drawing paper was placed on top and a design drawn on the back, the varicolored lines emerged. Display plate and print together.

PROJECT 3–7   I SAW A SHIP COME SAILING IN

Materials

pencil

pad of newspaper

light-colored chalk

crayons

9 × 12- or 6 × 9-inch construction paper

8-1/2 × 11-inch white drawing paper

ballpoint pen

masking tape

Directions

1. To prepare your construction paper for transfer, do the following:

   a. Place newspaper underneath the construction paper.

   b. Completely cover the construction paper with light-colored chalk (no paper should show through).

   c. Using light-colored crayons (pink, yellow, white, peach, pale blue), firmly color in one direction all over the construction paper.

   d. Turn the paper, coloring in the other direction with dark crayons (dark purple, dark green, dark blue, black, red), completely covering the light-colored crayons.

2. On a piece of drawing paper, do a completely detailed pencil drawing of one or more boats either in a harbor or near a beach. Think about details you find near the water, such as docks, pilings (wooden posts), boathouses, people fishing, beaches, lighthouses, buoys, waves, rocks.

3. Tape the white paper in two places along the top of the crayoned paper (with the pencil-side up). Retrace the picture you have drawn, pressing *very* hard. This will transfer the color from the underneath paper, and etch a drawing onto the dark paper.

4. If you peek from time to time, you will see that drawing firmly is important and that putting in enough detail is important before the two pictures are untaped. If the picture looks too plain, you can draw a fancy "frame" around the outside. When you have finished, display the two pictures side by side.

MARKERS

Most students have become accustomed to using crayons and markers well before they even enter elementary school. Choose assignments that draw students in, getting them enthused about using these familiar materials. If students will be coloring in solidly, avoid boredom by having them work on smaller compositions. Show students that neatness with markers will give much better results if the marker is applied in parallel lines rather than just scribbled on. Markers are also ideal for detailed drawings that ask students to recall places they have been such as a theme park or the circus.

Markers have changed enormously in the past few years, and offer potential far beyond being used to just fill in outlines with color. They can be used in combination with other materials, including being used in printmaking to "ink" a stamp or used in crayon-resist in place of watercolor.

To avoid the downside of markers (they run out of ink, caps get lost, and they don't store for long periods), date boxes of markers when they arrive and keep track of the inventory. Train students how to store a cap on the opposite end of the marker when it is being used, and appoint monitors to make sure caps are put on at the end of the class. Ask students to bring nonfunctioning markers to you so you can test them and throw them away.

The following listing gives some information about types of markers that are available. Manufacturers keep coming up with innovations yearly.

Tips. broad-line, thin-line, extra broad, brush, decorating (tips cut to make double or triple parallel strokes), stampers (tips have designs on them)

Inks. body doodlers (washable for drawing on skin), fabric, undercolor and overcolor markers, scented, unscented, permanent, washable, woodcraft (for use on wood projects), changeable, projection markers (for overhead plastic sheets), highlighter

Colors. bold, tropical, classic, multicultural, fluorescent, metallic

Applicators. air art gun (to aid in using markers like an air brush), poster applicator brushes, scholar art brushes (markers with flexible brush-like tips), GlassChalk™ sponge markers (temporary paint for signs on plastic, glass)

PROJECT 3-8
STUFFED FISH

FOR THE TEACHER   This project, developed by Marla Mayer of the Highcroft Ridge School in St. Louis County, Missouri, was part of a year-long theme about sealife. The stuffed fish take advantage of the qualities of Crayola Overwriter Markers® that cause any line they cross over to change in color. The project would be adaptable to any project that challenges students to use repeated line designs.

Vocabulary

form

variety

pattern

repetition

complementary

Preparation
Find books about different kinds of tropical fish and discuss the brilliant colors the students see. Point out the complementary colors one often sees in nature. If students are not yet familiar with the concept of pattern, demonstrate different patterns such as plaid, scales, stripes, checkerboard, spirals, etc.

The book *The Rainbow Fish* by Marcus Pfister is especially appropriate to read to students when introducing this project. In the story, a beautiful fish shares his shiny colors with all his friends. You could have small pieces of shiny paper for students to glue in only a few places.

Alternative Project
STUFFED PAPER SCULPTURES Although this stuffed-fish project is based on rather small creatures, older students also enjoy making huge stuffed sculptures to hang from the ceiling using colored roll paper filled with newspaper. Almost any theme is appropriate. These can be stuffed "people" (themselves, maybe), animals, or food.

PROJECT 3-8   STUFFED FISH

STUDENT PAGE

Materials

12 × 18-inch drawing paper
pencil
scissors
Crayola Overwriter Markers®
staplers and staples
newspapers
paper punch
string

Directions   Think about all the shapes in which fish come. Some are long while others are fat. What are some of their features? (tails, fins, scales [on some], eyes)

1. Fold the paper in half lengthwise or crosswise, depending on the shape of your fish. Use a pencil to draw a fish shape, using as much of the paper as possible. Start the design at the fold (you won't cut along the folded line). Cut through both layers of paper at once so both sides of your fish will be the same. Staple around the outside of the fish approximately 1/2 inch from the edges, leaving an unstapled opening about eight inches along one edge.

2. Although you may fill in most of the fish with color, make the eye and fin first on each side so that part will stand out from the rest by having some white in the eye and surrounding the fin.

3. Using the Overwriter Markers®, make patterns. You can fill in one entire side of the fish in stripes of different colors, then add some of the lines you know how to make such as spirals, scales, curving lines. Avoid simply scribbling, as you will be disappointed in the results. If the fish will be hung to be seen on both sides, then color the other side to be similar. Complete the coloring before stuffing the fish.

4. Wad newspaper into pieces that are small enough to fit into the opening you have made (it doesn't have to be overstuffed). Staple it closed. If it is to be hung, use the paper punch to make a hole near the top and put string through it.

PROJECT 3-9
TESSELLATIONS

FOR THE TEACHER   In the art world, tessellations have come to be associated with M.C. Escher, a Dutch artist who was born in 1908. He became fascinated with mosaics, another form of tessellation, while he was visiting the Alhambra in Spain, and made sketches of the tile patterns he saw there. Escher's black-and-white drawings and tessellations are frequently reproduced on calendars, posters, and in books.

Vocabulary

tessellate

balance

contrast

Preparation   Have a discussion with students about tessellations they have seen (floor tile, ceiling tile, a honeycomb, bricks). While this project is fun as an art project, ideally you would incorporate it as part of a math unit on geometric shapes and tessellation. After learning the process, students may work with shapes that—by themselves—will tessellate a plane such as triangles, quadrilaterals, squares, and hexagons. Shapes that do not by themselves tessellate a plane are: pentagons, heptagons, octagons.

Explain to students that tessellations are recognizable because they do not overlap or leave spaces and they can be extended infinitely in every direction. Demonstrate the procedure for students before they begin.

Several fine books are available on tessellation. One I especially recommend is *Introduction to Tessellations* by Dale Seymour and Jill Britton (Dale Seymour Publications, Palo Alto, California, 1989).

PROJECT 3-9 TESSELLATIONS

Drawn from Mrs. Ford's second-grade class at the Robinson School, St. Louis County, Missouri

Materials

masking tape

pencils

rulers

scissors

markers

12 × 18-inch drawing paper (or posterboard)

3 × 5 *lined* notecards cut to make 3 × 3-inch squares

Directions

1. On the lined side of the notecard, use a ruler and pencil to draw lines going the opposite direction of those printed on the card. This grid will make it easy to line up the shapes you have removed on the opposite side so they will tessellate perfectly.

2. Cut a shape from one side of the card. Move the cut shape to the opposite side of the card, matching the lines up exactly before attaching it there with tape. You may repeat this process from all four sides. Look at the shape and consider whether it resembles anything realistic. Could you draw details on it to make it resemble an animal or human? Would one more cut make it more interesting?

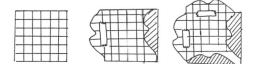

3. When you are satisfied with the shape, trace around it onto the sheet of drawing paper with pencil (you may start anyplace on the paper). It should line up perfectly in every direction. When you have finished drawing shapes onto the paper, use pencil to lightly draw details.

4. Draw details with marker on top of the pencil. You may simply choose to add color in the alternating shapes. When filling in shapes with marker, avoid scribbling; instead, carefully work in one direction, overlapping neatly.

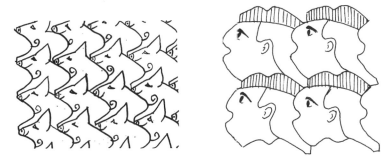

PROJECT 3–10
THE FACE OF A LEADER

FOR THE TEACHER   These outlines of faces will be filled with words either written/spoken by the leaders (for example: Lincoln and the *Gettysburg Address*) or contain the words of patriotic songs. Students become familiar at a very early age with the faces of our most famous leaders. Introduce this subject by discussing how every country honors its leaders by having their portraits painted or having sculptures made of them. Many countries put likenesses of their faces on coins and paper money.

Vocabulary

portrait

variety

emphasis

value

Preparation   This project is appropriate in February to celebrate Presidents' Day. Students could choose to draw any leader; or, if you prefer, each student could be assigned a different leader. The leaders could be famous men and women, including minorities and leaders of foreign cultures. Depending on the age of your students, they could do their own research or you could bring in photocopies of songs, speeches, quotes, or something else that could be repeatedly written either by hand or on the computer. Here is a list of documents or songs that could be interpreted.

DOCUMENTS AND QUOTES

Winston Churchill's *Iron Curtain* speech

Martin Luther King, Jr.'s *I Have a Dream* speech

Abraham Lincoln's *Gettysburg Address*

The Bill of Rights

The Constitution of the United States

The *Emancipation Proclamation*

George Washington's *Farewell* to his troops

SONGS

America the Beautiful

God Bless America

It's a Grand Old Flag

Over There

The Star Spangled Banner

Yankee Doodle

When Johnny Comes Marching Home Again

Alternative Projects

OVERSIZED HEADS If you wish to have these larger (on 12 × 18-inch drawing paper, for example), trace the leader's head on an overhead projector transparency and project it onto the paper to make it any size you want.

WALL-MURAL ESSAYS To make a wall mural, these small drawings with their writing could be copied onto an overhead projector transparency and projected directly onto a wall to be traced with pencil prior to painting.

COMPUTER-WRITTEN PORTRAITS To do this project on a computer, use a scanner to transfer photos of the leaders. If you do not have access to that technology, photocopy the outline onto overhead projector transparencies to be taped directly in front of a computer screen as a drawing aid.

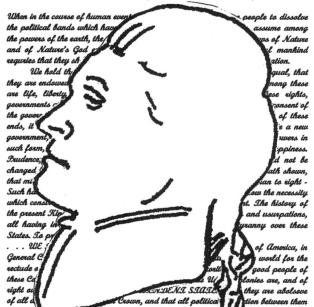

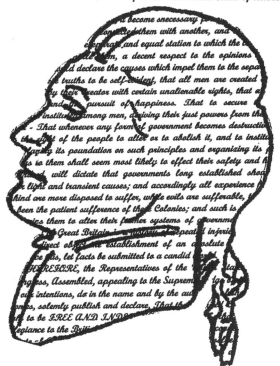

PROJECT 3-10   THE FACE OF A LEADER

STUDENT PAGE

Susan B. Anthony   Chief Joseph   George Washington

Materials

removable tape
dark fine-line markers
pencil
8-1/2 × 11-inch copy paper
8-1/2 × 11-inch narrow-lined tablet paper

Directions   This project involves continuous writing either within or surrounding the outline of the head of a famous leader. Ideally, the written words would relate to the leader whose face is used. You will find yourself repeating the words many times to fill the space you have chosen.

1. Use pencil to lightly draw an outline of the person's face in the middle of the plain paper (you may erase the outline afterwards). You may have to put some details such as glasses, hat, a mustache, or beard to identify the person.

2. Find information about this leader. It might be a speech he or she made, several patriotic songs that were popular during that leader's time, or even a copy of a document such as the Constitution of the United States or the Gettysburg Address.

3. Make a decision as to whether you will write within the outline of the head or surround the outline of the head with writing, leaving the head blank. It will take quite a long time to fill the background with neat writing, but neatness does count!

4. Tape the lined paper underneath the drawing of the head (you will be able to see the lines well enough to allow you to keep your writing straight). If you decide to work on larger paper, you may choose to lightly draw lines with pencil directly onto the drawing paper (to be erased later).

5. If you fill the inside of the face with writing, the paper may look somewhat empty outside. You could make a border by writing two or three rows of the same words all the way around the outside 1/2 inch of the paper.

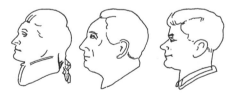

Thomas Jefferson   Franklin D. Roosevelt   John F. Kennedy   George Washington Carver   Louisa May Alcott

Abraham Lincoln   Thomas Jefferson   Theodore Roosevelt   Buffalo Bill Cody   John Paul Jones

PROJECT 3–11
I CAN DRAW A STRAIGHT LINE

FOR THE TEACHER   Many people claim they cannot be artists because they "can't draw a straight line." Ask students if they know of any way that they *can* draw a straight line. Most of them will quickly realize that they need a ruler. Have them talk about things that have straight lines; then discuss natural forms. Ask the students to name a few forms from nature (lakes, trees, animals, the human face, fish, an octopus).

Vocabulary

line	form
space	value
highlights	emphasis
rhythm	

Preparation   To have some continuity in your display, limit the selection to a theme such as sea life, plant life, the human form, wild animals, domesticated animals, dinosaurs—or anything else that this particular age group happens to be studying in science. If you have several classes, give each class a different theme.

Photos from magazines could be used here as a starting point. Tape the magazine photo underneath the copy paper for students to draw outlines (at a window), then have them notice differences in value as they draw. Lines placed close together will give darker values.

Alternative Project

LINE PORTRAIT ON A COMPUTER   This could be done on a computer with a drawing program, using only straight lines of various widths. Students can first draw an outline with the cursor, then fill in within the outline using only straight lines. If they don't want the outline to show, it can be erased when the drawing is done. Or a drawing could be put on a transparency and taped to the front of the screen, then "filled in" with straight lines.

These three straight-line drawings were done on a computer. Several individual drawings can be combined for a group portrait.

PROJECT 3–11   I CAN DRAW A STRAIGHT LINE

Materials

rulers

fine-line markers

9 × 12-inch drawing or construction paper

pencils

magazine photo (*optional*)

Directions You will be selecting a form from nature (where it is said there is no such thing as a straight line). It could be *plant life* such as trees, shrubs, or flowers; *sea creatures* (fish, octopus, whales, snails, seahorses, shellfish); or *animals* (cats, dogs, pigs, cows, elephants, humans).

1. Whether or not you use a magazine photo, use pencil to *very* lightly draw outlines on your drawing paper (because you will be erasing the pencil marks later). Notice differences in value (lightness and darkness of an area). To show differences in value, make parallel straight lines closer together for the darker areas, further apart for the highlights (lighter areas).

2. Before beginning to draw with marker, select one object that will be emphasized by having it a different color from the rest of the picture.

3. Use the ruler and a marker to make straight lines on top of your pencil outline. Some of your lines will be short, some long, some closely spaced, some with wide spaces in between. Just remember to keep the lines straight and all going the same direction.

4. Because a complete composition does not leave objects just floating in space, repeat shapes (perhaps making them bigger or smaller) or make other straight lines that will represent the environment. Even clouds can be drawn with straight lines.

© 2000 by John Wiley & Sons, Inc.

PROJECT 3–12
PIASA BIRD (THUNDERBIRD)

FOR THE TEACHER Because nature is so much a part of the life of Native Americans, they sometimes use symbols that represent animals to decorate pots, create pictographs (drawings), or petroglyphs (etchings on rock). This project is based on a painting found on bluffs above the Mississippi River near Alton, Illinois of a fantasy bird, the Piasa Bird.

As teachers, we must be aware that selecting projects based on a culture such as this can be meaningful to all students, but only if the time is taken to introduce something about the people who live the culture. It might be part of an ongoing unit of study within the regular classroom, or an art theme that explores contributions of Native Americans throughout the North American continent.

Chanter, 1991, Emmi Whitehorse, oil on paper on canvas, Saint Louis Art Museum. Ms. Whitehorse uses symbols of her culture in her contemporary paintings.

Vocabulary

pattern

color

repetition

abstract

stylization

limited palette

Preparation Discuss the fact that the designs that outsiders see on Native American artwork as purely decorative are meaningful symbols to Native American artists and viewers. Some of these would be mountains, warriors, sun, arrows, rain, serpents, feathers. Talk about mythical or extinct birds such as the Thunderbird or the Piasa bird, as well as existing birds such as the Eagle or Parrot. Designs used on Native American pottery can be used as inspiration for designs.

Interdisciplinary Connections
SOCIAL STUDIES
PETROGLYPH COMPARISONS Students can compare and contrast designs from pottery or petroglyphs of other cultures with those done by Native Americans. For example, how did Australian Aboriginal people depict a snake? a bird? a cat?

Drawn from *Fantastic Bird*, c. 1925–1930, Awa Tsireh

Native American Bird and Animal Symbols

Turtle

Turtle

Spider

Snake

Plumed Serpent

Fish

Lizard

Puma God

Bear

Lion

Goat

Buffalo

Puma

PROJECT 3–12   PIASA BIRD (THUNDERBIRD)

STUDENT PAGE

Materials

12 × 18-inch drawing paper

pencil

markers (or colored pencil)

Drawn from Piasa Bird, Mississippi Bluffs, Alton, Illinois, first seen by explorers in 1673

Directions   On a bluff over-looking the Mississippi near Alton, Illinois, there was for many years a Native American painting of a mythical bird, the Piasa (pronounced "pie-a-saw"). Although the original painting disappeared, a reproduction is currently seen in the same place. Elsewhere one sees drawings of Thunderbirds, that were also mythical birds in the Native American culture. What do you think would be the characteristics of a powerful mythical bird? Since no one has seen one, it might have a very long tail, be brightly colored, and have powerful claws.

1. Make thumbnail sketches of the outlines of birds on your paper. These outlines can represent real or imaginary birds. When you have selected a design, draw a large outline on the piece of drawing paper. Use straight or curved lines to make divisions within the body of the bird (wings, a line at the neck or legs). These lines will be helpful when you are making designs.

2. Draw designs within the body of the bird in pencil before coloring with the marker, using only a few colors. Colors typically used in Indian designs are tones of dark red, reddish brown, black, turquoise, and yellow.

3. Now let your imagination go. These birds are *stylized*. They may have more than the usual number of feathers on their tails. Some areas can be plain colored, while others have designs or patterns, or simply areas left uncolored to allow the paper to show through. Designs could be checkerboard, stair step, zigzag.

4. Although the background is plain, if you feel there is too much space, then make a border all the way around the outside of the picture by repeating some of the patterns.

PROJECT 3–13
POSTCARD ART—PUT IT IN THE MAIL

FOR THE TEACHER Even very young students have seen postcards and understand that one person can send a message to another person by placing a stamp on a piece of cardboard. What they may not have known is that they can make their own postcards, as long as a standard size (4 × 6 or 5 × 7 inches) is used. Many national art organizations have miniature art competitions. You might call your assignment *Postcard Art Competition*, complete with rules about deadline, craftsmanship, and originality.

Vocabulary

miniature

concept

craftsmanship

permanent medium

Preparation While your students can at least begin their postcard artwork at school, it would be fun for them to take it home and address it to you at school. You can then make an exhibit of this mail-in art. Suggest using permanent media such as ballpoint pen, ink, or permanent markers that would not be damaged by rain or rub off onto other mail.

Interdisciplinary Connections
SOCIAL STUDIES

INTERNATIONAL PEN-PALS This is an easy and interesting way to have an art exchange with a foreign country. Arrange in advance with a teacher at an international school to have the cards go both directions. Officials in your school district will have access to addresses of schools worldwide. With most schools having Internet capability, this project could possibly result in an international art exchange that would not mean that the student's work was gone for a lengthy period.

This scarecrow was drawn by a first-grade student of Debbie McConnell of the Barretts Elementary School, St. Louis County, Missouri.

PROJECT 3–13   POSTCARD ART—
PUT IT IN THE MAIL

STUDENT PAGE

Materials

newsprint

pencils

ball-point pen

colored pencils

ink

permanent markers

scissors

tape

tagboard or posterboard cut 4 × 6 inches or 5 × 7 inches

Wish you were here!

POST CARD

STAMP

DO NOT WRITE BELOW THIS LINE

Directions

1. On the newsprint, try out ideas with small thumbnail sketches. Your card can be an original cartoon, a design, an illustration of a story, a drawing of a place you have visited or would like to visit. Originality counts, so avoid often-used designs like hearts, rainbows, smiley faces, other people's cartoon characters.

2. The design will take up one entire side of the postcard. After you have worked out small designs and selected the one you like best, draw around the outside of the postcard on the newsprint and carefully draw your final design in complete detail in the correct size on the newsprint.

3. To transfer your design from the newsprint to the postcard, rub over the back of your design with pencil. Now cut out the rectangle from the newsprint and tape it onto your postcard with the original drawing facing up. Redraw over the original design, and it will be lightly transferred to the postcard.

4. Use pen, colored pencils, or permanent markers to carefully make this the most beautiful postcard anyone could imagine. On the back side of your postcard, draw a line vertically down the center. On the right side of the line, put the address to which you will mail the card. On the left side, send a brief message about your drawing and sign the card. Mail it.

PROJECT 3–14
FOLDED TISSUE DESIGNS

FOR THE TEACHER This project is easily and quickly done, so students may wish to do several, then select their best one for matting. Discuss the universal need for decorative design. Have students look at their own clothing to observe some designs, to think about nature's designs on animals, or to look around their own rooms for decorative objects. Help students think about ways to combine lines and shapes to make patterns.

Preparation Try this yourself with *your* markers, as each brand of marker gives a different result. You can use recycled copy paper underneath in place of paper towels, but caution students not to leave their designs in place very long, or else the color leaches out to the underneath paper. Their paper may tear if they are in too much of a hurry applying the marker, but since these will be mounted on white paper, it will not make much difference.

Lines and Patterns

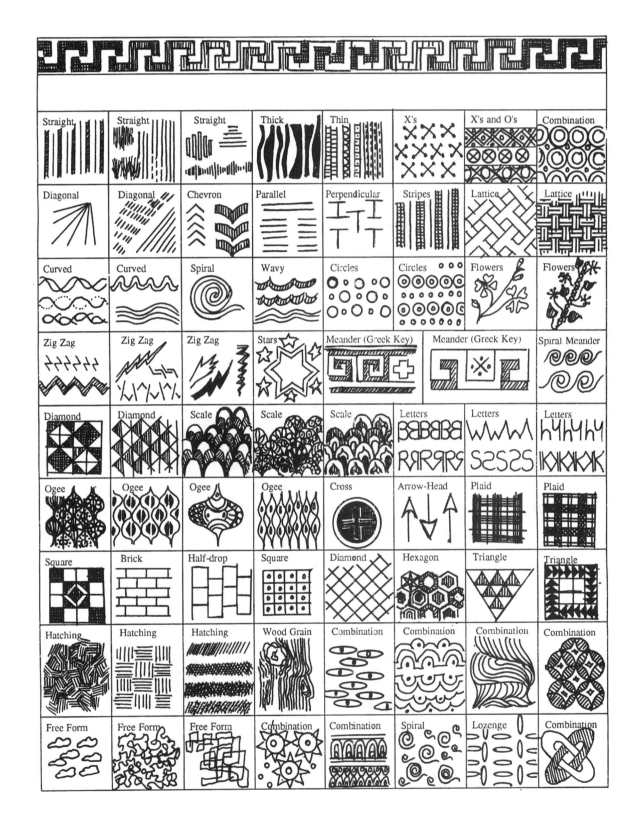

PROJECT 3–14   FOLDED TISSUE DESIGNS

Materials

spray bottles of water (1 per table)

broad-tipped watercolor markers

1/4 sheet white tissue paper

newspapers

Directions

1. Fold the paper to have two or four thicknesses. It can simply be folded in half lengthwise, crossways, a triangular fold, or folded in from all four corners.

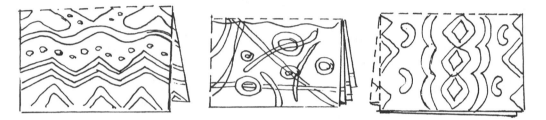

2. Place the folded paper on a paper towel, newspaper, or recycled paper. Spray it first on one side, then turn it over and spray the other side. Blot it slightly (it should be damp but not soaked).

3. Use a broad-tipped watercolor marker to carefully draw designs onto the paper. The marker will "bleed" and go through the first layer to the second layer. Use only a few different colors; some light, some dark.

4. When you are satisfied, carefully open the paper. If you let it set too long, the colors will drain onto the newspaper. When it is open, put it on a drying rack. Then mount your design onto white paper.

UNIT 4

PAINTING

No doubt about it, painting is a messy business (which is probably one reason for the popularity of markers with teachers)! There is also no doubt that it is one of the things students love the most about art, which makes it worthwhile doing. One of the greatest moments of teaching art is when a very young student "discovers" what happens when two colors—such as yellow and blue—are mixed together. It is also a certainty that students' painting improves as they have more opportunities to do it.

Simplifying the Process

CLEANUP There are many ways to make it easy on yourself. Experienced teachers learn how to dispense and clean up opaque (tempera or acrylic) paint in a variety of ways. You will need "table helpers" to get paint and water. You will also want two or three people who will help wash brushes at the end of the hour. It is recommended that you preserve your sanity by avoiding having primary students anywhere near a sink. Several teachers of my acquaintance purchase up to 30 inexpensive lightweight washcloths (towels could be cut up to serve the same purpose) that are kept damp in an open-sided plastic crate. These are rinsed daily and laundered weekly, and greatly simplify wiping hands and tables.

THE PAPER PALETTE My favorite method for students of all ages is to remove the staples from a weekly news magazine or catalogue. The double-folded pages are slick and make perfect palettes for mixing colors. Older students can take their colors from a "table palette" of pure hues to mix them on their own folded-page palettes. (The table palettes are refilled as needed.) When they are finished, the palettes are folded in half and thrown away. Brushes are collected and put in a coffee can filled with water to be washed later. Each student has a paper towel. A water container is on the table for rinsing brushes when changing colors.

PAINTING WITHOUT A SINK Diane Papageorge of the Lewis and Clark Elementary School in St. Charles County, Missouri has solved the problem of not having a sink in her room. She places four baby-food jars containing thinned acrylic paint on a paper plate. Each jar has a brush in it and each table's "palette" has been mixed with slight color variations from that of another table. After painting from one set of jars for ten minutes, these are passed on to the next table. The sets of jars are collected at the end of the hour and covered with lids. This avoids the problem of brushes drying out, or even of the need for water. Students are told they must use a small piece of cardboard that is moved along under the edge of the paper as they paint to protect the table. Many teachers routinely cover the tables for painting with newspaper, which is then simply wadded up and thrown away.

Another option for clean-up in a sinkless room is to have three buckets placed on newspaper. At the end of the hour, one bucket is used to collect dirty water. Water containers and brushes are rinsed in a semi-clean bucket, and hands are rinsed in the clean water. When students need clean water for painting, they get it from the clean-water bucket.

PREMIXING PAINT FOR YOUNGER STUDENTS Jay Morthland of the Bellerive School in St. Louis County has made a wooden box that holds small milk cartons from the cafeteria for each table. He mixes tempera colors for the cartons in advance, and each carton has its own brush. The brushes are washed and cartons closed at the end of a painting period. Students wipe their hands on the damp towels he keeps in the center of the table (which are washed and dried as needed in the school's machines).

When painting with kindergarten and first graders, Cathy Williams (of the Hageman Elementary School in St. Louis County, Missouri) has students first use a brush for one specific color (for example, white). She collects the brushes before having them do the next color (green), and so on. Students do not have to use water at all.

Teachers of older students sometimes use foam egg cartons, having students put tempera in the depressions and mixing color on the lid. The boxes are closed and put away for the next day's use. Or older students use commercial plastic reusable palettes with depressions that are washed at the end of each use. (This tends to be wasteful of paint.) Many teachers prefer to dispense paint on paper or foam plates.

This painting was done by a student in a primary grade at Barretts School, St. Louis County, Missouri.

TEMPERA AND ACRYLIC

PROJECT 4–1
ENLARGE A MASTERPIECE

FOR THE TEACHER   This project enables students to learn how to mix colors. Select a painting for enlarging that has sufficient variety throughout so each student will have something interesting to enlarge. It would surely be discouraging to have to paint a section that is absolutely plain. Artists whose work would be interesting and appropriate for this project are Vincent Van Gogh, Faith Ringgold, Henri Matisse, Henri Rousseau, Edward Hicks, Thomas Hart Benton, Grant Wood, Grandma Moses, and Paul Gauguin.

Vocabulary

grid

enlargement

proportion

hue

Preparation   Select a masterpiece to be enlarged and decide what the ultimate finished size will be. It can be large enough to go floor to ceiling or 3 × 3-feet square. Cut the drawing paper so it will be in exact proportion to the individual pieces of the original (for example, 1/4 inch = 2 inches). The individual pieces in the enlargement can be as small as 6 × 6 inches. Because colors are going to be mixed by the students, even a small painting may take two periods.

Make two color photocopies of the masterpiece(s) (or buy reproductions). Divide both with a ruler, making enough individual sections for each of the students in your class to have one. Number these identically. Cut up one photocopy and staple each individually numbered piece to a numbered index card. Write the student's name on the uncut photocopy for easy assemblage. When the paintings are complete, glue them together on a roll paper background (if it is not wide enough, glue strips of roll paper together, leaving room for a border for the students to sign). Or join pieces together with wide tape.

This delightful painting of a panda is one of many tempera paintings of animals done by Beth Goyer's students from Holman Middle School, St. Louis County, Missouri. The explorations encouraged students to draw animals in their environments.

Adaptations for Younger Students   Follow the instructions above, but enlarge a black-and-white high-contrast reproduction and allow students to do it either with paint or marker.

Alternative Projects

PROJECT IT ON THE WALL   Make an overhead transparency of the masterpiece on a copier. Tape a large piece of roll paper onto the wall and directly project the transparency from an overhead projector. Students may draw it with pencil onto the background. Several students can work together painting the picture to look as close to the original as possible. This method also works directly on a wall. Large pieces of primed canvas are also suitable for painting with acrylic paint, and can be rolled up and put away.

PUT IT ON THE CEILING Art Teacher Toni Wilson of North Kirkwood Middle School in St. Louis County, Missouri has her students paint personalized versions of masterpieces and project them onto ceiling tiles, which are reinserted into the ceilings of the art room and hallways.

OIL PASTEL ENLARGEMENT ON TAGBOARD This project is also appropriately done with oil pastels, although you may wish to work with tagboard rather than drawing paper.

SUBSTITUTE YOUR OWN FACE Each student can enlarge a masterpiece using the grid system, substituting his or her own face for one or all of the faces in the painting.

Interdisciplinary Connections
SCIENCE

ENVIRONMENTAL MURAL WITH ANIMAL LIFE Students may select a segment of the animal kingdom—such as undersea creatures or jungle creatures—and paint an entire wall. Simply draw these animals on 8-1/2 × 11-inch paper in black, photocopy it onto an overhead transparency, and then project it directly onto the wall for painting.

History

SCHOOLWIDE THEME MURAL Students at the Reed Elementary School in St. Louis County, Missouri transformed their entry hall by enlarging a George Caleb Bingham painting. Parents constructed wooden walkways, and placed barrels and ropes appropriately to make the entry hall resemble the authentic St. Louis riverfront of Bingham's time. Students researched and learned about the history of the city as part of this project.

The Cornell Farm, 1848, Edward Hicks, oil on canvas, 36³/₄ × 49 inches, National Gallery of Art, Washington, DC, Gift of Edgar William and Bernice Chrysler Garbisch

Peaceable Kingdom, c. 1834, Edward Hicks, oil on canvas, 29³/₈ × 35¹/₂ inches, National Gallery of Art, Washington, DC, Gift of Edgar William and Bernice Chrysler Garbisch

PROJECT 4–1   ENLARGE A MASTERPIECE

Materials

2 photocopies of a masterpiece

index cards

drawing paper cut to proportion

rulers

pencils

tempera paint

brushes

water containers

paper towels

The ceiling tiles in North Kirkwood Middle School, St. Louis County, Missouri, bloom with "take-offs" on masterpieces, changed slightly to reflect the student's input. Toni Wilson's students have painted everything from Picasso to a Greek Vase Angel–Bulldog (the school's mascot).

Directions   You will be enlarging a very small portion of this masterpiece, so it is important that you mix the colors to be exactly the same as your portion of the picture.

1. Use a pencil to measure and draw a grid over your portion of the picture. On the larger drawing paper, carefully draw a larger grid in exact proportion to your section of the original. For example, 1/4 inch on the original section could be equal to 2 inches on your enlargement.

2. Using a pencil, lightly draw in each large square on your drawing paper exactly what you see in the small square of the original. Before you begin to paint, have your teacher look at the drawing.

3. In mixing colors, you may find that rather than just adding black or white to change a color, the artist originally added the complement of the color to change the color (a touch of red added to green, for example). If you have difficulty mixing a certain color, ask your teacher for help.

4. To avoid constantly having to clean your brush and mix color again, mix the most-used color first, applying it to the drawing paper wherever it occurs. Then mix the second color, and so on. Continue painting until you have covered the piece of paper and it looks exactly like the small piece with which you started.

5. When all the squares are finished, they can be reassembled either by taping them together on the back or by gluing them to a large paper background. If a border is left around the outside edge, sign your name to the enlargement.

PROJECT 4–2
OPEN THE DOOR!

FOR THE TEACHER   Talk with students about how they feel when they go someplace they have never been to before. When the door is opened, is it different from what they thought it might be? Talk about styles of doors, and about some artists who have used doors as a device to frame a picture. Dutch artists Pieter de Hooch and Jan Vermeer specialized in painting interiors and scenes viewed through a doorway. Ask students to consider what they might find behind a special door.

Vocabulary

resist

fantasy

realistic

unrealistic

frame

imagination

interior

genre

Preparation   Try to find photocopies of various kinds of doors to whet the imagination of the students. The doors should be drawn first, with the character of the door determining what might be found behind it.

After the ink has mostly dried, I suggest you should be the one to rinse it off, as students sometimes are a little too enthusiastic and wash it all off. As an alternative to matting, you could have each student create a "door border" from colored construction paper decorated with marker.

Interdisciplinary Connections
LANGUAGE ARTS

OPENING DOORS IN LIFE   Talk with students about *doors* in their lives. Ask them to think and write about someone who opened a door to them in a special way, such as a relative who took them to a zoo, or the person who taught them to read. What are some symbolic doorways? Are they new experiences, new places, revealing glimpses into the past through looking at old photos?

PROJECT 4–2   OPEN THE DOOR!

STUDENT PAGE

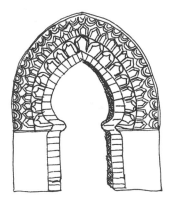

Materials

drawing paper

chalk

tempera

India ink

brushes

water containers

Directions   Where do you find doors? On the inside of a ship? a church? a home? a grocery store? a shopping mall? a gingerbread house? a candy store? a haunted house? a spaceship? through a giant redwood tree? between the cars of a train? Where are some other places? Think about what *might* be behind a door rather than what you know is there. Think about the shape of your door. It might be rounded on top, or actually be a "moon gate" (a round opening in a wall that surrounds a garden).

1. Using chalk, draw a door around the edge of your picture, then consider what you might see when you look through if the door were opened. You might see a secret garden, or there might be people behind your door. How would they be dressed? Use your imagination to develop a fantasy interior.

2. Select colors. You may use realistic colors (brown tree trunks, green leaves, blue sky), or they might be completely unrealistic—such as pink trees, yellow sky, magenta grass! Think about whether you could use patterns and bright colors to make your composition more interesting.

3. Use tempera paint to paint up to the chalk lines, but do not paint over the chalk. Try to have only one layer of tempera so the paint will not flake off. When you have finished, apply a coat of India ink, allowing it to become almost completely dry.

4. Gently rinse off the ink, rubbing slightly if necessary, but allowing it to mostly stay so that the black gives a batik effect.

PROJECT 4–3
LEGS, WINGS, CLAWS, AND ANTENNAE

FOR THE TEACHER   This project is appropriate for primary grades, although older children also enjoy seeing what they can create from an accidental beginning.

Vocabulary
symmetry

color scheme

line

shape

Preparation   Try this first yourself so you will be able to advise students about the proper amount and placement of the tempera paint.

Interdisciplinary Connections
SCIENCE
FLYING AND CRAWLING CREATURES This project could be made more specific with a study of flying insects, butterflies, spiders, or crawling insects. Habitat such as a spider web, grasses, flowers, or tree branches could be added to the background.

LANGUAGE ARTS
SHORT STORY ABOUT "MY CREATURE."   When students have "discovered" what their creature is, they must give it a name and a personality, and write a short story about where it lives and what its family is like. Students are certainly familiar with stories and songs about animals.

 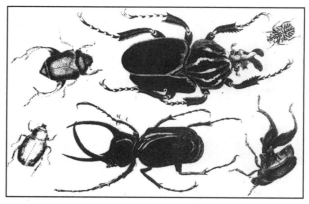

Print from *The Earth and Animated Nature* by Oliver Goldsmith, 1849. From the collection of Carl and Helen Christoferson.

PROJECT 4–3 LEGS, WINGS, CLAWS, AND ANTENNAE

Materials

drawing paper

tempera paint

newspaper

brushes

Directions You will be using your imagination to discover creatures that suddenly appear when you use your fingers to push paint around on the paper. You may find antennae, eyes in strange places, and interesting blends of color.

1. Fold your paper in half horizontally. Put drops of several colors on one side of the paper near the crease. Do not put one color on top of another, but at intervals that will allow colors to blend when the paper is closed and you use your fingers to move the paint around.

2. Close the paper and turn it so you can see the underside of the paper where you placed the paint. Use your fingers to ease the paint out from the center toward the edges of the paper.

3. Open the paper to discover the butterflies, fish, bugs, or animals you made. If you feel you did not have enough paint for a creature to emerge from its cocoon, add a little more paint.

4. Allow the paint to dry slightly, then outline your creature in black or bright colors. Add eyes, antennae, wings, and/or legs.

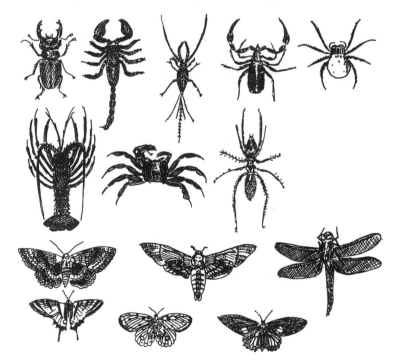

PROJECT 4—4
WINTER WHITES: ANIMALS
OF THE FAR NORTH AND SOUTH

FOR THE TEACHER   This project is about winter animals of the Arctic or Antarctic, many of which are white or may have white winter camouflage. While your students may not live where there is snow, they can still learn to enjoy painting it while learning about animals of these regions.

Vocabulary

form

value

palette

variety

emphasis

Preparation   Discuss a limited palette. White is to be the predominant color, so discuss how one might show shadows and the differences between the animal's camouflage and the snow that surrounds it. I recommend having each student use a paper palette (two folded magazine pages) with mostly white, brown, orange, yellow, blue, and violet to make this painting.

Interdisciplinary Connections
SCIENCE

WINTER CAMOUFLAGE This project will involve research on your part or that of your students to find out which animals change color in the winter. Polar bears are white year-round, but other animals may develop winter coats for camouflage. Winslow Homer's *Fox in Winter* happens not to be in camouflage, but he is a beautiful sight against the white snow. The painting could show any animals from the Arctic or Antarctic regions silhouetted against snow.

HIBERNATION HABITS This also offers an opportunity to study about winter hibernation, the effect of population growth into the animals' habitat, animal adaptation to city life, the number of animals that are now extinct.

Chilly Observation, 1889, Charles S. Raleigh, oil on canvas, 30 × 44 inches, Edgar William and Bernice Chrysler Garbisch Collection, Philadelphia Museum of Art

Arctic Hare, c. 1841, John James Audubon, 24 × 34$\frac{1}{4}$ inches, pen and black ink and graphite with watercolor and oil on paper, National Gallery of Art, Washington, DC, Gift of E.J.L. Hallstrom

PROJECT 4-4   WINTER WHITES: ANIMALS OF THE FAR NORTH AND SOUTH

STUDENT PAGE

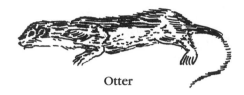

Otter

Materials

18 X 24-inch paper

yellow chalk

tempera paint

brushes

Directions   This will be a quiet painting, just as snow and the outdoors seem quiet in the winter. While white will be the main color, you will be able to add other hues to the white to show shadows or sunlight. Winter white animals might include polar bears, white rabbits, snowy owls, white foxes, wolves, sea lions, and mink. Other animals from the cold regions of the world include caribou, moose, buffalo, elk, otters, fish, penguins, and walruses.

1. Use yellow chalk to draw the animal(s) you will be painting. Think about where the horizon line will be, and draw some trees in the background. You may later add a few weeds poking through the snow for balance. Think about the colors of a winter sky.

2. Give the animal a first coat of paint, then paint in the background. Think about a direction of the light to decide whether to put a shadow in front of or behind the animal. You can indicate light and shadow by adding a small amount of yellow or orange to the white for sunlight, and violet or blue for shadow. In some places you will use white without any color added at all.

3. Now reconsider the animal(s). Darken around the edges to show form (roundness). If the animal has long hair, dip the brush in white pigment and use a dry-brush technique to create the appearance of fur. Almost the only color we will see of some animals is a nose and the color of the eyes!

4. If there are trees or bushes on the horizon, paint those with darker colors. Limbs of trees might have snow on them. Stand back and look at the painting to see if you have made enough differences in value between the animal and the snow so the animal is visible from a distance.

Wolf

Beaver

Sea Lion

Bear

PROJECT 4–5
TABLITA

FOR THE TEACHER   The tablita is a flat headpiece made of wood that continues to be worn today in traditional ceremonial dances in the Southwestern pueblos. Often worn by Kachina dancers, you may have seen tablitas on miniature Kachina figures. Many contemporary tablitas are based on ancient designs.

Vocabulary
symmetry

form

balance

Preparation   This project could be part of a unit of study about Native Americans of various regions. Suitable materials might be cardboard, matboard or foamboard, tagboard, and construction paper. If you intend the tablitas to be worn, they will need to be of heavier material such as cardboard or foamboard. You could prepare for this in advance by collecting and cutting up cardboard boxes so the tablitas could be large enough to actually be worn. For adults, these designs are approximately 22 to 24 inches high, with an opening cut to fit around the head, and are held in place with twine. Adjust the general size according to the age of your students. **SAFETY NOTE: If using cutting knives, be sure to give the students proper instructions for keeping the non-cutting hand behind the knife.**

Adaptations for Younger Students   This design project could easily be interpreted with cut construction paper mounted on black, tan, or white paper.

Alternative Projects
CORN-DANCE STICKS These sticks, decorated with the symbol for corn, are also carried during pueblo ceremonies. They could be made on wooden paint paddles (perhaps your local paint store could donate some) or on cardboard that has a "handle" cut at the bottom.

COMPUTER GRAPHICS TABLITAS Because of the symmetry and basic geometric forms used on the tablita, it is a natural for students to draw on the computer. These could be printed out in color or black and white (colored later with crayon or marker). They would be effective mounted on black construction paper.

PROJECT 4-5 TABLITA

Materials

scissors or cutting knives

cardboard or posterboard

gesso or white tempera paint

tempera paint in earth tones

pencils

chalk

newsprint

black permanent marker

twine or heavy string

Directions Tablitas are decorative wooden headdresses that have been worn for centuries in traditional Southwestern pueblo ceremonies. They are admired for their simplicity and beauty.

1. Make several thumbnail sketches to decide on your symmetrical design. Draw an opening for your head, then make a design that will extend out to both sides and approximately 12 inches above your head. These are often based on simple geometric forms, but could have a face or the wings of a bird on them. The sketches on this page show some typical designs.

2. After selecting a design, draw the outside shape onto cardboard or poster-board, then cut around it. To keep it from curling under, as it sometimes does when only one side is painted, cover the cardboard with gesso or white tempera paint on both sides. Lightly draw the design with chalk on the front.

3. Paint your design using traditional colors that were formerly made from natural pigments—such as turquoise, black, brown, reddish-brown, deep yellow, and dark red. These were usually painted on top of the white clay-painted background. When the colors are painted on, outline the design in black permanent marker.

4. Punch holes at the inside bottom and two holes at the top, inserting twine (heavy string) to hold the tablita in place.

PROJECT 4–6
THE MYSTERIOUS JUNGLE

FOR THE TEACHER Henri Rousseau, who is best-known for his paintings of jungle scenes, was sometimes called *Le Douanier* (the French translation for his occupation as a tollkeeper). He was a so-called primitive or "naive" artist, which simply meant that he did not have formal art training. Not only that, he probably never saw a jungle! He visited the Paris Botanical and Zoological Gardens frequently, and his plants and animals are based on his observations there. Although he did not always have animals in his pictures, sometimes one might see a monkey, lion, or panther peering through the leaves.

Vocabulary

foreground

middle-ground

background

value

variety

emphasis

shade

tint

complementary color

gradation

overlapping

stylized

repetition

Preparation This assignment is to create a jungle painting. Show students as many reproductions of Rousseau's work as are available, then borrow plants from around the school and have them do drawings of real plants (or fake silk plants). Have the students observe the variations in the colors, sizes, and shapes of the leaves, even in the same plant. Tell students they need to have at least three plants in their painting, using dark, medium and light tones, and that they need to fill the whole page.

Alternative Project

OIL PASTEL/BLACK TEMPERA RESIST This same project can be done on 9 X 12-inch construction paper using oil pastel/black tempera resist. Students can draw their compositions with chalk, then color almost to the chalk lines. Jungle animals, flowers, or fruit can be included. Plants can even run off the top of the page. Encourage students to blend colors, beginning with darker ones, then adding lighter ones on top. When the pastels have been firmly applied, the chalk lines should be wiped off with a tissue. Have students paint the entire picture with black tempera paint. Tempera will "crawl" when applied, but this will not be a problem. After the paint has dried, you should gently wash off the tempera under running water.

The Equatorial Jungle, 1909, Henri Rousseau, oil on canvas, 55¼ × 51 inches, National Gallery of Art, Washington, DC, Chester Dale Collection

The Waterfall (La Cascade), 1910, Henri Rousseau, oil on canvas, 116.2 × 150.2 cm, Art Institute of Chicago, Helen Birch Bartlett Memorial Collection

PROJECT 4–6   THE MYSTERIOUS JUNGLE

STUDENT PAGE

Materials

18 X 24-inch paper

tempera

brushes

chalk

Directions   This project, which is based on the work of French artist Henri Rousseau, calls for painting a forest. Rousseau based most of his plant drawings on plants and grasses he saw or picked up at the Paris Botanical Garden. His animals were based on his visits to the Zoo and pictures from books. He was sometimes called a "fantasy artist" because so much of what he painted came from his imagination.

1. With chalk, loosely compose your drawing. Perhaps "frame" your picture with tall plants on the sides, and include a foreground, middle-ground, and background. A portion of sky with the sun or moon showing reveals the time of day or night. To show depth in the sky, it is usually darkest toward the top of the page, lighter as it nears the horizon.

2. Rousseau sometimes used as many as 50 different shades of green in a single composition! Individual leaves had more than one shade. Plan for light and dark areas of the composition. Green can be changed by adding small amounts of another color such as blue; made darker by adding black or violet; or made lighter by adding white or yellow. Plants could also be painted pure blue, violet, yellow, or white.

3. In addition to the green plants, you might want to include a "surprise," as Rousseau often did. It could be animals peeking out through the leaves or partially hidden. A tree might be filled with oranges, or beautiful exotic flowers might be growing. Even in a mostly green painting, many different colors can be included. "Artistic license" is a term that means the artist has the freedom to do whatever he or she thinks will make the picture more beautiful.

4. When you feel you are almost finished, step back and look at your painting. Do you have some areas of light? Are there enough differences in your greens that you can see individual leaves of the plants? Where could you touch up things to improve them?

PROJECT 4–7
HOW DOES YOUR GARDEN GROW?

FOR THE TEACHER Many artists used flowers and plants as their subjects, including Monet with his haystacks and his fields of poppies; Emil Nolde and Georgia O'Keeffe with their beautiful flowers; Odilon Redon with his mystic paintings of people and flowers; and Henri Rousseau with his jungle scenes. Show students such paintings, or photos of beautiful flowers in a natural setting.

Apple Blossoms, 1930, Georgia O'Keeffe, 36 × 24 inches, The Nelson–Atkins Museum of Art, Kansas City, Missouri (Gift of Mrs. Louis Sosland)

Vocabulary

depth

variety

emphasis

three-dimensional

Preparation Not too many years ago, artists painted one subject on several layers of glass to create depth in a painting. This same technique is suggested here, but the painting is to be first on paper, then on layers of overhead transparencies separated by cardboard spacers. This process develops as the students go along, so it cannot be totally planned. Younger students might work better with small pictures. Cardboard supports for overhead transparencies make perfect, inexpensive frames for a small project and hide the cardboard between the layers. However, you can create larger sheets of plastic on a school laminating machine by simply running the two layers of plastic through the lamination rollers with nothing between them. These sheets of plastic can be cut to any size to fit within a standard mat.

Show students varieties of flowers and talk with them about differences in stems, leaves, and colors. You may find that plant catalogue examples will be helpful in showing them differences. Another option is to have a variety of silk flowers around the room for them to look at.

It is recommended that *you* first try this project using the same materials your students will use. If acrylic paint is not available, mix tempera with polymer medium or liquid soap to make it adhere to the plastic transparencies.

Alternative Projects

FOIL-BACKED PAINTING This project resembles the Victorian technique of painting on glass, backed by tin-foil. Students could paint on only one layer of plastic, placing a layer of aluminum foil and a layer of paper to protect the foil underneath. Hold the layers in place inside a mat.

LAYERED CITYSCAPE Another possible subject is a cityscape, with buildings in the distance painted on the underneath layers, and closer buildings added on succeeding layers.

Interdisciplinary Connections

SCIENCE

BOTANY STUDY This can be the culmination of a botany unit in which students learn about the parts of a plant. If students understand the parts of a plant, they will be much more careful to make their flowers look realistic.

PLANT STUDIES Introduce research about plants done by Gregor Johann Mendel or Booker T. Washington.

These photos show the finished picture done in three layers and put together in a mat.

PROJECT 4–7 HOW DOES YOUR GARDEN GROW?

Materials

9 X 12-inch drawing paper
sheet plastic (overhead transparencies or laminating plastic)
masking tape
corrugated cardboard cut in 1/2-inch strips to fit inside the mat
glue
acrylic paint
pre-cut mats or overhead transparency holders

Directions You will be painting flowers on paper, then adding two or three layers of plastic to show depth and variety. The bottom (paper) layer will be the most complete.

1. On drawing paper, paint an interesting sky, using more than one shade of blue. Consider adding some violet or even a tiny bit of red to it. Use chalk to draw the outlines of flowers, stems, and leaves, then paint them. Think about how flowers grow. Some are low to the ground and large, while others have tiny star-like blooms. Stems and leaves also show great variety.

2. When the painting on paper is dry, use two small pieces of masking tape to cover the original painting with a sheet of plastic. Use similar colors and paint on the plastic layer directly on top of a few of the underneath flowers. Add several new flowers. You might want to add a few clouds in the sky.

3. *Optional:* Tape a third layer of plastic on top of the first two layers with masking tape. Again, paint this layer to fill in spaces on the first two layers, or to accentuate the flowers on the underneath layers. This will be your last layer. Space will be maintained between the layers by using thin cardboard strips to hold the layers apart.

4. When the painting is complete, you are ready to mat the painting so it will be three-dimensional. Place a mat on the table so it is face-down.

   - Tape the top layer of plastic firmly in place directly to the back of the mat with masking tape.

   - Put a line of glue on 1/2-inch corrugated cardboard strips the size of the transparency. Glue the strips in place on top of the mat.

   - Add the second layer of plastic, using glue to hold it in place on the strips.

   - Again, add corrugated cardboard strips. (These strips should be near enough to the edges of the plastic that they are hidden by the mat.)

   - Put a bead of glue all around on the second cardboard layer, and place the paper layer on top.

   - Put a weight on top of the painting until the glue has dried.

PROJECT 4–8
MOCK AIRBRUSH SPACE PAINTING

FOR THE TEACHER   This project was inspired by observing airbrush painters from California painting faces at an art fair. They simply airbrushed base colors (such as blue, violet, and green) on one side of the face, then airbrushed stars, planets, comets through or around stencils to create a space fantasy. The "airbrush" in most classrooms is a toothbrush rubbed with the thumb or a Popsicle stick, or by using a variety of spray bottles. The stencils will be cut-out from tagboard, but the end result is similar. Introduce students to the work of Peter Max, whose artwork has this same "futuristic feel."

Vocabulary

variety	emphasis
value	unity

Preparation   To avoid waste, acrylic paint could be thinned with water in baby-food jars, using "sky" colors such as light and dark blue, light and dark violet, light and dark green. Keep white and yellow colors thick enough so they will cover the underneath colors when sprayed on top. Have students wear smocks to protect their clothing. Spray bottles of various types could also be used. While this may lead to some splotches, it can be a wonderful opportunity to teach students to *use* their mistakes.

Adaptations for Younger Students
STICKERS, STENCILS, SPONGES Put stickers on the paper (circles, stars) and have the students sponge-paint on top of them. Then remove the stickers. Or have students use purchased or pre-cut "space" stencils for sponge-painting.

Alternative Projects
THE STARS AT NIGHT ARE BIG AND BRIGHT A variation of this could be done on black paper with light-colored paint. While there will be splotches, they can either look like the sky on a brightly moonlit evening or a pitch-black night in the desert.

INSECT SPRAYER AND STENCILS To make a large all-class space painting, tape two 36-inch lengths of white kraft paper together and hang on the wall. Spread paper on the floor underneath. Have each student make one or more large stencil cut-outs of stars, comets, planets, the moon, etc. Use insect spray guns (available at hardware stores) as your "airbrushes," filling three with dark tempera paint. Tape the stencils to the paper with loops of masking tape, then spray with tempera around them. When you have finished, mist white paint over all for the Milky Way.

Interdisciplinary Connections
SCIENCE
CONSTELLATION PICTURES This project could be the culmination of a unit of astronomy, studying stars, planets, comets, constellations, and phases of the moon. Students will have an understanding of the varied appearance and sizes of stars. Each student could make an individual "constellation" picture.

SOCIAL SCIENCE
THREE COMPANIONS IN SPACE Have students write a paper about which three people from history they would want to have with them on a voyage in space, and why those three (along with themselves) would form a valuable team.

PROJECT 4–8   MOCK AIRBRUSH SPACE PAINTING

Materials

drawing paper or black construction paper
thinned acrylic or tempera paint or ink
tagboard
round and star stickers in various sizes
X-acto® knives (for older students)
toothbrushes
spray bottles
brushes
newspapers

Directions   You will be building up layers of designs to create a space fantasy that will include stars, comets, the moon, and planets.

1. Decide in advance if you want to leave part of the paper white. Place stencils (cut-out comets, moon, stars) on the paper with rubber cement or a removable glue. Dip a toothbrush in paint and rub it with the handle of a brush, spattering with the darkest colors first. Or use a sponge brush to apply and blend background colors such as dark and light blue, green, violet, and turquoise.

2. Continue building up colors by spattering all over the paper. Leave the stencils in place even when you apply new stencils. You can control where the spatters go by spattering only in the place where you are holding the screen over a stencil.

3. You can make open stencils by cutting comet or star shapes in a piece of tagboard or heavy plastic. Hold this over the colored paper and use white or yellow paint to spatter or sponge-stencil through the opening, applying the paint thickly so it will cover the dark colors.

4. Because you will get some spatters where you do not want them, these areas can be cut up and used in collage fashion in other areas or another composition.

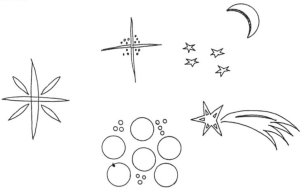

WATERCOLOR

PROJECT 4–9
WATERCOLOR CHART

FOR THE TEACHER Although we tend to think of watercolor as a nonpermanent medium as compared with oil paint, transparent watercolors of at least 400 years of age still exist in all their brilliance. Some of the great watercolorists are Mary Cassatt, Raoul Dufy, John Singer Sargent, Edgar Degas, John Marin, Winslow Homer, Alexander Calder, and Joseph Mallord William Turner. Often artists made watercolor sketches "in the field," then turned these into larger paintings in their studios. To introduce students to the use of watercolor, have them make a "chart" using techniques listed here.

Vocabulary

wet-in-wet	wash
hue	value
dry-brush	dilute
resist	stipple
unity	

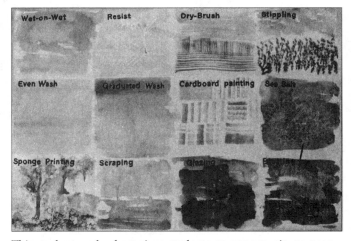

This student-made chart gives students an opportunity to practice different ways of working with watercolor. Fine-line marker letters are traced from computer-printed letters.

Preparation Demonstration in these various techniques will be helpful to students as they prepare their own charts. Because this is simply to introduce them to the techniques of watercolor, the students will label each experiment. Suggest they might have unity in their chart if they were to use warm *or* cool colors, or use similar subjects such as landscape, seascape, faces, or flower garden in each square.

Have students begin by adding a few drops of water directly to each pan of watercolor to soften the paint. Explain to them that when they are finished, they should make sure the color pans and the lid are clean so the paint will be ready for the next person. Show students how to dilute and mix the color in the lid of the pan. Watercolor is distinguished from tempera by its transparency. Acrylic paint can also be thinned with water to be used as watercolor.

Adaptations for Younger Students
EXPERIMENTS IN MARK-MAKING Rather than attempt to make a "chart" for future use, simply introduce younger students to one process at a time, encouraging them to place these painting "marks" anywhere on one sheet of paper. Allow the painting to dry before trying to pull it together by "taking a walk with a crayon."

Interdisciplinary Connections
SCIENCE
PIGMENTS Students could work as a group to research the source of pigments used prior to artificial minerals. Or, as early artists in all cultures have done, students could make dyes from such things as onion skins or beets, or pigments from earth, rocks, or charcoal.

PROJECT 4–9   WATERCOLOR CHART

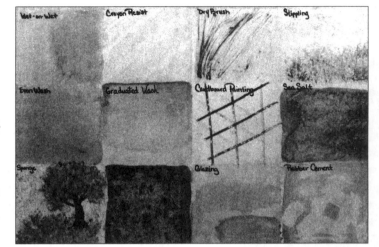

Materials

watercolors

crayons

12 × 18-inch watercolor or
drawing paper

newspapers

2 containers per table (one
with clean water)

brushes

black marking pen

Directions   The chart you will be making will allow you to see all the different possibilities for working in watercolor. You could use warm colors on half of the paper and cool colors on the other half. You may prefer to have a "subject" for some of these, such as a flower or tree.

1. Fold the paper into twelve sections by folding in thirds lengthwise, then in fourths horizontally.

- *Wet-in-wet.* Especially good for skies and water. Dip a brush in clean water and brush it on one segment of the paper. Now dip the brush into a color and touch the tip into the wet section. The pigment will spread. Add a related color (for example: red/orange or blue/violet).

- *Watercolor resist.* Use crayon or oil crayon to draw a design. Go over the design with watercolor of two different values. White crayon is especially good for this.

- *Glazing.* Colors are made darker by beginning with a light color, then after the paint has dried slightly, more pigment is added to intensify it. If using *drawing* paper, this can be overdone.

- *Even Wash.* Paint even horizontal brush strokes of the same value across the section.

- *Graduated Wash.* Select one hue. Paint the darkest value at the top, then dilute the brush slightly and overlap the darkest place. Dilute again, then make another stripe. Continue diluting with water until there is almost no color at the bottom. Great for skies.

- *Sea Salt.* Use two analogous (for example: red, orange, or yellow) colors to cover an area with paint. While it is wet, sprinkle the watercolor with sea salt (or Kosher salt). Allow the salt to dry completely before brushing it off.

- *Dry Brush.* Remove most of the water from the brush before dipping it in pigment. Brush it on newspaper before applying it to the watercolor paper to remove most of the liquid. Drag the tip of the brush across the section, leaving streaks of pigment. Excellent for fur or grass.

- *Printing or painting with cardboard.* Dip the edge of a small piece of cardboard into watery mixed pigment in the lid of the paintbox. Drag the paint on the paper with the cardboard, or use the edge of it to print details such as fences, bricks, shingles, or windows.

- *Sponge printing.* Dip a small piece of sponge into watercolor and use it to print details such as tree leaves or clouds.

- *Plastic wrap or bubble wrap.* To make rocks, apply pigment and, while it is wet, use crumpled plastic wrap to press into the surface, leaving it in place to dry. Bubble wrap laid across a wet surface and left for a time gives an entirely different effect.

- *Scratch into dry paint.* When an area is completely dry, use a sharp instrument, such as scissors, to scrape detail into an area, or remove pigment altogether for highlights.

- *Blotting.* Use paper towel to blot areas of wet paint.

2. When the paint has dried, use black marker to label the sections. Computer-printed lettering could be placed underneath each section for tracing.

PROJECT 4–10
WEAVING WITH THE HAPPY ACCIDENT

FOR THE TEACHER   Taking advantage of the happy accident is a familiar technique for watercolorists, and many of them tilt their paper to encourage drips and runs, or spatter the paper with dark values or white opaque paint. They blot it; scrape it; print on it with sponges; use a comb to create texture; use masking tape, crayon, rubber cement, or mastic as resists. **NOTE: Use rubber cement only in a well-ventilated room and not at all for students under 12 years of age.**

Students will compose their paintings with lights and darks. Tell the students that after their paper has dried, they will be cutting it up to make an entirely different composition by weaving the paper.

Vocabulary

harmony

variety

emphasis

texture

form

shape

warp

weft

Preparation   Before the weaving portion of this project, students should prepare two 12 × 18-inch sheets of paper or one 18 × 24-inch sheet cut in half. If time allows, they may make several sheets, keeping the best composition simply as an Expressionistic watercolor. Talk with students about artists whose work was Expressionistic, such as "stain painters" Helen Frankenthaler and Kenneth Noland. Allow students to paint to music to inspire them to use rhythmic gestures or to create emphasis.

Alternative Projects

LANDSCAPE OR SEASCAPE   Use the wet-in-wet technique to paint cool colors such as blue, green, or violet horizontally on a piece of 9 × 12-inch watercolor paper. When it is dry, tell students to tear the paper horizontally toward themselves to create a white edge along the torn surface. Mount three pieces together on a cool-colored construction paper background to make "hills" or "waves." Draw on these with fine-line black marker to make trees, small houses, ships.

WOVEN PAPER BASKET   Students of Leigh Mincks of the North Kirkwood Middle School, St. Louis County, Missouri make woven baskets with watercolored paper. The paper is painted on both sides before cutting into even strips. The weaving begins by interweaving strips in the center to make the bottom, then bending these up to form the weft and weaving around the sides of the basket. The baskets are then decorated inside and out with found objects such as buttons, pearls, or fringed paper.

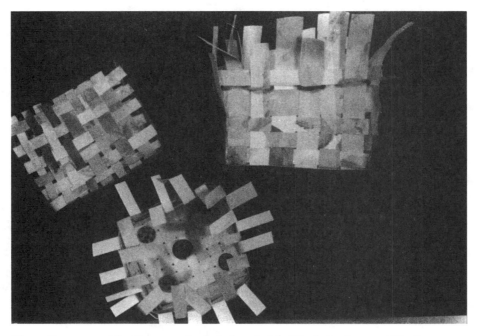

These "happy accident" woven baskets fromLeigh Mincks's classes at North Kirkwood Middle School, St. Louis County, Missouri include strategically placed "extras" such as buttons, woven yarn, glitter, or jewels.

Nine Anemones, 20th century, Emil Hansen Nolde, Watercolor, Bequest of John S. Newberry, © The Detroit Institute of Arts. Although Emil Nolde's work was anything but accidental, he exploited the fluid qualities of watercolor.

PROJECT 4–10   WEAVING WITH THE HAPPY ACCIDENT

Materials

watercolor or white construction paper

watercolors

brushes

paper towels

yarn

raffia

miscellaneous materials for changing the surface: crayons, cotton swabs, sea salt
(or table salt), combs, watercolor pencils, toothbrushes, X-acto® knives,
nails, scissors, feathers, masking tape, eye droppers, sponges, rubbing alcohol (in a spray bottle)

Directions   You will be decorating paper through the happy accident
"method," which means that almost anything you use to change your paper is acceptable. It is still important to think about differences in light and dark areas (value), and
to emphasize some areas.

1. Decide before beginning whether you want to have a warm or cool color
    scheme, and limit yourself to only a few colors. Remember that you can
    make these lighter or darker by adding more or less water. If the composi-
    tion calls for it, you might also use a complementary color for emphasis.

2. Prepare the paper through such techniques as varying the intensity of water-
    color pigment, wet-in-wet, dry-brush, blotting, scraping with the brush han-
    dle or scissors, spattering, stippling (creating dots with the end of the brush),
    tilting the paper to make drips, spritzing with alcohol, or making watercolor
    resist through the use of crayon, masking tape, mastic, or rubber cement.

3. Allow the paper to dry overnight. Tear or cut the paper into strips of varying
    widths. If you tear it, you can make a white border on one side of the strips.
    In weaving, whether it is with paper or yarn, establish the warp (vertical
    strips) first. Lay the vertical strips side by side. Some of these will be wide,
    some narrow. Lay them on a strip of masking tape placed underneath the
    top edge to hold them together.

4. Start at the top and do an in-and-out (tabby) weave going horizontally, vary-
    ing the width of the horizontal strips. Instead of having this a purely flat
    weaving, as you weave, pull some of the strips up to make a loop big
    enough for your finger to fit inside, then continue weaving. Sometimes you
    might have loops all the way across one strip (you may have to glue two
    similar strips of paper to do this).

5. You might even center a length of yarn on a strip and weave strips of yarn
    across at the same time you are weaving the paper. Or simply weave the
    yarn by itself (forming loops as you go).

6. When you have finished weaving, push the strips toward the top to make
    sure they are tight. Then glue the ends of the weft (crosswise) strips to the
    warp strips front and back.

PROJECT 4–11
DRESSED FOR SPORT, A SELF-PORTRAIT

FOR THE TEACHER   Self-portraits have been painted by most painters because they are their own most willing models! Artists often draw themselves while looking in a mirror, holding a palette. They often are in special clothing, or show a background that tells something about themselves. Artists whose portraits are of special interest are Henri Rousseau, Marc Chagall, Rembrandt, and Albrecht Durer. Discuss self-portraits with the students, and talk about how the clothing and background selected tells something about the artist.

Vocabulary

emphasis

balance

proportion

depth

contrast

detail

value

resist

space

intensity

dominance

Preparation   Let this project follow brief lessons of students drawing their own faces while looking in a mirror (or working from their own school photos if you don't have mirrors). Help them to notice the general egg shape of the head, that the eyes are located halfway down. Demonstrate how to draw the nose by showing the lines between the eyes and the nostrils, and point out how the most noticeable part of the mouth is the dark line between and extending beyond the lips. Point out value differences in hair, how it grows, and how to draw it. Have them feel where their ears are in relationship to their eyes and noses. (One colleague says she prefers *not* to use mirrors with older students because they become *too* preoccupied with their own images.)

At a young age children become aware of uniforms and sports clothing worn when participating in some activities. Even such non-team activities as ice skating, gymnastics, ballet, roller blading, building a snowman, swimming, ice skating or bicycling call for special clothing or protective headgear. Playing "catch" outside might require a baseball glove and hat. Talk with students about seasonal sports, and help them to become aware of the clothing that they wear for these activities.

Interdisciplinary Connections
HEALTH AND PHYSICAL EDUCATION
PICK A SPORT Discuss appropriate dress for a variety of sports, rules, safety gear, sportsmanship.

DESIGN A SCOREBOARD Pretend a wealthy person or a soft-drink company has offered to pay for a scoreboard for your favorite sport. Design one that will allow for the teams' names, scores, time, etc.

This action drawing by Carolyn Baker's students at the Shenandoah Valley School in St. Louis County, Missouri stresses the use of pattern in clothing.

This tempera painting from Beth Goyer's student at Holman Middle School, St. Louis County, Missouri, shows a youngster enjoying winter sports.

Libby Cravens's students of the Claymont School in St. Louis County, Missouri drew themselves as cowboys ready for a ride.

PROJECT 4–11 DRESSED FOR SPORT, A SELF-PORTRAIT

STUDENT PAGE

Materials

white drawing or watercolor paper

crayons

pads of newspaper

watercolors

brushes

bowls for clean and dirty water

paper towels for cleaning brushes

Directions   This self-portrait will be a combination of crayon and watercolor (a watercolor-resist). Think about yourself, your favorite season of the year, and the sports that you can do in that season. In the warm seasons you swim, inline skate, play ball, go barefoot, bicycle. If you live where there is snow in the winter, you might ice skate, go sledding, play ice hockey.

1. You are the dominant person here. Draw yourself so large that the paper is almost filled. You might even make yourself so large that only half your figure is visible. You could place friends or teammates, a goal, or a house far off in the distance.

2. Of course, you want to draw your face and hair so we recognize you, but also think about what you are wearing. If you have a uniform, a hat, or special clothing, try to draw every detail that you can think of on that clothing. Does it have zippers, pockets, quilting, a collar, cuffs? Even the stitching can be shown.

3. Firmly outline and put details on your drawing with crayon. You need to leave enough wax from the crayon on the paper so that it will *resist* the watercolor. When you have finished the crayon drawing, brush off the excess before beginning to paint.

4. Paint over the crayon drawing with watercolor, varying the intensity of the color. Be aware that if you go over the paint too often, the paper begins to ball up. You may even prefer to leave some areas unpainted.

PROJECT 4–12
SUNFLOWERS AND IRISES

FOR THE TEACHER   A painting lesson about flowers gives you a chance to teach about Vincent van Gogh and his obsession with light and working outdoors.

Note: Prang® Payons™ or Holbein Water-soluble Crayons may be used to color dry paper. When clear water is added with a brush, the crayons dissolve to resemble watercolor. These crayons may also be used to draw on paper that has been wetted.

Vocabulary

still-life

variety

watercolor crayons

Preparation
Show students a reproduction of van Gogh's paintings of irises or of sunflowers. Try to time this project for a season when sunflowers, irises, or wildflowers are available. (**Note:** Funeral homes sometimes will save flowers for you if you contact them in advance and request them.) Silk flowers are also an acceptable substitute. Place containers of the flowers close to small groups of students so they can really paint from observation. Have them look carefully to see that some of the flowers will be in buds. Students might do only the portion of the flower that they actually see. If circumstances allow, show students flowers or weeds growing in the ground. Point out variations in colors to the students and encourage them to color vigorously, combining colors before adding the water. (This is based on a project developed by practice teacher Jennifer Feise when working with Marla Mayer at Highcroft Ridge Elementary School in St. Louis County, Missouri.)

Adaptations for Younger Students
Have students accordion-fold a piece of 12 × 18-inch drawing paper in fourths horizontally to make a "book" about sunflowers. On the first page they may draw a seed being planted; on the second page, the seedling coming up; on the third page; a half grown plant and bud; and on the fourth page, a fully open sunflower. If students have learned to write, they can print an explanation at the bottom of each page.

Alternative Project
GIANT FLOWERS   Georgia O'Keeffe's giant flowers are also a source of inspiration for students. When forced to look closely at a flower, they have an appreciation for the exquisite details they see. Suggest they force their flower to "bump the edges" or run off the page, or to make their flower so large that only a portion of it shows.

Interdisciplinary Connections
SCIENCE

PLANT YOUR SUBJECT   Allow students to plant their own sunflower seeds or bulbs either indoors or outdoors. Many elementary schools have a small garden plot and outdoor learning center. Planting bulbs in the fall gives students something to look forward to for the spring, or plant sunflower seeds in the spring for a fall crop.

BOTANICAL DRAWING   Students can draw a flower carefully, then identify its various parts by writing directly on the page, in the manner of a scientific botanical drawing.

LANGUAGE ARTS

TELL ME ABOUT VAN GOGH   Students might enjoy researching the lives of several Impressionists and Post-Impressionists, making posters for the entire class to use. These could include a brief biography, a photocopy of the artist, a photocopy of samples of the artist's work, and the student's painting based on the work of that artist.

PROJECT 4–12 SUNFLOWERS AND IRISES

STUDENT PAGE

Materials

12 × 18-inch or 18 × 24-inch drawing paper

watercolor crayons or Payons™

brushes

newspaper

Directions Vincent van Gogh loved to paint in the outdoors. He painted fields of growing crops, and was especially fond of painting sunflowers and irises.

1. Look carefully at the flowers you will be drawing. You may draw the flowers in a vase on a table, or as if they are growing in the ground. Plan the composition carefully before you begin. Use your finger to "trace" the flowers on the paper, thinking where you will place the largest flowers. Think about how you will use the space.

2. Draw the flowers (using watercolor crayons).

    Irises. Irises can be almost any color, but some are a combination of white and purple petals. Flowers that are one hue will still have light, middle, and dark values on each petal, and often have a fuzzy yellow area on the inside of the lowest petals.

    Sunflowers. Although they are basically yellow, if you look closely, you will see the petals also have areas that are green or orange. Some of the shadowed areas in the flower might also be interesting if you add a little violet to the petals. The centers might be green or brown. Although you will be coloring the stems and leaves green, they will be more interesting if you also combine blue and yellow with the green.

3. If you decide to draw your flowers in a vase, don't forget that your container is resting on a table. Draw a line on the page that will represent the table, to avoid having the flowers simply "float" on the background.

4. When you are satisfied that you have applied enough color with the watercolor crayon, dip the brush in clean water and apply it on top of your drawing. The watercolor crayons will dissolve to appear like a watercolor. To emphasize an area, you can draw into the wet areas with these crayons to add more color.

Drawn from *Sunflowers*, 1888, Vincent van Gogh

Drawn from *Irises*, 1899, Vincent van Gogh

INK

Drawing ink, which was used by the Romans, continues as a popular medium today. Black permanent inks such as India, China, and Japanese (Sumi) inks are made from carbon pigment such as lampblack combined with a wetting agent and a preservative. Inks are popular for washes or to be used in combination with watercolor. From Roman times until the 1900s, brown inks—sepia (made from cuttlefish) or bistre (from burned beechwood)—were also popular and frequently used by such artists as Rembrandt van Rijn and Peter Paul Rubens, but these were not so lightfast as the black inks. An example of a brown ink drawing is the Vincent van Gogh drawing seen here. Washes, applied with a brush, are often used in combination with strokes from a pen, bamboo pen, sharpened sticks, or bamboo skewers.

Inks also come in a variety of colors, and are popular for illustration or artworks where permanence is not of great importance. Some opaque colored inks are considered permanent and fadeless. Some of the "dye-inks" (such as Dr. Martin's Dyes) are concentrated and can give startling effects.

Because of the popularity and ease of use of markers, ink is primarily used today for calligraphy or in doing Sumi-e Japanese painting. When working with ink, caution students to always hold the bottle on the table while removing the cap. If using permanent inks, have students wear smocks. Insist they clean and dry pens and brushes before returning them to you.

The Harvest, 1888, Vincent van Gogh, pen and brown ink over graphite, 12$\frac{1}{2}$ × 9$\frac{1}{2}$ inches, National Gallery of Art, Washington, DC, Collection of Mr. and Mrs. Paul Mellon

PROJECT 4–13
THE THREE PERFECTIONS: ASIAN CALLIGRAPHY, POETRY, AND PAINTING

FOR THE TEACHER In China, all civil servants were trained as scholars, and among their accomplishments were what they called the *Three Perfections:* calligraphy, poetry, and painting. Poet–painter societies might go out to the country for the day to paint, write poetry, and admire each other's work. Owners of scrolls displayed their work to others. The viewer of a work of art might actually write a poem directly on a scroll and then affix a personal seal in red. Writing was done vertically and from right to left, exactly the opposite of Western writing (the vertical columns were possibly a result of originally writing on flattened vertical sections of bamboo). Horizontal scrolls were sometimes 18 feet long. Paintings were also done on long, vertical rectangles. These were usually mounted on paper-backed silk. The *Four Treasures*—brushes, inksticks, inkstones, and paper—were used in these scholarly pastimes.

Subject matter varied, but often portrayed landscape such as mountains, a waterfall, farmland, lakes, trees, or streams. In such paintings, people were quite small. Other favorite themes included portraiture, *100 Children Playing*, cats, tigers, monkeys, fish, bamboo, flowers, and trees.

Modern Asian painters choose a variety of subject matter and ways of presenting it. Historically, however, painters used styles and symbols that were understood by everyone who looked at the artwork. In fact, imitating someone else's style was considered a valid way to learn to paint. Brushstrokes even had specific names. Painters and calligraphers patiently learned to do certain strokes perfectly by repetition and practice.

Vocabulary

value

line

shape

perfection

strokes

characters

seal

Preparation Show students the "look" of Far Eastern painting from slides or reproductions in a book. Have them observe the differences between Asian and Western paintings. Point out how portraits seldom have a background, and how simplified most paintings are. Subject matter (often of nature) was frequently symbolic. Certain trees, flowers, birds, and bamboo represent different ideas or seasons of the year. For example, cranes and pine trees used together represented old age.

There are 40,000 characters in the Chinese alphabet, which was said to have been invented in 2000 B.C. If you are fortunate, you may have a resource (a parent or a book) from which you could write a few Chinese characters for students to practice. If Chinese characters are not available for copying, students could write their own names or a poem with fine-line marker, using the font shown on the student page.

Students can "engrave" a Chinese character on a personal seal formed from plasticine clay (use a toothpick) or an argum eraser (use a nail). This can be stamped from a red stamp pad or a folded paper towel on which red tempera has been poured.

Adaptations for Younger Students

CHINESE FABLE Tell students a Chinese fable and ask them to illustrate it. Even young children do delightful watercolor, and can be taught to do one or two simple Chinese characters. Mount these small works of art together on a long piece of wallpaper to form a scroll. For the seal, have them paint their initials inside a 1-inch square with red paint.

These tools are similar to those used by Chinese scholar–painters. Clockwise: ink and inkstone, brushes, box for inkstone, liquid ink, cinnabar paste, and individual alabaster seal (square form).

Scholars and Waterfall, 1947, Yang Shanshen, hanging scroll: ink and color on paper, 38³/₄ × 15 inches, Museum purchase, by exchange, Saint Louis Art Museum

PROJECT 4–13 THE THREE PERFECTIONS: ASIAN CALLIGRAPHY, POETRY, AND PAINTING

STUDENT PAGE

Materials

newspaper

rice paper

9 × 18- or 18 × 24-inch drawing
or watercolor paper

India ink

small foam butcher trays

water containers (2 per station)

paper towels

brushes

wallpaper

glue sticks

dowels

art gum erasers

1-1/2- to 2-inch nails

red ink pad (or red paint on a sponge)

fine-line black markers

Drawn from *Composing Poetry on a Spring Outing*
(detail), c. 1189–1225, Ma Yuan, Nelson–Atkins
Museum of Art, Kansas City, Missouri

Directions   Pretend you are an Asian painter–poet, and you are going to go out into the country with your friends and have an *artistic* afternoon. You will paint either what you see or from your imagination. You may even write a poem about your work, or about the work of your friends.

1. As Chinese calligraphers and painters used to do, sit straight forward with both feet flat on the floor. Hold the brush straight up and down in order to be able to use the tip of it. Wet the brush and use your fingers, or wipe off excess water on the container to make a point on the brush. If you wish to have a "wash," leave more water on the brush. Make the strokes once. Try not to go over an area once it is covered. Keep the painting simple.

2. On a practice sheet of paper, make different values (shades) of wash and line drawings. Apply a light wash, then draw into it with the tip of the brush and undiluted ink (wet-on-wet). Try dry-brushing the ink. Wipe the brush with a paper towel from time to time. If you have Chinese alphabet characters, try calligraphy with the tip of the brush. Or write your own name vertically using the "fake Chinese" alphabet that is shown here.

3. Decide on a subject before beginning the painting. A *very light* drawing should be made on the paper before painting. In Chinese landscapes people often were quite tiny, and the scene was dominated by mountains, water, and trees. In portraits, which were done vertically, the figure fills the page,

with almost nothing in the background. An animal might be portrayed large, with something such as a branch to fill a corner, but still quite a bit of open space.

4. Draw a Chinese "seal" on an art gum eraser. Use a nail to make a design (it could be your initials drawn *backwards*). When you have finished the painting, use the tip of the brush (or fine-line black marker) to make your name on the upper right corner, printing vertically. Below your name, use the seal and carefully impress it one time (the seal is usually in red).

5. If you wish to share your painting with a fellow artist, have that person also write a name or poem vertically (and small), and stamp his or her personal seal. The writing is always done only at the edges, and some paintings have up to 15 or 20 "poems" and seals.

ABCDEFGHIJKLMNOP
QRSTUVWXYZ

PROJECT 4–14
JAPANESE SUMI-E:
SEVEN SHADES OF BLACK

FOR THE TEACHER Sumi-e (literally "pictures with ink") is primarily a Japanese form of painting that has very specific methods to follow. The same general materials are needed for Sumi-e that would be used in Chinese painting, and they differ very little. Japanese paintings are also done in scroll form, and are sometimes presented on six-fold screens. Gold paper is sometimes used as a background rather than rice paper. These paintings are often quite spare, with simple designs and quite a bit of open space. The reverence for nature and its beauty is explored to its fullest in Sumi-e painting.

Vocabulary

value

line

form

space

variety

balance

Preparation Ink may be purchased in liquid form for use in the classroom, and a watercolor brush that will form a point is an acceptable substitute for a bamboo brush. Students should practice making both line drawings and graduated washes, as these are both used in this form of painting. A Japanese painter once said that there are seven shades of black. Have students experiment in making seven different values with ink, using both wash and line techniques. Practicing with the traditional brushstrokes shown with the student page will aid in simplifying the application of paint. Watercolor is an effective substitute for traditional Japanese pigments.

Find postcards and reproductions in books of typical Asian painting. Discuss ink stones and ink, seals, brushes, rice paper, and scrolls, and the place of the artist–poet in Asian society. Explain the niche set aside in Japanese homes (the *Tokonoma*) for the display of a beautiful scroll and perhaps a simple flower arrangement.

Interdisciplinary Connections
LANGUAGE ARTS
HAIKU POETRY Invite students to write a haiku poem to accompany their painting. It should be written rather small, near an upper edge. (Refer to Section 2, "Writing About Art.")

Multicultural Connections
THE ASIAN PAINTING TRADITION Students can compare and contrast landscape paintings done in the Eastern cultures with those done in Western cultures. Help students notice differences in color, space, value, subject matter, etc. Discuss the value ancient Eastern societies placed on the written word, the beauty of nature, and poetry. Ask for comparisons to Western standards.

These llamas were captured in the Sumi-e watercolor technique by artist Mahala Cox. Collection of the author.

Old Badger in Misty Bamboo, early 20th century, Okoku Konnshima, ink on silk, hanging scroll, $56\frac{1}{2} \times 20$ inches, Mr. and Mrs. Oliver M. Langenberg Endowment and Museum Shop Fund, Saint Louis Art Museum

PROJECT 4–14   JAPANESE SUMI-E: SEVEN SHADES OF BLACK

STUDENT PAGE

Materials

newspaper

rice paper

9 × 18- or 18 × 24-inch paper

India ink

small foam butcher trays

water containers (2 per station)

paper towels

brushes

wallpaper or wrapping paper

glue sticks

dowels

art gum erasers

$1\frac{1}{2}$- to 2-inch nails

red ink pad (or red paint on a sponge)

fine-line black markers

Directions

1. The standard hand position for line drawing is to hold the brush halfway up the handle, with the thumb and forefinger in front and the middle finger behind (as in holding a pencil). Hold the brush vertically, using the tip for drawing lines. For a wash, add water and hold the brush at an angle. To allow freedom of movement, keep the arm off the table.

2. On a separate piece of paper, practice making circles and curved marks in a *graduated wash* (dark on one side and light on another) with the brush. These should be made in one stroke, without overlapping. The brush is cleaned in water, then the tip dipped in ink for a graduated wash. Practice making differences in lines by how hard you press on a brush or by using only the tip.

3. Use the brush to make a few of the following objects listed here: rocks, willow trees, branch with leaves, mountains, pine trees, rocks. In painting a tree, paint it the way the tree grows: first the trunk, then larger branches, smaller branches, twigs, and leaves.

4. Animals (cats, monkeys, raccoons, tigers), birds, butterflies, and fish are perfect subjects for Sumi-e. Decide whether *your* animals are the solitary kind (such as a cat or raccoon), or those that are normally found in groups, such as monkeys. Draw one or more animals. The animals are usually done with a combination of wash and line, and often a hint of their habitat is included. This might be a bamboo grove or a tree limb coming in at an angle. When your painting has dried, you may choose to add one or two soft colors over the ink.

5. Mount the finished painting on a vertical "scroll" of wrapping paper or wallpaper (that contains a small pattern), and fold down the top and bottom to insert a dowel or stick for hanging.

Traditional Japanese Brushstrokes

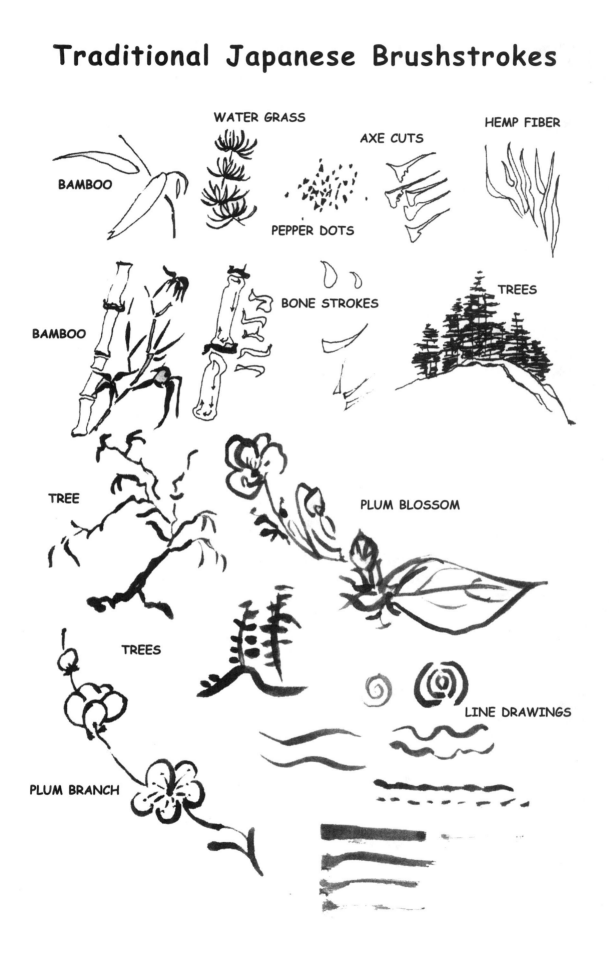

WATER GRASS

HEMP FIBER

AXE CUTS

BAMBOO

PEPPER DOTS

BAMBOO

BONE STROKES

TREES

TREE

PLUM BLOSSOM

TREES

LINE DRAWINGS

PLUM BRANCH

PROJECT 4–15
FANTASY/SURREALISTIC ART

FOR THE TEACHER   Artists often have been been compared to children for the sense of playfulness they show in their artwork. Fantasy and Surrealism are normal ingredients in the early art of many children, but unfortunately become lost as the children grow older.

Vocabulary

stream of consciousness writing

mixed media

collage

texture

contrast

Preparation
Show pictures of some fantasy artists throughout the history of art. Renaissance artist Arcimboldo did fantasy faces, and two artists whose work was often based on childhood memories were Marc Chagall and Salvador Dali. Other Surrealists were Giorgio de Chirico, Max Ernst, and René Magritte. Modern artists also create unlikely combinations, such as Meret Oppenheim's mink-lined teacup or Jeff Koons's giant *Energizer Bunny*. Talk about the concept of mixed media. It simply means that any combination of materials can be used by an artist. Suggest students may want to use portions of a previous artwork, one magazine cut-out, handmade paper, or any other collage materials for this project.

Suggestions for Leading Students to Surrealism

- Have every student write three nouns on three separate pieces of paper. Fold these and put them in a "hat." Then have each student pull three pieces of paper from the hat. Those three nouns would be the basis of the composition. (*Examples:* bicyle, ice cream cone, flower; car, grandmother, wristwatch).

- Have a student write three headings on a piece of paper: NOUNS, VERBS, ADJECTIVES. Without telling them what they will do, have the students make lists of at least six items under each heading. They then must select one item from each list from which to make a fantasy composition.

Interdisciplinary Connections
LANGUAGE ARTS
STREAM OF CONSCIOUSNESS WRITING Surrealism (a French word that literally means "above reality") was an outgrowth of a writing movement that explored the subconscious. Suggest students try writing words as they come to mind, allowing one word to lead to another, not even trying to make connections, but just as their minds constantly jump from one subject to another, allowing those thoughts to be put on paper. After a five-minute session, suggest they compose a sentence using at least three of the words they have written.

This artwork was created by eighth-grader Meghan Sullivan in Nancy Raleigh's art class at LaSalle Springs Middle School, St. Louis County, Missouri. Students' work was inspired by the fantasy art of Marc Chagall.

The Juggler, 1943, Marc Chagall, oil on canvas, 109.9 × 79.1 cm, Art Institute of Chicago, Gift of Mrs. Gilbert W. Chapman, © 1999 Artists Rights Society (ARS), New York/ADAGP, Paris. This painting shows that Marc Chagall was not concerned with objects being the "right" size. Chickens in the air, upside-down houses, people flying were all from memories of his Russian childhood.

PROJECT 4–15 FANTASY/SURREALISTIC ART

STUDENT PAGE

Materials

newsprint
drawing paper
pencils
materials for collage
tempera paint, marker, ink, colored pencils
scissors

Drawn from *The Librarian*, 1566,
Arcimboldo, Skokloster, Sweden

Directions   In creating an artwork from your
imagination, remember that it doesn't need to look real.
Fantasy or Surrealistic art comes from the imagination, and
can have a dreamlike quality where nothing really makes
sense. Here are some ways to approach a composition.

- Transform something real by combining it with something totally foreign (for example: a human form with a flower face; a car with feet instead of wheels).
- Take something real and have it do something "unreal." (Salvador Dali's melting watches would be a good example.)
- Make the subject much larger than anything else in the picture.
- Make a realistic background, with strange objects in the foreground.
- Select totally unrelated objects and group them together.

1. Draw several thumbnail pencil sketches on newsprint before trying your idea on good paper. Remember, you will probably have some wild ideas while you are doing these sketches. Sometimes you can combine several sketches to make a total composition.

2. You could enlarge some of the objects on newsprint, then cut them out and move them around to find where they look best before tracing around them. You can overlap objects or combine them.

Summer, Giuseppe Arcimboldo, 1563,
Kunsthistorisches Museum, Vienna

3. Make the main objects large enough so you don't have a tremendous amount of empty space. You might want to consider having size differences with a foreground, middle-ground, and background.

4. Paint or color the composition, considering that color can be used to make something stand out or be almost hidden. Although you may choose to make a realistic landscape in the background, remember that it is important not to just have objects "floating" in space.

Winter, Giuseppe Arcimboldo, 1563,
Kunsthistorisches Museum, Vienna

Unit 5

Printmaking

Printmaking is one of the staples of most elementary and middle school art programs. It ranges from basic stamping with thumbprints or "found" objects at the primary levels to more sophisticated relief printing such as the lino-cut at higher levels. It is this repetition and inherent building process that helps students develop confidence in their skills, and helps them become increasingly more adept as they get older.

Many well-known painters also make prints, enabling their work to be more widely seen. Listed here are some representative painter–printmakers: Jasper Johns, Sam Francis, Mary Cassatt, Pablo Picasso, Charles Sheeler, Stuart Davis, Edward Hopper, Yasuo Kunioshi, Ben Shahn, Louise Nevelson, Jim Dine, Robert Rauschenberg, Roy Lichtenstein, Andy Warhol, Romare Bearden, and Chuck Close.

Vocabulary

unity

variety

repetition

color

line

relief

collagraph

edition

emphasis

brayer

ink

printing press

baren

monoprint

printing plates

texture

These are the tools that would be commonly used in relief printmaking. Shown here are tubes of water-soluble ink, plastic for inking, brayer, and bench hook (for holding plate and to assist students in keeping their hands behind the cutting tools).

METHODS OF PRINTMAKING

Collage Prints   Commonly called collagraphs, these are made of a raised surface that, when inked, transfers differences in surface. Examples would be string prints, tagboard or corrugated cardboard cut-outs glued in place, or a variety of textures using cloth or paper. Most of these are varnished before inking to preserve the surface for many printings. Often the well-inked plate is as interesting as the print, and they are displayed side by side.

Embossed Prints   After a relief design has been created on a plate, but before ink has been added, dampened paper can be placed on the surface of the plate. It is then printed with sufficient pressure to force the paper into the recessed areas, giving a low-relief print.

An embossed print could later be sparingly hand-colored with a brayer or watercolor brush. Phyllis MacLaren's students in the University City School District in Missouri discovered that placing a piece of colored tissue paper between their printing plate and the dampened paper resulted in soft colors being transferred to the embossed print. Some of them then colored areas of the dried print with Prismacolor® pencil.

Monotype   A monotype literally means that it is the only one of its kind. A design can be painted with ink or paint on a surface such as plastic, then a damp piece of paper placed on top and the back of it rubbed to transfer the print. Another method is to completely ink the surface of glass or plastic, then place a piece of paper on it, and draw on the back of the paper with pencil to transfer ink from the plate to the print. A monotype can even be made by rubbing a paint design onto fingerprint paper, then placing clean paper on top of it, and rubbing on the back, thus transferring the design to the clean paper.

Monoprint   A monoprint is also one of a kind. However, it incorporates a traditional printing plate such as a relief print, etching, or lithograph, but is changed slightly each time it is printed. It can be printed on top of a monotype, or paint applied directly to the plate to give different effects.

Printing "Plates" for Monoprints or Monotypes   Plates can be made on paper, cardboard, Mylar, acrylic, unmounted linoleum, white-coated Masonite wall panels (cut to size), aluminum foil, or aluminum offset plates (sometimes available from newspaper printers at low cost). A new material, the flexible printing plate, can be cut with scissors and has an adhesive backing to allow it to be mounted on wood or cardboard. If the plate is to be run through a press, the edges of thicker materials must be beveled (sandpapered or scraped at a 30- to 45-degree angle). Fast-drying acrylic spray can be used to seal paper or cardboard before painting to prevent absorbing ink. A slick plate (such as Mylar) or sheet plastic can be coated with liquid detergent, starch, or gum arabic and allowed to dry. This can be painted on thickly with watercolor and printed onto dampened paper. The coating leaves less of the paint on the plate and therefore transfers more to the paper.

Relief Prints   Although technically a relief print can be anything that has a raised design such as fingerprints or glue-line prints, most relief prints are incised either by cutting or drawing into the surface of a plate. An effective relief print sometimes has as much as 50% of the surface white and the other 50% in color. Manufacturers have responded to needs of art teachers through innovations in materials and cutting tools. The following list contains some of the materials you can use for relief-printing:

- Foam meat trays, soap blocks, paraffin, plaster of Paris, erasers, or wood blocks
- Battleship linoleum, available in pre-cut sizes or 12-inch × 50- or 100-foot rolls. This material is suitable for older students, although they also enjoy using Soft-Kut Blocks®.
- Scratch Foam Board® Printing Plates can be shaped with scissors. Designs are impressed with ballpoint pens or sharpened dowels.
- Soft-Kut Blocks® range in size from 4 × 6 inches up to 12 × 18 inches. Some teachers purchase the largest blocks and cut them (with scissors) to the desired size for the students. These are worked with traditional cutting tools. Although expensive, both sides can be used.
- Flexible printing plates, 1/16-inch thick, have a smooth white surface that can be mounted on ordinary cardboard. Can be cut with traditional printmaking tools, scissors, or X-acto® knives. Art teacher Phyllis MacLaren has her students carefully remove the cut-away portion, gluing it onto a second piece of cardboard to print both the positive and negative designs on separate plates.

Rubbings (Frottage)   Rubbings made with crayon or candles on paper are frequently cut out and used as part of a collage, or used in a resist painting. Adapt various plastic texture screens, plastic ceiling fixtures, or mesh shelf covering (found at hardware stores). Textured plastic kits may be purchased at art supply houses or textured wallpaper samples can be mounted on tagboard for frequent reuse. Consider combining textures with brayer printing.

Serigraphy (Silkscreen Print)   Prepared silkscreens are available in many sizes. They consist of a wooden frame over which a fine cloth such as silk, organza, or nylon filament is stretched and attached with staples. A small amount of washable ink is placed on the silk inside the frame, then a squeegee is used to draw ink across the filament, leaving a fine coat of ink on a piece of paper placed underneath.

For the elementary school, you could substitute nylon hosiery stretched between embroidery hoops or use organdy stretched and taped on the underside of a box lid that has a rectangular hole cut in it. Use matboard pieces as squeegees to spread ink. The advantage to purchased screens is that they are reusable year after year.

Intaglio Printing (Etching Process)   This printing differs from most in that the ink is forced into the lines that have been etched or engraved into the surface. Ink is applied, and the surface of the plate is wiped clean. Damp paper forced into the inked recessed lines gives a print. This method includes engraving, drypoint, etching, aquatint, sugar-lift, soft ground, and hard ground.

Stamping   Almost anything that can be inked can be stamped. This would include fingers; sponges; found objects such as corks, forks, potato mashers, coins, buttons, toy car wheels, screw heads; dowels; bottoms cut from Christmas trees; leaves; cut vegetables (green pepper, carrots, potatoes are especially good); erasers; wood blocks covered with string or rubber bands; bubble wrap; jar lids; washers or keys glued on the ends of dowels; plastic of almost any kind; Lego® blocks; berry baskets; wooden kitchen tools; even the bottoms of athletic shoes. You could make groupings of stamping items in trays, allowing students to use one grouping for approximately ten minutes before passing that tray to the next table.

While stamp pads are a nicety for small items, they are usually limited in color, and have to be re-inked frequently. Instead, use folded paper towels, large sponges, or 3/4-inch thick foam rubber carpet padding cut to fit a foamboard tray, keeping them "charged" with tempera (turning over from time to time, as the tempera seeps downward). To keep from drying out, simply cover with plastic wrap overnight. Or use a brush to *paint* ink or tempera onto the object for stamping.

These delightful "moving" figures were created in the fourth-grade classes of Beth Scott of Ross School, St. Louis County, Missouri. A large stencil was created of a figure in action, then the students used a sponge to stamp progressively lighter colors as they moved the stencil along to show action.

Stenciling   Use an X-acto® knife to cut designs in a piece of plastic or tagboard (oil the tagboard with vegetable oil if you plan to use it repeatedly; you can also purchase stencil paper). Simply use a sponge or a stenciling brush to apply paint, mostly working from the outside of the stencil opening toward the center. For stenciling large areas, tape stencils in place and use a spray bottle or pump-action bug sprayer filled with paint.

GENERAL INFORMATION

Inking Stations   The whole process of printmaking can be greatly simplified if you have an area for inking the plates, a separate area for actually printing, a third for placing wet prints, and a fourth for cleanup. Water-based inks are adequate for any need in elementary or middle school. This way you avoid having solvents in a classroom. The inks come in a wide variety of colors and can be mixed to provide interesting results.

To avoid chaos when an entire class is inking, set up each work station with one color of ink, having the brayer remain with the ink color rather than having to be washed out if the student wishes to change color. Cover tables with paper and use washable inking plates (heavy-duty plastic, metal bench-hooks, or glass).

Mess Control   Ideally water is used only at the end of the hour, no matter what age your students. If each student has a brayer, it is relatively easy to have each one return a brayer to you that has been cleaned, washed, and dried. To avoid last-minute pile-up at the sink, fill two trays or buckets with water and put them and paper towels on newspaper on a table near the sink. Students can wash and dry the inking plates, their own printing plates, brayers, and brushes. If you have covered the tables with newspaper, students can throw away the newspaper and put out fresh for the next class.

Preparing Dampened Paper for Monoprinting or Embossing   To prepare paper immediately prior to printing, put a piece in a tub of water, place it between two blotters or clean sheets of newsprint, then remove excess water by using a rolling pin. You could use newspaper in place of blotters by placing the dampened paper between newsprint sheets to keep it clean. Large quantities of evenly dampened paper can be prepared the previous day by alternating damp and dry sheets and storing them in a plastic bag. The paper should not have shiny spots on it, which would indicate that it is still too wet in some areas.

Inking Techniques

- Remind students that the front of a print should be completely clean and free of fingerprints. You could encourage printing with a partner so one would have clean hands and handle the paper while the other takes care of inking. Or make a "grabber" of a 1 X 3-inch piece of matboard folded in half.

- Caution students to squeeze ink from the bottom of the tube, and to put out a "toothpaste-on-a-toothbrush" amount at a time (approximately 1 teaspoon). Put someone at each table in charge of collecting ink and putting lids on properly, as well as flattening the partially empty tubes from the bottom.

- When inking the print, use a brayer to distribute a small amount of ink until it has a tacky sound, a "snap." The brayer should *roll*, not slide. If the ink is too thick, it affects the surface of the print and fills in all the lines. It may be necessary to coat the plate several times to get enough ink on it. You may notice that a second or third print is better than the first one because the plate is well "charged."

- Ink can also be applied by using scraps of matboard to "card" ink onto a plate. Simply get ink on the bottom edge of a piece of matboard and drag the ink across the surface. This is not so satisfactory as a brayer, but sometimes one must improvise.

Multiple Color Prints   Some teachers prefer for students to mix their colors with the brayer to make the plate more interesting. Although this would mean you would need enough brayers for everyone in the class to have one, it would give them more flexibility. To change color, students can mostly empty a brayer of color by rolling it on the plate, then newspaper, then simply roll it in a new color. Sometimes after a plate has been printed, a second or third color is added. Another method of using more than one color is to make a *rainbow roll* by placing small amounts of two or three colors side by side at the top of the inking plate, then using the brayer to go straight down the plate, allowing the colors to mix where they overlap. This is somewhat wasteful of ink, but if students do it carefully, the rainbow can be used several times.

Registration   When the same piece of paper is printed more than one time, registration (lining up the plate on the paper to match) is important.

Printing Techniques   The tried-and-true techniques of using the back of a spoon, a baren (a round, flat Japanese tool that is used for rubbing on the back of a relief print), rubbing with the hand, placing the paper on the floor and standing on the back of the plate, using a Rubbing Stick™ that has a flat surface on the bottom (a new tool available through art supply stores), or using old-fashioned wringer are all effective methods for transferring prints. Students can improve pressure by pressing down firmly with both hands.

Signing Prints   Printmaking is a technique that is several hundred years old. Some traditions continue to be followed by modern printmakers. An *edition* of prints signifies that a certain number of identical prints are made from the same plate. These are always signed in *pencil* directly under the print, with the artist's signature on the right, and a number on the left side or middle. A title might be written on the left side.

An edition is numbered with the left number signifying the order in which the print was made, and the right number signifying the number of prints made. For example, a number of 3/7 means that this was the third of seven prints made. If different colored prints are made from the same plate, these are signed AP in the center, which means "artist's proof."

Storing Plates   If linoleum plates will be reprinted, they should be washed and dried. Allow them to dry thoroughly before stacking them for storage; otherwise, they will stick together. Even though they may curl, eventually they will flatten. For a collagraph plate, allow it to dry with the ink on it. Sometimes the inked plate is as interesting as the print.

This print, by artist Joan Larson, demonstrates the traditional method of signing a print.

Transferring a Design   If the original drawing is done in soft pencil and you are working on Soft-Kut Blocks®, simply turn the design pencil-side down on the plate and press firmly around the lines to transfer it. Then redraw the design directly on top of the plate. Linoleum is harder, so it may be necessary to scribble on the back of the original design, then redraw from the front to transfer it. Another method is to place transfer paper or carbon paper between the original design and the plate, then redraw.

Prints are backwards! Students sometimes insist they want to use words. They are difficult to cut out, but sometimes students cannot be talked out of them. Allow them to write the letters normally, but turn the design over so it will be transferred onto the plate *backwards* from the original drawing. If they hold their design to a window, they can trace over the lines on the front, thus having graphite front and back.

What to Print On   Just about anything! . . . drawing or block-printing paper, kraft paper, graph paper, rice paper, paper decorated with watercolor, paper that has been decorated with a brayer, cloth, T-shirts, on top of colored magazine pictures, fadeless paper, wrapping paper, plastic overhead transparencies (mounted later on colored fadeless paper).

Improving a Print   Although purists accept the print "as is," it isn't a sacred object, and sometimes can be much improved with minor changes, such as:

- Combine prints with other materials to make a collage.
- Neatly cut two prints into equal strips, one horizontally and one vertically, then weave them together.
- Reserve prints for overprinting later.
- Incorporate prints into a book.
- Draw on prints with ink, colored pencil, oil pastels or crayon, filling in blank areas with color or pattern.
- Emphasize certain areas with fluorescent paint.

What to Do When Prints are Done   For older students, request them to turn in at least six signed prints, with two prints using more than one method of printing (for example, combining brayer and stamping).

Have every student turn in one print to be mounted all together on one large sheet of butcher paper.

This group project was done at a workshop at the Saint Louis Art Museum under the direction of Sue Trent. Each participant made a drawing in Styrofoam, which was then printed on black paper. The separating lines were made with the edges of a piece of cardboard.

PROJECT 5–1
COLORFUL TILES

FOR THE TEACHER   This project is a variation on techniques with which most students are already familiar, so it can lead to exciting experimentation. Neither stamping nor painting with a brayer requires the prior preparation of a plate, and each is an interesting printing method. Combining the two gives rich, intricate surfaces.

Vocabulary

abstraction	Expressionism
brayer	line
stamping	radial
symmetry	balance
rhythm	variety
unity	movement
opaque	emphasis

Preparation   Brayer printing is fun for students as they find out that simple techniques can lead to the creation of beautiful paper. Demonstrate how to charge the brayer with ink and how to vary the results. To get students into the swing of brayer painting, lay out several long sheets of kraft paper on the floor or a large table and let everyone experiment printing brayer marks anyplace on the paper. Students could later use the same sheet of paper for experimenting with stamping.

Stamping is equally fun, and while random stamping leads to interesting results, this project emphasizes the techniques of repetition and symmetry. This method leads to geometric designs and patterns such as one might find on Turkish tiles. Let students use small mats to "select" a perfect portion for matting.

Alternative Projects

STAMPED CITYSCAPE Cut the brayer-printed paper into rectangles of various shapes to represent buildings. Have students arrange and glue these on a plain background. If they wish, they can glue additional cut-outs of the printed paper onto some of the buildings *prior* to stamping. Use found objects or stamps made from art-gum erasers to print with black or white ink. Make decorative details such as doors, windows, columns, and "gingerbread."

ABSTRACT EXPRESSIONIST PRINTING Students are sometimes uncomfortable when just "making a design." Expose students to work by Abstract Expressionists of the 1940s, 1950s, and 1960s whose artwork showed greater concern with line, shape, and composition than with specific subject matter. The techniques in this project could be used to make an Abstract Expressionist print in the manner of Franz Kline, Hans Hofmann, Jackson Pollock, Robert Motherwell, Willem de Kooning, or Jean Dubuffet.

The stamping with found objects done by Debbie McConnell's kindergarten students at Barretts School, St. Louis County, Missouri, was done on painted rather than brayer-applied shapes, but shows how resourceful students can be.

Libby Craven's students at Claymont School, St. Louis County, Missouri, used the brayer printing as a background for action pictures.

PROJECT 5–1   COLORFUL TILES

Materials

kraft paper

viewfinders (tagboard with 8-inch squares cut from the center)

soft and hard brayers

inking plates

polymer medium or thinned white glue

Pritt® or Ross® art paste

12 X 18-inch drawing paper

stamping tools: hands, sponges, erasers, metal objects, Popsicle sticks, dowels, jar lids

tempera paint

chalk

sponges or paper towels to hold ink for stamp printing

containers for mixing tempera

Directions

1. Combine the tempera with polymer medium or Pritt® or Ross® art paste. Use brushes to transfer a small amount to an inking plate, then use a brayer to spread it to inking consistency prior to transferring it onto a piece of paper.

2. Printing with a brayer allows you to experiment with many different techniques:

   - Print first with a soft brayer, then a hard one. The two different consistencies printed on top of each other will give a soft, layered effect.
   - *Plaid.* Print one line horizontally at the top of the paper, then a different color vertically. Alternate vertical and horizontal lines until you get to the bottom of the paper.
   - *Swirls.* Hold one end of the brayer in place and swirl the other end around in a circle.
   - *Lines.* Print only with one edge of the brayer.
   - *Interrupted lines.* Apply ink only to one side of the brayer.
   - *White lines within brayer marks.* After inking the brayer, use a pencil to draw on it.
   - *Repeat patterns.* Glue string in a design on paper, then tape the paper onto the brayer before inking.

3. After the background has been printed with a brayer, use a viewfinder (piece of paper with an 8-inch square cut from the center) to find the two most beautiful portions of your design. Draw around the inside of the viewfinder with a piece of chalk. These two squares will be your tiles.

4. The design you will stamp on the tiles can be *radial* (starting at a point in the center and going in a circular design), *symmetrical* (divided in the center, and the same on two or four sides), or *rhythmic* (stamping repeatedly in a pattern). Use one stamping tool on top of another to make interesting combinations. Use colors that contrast with the background so the stamped designs will stand out.

5. When your design is finished, neatly cut it out. Mount the best of the two prints on colored construction paper. Keep the scraps of printed paper to be used later as part of a collage.

PROJECT 5–2
RELIEF PRINTS

FOR THE TEACHER   Show students reproductions of the work of some of the great European wood-cut artists such as Paul Gauguin, Albrecht Durer, and Kathe Kollwicz. The Japanese ukiyo-e prints that depicted everyday life and interests of the ordinary person popularized printmaking and were a great influence on the prints of the Impressionists. Pablo Picasso made many linoleum relief prints.

The most common relief print in schools is the lino-cut. This method is recommended for students fifth grade or older. In this technique, a V-shaped line is cut into the surface of a piece of linoleum, Soft-Kut®, or wood. When the surface of the plate is inked, the area that is cut away remains white. Part of the charm of a lino-cut are the lines that remain in some of the cut-away areas as a result of the cutting techniques.

Vocabulary

relief print

positive space

negative space

symmetry

Preparation

Set up inking stations by covering tables with newspaper. Tell students they are not allowed to throw away any prints, as they may be cut up and used later in collages or book-making. If you do not have a drying rack, have each student put a name on a piece of newspaper on the floor or hall where prints will be placed to dry to be gathered up later.

Demonstrate how to squeeze ink onto the inking surface so it is not too thick. At the same time, explain the necessity of squeezing from the bottom of the tube and of always replacing the cap on the tube. Demonstrate how to use a brayer and how to *charge* a plate for printing by inking first horizontally, then vertically. Then show students how to lay the paper on the inked plate and how to rub the back of the paper to transfer the print.

Draw an example on how to sign and number an edition and put it where it can be referred to when they are ready to sign (even the most mature students find this difficult to remember).

Alternative Projects

REPEAT PATTERN   Small plates, such as 2 × 3 or 3 × 3 inches, are ideal for printing an overall pattern on one large piece of paper. By carefully planning the design, an overall pattern will develop when one print meets the one above or below it. The plates are inked each time, then lined up to print repeatedly. A checkerboard pattern could also be created by leaving a blank space of the same size between each print (use a blank plate to mark where each print will be placed).

ERASER STAMP/WATERCOLOR MARKER   Eraser stamps can be used for repetitive patterns. Encourage students to use 4 × 6-inch cards to experiment with a variety of patterns using only one stamp. Color different portions of the stamp with watercolor markers and quickly stamp the design before the marker dries.

GROUP PRINT   For group prints, use the edge of a piece of matboard to stamp a decorative border and divisions on separate pieces of paper so each student will have a print to take home. This could be done using only one color of ink. Divide a piece of paper into as many sections as you have people in a group. For example, using 3 × 4-inch plates, nine students could each print their plates on nine pieces of 9 × 12-inch paper.

REDUCTION PRINT A *reduction-relief* print is created when a linoleum plate is printed in several colors, usually working from lighter colors underneath to darker colors on top of the original print. It is recommended that you begin with approximately six prints in the lightest color, then remove a portion of the plate before printing each time with a new color.

INCISED SOFT SURFACES Other methods of relief prints that take less time and do not require cutting tools rely on incising into the surface of a soft surface with a pencil or nail. Suitable materials are potatoes, artgum erasers, blocks of paraffin, commercially available foamboard or the bottom of foam meat trays, Styrofoam picnic plates (cut away the raised sides), plaster of Paris forms made in paper cups or oiled box lids, or squares made on glass using oil clay to make boxes.

Barber Shop Chord, 1931, Stuart Davis, lithograph on zinc, printed in black, 14 × 19 inches, The Museum of Modern Art, Gift of Abby Aldrich Rockefeller. Photograph © 1999, The Museum of Modern Art, New York.

Swiss Peasant—The Blacksmith, 1917, Ernst Ludwig Kirchner, 50 × 40 cm, woodcut, printed in black through rubbing, Art Institute of Chicago, Gift of Prints and Drawing Club.

PROJECT 5–2   RELIEF PRINTS

Materials

foam printing plates

pencils

ballpoint pens

ink

masking tape

newsprint

drawing paper (slightly larger than the printing plates)

brayers

Student Jennifer Watson's print reflects her own personal interests.

Directions

1. Make a series of small sketches the same shape as the printing plate you will use. Know in advance what you are going to scratch into the surface. When you have a design with which you are satisfied, redraw it on newsprint the exact size of the plate. Scribble over the back of the drawing with pencil and tape it to the plate.

2. Transfer your design by pressing firmly on the front of your drawing with a ballpoint pen or sharp pencil. Lift the corner of your drawing to make sure the design is transferring. When it is completed, remove the original drawing. To make sure the lines are deep enough, go over the printing plate with a pencil or pen.

3. Roll ink onto the plate with a brayer, going all the way to the edges. If your first print is a little light, just go back and re-ink. Remember that if you roll the ink on too thickly, it will fill in the lines and you won't see them on the print.

4. To print, place the plate face down onto the paper. Turn the paper over, holding the plate in place. Rub on the back of the paper to transfer the ink, giving even pressure all around the edges. You should do several prints while you are at it, and trade some with friends.

5. When the prints are dry, sign them in pencil directly underneath the print. The name goes on the right, and a title (if any) on the left. If the prints are all exactly the same color, you have printed an *edition* and the prints should be numbered. For example, 2/8 means that this was the second of eight prints made (the edition in this case is eight). AP (artist's proof) would be written in place of the numbers if each print is a different color.

PROJECT 5-3 PROVINCETOWN PRINTS

FOR THE TEACHER "Provincetown Prints" refers to relief-printed woodcuts that were made popular by a group of artists working in Provincetown, Massachusetts approximately 1914–1917, during and after World War I. The prints had a wider-than-usual white line, separating different areas. In contrast with most prints, which are done in one color, several colors of watercolor were painted on one plate before printing. Subjects were of local scenery and people, grazing cattle, washing hanging on a line, boats at the wharf, frame houses, flowers, and gardeners.

Vocabulary

genre

emphasis

Preparation Ask students what some "local" scenes are where they live. Soft-Kut Blocks® work very well for this technique, but it will also work on wood or battleship linoleum. Emphasize that the lines should be wider than usual to allow for the separation of colors. **SAFETY NOTE: Exercise every precaution, making sure the students understand that the non-cutting hand is always behind the knife. If possible, provide bench hooks that will keep the plate in place during cutting.** To make curved lines, the cutting tool is held facing forward and the plate is turned.

The plates can be inked in the traditional method discussed in the previous project, or by a method used by a colleague, Marilynne Bradley, formerly of the Webster Groves School District, St. Louis County, Missouri. Different colors can be applied with watercolor markers (which

The Violet Jug, 1919, Blanche Lazzell, 12 × 11½ inches, color woodcut, © The Detroit Institute of Arts. This multi-colored Provincetown woodcut is typical, showing areas of varied color, separated by wide white lines.

quickly dry). The printing is done on dampened paper. To prepare paper as needed, one sheet at a time, put wet paper between two blotters, using a rolling pin to roll out excess water. The paper should not have shiny spots on it. To prepare evenly dampened paper in advance as printmakers do, wet paper in a tray of water, then take it out and alternate wet paper between sheets of dry paper, wrapping overnight in a plastic bag.

Alternative Project

ALPHABET STAMPS Have students use pencil to draw or trace one alphabet letter from a wide variety of alphabets. The size might be 2 × 2 inches. Turn this tracing over and simply rub the back of it to transfer the drawing backwards to a Soft-Kut Block®. Carefully cut it out. A group of these stamps can be combined to make portraits, buildings, landscapes, or still-lifes.

Multicultural Projects

ADINKRA CLOTH STAMPS The St. Louis Art Museum Education Department presented a lesson on cutting Adinkra designs on Soft-Kut Blocks®, using special lino-cutting tools. These African designs, originally carved on calabashes, were used to print cloth for significant occasions. Each of these designs, a symbol with specific meaning, can be printed on cloth or paper.

Student Susan McCutchen's white-line lino-cut was a one-process multi-color procedure. She used several different watercolor markers to color the surface. Even though the marker had dried, when she printed it with dampened (and blotted) paper, the color transferred perfectly.

PROJECT 5–3 PROVINCETOWN PRINTS

Materials

newsprint

pencils

transfer paper

Soft-Kut Blocks®

linoleum cutters

dampened drawing paper

water-soluble markers

The Violet Jug, 1919, Blanche Lazzell, The Detroit Institute of Arts

Directions Be a "Provincetown Printer."

Provincetown printers differed from most printmakers because they used wider V-shaped lines in their lino-cuts that caused the lines to print white. They used a single plate, but had different colors in various portions of their prints.

1. Do several thumbnail sketches to get ideas. Good subject matter for prints could be almost anything that is special to you, such as animals, birds, friends, lighthouses, landscapes, etc. Avoid putting a sun in the corner to fill space. Instead, think about the shapes of clouds or the use of lines to show differences in value.

2. When you are ready with a design, trace around the plate you will use, then redraw your design to the exact size. Remember that the design will print backwards. If it doesn't make any difference which direction your design faces, simply scribble over the back of the design with pencil, or use transfer paper, and redraw the design onto the plate. If you have lettering, then the design must be applied to the plate backwards.

3. When the design is drawn on the plate, use a cutter to remove the part that you want to remain *white*. To make a "proof," simply put a piece of paper on the plate and make a rubbing of it with pencil to get an idea how the finished print will look.

4. True Provincetown prints were made with watercolor thickly painted on the single woodcut, enabling the artists to get differences in color. Instead, color different areas of the linoleum plate with washable marker.

5. Place the plate in the middle of a sheet of dampened paper, then turn over the plate and rub over the back of the paper with your palm or a wooden spoon to evenly distribute the color. Because each print will vary slightly from others, this will not be printed in an edition, but rather will be an "artists' proof." Therefore, it will be signed in pencil with AP in the middle, the title directly under the print on the left, and your name on the right. Sign all your prints, then select one for matting.

© 2000 by John Wiley & Sons, Inc.

PROJECT 5-4
JAPANESE FISH PRINTING

FOR THE TEACHER Japanese fish-printing is an ancient technique said to have originated when fishermen wanted to record a catch. Show reproductions of Japanese screens and artwork that include paintings of fish in a simple environment of reeds or water. Discuss with students the Japanese reverence for nature that is frequently seen in the simplicity of their artwork, gardens, and poetry.

Preparation Although the experience will be more memorable to students if they use real fish, you are limited to reusing the same fish for a relatively short time, and may prefer to use plastic fish that are available from art supply houses. In either case, use a variety of sizes. Think about the individual fish as *printing plates*. The ink needs to be evenly applied, the paper placed on the inked surface, and the back of the paper rubbed until all details are on it. In the normal tradition of print-making, the print is usually left untouched after it has had the ink transferred from the plate. In fish printing, it can be exciting to enhance a composition after the inked plate (fish) has been transferred to the paper. Using metallic ink in printing adds a special touch.

Vocabulary

plate

inking

composition

variety

emphasis

Alternative Project

FOAMCORE FISH PRINT Students can do research and draw one fish in detail on paper, including fins, scales, and eyes. This can then be transferred to foamboard by going over the original drawing with a ballpoint pen (or by scribbling over the back with pencil or using transfer paper). The foam-fish can be cut out around the outside. Students can then ink it and print repeatedly over a prepared background such as a watercolor wash or tissue-paper collage.

Interdisciplinary Connections
SCIENCE

UNDERWATER HABITATS Students can study the habitat (ocean, river, pond, lake) of fish in the region where they live. They can learn to identify by size, scales, color, and shape a variety of local fish.

SCIENTIFIC FISH ILLUSTRATION Students can turn one of their prints into a *scientific illustration* by labeling the species or different parts of the fish.

LANGUAGE ARTS

HAIKU POETRY CELEBRATION After mounting a print from each student, ask the students to write a Haiku poem to be read. Japanese music playing in the background would be a nice touch.

RAINBOW FISH Read *The Rainbow Fish* by Marcus Pfister to younger students. Give each student a shiny piece of Mylar to use as a fish scale on one of their fish prints.

These fish were printed with water-based paints, including metallic paints. Extra details such as outlining fish and adding seaweed or water effects were done with watercolor.

PROJECT 5–4   JAPANESE FISH PRINTING

STUDENT PAGE

Materials

fish (frozen or soft plastic)

paper (rice paper, paper towels, tissue, newsprint, drawing)

ink (water-based cool colors, metallic)

foam brushes

watercolors

watercolor brushes

ice-filled cooler (for storing fish when not in use)

paper towels for clean-up

Directions   Although you are not Japanese fishermen, you can still "record" a fish, just as they did many generations ago. You can print the fish more than one time on a piece of paper, overlapping them, or print fish of different sizes on the same piece of paper.

1. Select the fish you will print. Use paper towels to dry it carefully. Use the foam brush to carefully apply ink to the fish, making sure all surfaces including fins, eyes, and mouth, are coated.

2. Move the inked fish to a clean piece of newspaper to avoid accidentally getting ink on the background of your printing paper. Because this is a curved surface, put the paper on top of the fish and carefully rub the paper, making sure that the paper touches the fish all the way around, taking special care with eyes, mouth, and fins.

3. Look at your paper and decide if you would like to have more than one print of the same fish, or if a "school" of small fish near the top of the paper might be interesting.

4. Although normally a print is not touched after the ink has been transferred, in this project you may use watercolor to make a complete composition. Using the tip of the brush, make a few strokes to represent grasses coming up from the bottom of a pond, or make horizontal strokes to show ripples in the water. Leave most of the background untouched. The small amount of painting you will do is just to place the fish back into "water."

PROJECT 5-5
COLLAGRAPH

FOR THE TEACHER The word "collagraph" comes from the French word *coller*, which means "to paste." The technique offers unlimited possibilities for artists of all ages. The process simply consists of gluing objects onto a supporting piece of cardboard, inking the resulting plate and transferring the image to paper. Collagraphs can be made of only one material such as tagboard, which is layered to give detail, or a combination of materials such as cloth, yarn, cardboard, aluminum foil, flowers, Mylar®, etc., glued onto a piece of cardboard. Often the plate becomes more beautiful than the print as successive layers of ink are built up. It is interesting to display the plate and the print side by side.

Vocabulary

plate

collagraph

texture

Preparation Send home a note at the beginning of the year asking parents to save supplies. If you're lucky, someone might have access to pieces of heavy cardboard. Cut and save large pieces of corrugated cardboard as you unpack your supplies at the beginning of the year.

This assignment might be more satisfactory if a general theme is used. If the theme is tied in with something else you are teaching, students sometimes get better results. Suggestions include animals, birds, landscape, the harbor.

Adaptations for Younger Students

POLYMER-MEDIUM MONOPRINT Students could use polymer medium to glue leaves on a small piece of matboard. The leaves should then have more than one coat of polymer medium applied to seal the plate for printing. When the polymer is dry, apply tempera paint for a monoprint.

FLATTENED STRAWS Cut and flatten straws to make interesting collagraphs. These can be done in a radial design or simply create patterns by grouping various lengths together.

Alternative Projects

ALUMINUM-FOIL RELIEF A simple tagboard collagraph (several layers of tagboard) can be transformed into a completely different work of art after all prints are made. Cover the collagraph with aluminum foil and carefully smooth it, tucking the edges over the back and taping them. Use a dull pencil to make textures and pattern in the foil. Paint over the foil completely with India ink. After the ink has dried, use fine steel wool to rub the high spots, allowing the ink to show through. (This project was developed by Debbie McConnell of Barretts School in St. Louis County, Missouri.)

INNER-TUBE PRINTING If you can find inner tubes, this wonderful material can be cut into designs with scissors. (Sometimes trucking companies or your own school's transportation department have them.) Glue the designs to cardboard and ink them either with a brayer or by applying ink with a brush. One simple motif can be re-inked and repeatedly printed on the same piece of paper.

TAPE PRINTING Make patterns by applying different types of tape—such as masking, strapping, or Mystic Tape®—to tagboard. Different types hold ink differently. After printing, challenge students to use colored pencil to draw something unique or personal in one of the openings created by the criss-crossed tapes.

MATBOARD AND GESSO PRINT Change the surface on matboard by cutting with a knife and removing the top layer in some areas. Or add other materials on top of the matboard. Cover everything with a layer of gesso, impressing various objects into it while it is wet, or using the brush to create interesting textures. Spray outside with polyurethane varnish to seal the surface. **SAFETY NOTE: If students are using cutting knives, remind them that the non-cutting hand is always held behind the blade.**

Carolyn Baker's students (of Shenandoah Valley School, St. Louis County, Missouri) made animal collagraph prints simply using tagboard mounted on cardboard.

PROJECT 5-5 COLLAGRAPH

Materials

cardboard: corrugated, tagboard, railroad board

fabric: cotton, organza, corduroy

yarn

hammer and nails (*optional*)

scissors

white glue

polymer medium

water-based ink

brayers

drawing paper

newsprint

Directions

1. On newsprint, make several small drawings to help develop your ideas before you begin to add materials to the printing "plate." When you have decided on your design, select a piece of cardboard (tagboard, corrugated board, or railroad board) to use as a base. Try to keep all your materials about the same thickness so the plate will be easier to print.

2. The first layer of the design can be applied by cutting out pieces of tagboard or cloth. Arrange these carefully, then firmly glue down with white glue (taking special care with the edges). Third and sometimes fourth layers are added to give more detail. Yarn or strips of tagboard are effective to create the element of line. You can use a nail to punch indentations in the surface to give an interesting texture.

3. When everything is in place, the plate needs to be "sealed" by coating it with at least one coat of polymer medium or spray varnish. This is to avoid having the tagboard or other glued pieces stick to the printing paper when the paper is removed from the plate.

4. Avoid applying the ink too thickly. Rather, use the brayer to apply a thin coat more than once. You may find that the first print is a bit "thin," and that several printings are necessary to get the plate completely covered. For variety, two different colors can be applied with the brayer, one on top of the other. Or you may prefer to paint ink on the surface for even thickness.

5. When the plate is inked, carefully place it (ink-side down) in the middle of a piece of paper. Reach your hand under the paper and hold the plate in place as you turn it over so the paper is on top. Carry it to a clean surface to keep the rest of the paper clean. Then use the back of a spoon, a brayer, or your hand to firmly rub over the back of the paper, making sure to go all around the edges. Remove the print and put it on a drying rack.

PROJECT 5–6
THE MONOTYPE, IN THE MANNER OF DEGAS

FOR THE TEACHER   The *monotype* was popularized by Impressionists Edgar Degas, Paul Gauguin, and Maurice Prendergast (an American). It is created by painting ink or paint on a hard surface, such as glass or plastic, then laying paper on the painted surface and rubbing or drawing on the back of it

to create a one-of-a-kind print. While best results are obtained by running the plate and damp paper through a press, adaptations can make it usable for the classroom.

A *monoprint* is also one-of-a-kind, but a standard printing plate (lithograph, relief, intaglio [etching]) is used in combination with the monotype process. It can be printed on top of an existing monotype, or paint can be directly applied to the plate prior to printing. A second, softer print can sometimes be made without re-inking the plate, which is called a *ghost print*. Degas sometimes used ghost monoprints as the basis for some of his pastel drawings.

Vocabulary

monotype

ghost print

printing press

Ballet Dancers in the Wings, 1900, Edgar Degas, pastel on paper, 28 × 26 inches, Saint Louis Art Museum. Degas sometimes used his monotypes as a base on which he drew with pastel. His method of monotype was to cover the plate with ink, then use a rag to remove areas that he wished to be white.

Preparation
Water-based inks are ideal for this project because they do not dry so rapidly as the other water-based materials and would not necessitate using dampened paper. New water-miscible oil paints and serigraphy inks are also suitable. Other materials such as watercolors, watercolor markers, or water-sensitive crayons would necessitate using dampened paper. To reactivate dried pigments, it is necessary to put evenly dampened paper in contact with the plate under pressure.

Alternative Projects
SUBTRACTIVE PRINT AND GHOST IMAGE Restrict students to one color for this technique. Degas sometimes first applied a layer of black to his plates, removing the black in some areas with rags or a paper towel (a subtractive method of working). He sometimes added color during this step, or added color to a ghost print (a second print made without re-inking). Students could make a first print, then reprint the plate on a second piece of paper to make a *ghost* image, which would be light. Color could then be added to the dried ghost print with pastels or colored pencil.

PAPER-TO-PAPER OR PLASTIC MONOTYPES Fingerpaint on slick fingerpaint paper is excellent for monotypes because the paint doesn't dry so quickly as other paint.

Témpera and watercolor paint may also be used on paper that has been sealed with polymer medium to prevent absorption of the paint, but the work must be smaller because the paints dry quickly.

Watercolor can be painted on 5-mil Mylar® to make a monotype. Apply the paint thickly, allowing it to dry; then make a print on dampened paper.

PROJECT 5-6   THE MONOTYPE, IN THE MANNER OF DEGAS

Materials

newsprint

pencils

brushes

paper

plastic overhead transparencies

masking tape

water-based ink

water-based markers, watercolor crayons (*optional*)

crayons

brayers

spoon (*optional*)

Directions   Because you will use the three techniques of drawing, painting, and printing all on one plate, you will create a one-of-a-kind print—a monotype. There is only one that will be *exactly* like this.

1. Draw a picture that you will transfer to your transparent plastic plate. Remember that if you draw it exactly the way your drawing looks, it will print backwards. If having it be exactly the same as your drawing is important, put the original drawing against a window and draw over the back of it. Paint this *reversed* image on the plate.

2. Tape the transparent plastic sheet on top of your drawing. Use a brush to *quickly* apply water-based ink to the plastic. Put it on thickly enough so it won't dry too quickly. The brushstrokes will show, but that is part of what will make it wonderful and spontaneous.

3. Lay a clean piece of paper on top of the plate and use a spoon or your hand to rub hard enough to transfer the paint to the paper. You can lift up a corner to see if it is working well. Pull the paper off the plastic.

4. Now look at the plastic plate. It has a *ghost image* on it. If you reprinted the plate immediately, you would have a faint image of your original painting. Instead, consider whether you would like to add different colors, changing it slightly. Print it again.

5. After the monotype has been printed, you could still make changes if you wish. Colored pencil, oil pastels, watercolor, fine-line marker, or ink could be used to make a print more interesting.

PROJECT 5–7
THREE TREES

FOR THE TEACHER Rembrandt van Rijn became a famous artist through his paintings, drawings, and prints. He was quite popular in his time, and his artworks are in collections around the world. His etching *Three Trees*, a simple landscape, was done in 1643. The scene is rich in light and shadow, incorporating tiny details such as windmills and horses in a field off in the distance. He was particularly known for his use of *chiaroscuro* (use of light and dark areas to call attention to the subject). Rembrandt is probably one of the most famous artists to use *drypoint*, which he mostly used to "finish" some of his etchings. He used a sharp tool to scratch a design in a metal etching plate, leaving a *burr* (metal shaving). The burr gave an interesting textured line.

Olive Orchard, 1889, Vincent van Gogh, oil on canvas, $28^3/_4 \times 37$ inches, The Nelson–Atkins Museum of Art, Kansas City, Missouri (Purchase: Nelson Trust). Although van Gogh's trees in an olive orchard are a totally different style from that of Rembrandt's, they show life and movement.

Vocabulary

drypoint	burr
intaglio	etching
chiaroscuro	daubers

Preparation Trees are suggested for this project because they exist everywhere, and students might enjoy going outside to do their preliminary drawings from real trees. Transferring their drawings to make drypoint etchings is not difficult, and will give students the experience of intaglio printing, without having to make too many decisions about subject matter. Other appropriate subjects could be anything complex, such as sailing ships, train engines, factories, insects, butterflies, furry animals, fruit, or flowers.

Most etching processes are unsuitable for elementary and middle school levels because they involve changing the surface of the plate with chemicals. The drypoint process is good for students above the primary level. Drypoint is an etching process that involves scratching a design into the surface of a plate. The plate is inked and the surface wiped clean, leaving ink in the *etched* lines (an intaglio print). The plate is printed by putting damp paper under pressure, preferably in a printing press.

Make "daubers" to apply ink (to force it into the etched lines) by rolling a piece of felt approximately 3 inches wide by 12 inches long, secured by rubber bands. The ink is applied in a circular motion, dipping the daubers in ink as more is needed. Wipe excess ink from the plate's surface with telephone pages (held flat, not crumpled).

Alternative Project

SCRIMSHAW The technique of drypoint is exactly the same process used by *scrimshanders* (usually sailors) as they etched walrus ivory, whale ribs and teeth, or ivory. Their work had detailed etchings with designs. Subject matter might be ships, women, flowers, or geometric designs. Although they did not *print* their etchings, they left ink in the lines and wiped the surface clean. Students can make scrimshaw on rounds of plaster of Paris (made in paper cups), plastic switch plates, pieces of plastic bottles, or white sheet plastic.

PROJECT 5–7   THREE TREES

STUDENT PAGE

Materials

clear 10-mil polyester plastic sheet
masking tape
scratch knives, nails, or a stylus
water-based ink
daubers (to apply ink)
phone book pages (to wipe off excess ink)
printing paper
tray for dampening paper (a cat's litter tray works)
blotters or newsprint
rolling pin or dowel
baren (or spoon for rubbing on back of print)

Drawn from Rembrandt van Rijn's
Three Trees, 1643

Directions

1. Do a detailed drawing of one or more trees, using only lines. Look carefully at how a tree grows, with the trunk the widest, then thick limbs, smaller branches, and twigs at the ends. Even if a tree is fully leafed out, you can still see some of the branches through the leaves. When Rembrandt wanted to show leaves, he made some in complete detail, but used *scribble strokes* for others.

2. Tape the drawing to the underside of a piece of clear plastic. Use a scratching tool to reproduce the drawing as faithfully as possible. To show how dark some areas are, use either cross-hatched lines or parallel lines close together. Rembrandt even put parallel lines in the *sky* of his print of *Three Trees* to show that a storm might be approaching.

3. Use a dauber to apply ink to the plate in a figure-eight motion to make sure ink is in all the lines. To remove the ink from the surface of the plate, use a page from a telephone book, holding it flat in your hand and wiping just the surface. If you crumple the page, you may accidentally remove some of the ink in the lines. It is okay to leave some of the ink on the surface of the plate, especially in the corners, as it makes the print more interesting.

4. Pull a proof! This means to place a damp piece of paper on the plate, rubbing firmly on the back of the paper or running it through a press to see what your plate looks like. Perhaps it needs more detail. This first print is called a *state* or *artist's proof*, when the artist is deciding whether to make changes.

5. If you are satisfied with the way the plate looks, you can print it several times, inking, wiping, and printing. These identical prints are called an *edition*. Use pencil to number it in the center directly under the print, and sign it in the right-hand corner. A title could go in the left corner. If you make only one print, this has AP (artist's proof) in the center.

6. Prints are properly matted leaving a 1/4-inch border on the sides and top, and 3/4 inch on the bottom (so the signature is visible). This means that you need to be careful not to get ink on the edges of the print.

Unit 6

Three-Dimensional Design

Three-dimensional (3-D) design offers great rewards to students. It encourages abstract thinking and visualization. Many students love drawing and two-dimensional work, so they should also be encouraged to work "in the round." For students who draw with less skill than others, three-dimensional work often allows them to shine. To give all students a chance to develop fully, art teacher Nora Olive of the Remington Traditional School, St. Louis County, Missouri (grades 1 to 8), alternates two-dimensional and three-dimensional projects. The 3-D experience is especially important in the upper elementary and middle schools.

Storage can be a primary problem while work is in process. Marla Mayer of Highcroft Ridge School in St. Louis County, Missouri allows work (such as papier mâché) to dry, then puts it into a labeled trash bag until the class returns the following week. Sometimes it is necessary to clear the counters until a three-dimensional project is over, or have only one grade level at a time do a 3-D project. Works-in-progress can be put on walls, or in plastic bags hung from lines strung across one corner of the room. If your halls are wide, larger work might be placed outside the room on the floor to dry.

Use the ceiling to display 3-D work. It greatly enlivens the art room and makes it an exciting place to be. Suspend the work from strings looped over the grids, or use special hooks (for plants) that are made to attach to ceiling grids.

For small sculptures, Crayola's Model Magic™ is clean and easy. But because it is relatively expensive, I have substituted papier mâché for many of the projects that could be done with Model Magic™. It would be an ideal product to use to make miniature masks, small chairs, gargoyles, or the tops of the Walking Sticks. It is easily worked by adding on and refining with simple tools.

An entire class of Beth Knoedelseder's third graders from the Reed School, St. Louis County, Missouri created these individual dragons to illustrate a unit on the Middle Ages.

ASSEMBLAGE

PROJECT 6–1
IMAGINATION STATION

FOR THE TEACHER   Even the youngest students enjoy manipulating paper. They can learn to accordion-fold, plait, curl, or wrap a strip around a pencil. Students will astonish you with their ability and imagination as they combine paper forms.

Artist Frank Stella does colorful abstract sculptures in metal that could serve as inspiration for students of all ages. A former painter, Stella's sculptures are flat on one side, but reach into space as all parts of the whole come together.

Vocabulary

scoring

curling

plaiting

space

repetition

Preparation   This is an ideal project for using all those scraps of paper. By planning ahead, you can have older students cut paper into strips and squares on the paper cutter for younger students to use. **SAFETY NOTE: Be sure a cutting guard is always in place on the paper cutter, and give students frequent instructions on its use.** Students also enjoy doing their own cutting with scissors.

Alternative for Younger Students   When they are finished, allow the young ones to make imaginative animals by adding printed sticker eyes and mouths where they think these features should be on their creations.

PROJECT 6–1   IMAGINATION STATION

Materials

scissors
glue
rulers
8-inch black or white posterboard squares
construction paper (could be cut strips)

Directions   You will be creating sculpture of construction paper that can be cut into strips or various shapes. Use your imagination to see all the ways you can manipulate the paper. Although most colors go well together, just as they do in a flower garden, this project might be more interesting if you used only warm or cool colors.

1. Experiment with some of these manipulations:
    a. *scoring*. If you wish to make a sharp-edged bend, use a ruler and the tip of scissors to score the strip.
    b. *curved strip*. Snip the edges at 1/4-inch intervals to the scored line, then bend the snipped edges to the line. This flexible strip can then be glued in any curved or rounded shape you want onto the background.
    c. *curling*. Wrap a strip around a pencil to make a tight curl. To make an "eye," flatten the curl and set on its side to glue down.
    d. *accordion-fold*.
    e. *plaiting*. Glue two pieces together at one end and bend them back and forth over each other. Glue at the finished end.
    f. *Curl* by holding one blade of a pair of scissors against a thumb and pulling the paper between your thumb and the scissors.
    g. *spirals*. Make a circle or square and begin at one corner, cutting in towards the center.
    h. Make tubes by rolling around a pencil and gluing the two edges.
2. An 8-inch square will be the base for your paper sculpture. You might want to plan whether it will be suspended from the ceiling, hung on the wall, or placed on a table. Fold under 1/2 inch on the ends of the manipulated pieces and glue these to the cardboard. Or you can put a line of glue directly on the cardboard and put a shape, such as a spiral, on its side.

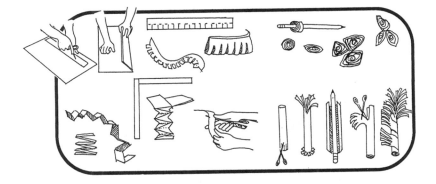

PROJECT 6-2
ROLLED PAPER-TUBE SCULPTURE

FOR THE TEACHER   This three-dimensional design project allows for individual problem-solving. Some students may have to struggle for awhile before finding a solution, but that is part of the process. Show them work by David Smith, Alexander Lieberman, and other nonobjective sculptors.

Vocabulary
emphasis

repetition

craftsmanship

negative space

positive space

unit

Preparation   Rolling the copy-paper tubes is best done in advance. Students may do it during their spare time or while watching television at home. Colored, fluorescent, or recycled paper works just as well as new white copy paper. Encourage students to bring medium-weight string from home, or purchase some that has interesting texture or color (but is soft and easy to tie). The excess raffia or string should remain on each individual knot (don't trim) and is an important part of the decoration. Try this yourself first, but it is best not to show students a sample, or they will be inclined to copy it. If someone is having trouble getting started, suggest they tie just two pieces together (about 1 inch from the ends), then tie two more together. They could also place the tubes side-by-side and weave raffia to make a mat-like base, or they can make units. Eventually they will figure out how to combine them, and each student will have a unique solution.

Alternative Projects
NEWSPAPER TUBE SCULPTURE Students may make larger individual projects of full sheets of newspaper rolled into 1/2-inch tubes. These are effective left plain with raffia and string, or painted with tempera or spray paint.

ALL-CLASS TUBE SCULPTURE Divide students into groups to make five tubes each. They will then work as a group to make a larger sculpture. Each group's sculpture could be combined into a large all-class sculpture.

HOUSE-OF-STRAW GROUP PROJECT Pre-rolled "tubes" (straws) can be used in somewhat the same way, but can also be used for a cooperative learning game for older students. Divide students into groups of four, with the purpose of the game to build the tallest structure, using only straws, masking tape, and string. A leader usually emerges from the initial chaos, and a lot of discussion is necessary. **Hint:** Geometric *units*, such as squares or triangles, usually have the greatest strength.

Rolled newspaper strip sculptures shown here are transformed with a variety of materials such as raffia, brightly colored yarn, tempera, or spray paint. The lower left photo shows a sculpture made of rolled white copy paper combined with raffia.

PROJECT 6–2 ROLLED PAPER-TUBE SCULPTURE

STUDENT PAGE

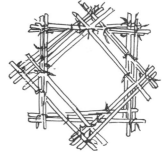

Materials

clear tape

pencils

raffia

tempera paint (*optional*)

brushes

medium weight string (colored, natural, yarn)

8-1/2 × 11-inch copy paper (new or recycled)

Directions

1. Place a pencil in one corner of the paper. Roll the paper tightly around the pencil until you have a tube (cylinder) of paper. Loosen it slightly to release the pencil, then tape the tube shut with clear tape. Make 25 to 30 of these tubes.

2. There is no right or wrong way to assemble these tubes. Some people make units to assemble (such as tubes tied together 1 inch from the ends in a triangle, square, or octagon). You can also drop a needle attached to string through three separate tubes, then tie the string to form numerous triangles that are then assembled. When you tie the tubes together, allow excess string or raffia to remain as part of the decoration.

3. Your sculpture can hang from the ceiling or, if it is flat on the bottom, it could hang on a wall. Display a tall sculpture on a table. To extend tubes in a standing sculpture, simply drop the bottom of one tube into the top of one you wish to make longer.

4. The plain paper tube sculpture tied with string or raffia is beautiful without any extra embellishment, but if you wish, you could paint the tubes with tempera or spray paint or use marker to make decorations such as stripes. If you have leftover tubes, make a second sculpture in a different style.

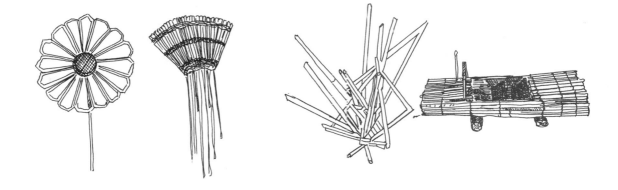

PROJECT 6–3
GEOMETRIC UNITS

FOR THE TEACHER This is a true interdisciplinary lesson, yet it challenges the students to go beyond simply making three-dimensional geometric forms. They must use their imaginations to transform geometric units into sculpture. This project was presented by art teacher Nancy Chrien at a National Art Education Convention.

Vocabulary
units

form

contrast

emphasis

scoring

geometric

Preparation Demonstrate how to measure, score, and glue the geometric forms. From the beginning of this project, challenge students to do something unique, even though all will use geometric forms. Encourage them to look around their homes for something that can be added to make the finished sculpture bizarre. Glue guns could be used to hold these together. The sculptures could hang from the ceiling or be free-standing.

Adaptations for Younger Students
WEIRD GEOMETRIC SHAPES Have the students cut out geometric shapes in different colored construction paper, then make a collage of them on a 9 × 12-inch piece of paper. Challenge students to cut out one thing from a magazine to hide somewhere within the geometric shapes to make it *weird*.

GLUED TOOTHPICK GEOMETRIC SHAPES Have students glue toothpicks with white glue to one 6 × 8-inch piece of tagboard to make a square, equilateral triangle, polygon, or rectangle. Show them how they can combine shapes to make pine trees (triangles and rectangles), house (squares and triangles), fish (diamonds). These are effective colored with marker, or with marker lines drawn on the tagboard on either side of the toothpicks.

Alternative Projects
GROUP SCULPTURE OF GEOMETRIC SHAPES If time is a problem, this would be an ideal group project. Each group of students could make a specific geometric figure (such as square boxes) to combine in a group sculpture. Or they could unify different geometric forms by using one color only.

CONSTRUCT A FAMOUS BUILDING WITH GEOMETRIC SHAPES Nancy Chrien challenges her students to work in groups of four to recreate a famous building by combining geometric shapes.

Geometric Units

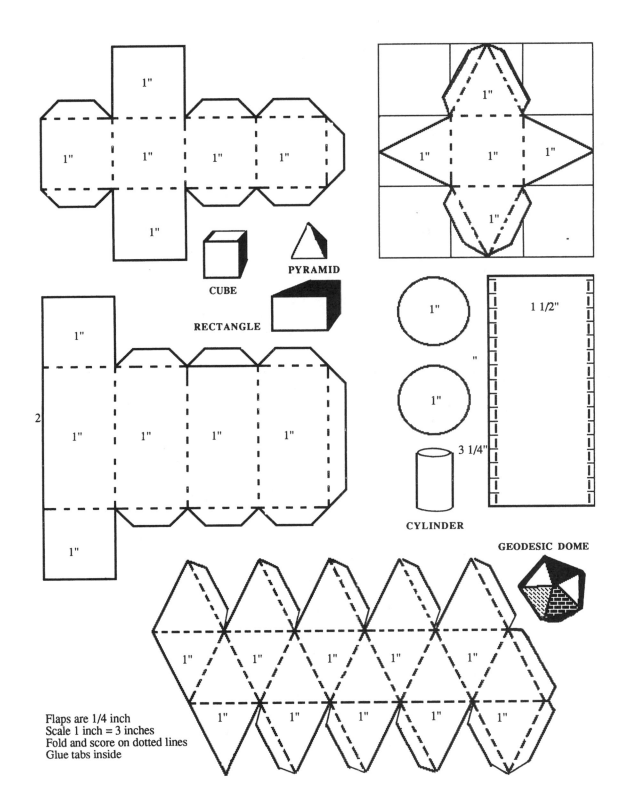

CUBE

PYRAMID

RECTANGLE

CYLINDER

GEODESIC DOME

Flaps are 1/4 inch
Scale 1 inch = 3 inches
Fold and score on dotted lines
Glue tabs inside

PROJECT 6–3 GEOMETRIC UNITS

Materials

tagboard or railroad board in bright colors

rulers

scissors

white glue, tacky glue, or a glue gun

straight pins

plastic bags (for each student to store units while they are being constructed)

Directions   It will take awhile for you to complete all the units that you will need for your sculpture. As you work, consider some of the things that could be added to your sculpture that might make it *weird*. Suggestions are toy dolls, cars, plastic fruit, playing cards, clothespins, straws, cotton swabs, workbench items, plastic containers, oversized dice, or magazine cut-outs (for decorative use).

1. If you will be working with colored board, select one or several colors, but plan your overall color scheme. It is recommended that you simplify your structure by using only one shape such as a cube, pyramid, cylinder, or cone.

2. Do your drawing and cutting from the underside of the cardboard so pencil marks will be hidden on the inside. Be sure to allow a tab on each side to be glued. (If you forget and cut off a tab, you can cut and score a piece of cardboard to glue on the inside of the two surfaces.)

3. To make tabs fold inward easily, draw the point of a pair of scissors along a ruler held in place on the fold. This is called *scoring* and will make the cardboard fold easily. Glue the units together as you cut them out, then store them in a plastic bag until you are ready to combine them.

4. When the units are completed, consider different ways they can be glued together that will make them interesting. You may have to use pins to hold two pieces together until the glue dries. Also remember that you are to bring "found objects" from home that can be combined within the body of the sculpture to make it unique.

PROJECT 6-4
3-D SPORTS HEROES

FOR THE TEACHER Students are familiar with sports—they play them, they watch them on television, and they read about sports heroes in books and newspapers. Popular artist Leroy Nieman has made a lucrative career portraying sports figures in action.

Vocabulary

variety

emphasis

rhythm

movement

shape

These silhouettes, traced from newspaper pictures onto tablet backings, are easily cut out and painted. They can be assembled in a variety of configurations.

Preparation Tell students that they are charged to create a cardboard "maquette" for a steel sculpture that will stand in front of a sports arena. Railroad board can be cut with scissors, yet is strong enough to support itself. Have students save lightweight tablet backings, which work very well, and are large enough for three figures.

Also have students bring in photos from the newspaper or sports magazines of sports figures in action. The action figures that will be based on these pictures will be painted solid colors. Details such as sports caps or helmets and the sports equipment will distinguish one sport from another. If you are in a hurry, magazines devoted to just one sport should have more than enough images for that sport. These completed, painted figures can be displayed in many different configurations. Challenge students to come up with ideas for assembling them using foamboard bases or dowels with slits. A simple square of foamboard works well.

Interdisciplinary Connections
PHYSICAL EDUCATION
SPORTS HEROES Students can give a report on the outstanding heroes of their sports, both those of the past and the present.

MATH
SPORTS STATISTICS Students can use figures from the newspaper to calculate sports statistics in many different sports. They can figure out batting, slugging, and earned-run averages in baseball; yards per carry, yards per pass, and pass completion percentages in football; and points, rebounds, and fouls per game in basketball.

These red, yellow, and blue tablet-board figures are mounted on a small square of Foamcore®.

PROJECT 6–4 3-D SPORTS HEROES

Materials

thin cardboard (tablet backings are good)

foamboard

scissors

newsprint

tempera paint

brushes

Directions You will be creating a maquette (model) sculpture of sports heroes from cardboard. This material is self-supporting, easily cut, and can be painted. Pretend this is a sculpture to be placed outside a major sports facility.

1. On newsprint, draw three figures of the same general height (approximately 6 inches) participating in the same sport. Each one should be doing a different action. For example, you might show baseball players pitching, batting, and running, or hockey players goal-tending, or hitting the puck. Don't be concerned about anything but the outlines of the figures, as you will be painting them in solid colors.

2. To transfer, scribble on the backs of the drawings with pencil. Place the drawings on the cardboard and redraw your original drawings transferring them to the cardboard. To make them easy to see for cutting, redraw the figures on the cardboard.

3. Cut the figures out as neatly as possible with scissors. Rather than cutting *all* the way around the outside, remove a small area at a time out to the edge, then go back over to carefully trim when it is roughly cut out. Each of the figures will need to have at least one foot touching the ground.

4. Paint each of the figures a different bright color (for example, red, blue, and yellow), front and back and including the edges. The three colors should harmonize. Cut a foamboard 3-inch square or round base. Use an X-acto® knife to make a slit in the foamboard in which each figure will stand upright behind another, yet allowing each to be seen.

© 2000 by John Wiley & Sons, Inc.

CARVING

PROJECT 6–5
INUIT CARVINGS WITH SOAP

FOR THE TEACHER   The Inuit people of North America have a tradition of carving beautifully simple figures from soapstone (a soft stone). Most Canadian Eskimos call themselves Inuit, which translates as "humanity" or "the people." The figures they carve are based on life around them, such as themselves or Arctic animals.

Soap carving teaches the same lessons that students would learn when using other, more expensive materials. For example, the material needs to be removed a little at a time. As Michelangelo said, when asked how he carved the famous *David*, "I simply took away everything that wasn't David." He envisioned the form that was inside the huge block of marble, and carefully worked the entire block, taking away small amounts at a time all over, then going back and refining it.

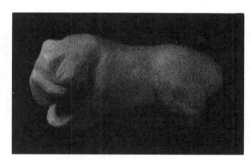

This soap carving touched all the outer edges of the soap and was done with a plastic restaurant knife. It was smoothed with a kitchen scrubber.

Vocabulary

form	plane
depth	contrast

Preparation   As always, try this yourself before you try to teach it to your students. Have a large jar in which students can dump their soap chips when they clean up. Later they can slightly moisten the scraps and form soap balls from the scraps. Tell them that if they try to take away large amounts at once, *all* they will create is soap chips. If these have a nice smooth finish, it isn't necessary to paint them. If some students have difficulty envisioning what the carving will look like, they can first model a figure in oil clay. Prepare them for change! Tell them that even though they may know exactly what the animal will look like before they begin, chances are good that it will be considerably different from what they envisioned!

Note: Depending on the ages of the students, they will use either potato peelers or plastic (or paring) knives for carving.

Alternative Project

PLASTER CARVING Instead of carving soap, make plaster blocks in cardboard milk cartons. Add vermiculite (available at garden stores) before pouring to make carving easier. The principle of carving is the same. Use a knife (plastic or kitchen) or file to take away small amounts at a time to avoid breakage. Sandpaper can be used to refine the finish. Seal it with polymer medium. This generates dust, so have students work on newspaper to be thrown away after working periods.

Interdisciplinary Projects
SCIENCE
ARCTIC ANIMALS Teach students about animals of the Arctic. Include *sea creatures* such as the walrus, sea lion, otter, and whale, and *land animals* such as the fox, polar bear, rabbit, etc. Discuss hibernation, migration patterns, and color adaptations.

SOCIAL STUDIES
MODERN LIFE IN THE FAR NORTH While teaching students about what life formerly was like in extreme northern regions, discuss with them what life is like there today: why it has changed, whether these changes are or are not for the better, etc.

PROJECT 6–5   INUIT CARVINGS WITH SOAP

Materials

bars of soap (students bring from home)

newsprint (for working on and saving chips)

toothpick or nail

potato peelers, plastic knives or paring knives

plastic kitchen scrubber

Directions

1. Work on a piece of clean newsprint so you can save your soap shavings. Make a "working drawing" by first drawing around the outside of the bar of soap on newsprint. Think about what kind of thing is hidden in there. It might be an animal such as a bear or walrus, that is lying down. Try drawing the creature first, deciding which direction its head will face. Draw your design on the soap with a toothpick or nail.

2. Several reminders that will help you while carving:
    *   Plan to cut away as little of the bar as possible, making legs and heads go to the edges, and keeping the full thickness of the bar.
    *   *Shave* away the soap a little bit at a time. Avoid trying to cut away an entire corner or a big shape, because this almost surely leads to a broken bar of soap.
    *   Draw the design on both sides. Then work on the entire bar, shaving away a little at a time and turning it frequently.
    *   If you have an area that will have to be thin, leave it until last to carve.
    *   Make a "stop cut" if you need to carve a delicate area, gently bring the knife blade straight down in front of the area, then cut toward the stop cut from both directions.

3. After you have completely rounded the form with a knife, use a plastic abrasive kitchen scrubber to round the entire figure. Inuit stone sculptures are smooth and rounded, and it is possible to get this same effect with soap.

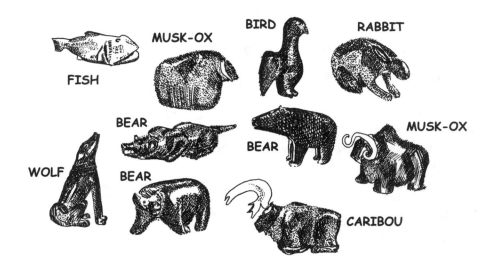

FISH   MUSK-OX   BIRD   RABBIT

BEAR   BEAR   MUSK-OX

WOLF   BEAR   CARIBOU

PROJECT 6–6
PLASTER OF PARIS "BAG MOLDS"

FOR THE TEACHER   Plaster of Paris is the common name for gypsum, which was originally mined in Paris. In the United States in the late 19th century, many of the sculptures found in museums were plaster casts of famous Roman and Greek sculptures. Students of that time were introduced to drawing the human form through drawing from plaster sculptures.

Casting is most commonly done with liquid plaster. It can be poured into molds formed of something as simple as damp sand, paper cups, cardboard milk cartons, boxes, or molds made of plaster, clay, or wax. If vermiculite (found in garden-supply shops) is added while the plaster is liquid, carving it becomes relatively easy. Tell students that although plaster will break if dropped, it is a permanent medium that could last for centuries.

Introduce students to the sculpture of Henry Moore, who based most of his large sculptures on the human form. Much of his work is totally abstract, often with holes. His works would help students to realize that they too can create *real* sculpture, even though it is not large in size.

Vocabulary

form

emphasis

casting

plaster

planes

chemical reaction

Preparation
  This method of mixing plaster allows all students to mix their own plaster at the same time, and should give each student a rough sculpture that can be refined in another session. Try this first so you know how the mixing feels at each stage, and how simple it is. From mixing to bag-removal stage takes approximately 20 minutes. Cover tables with newspaper and have plaster and warm water (about body temperature) ready. You could already have the plaster measured into 1-cup portions. Add the *plaster to the water* rather than the other way around. Request the students to be silent during the mixing process so they will have time to consider the shape they want. Once the plaster begins to set, they have only a minute or so for decision-making.

CAUTION: Never pour plaster down a sink. If you mix plaster in a plastic container, wait until the plaster has dried, then "thump" the plastic container into a wastebasket to release the dried plaster.

Alternative Project
LARGER FORMS Although instructions are given for making a mold supported by hands, if you used larger bags and increased the amount of plaster, the bags could be placed to harden over a knee, inside a bent elbow, on the side of the neck, etc., or formed over a tennis ball, baseball bat, or other rounded object. Be careful of *undercuts* (the liquid plaster creeps underneath an object, making it impossible to remove without breaking).

Interdisciplinary Connections

SCIENCE

MEASURE CHEMICAL-REACTION TIMES Plaster of Paris is slightly hydrated Calcium Sulfate ($CaSO_4 \cdot 1/2\ H_2O$). When water is added, it causes a quick-setting chemical reaction that generates heat. Students might like to measure different setting times when cold or hot water is used in place of water at body or room temperature.

PLASTER LEAF OR HAND PRINTS Students can pour plaster into shallow aluminum pie tins and make hand or leaf prints. Wait until just before the plaster sets up to make the impression.

SAND CASTING Do sand casting by filling pie tins with sand and dampening the sand. Natural items such as shells and stones may be placed face down on the surface. Animals can be drawn within the sand (make the depressions deep enough so the plaster is at least 1/2-inch thick overall). Put a large "opened" metal paper clip in the smooth plaster back just as it sets to make a hanging plaque. Use pencil to write names and dates on the back just before the plaster sets.

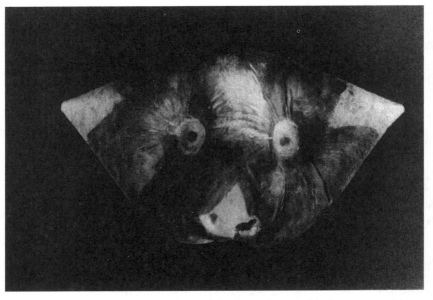

The eyes of student Joyce Mandernach's plaster bag-molded creature were created by holding the fingers and thumbs together as the plaster set up. The sculpture was later decorated with marker.

PROJECT 6–6   PLASTER OF PARIS "BAG MOLDS"

Materials

water
1 cup measures
twist-ties
newspapers
plastic knives with serrated edges
plaster rasps or coarse *wet and dry* sandpaper
plastic containers (margarine tubs, etc.)
1 quart sandwich bags (not self-sealing)
spray paint, shoe polish, or acrylic paint
quick-acting plaster of Paris (1 cup water:1 cup plaster)

Directions   You will be forming a material that will harden in a particular shape within your palms.

1. Place an open plastic bag inside a bowl. Pour in one cup of water. Gently sift one cup of plaster of Paris into the water. Try to get as much air out of the bag as you can, then use a twist-tie approximately two inches from the top of the bag.

2. Remove the bag from the bowl and cradle the bag full of liquid in your palms. Use your fingers to dissolve the lumps. Continue to gently move the liquid around with your hands. After a time (approximately ten minutes) you will begin to notice that the bag is getting warmer and is beginning to feel thicker and heavier. You should consider how you could move your fingers to make some depressions in the mold on both sides.

3. Test to see if the plaster is ready to harden by pushing the bag with a finger. If a hole remains where you touched, then the liquid is ready to set up. Try to pull out the top and corners of the bag and as many wrinkles as you can, as this will save you time later. Use both hands to support the mold. By touching a finger of one hand to the finger of the other through the bag, you would create a hole that would go through the sculpture.

4. The plaster will harden within a few minutes. If you feel the sculpture a little later, you will notice that it has become quite warm. That is the sign that a chemical reaction has taken place. When it has hardened sufficiently that the form doesn't change, carefully remove the bag.

5. While the plaster is somewhat damp, you can use the plastic knife to gently shave off some of the rough spots. You may notice that you will now have a straight edge or two. These are called *planes*. They make a rounded piece of sculpture more interesting because of the contrast of flat and curved sides. Remember to work over the newspaper so clean-up will be easy. Later, use sandpaper to smooth the sculpture.

6. When the sculpture is dry, it can be finished many different ways. You can put shoe polish on it, paint designs with acrylic paint or paint-markers, stain it with tea or coffee, or spray it with gold or silver paint.

MASK-MAKING
GENERAL INFORMATION

Masks continue to be popular in many cultures around the world although the reasons for wearing them and the materials used to create them may have changed. To provide purpose and unity to a mask unit and for the masks to display well together, select a theme such as *animals, carnival,* or *Mardi Gras*. You might prefer to relate them to one culture, perhaps one with which your students may already be familiar, using similar colors, materials, and decorative additions. Consider how you will display masks, and whether this will also involve writing about customs of the group on which the masks are based.

Vocabulary

form

shape

contrast

texture

tradition

THEMES AND MATERIALS

Here is a short list of mask-making themes or cultures and the commonly used materials:

Africa. primarily carved wood, might include headdresses

Kuba (Democratic Republic of the Congo). cloth and shells

Cajun (primarily Louisiana). screenwire; paint; raffia; sequins

Carnival. plastic; feathers; glitter; shiny; metallic materials

Caribbean. wood; feathers; fluorescent paint; glitter; screenwire

China. clay masks; papier mâché

Egypt. gold repoussé masks

Greece. metal repoussé; comedy and tragedy; masks of the gods

Indonesia. brilliantly painted carved wood

Italy. papier mâché masks, constructed in molds—often half masks, traditional theatrical characters

Melanesia (including New Guinea). carved palm fibers; boars' tusks; painted in red, black, white

Mexico. tin; carved wood; papier mâché; jade or turquoise mosaic

North America.

    Northwestern Native Americans. usually made of cedar, might include feathers and pieces of copper

    Plains Indians. mostly carved of wood; some made of leather or shell

    Southwestern Indians. kachina masks (wood, leather, feathers)

    Eastern. carved wood

Iroquois. corn husks

Inuit. carved wood; feathers; bone

ARMATURES FOR THE MASKS

Aluminum cans. These masks, based on Mexican tin masks, should not be worn.

Aluminum foil. Ordinary kitchen foil can be shaped over students' faces, then placed over a wad of newspaper for support before being used as the armature for papier mâché masks.

Balloons. Cover with papier mâché or plaster-gauze. Rest the balloon on a bowl while working.

Cardboard. Simply cut into mask shape and decorate. A split-and-taped fold under the chin could make it curve.

Cardboard boxes. Use small boxes, or corners and portions of a shoebox bottom for larger ones.

Cardboard strips and masking tape. Cut 1- to 1-1/2-inch wide cardboard strips to use as bands formed on the students' own heads. Put bands around the forehead and back of the head, in front of the ears to the top of the head and under the chin, a band across the top of the head, and one across the nose and chin. Anchor these strips with masking tape, and fill in between with papier mâché.

Gallon plastic milk jugs. Split in half vertically, with the opening facing up or down. Use the handle for a nose. **Note:** These are also effective simply painted, without the papier mâché.

Metal-tooling foil. Not to be worn, symmetrical shape can be drawn on paper and transferred.

Plastic masks (available from art suppliers). Cover with papier mâché or plaster-gauze (can be reused).

TO DISPLAY

- Mount a metal-foil mask on successively larger layers of fringed burlap (each could be a different color).

- Make a headcloth or costume of colorful long narrow strips of scrap cloth, as is done in the Caribbean and Cajun cultures.

- Display each mask on a cardboard or painted "headcloth" that complements the designs on the masks.

- Place Southwestern Native American masks within a *tablita* (cardboard headdress drawn, painted, and cut out). (Refer to Project 4–5.)

- Drill a hole in the sides and put a string through to hang on a nail.

- Make a hole in a wooden base (or a box filled with plaster), and insert a dowel or broom handle, attaching the mask to it for table display.

ALTERNATIVE MASK PROJECTS

Masks as Sculptural Objects   Because many masks created today are made simply to be displayed as decorative objects
rather than worn, consider a sculpture unit in which the masks *are*
sculpture made from found materials such as wood scraps. Even
though they wouldn't be worn, they are still masks in that they are
one-sided, have features, and involve a variety of materials.

Gigantic Papier Mâché Masks   Have two or three students work together to make oversized papier mâché masks for a
"parade." Formed over a base of chicken wire, they could be worn
on the shoulders or left large enough at the bottom so that only the
wearer's legs would show. These could be realistic humans or animals. Such masks were formerly created by school children for the
annual St. Louis Riverdance parade that had a theme such as *Water*
or *Humanity*.

Frontlets   Instead of masks, students may make headdresses
or "frontlets" (from Northwest Coast Native Americans) that also
were worn on the forehead and top of the head. These sometimes
represented animal totems.

Mask, Middle Sepik, Iatmul People,
wood, clay, shells, boar's tusks, yarn and
feathers; red, black and white paint,
93.0 cm. Saint Louis Art Museum, Gift of
Morton D. May. This mask demonstrates
the many different media used by artisans of Oceania.

INTERDISCIPLINARY PROJECTS

Social Studies
Mask Research Project   Classes could be divided into
groups, with each group researching and making masks from a different culture. They could obtain information about dances, rituals, cus-
toms, when masks would be worn, who would wear them, what the religion is. They could further
learn about natural resources and trade and differences between specific cultures today as compared with those of a century ago.

Language Arts
Write a Play   Students can write a story about the personality their mask represents, or
write a play in which they can perform with their masks.

Masks of the World

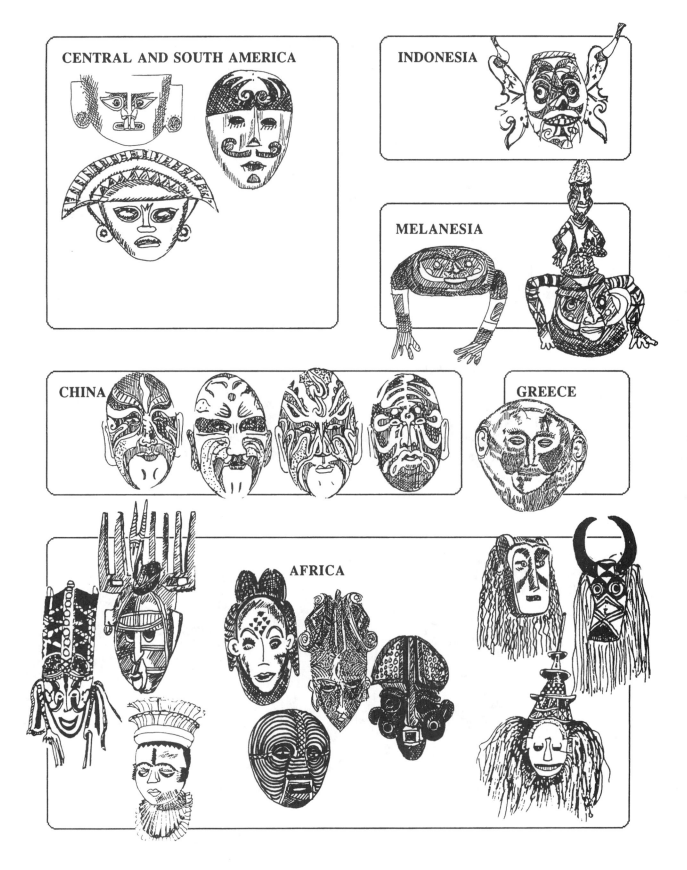

CENTRAL AND SOUTH AMERICA

INDONESIA

MELANESIA

CHINA

GREECE

AFRICA

Masks of
North America

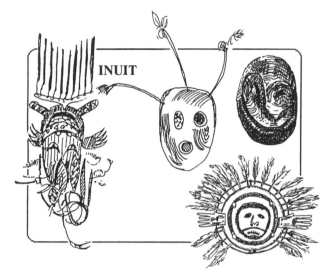

INUIT

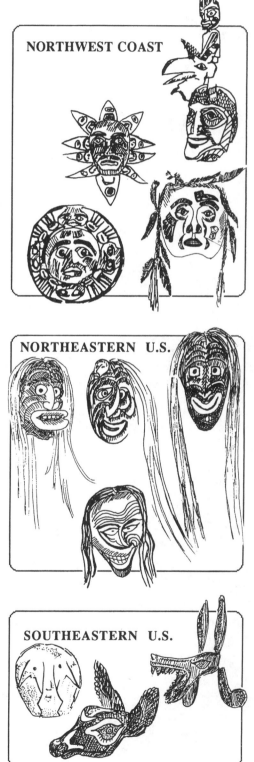

NORTHWEST COAST

NORTHEASTERN U.S.

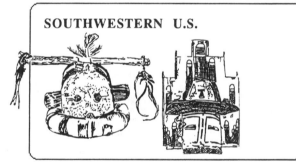

SOUTHWESTERN U.S.

MEXICO

SOUTHEASTERN U.S.

Map of Masks Around the World

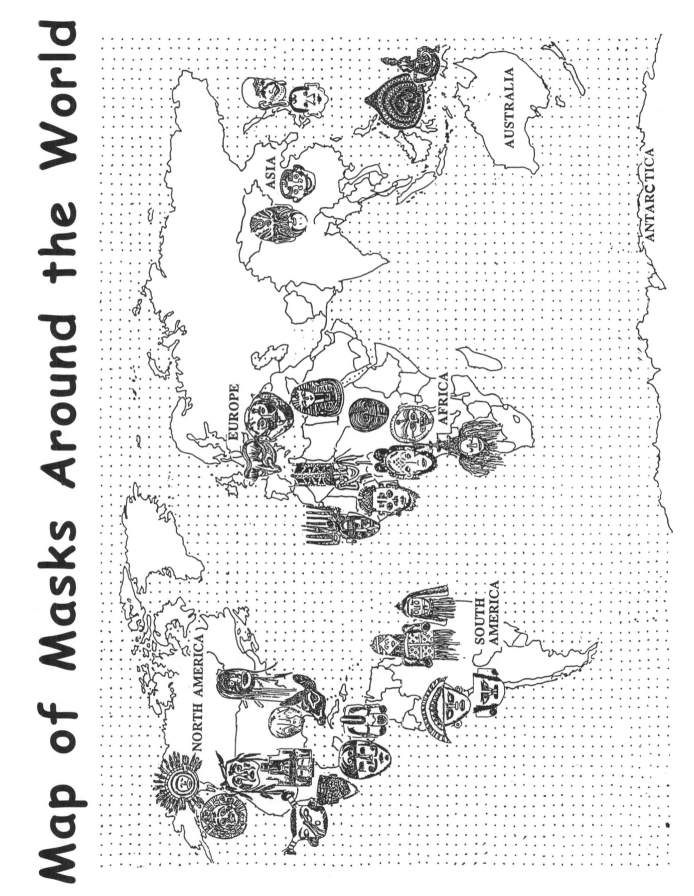

PROJECT 6–7
SYMMETRICAL PAPER MASKS

FOR THE TEACHER   These simple paper masks are suitable for most levels, varying only in the degree to which you wish to develop them. Older students could manipulate paper to make them more three-dimensional. For upper levels the masks could serve as an introduction to more complicated mask-making, such as copper tooling repoussé.

Vocabulary

symmetry

positive–negative

balance

contrast

Preparation   Hang pictures of masks from various cultures around the room. Discuss with students the fact that masks are often part of a costume, with "maskers" often wearing headdresses or hats of some type. Talk about similarities and differences between the masks of different cultures. Discuss hats for men and for women, what might be differences in hair and hair styles. For very young children, pre-cut the vertical folds on a paper cutter. Remind students to glue the outer (pre-cut) edges of the paper in the center because the outer edges of the paper are already straight.

Alternative Project

SHAPED CONSTRUCTION-PAPER MASKS Doris Vaughn's students of the Jefferson Elementary School in St. Louis made charming three-dimensional masks. Students folded construction paper in half lengthwise, making eyes, noses and mouth at the appropriate places, then tucking the chin inside to give a rounded effect. They cut out eyes with scissors, sometimes outlining them with paper, and made paper noses to go on the center fold. Curled hair, cones for cheeks, and lips of contrasting colors gave each face a unique appearance. Hair was curled or braided paper.

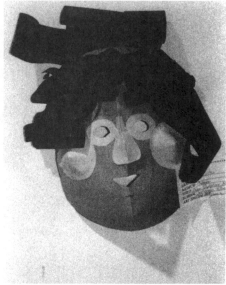

These three-dimensional sculptured masks were created by students of Doris Vaughn, Jefferson Elementary School, St. Louis, Missouri.

PROJECT 6–7   SYMMETRICAL PAPER MASKS

STUDENT PAGE

Materials

glue

scissors

chalk

9 X 12-inch construction paper, cut in half vertically (2 sheets per student)

12 X 18-inch drawing or construction paper

Directions

1. Carefully fold two sheets of contrasting construction paper exactly in half lengthwise (a hot-dog fold). Cut the two sheets in half vertically. On one of the halves, use the chalk to draw the *outer* part of a head (from the chin, around the back, including ears, to the top of the head).

2. Firmly hold a contrasting half of paper next to the one on which you have drawn, and cut around the chalk outline through both layers. Place the uncut (outer) edges next to each other and glue the two halves side by side on a background sheet of paper.

3. Use the other two halves of the sheets of paper to make details such as hats, noses, mouths, eyes, mustaches, ties, etc., again cutting through both layers at once so you have two identical shapes. Remind students to place the eyes halfway down the face. Glue these details on the opposite color paper.

4. If students want to wear their masks, have them determine where their own eyes will be, then cut these out before gluing on other features. Or mount the mask on drawing paper for display.

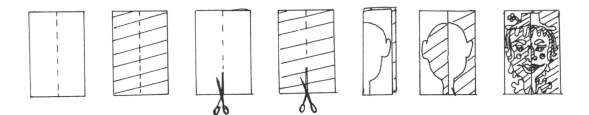

PROJECT 6-8
PLASTER—GAUZE MASKS

FOR THE TEACHER   These masks can be adapted to any of the themes listed in the introduction to mask-making.

Vocabulary

form

texture

emphasis

pattern

craftsmanship

Preparation   Directions given here are for making masks directly on students' faces, covered (*except for nostrils*) with plastic wrap. Half the class can make masks one day; the other half, another day. This project takes approximately 45 minutes. Students will need to spend one day cutting plaster—gauze and designing the masks. Two more days will give time to make the masks, reinforce and make additions, and decorate them.

If working in the "direct" method (appropriate from fifth grade and up), it is important to stress to the student "patients" that they can take the mask off any time in the whole process and that they are in charge. The "surgeon" should constantly reassure the "patient." The students' faces will be covered for approximately 15 minutes. Consider playing soothing music to relax the students. **NOTE: If you sense that a student is anxious about having his or her face covered, suggest that the student bring in a coffee can, box, or a balloon on which to form a mask. Ask students to wear old clothes or smocks.**

You, the teacher, should demonstrate how the plastic wrap has to be placed in order to leave the nostrils open, and then make a quick check before students begin. This method is preferable to working directly on the student's skin so you avoid plaster in hair, eyes, ears, etc. Tell students you will ask from time-to-time for a thumbs-up sign to make sure they are feeling all right. Continually check to encourage students to work over the entire mask, not just the center portion. Neatness definitely counts. Remind students not to pour plaster-water down the sink, but rather into a bucket, to allow it to settle.

Have an area cleared for the damp masks to be placed when they are finished. Make sure names are marked on the inside.

When the masks are slightly hardened, use a Phillips screwdriver to punch holes on the sides for hanging (or an electric drill, if they have already hardened).

Alternative Project

MASKS FORMED OVER PLASTIC MOLDS   If you prefer, you may purchase enough individual plastic reusable mask forms from an art supply house for an entire class to use. Although these all look alike in the beginning, students can change their own masks by adding aluminum-foil or cardboard features (hair, mustaches, beards), which are then covered with plaster—gauze.

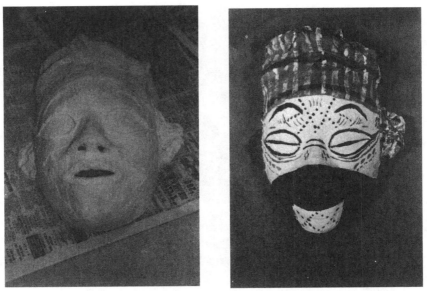

Student Dionna Arnold's plaster–gauze face mask was changed by adding string, cardboard, and aluminum foil.

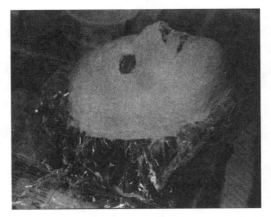

This mask, formed with plaster–gauze on student Rachel Scharf's face, was then transformed by the addition of aluminum foil hair.

These masks of plaster–gauze were formed on purchased plastic forms, then cardboard features added prior to covering with plaster–gauze. Courtesy of Marla Mayer, Highcroft Ridge Elementary School, St. Louis County, Missouri.

PROJECT 6–8   PLASTER–GAUZE MASKS

Materials

plastic wrap
aluminum foil
cardboard
plaster-impregnated gauze
newspaper
containers for warm water
jute, raffia, yarn
scissors
hand mirror
9 × 12-inch newsprint with each student's name on it
bucket (to pour plaster-water into and allow it to settle)

These Chinese masks demonstrate a variety of designs that can be painted on face masks.

Directions

DAY 1. PREPARATION

1. On newsprint, draw how you will decorate your mask, designing any additions you will make such as hats, horns, ears, beards, or mustaches. Cut plaster–gauze into at least 50 pieces approximately 3 × 6 inches and wrap into newsprint (taped shut), with your name on the outside. Make four strips approximately 2 × 24 inches to go around the outside (under the chin and on top of the head).

DAY 2. "SURGEONS" AND "PATIENTS"

2. Cover the tables with newspaper. The "patient" lies down with eyes closed, and two long pieces of plastic wrap are draped over the head all the way to the tabletop. One piece goes across the top of the nose to the tip, *leaving the nostrils uncovered*, and the other piece begins underneath the nose so the patient can breathe. It is tucked under the chin and around the neck.

3. Dip a long piece of tape in warm water and draw it between your thumb and index fingers over the bowl to smooth it, getting rid of excess water. Take the time to open the gauze so it is flat before you apply it. Start at one side in front of the ears, go under the chin, and on top of the head just above the forehead. Do this again to reinforce the edges. Next apply the tape around or over the eyes, then the nose, then cover the entire mask with one coat before beginning a second layer. You should have at least three layers over the entire mask to give it strength. This step needs to be done in one day.

4. When the nose has begun to get firm, cut a piece of tape 3/4 inch × 3 inches. Fold it and place it down the center of the nose between the nostrils. Add horizontal tape at the top of the nose and the upper lip to hide those edges. After allowing the mask to harden, you and the patient remove it together and set it aside to harden overnight.

5. When the masks have cooled, strengthen any weak areas. You may make additions by attaching aluminum foil or cardboard shapes such as hair, beards, mustaches, or hats that are covered with more plaster tape. To conserve paint, coat the entire mask with polymer medium or thinned white glue before painting with tempera or acrylic paint. Think about how you can paint the eyes to make them important. You could make hair with yarn, jute (fringed), or raffia.

PROJECT 6–9
ALUMINUM CAN MASKS

FOR THE TEACHER   Mask-making is a universal art form that has been passed down through the generations. This project, based on Mexican tin masks, was developed and shared by art specialists Nora Olive and Beth Goyer in the Pattonville School District, St. Louis County, Missouri. These masks were not meant to be worn, but were created as wall decorations.

Vocabulary

form

shape

variety

contrast

texture

emphasis

Preparation   Talk with the students about the different purposes of masks (religious cere-monies, celebrations, carnival, or only for display). Photocopies may be made of masks from many different cultures, or this project can be based on masks of only one culture. Have students recycle aluminum cans (after first rinsing and draining them). Use ordinary classroom scissors to *carefully* cut off the top and bottom. **SAFETY NOTE: If students are alerted to safety procedures, and you closely supervise the can cutting, this material can be safely used with children as young as fourth grade.** Plan ahead for this project in order to have enough cans available. Have students bring in materials from home for trim, and ask them to think of ways to utilize the tops and bottoms of the cans (for eyes, ears, etc). Beth Goyer said that in addition to assembling these masks with brads, she often simply used a paper stapler.

Alternative Project
TIN HANGING ORNAMENTS   Tin decorations have been made in Mexico for purposes other than masks. Hanging ornaments in the forms of stars, pine trees, and decorated fringed circles are also very popular. Make a version of these ornaments from recycled soft-drink cans. They may be cut out with school scissors, fringed, and left plain or colored with permanent markers. Often several con-secutively smaller layers are placed together and joined with a brad in the center.

Interdisciplinary Connections
SOCIAL STUDIES
THE UNIVERSAL LANGUAGE OF MASKS   Study differences and similarities of uses for masks throughout cultures around the world. For example, Italian and Japanese dramas have traditional characters whom everyone in these cultures recognizes.

LANGUAGE ARTS
MASKS OF ONE CULTURAL GROUP   Research the masks of one culture, making photocopies and sharing the results with the class before beginning a mask-making project.

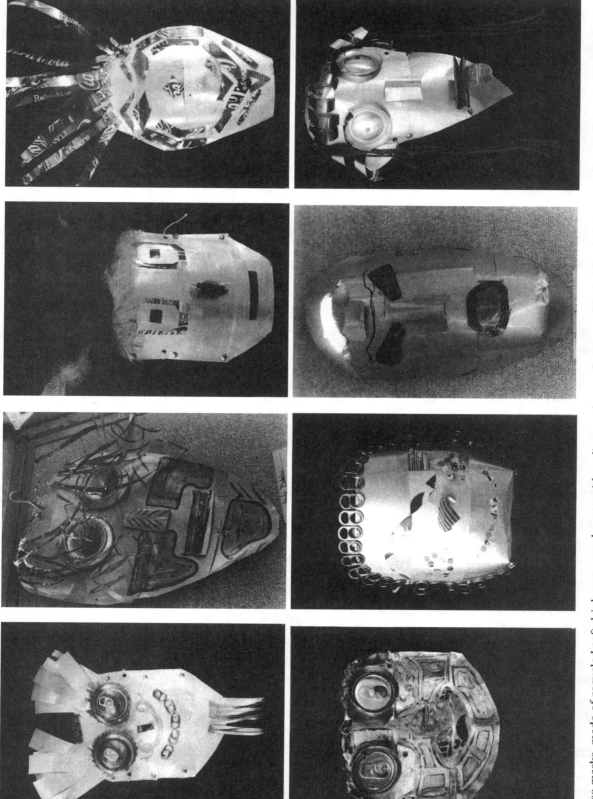

These masks, made of recycled soft-drink cans, can be cut with ordinary scissors. Courtesy of Beth Goyer, Holman Middle School, Pattonville District, St. Louis County, Missouri.

PROJECT 6–9   ALUMINUM CAN MASKS

STUDENT PAGE

Materials

3 to 4 clean aluminum cans per mask

scissors

rulers

pencils

permanent markers

cotton gloves (students wear when cutting tops and bottoms
from cans)

brads

other decorative items: "jewels," yarn, sequins, leather scraps,
feathers

hole punch

low-temperature glue guns

Directions   Masks have been used in cultures around the world for many different purposes. These include religious ceremonies, the theater, carnival celebrations, or simply as decoration. Mexico has long had a tradition of creating masks from
tin. Metal can be fringed and curled around a pencil, or the masks can have such
things as beads, jewels, color, and feathers added.

SAFETY NOTE: The edges of cut aluminum cans are sharp. Be careful!

1. Before beginning your mask, make several drawings to get an idea of what is
    possible. To make life-sized masks, cut the tops and bottoms from three alu-
    minum soft drink cans. *Carefully* trim these pieces neatly with scissors or a
    paper cutter. To flatten, grasp each end of one piece, and run the curved
    side back and forth on the edge of a table.

2. To join horizontal strips together, slightly overlap two pieces (plain side up)
    and use a hole punch to make holes through two corners. Insert a brad
    through the pieces to be joined (three aluminum strips used horizontally are
    big enough for a mask). These may then be gently
    curved to the shape of a face. Set aside the tops and
    bottoms you cut off, and any tabs you can get. You
    may be able to use these later for decorations.

3. Think about the personality of your mask. It could
    be young or old, male or female. Decorations are up
    to your imagination. Some suggestions are:

    - Add a headdress (feathers, more foil, yarn).

    - Instead of only two brads to join a strip, put brads
      all along the edges at close intervals.

    - Use extra cans to make such decorations as
      fringes, beards, or curls from strips of metal.

- Use tabs from many soda cans as decoration, or combine the tabs with yarn for hair.
- Use the colored outsides of soda cans as decorations, cutting them into thin strips for hair.
- Use the bottoms of cans as eyes, carefully drawing a circle for the eyeball.
- Draw feathers with permanent marker.
- Add feathers, "jewels," or sequins to make a fancy mask.
- Insert colored raffia through punched holes.
- Use the hole punch to create dozens of metal dots to glue onto the mask.
- Color certain areas with colored permanent markers.
- Use brightly colored marbles for eyes.
- Add ears, and hang strips of aluminum for earrings.
- Work with the three strips of aluminum vertically.
- Add a nose.

4. Display masks together on a black background or on fringed layers of burlap.

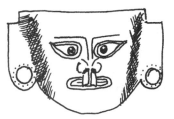

PROJECT 6-10
NORTHWEST COAST REPOUSSÉ MASKS

FOR THE TEACHER   Rather than basing features of these masks on human faces, adapt Northwest Native American designs based on animal totems (symbols) such as birds and fish of the region, raven, bear, beaver, whale, fish, and wolf. Some of the stylized animal designs have features that look surprisingly human.

Although Northwest Coast Native Americans used copper as decorations on masks, rather than entire masks, metal-foil masks have been found by archaeologists in several places around the world. Most are of solid gold foil that have been shaped into portraits of the deceased. Young students may already know about the Egyptian boy king, Tutankhamen, and many have seen pictures of his famous mask. Other gold masks have been found in China, Greece, Peru, and Central Europe.

Vocabulary

totem	repoussé
texture	bas-relief
embossing	stippling

Preparation   Give students a 2 × 6-inch rectangle of metal on which they may practice textures (this can be used later as a bookmark). Copper was an especially significant metal to Northwest Coast Native Americans. In Potlatches (Northwest Coast Native American festivals), a "copper" (shield) might be given as a token of esteem. Copper may sometimes be found on masks.

Interdisciplinary Connections
SOCIAL STUDIES

SPECIAL FESTIVALS In connection with making Northwest Coast masks, students could compare and contrast some of the different celebrations held by Native American cultures throughout North America. For example, the Potlatch of the Northwest Coastal Indians was considerably different from the Corn Dance of Southwestern Native Americans. This study could extend to various cultures around the globe.

This life-size copper repoussé mask is colored with permanent marker.

This carved wooden Northwest Coast mask is based on "Raven." It has cedar braids, a "copper" on one cheek, inlaid mother of pearl for eyes and forehead, and, of course, Raven feathers. Carved by Joe Bolton, Collection of the author.

Headpiece, 19th century, Bella Coola People, wood, paint, abalone shell, copper, mirrored glass, Saint Louis Art Museum, Gift of Morton D. May

House Post, mid-nineteenth century, Northwest Coastal Indians, $110 \times 37^{1}/_{2} \times 13$ inches, top; $35^{1}/_{2} \times 36^{1}/_{2} \times 13$, bottom; The Nelson–Atkins Museum of Art, Kansas City, Missouri (Purchase: Nelson Trust). Student-made totem masks can be displayed to resemble a totem pole by mounting on construction paper.

PROJECT 6–10   NORTHWEST COAST REPOUSSÉ MASKS

STUDENT PAGE

Materials

copper-colored aluminum foil or copper foil

burlap in several colors

newsprint

8½ × 11-inch paper

tools: dull pencils, tongue depressors, sharpened dowels, brush ends, mechanical pencil

black and red permanent markers

newspaper pads

pencils

Directions

1. Decide what "totem" will be used on your mask and make several thumbnail sketches. It could be a bird, fish, or animal, and often might have almost human features. Eyes and mouth are often exaggerated. Experiment with textures on a small piece of foil, giving depth by working on both back and front to push and repush (repoussé in French).

2. After you have selected one of the designs, fold a piece of white paper in half and draw half the design (with half the nose on the fold). Take the folded piece of paper to a window and trace the same features on the other half of the paper. Make the features exaggerated and interesting.

3. Tape the pattern onto the foil and trace around it to transfer the design to the foil. Place the foil on a pad of newspaper and use an embossing tool (pencil) to push the features. Work first on one side, then on the other to stretch the foil. This repushing on both front and back creates depth and contrast. Use a flat tool to smooth some areas.

4. If you wish, use black or red marker to emphasize *some* of the features such as the eyes, mouth, eyebrows, and ears. Shape the mask by cutting out around the outside. Glue the finished mask onto two or three burlap circles cut several inches larger than the masks. Fringe the burlap to make hair. Or simply mount on black paper or posterboard.

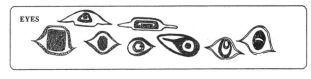

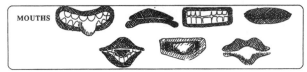

PROJECT 6–11
CAJUN SCREENWIRE MASKS

FOR THE TEACHER   The Cajuns of the Southwest part of Louisiana settled there when they were forced to leave the Arcadian (Cajun) region of Canada. Their customs at Carnival time date back to the Medieval Age of Europe, and are reflected in the traditional religious hats of a miter (a Bishop's Hat) and a cone (worn by ladies of Medieval times) that are often worn with the masks. The Cajuns see Mardi Gras as a time for laughing, teasing, and fooling their friends. They disguise themselves completely, wearing masks and costumes made of strips of cloth. Their masks are traditionally made of screenwire (as are some masks created in the Caribbean). Some of the masks are lined with plain cloth with holes cut for eyes so there is no chance of recognition. They also wear gloves so friends won't recognize their hands when they go begging for a Guinea (money), chicken, or a bag of rice for the pot.

> ***Vocabulary***
>
> tradition
>
> score
>
> emphasis
>
> pattern

Preparation   To help the process along, pre-cut the wire into mask-size pieces (sizes vary according to the age of the students), and make a sample yourself so you will have solved some problems that students might encounter. Students will have an opportunity for individual expression when it comes to completing the masks, but the general shapes will all be the same.

Pitchy Patchy Costume/Jonkonnu Masquerade, 1990, Millicent Matthie, Saint Louis Art Museum. The screenwire mask and strips of cloth on this costume closely resemble the Carnival costumes of the Cajun tradition.

PROJECT 6-11   CAJUN SCREENWIRE MASKS

STUDENT PAGE

Materials

metal screenwire

acrylic paint (or gesso)

permanent marker

tape (or cloth)

scraps of cloth

glue or glue gun

scissors

sequins

brushes

feathers

stapler

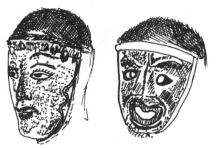

These drawings are based on Cajun masks from a workshop at the National Art Education Convention in New Orleans.

Directions   Screenwire masks allow the wearer to see out and talk, but people cannot really see who is wearing them. Paint features on them, then put trim around the edges. **SAFETY REMINDER: Be very careful handling the wire until you have had an opportunity to fold the edges and cover them.**

1. Leave the top of the mask in a straight line, and draw an oval-shaped face. The face could be a human face with funny designs, a clown, or something like a cat or bird. Pinch the screenwire in the center to form a nose. Then gently bend the wire in and out to form eye sockets, cheeks, eyebrows, mouth, and chin. Coax the screenwire edges to bend to fit the face. To make the chin and forehead rounded, make slits, then place one slit edge on top of the other and staple them.

2. To make this a wearable mask, use the tip of a pair of scissors to score 1/2 inch around the outside edges of the mask. This will help you to finish the edges by neatly folding the screenwire toward the *outside*. These edges should be bound on both sides of the mask with tape or cloth to prevent scratching.

3. Use a brush to coat the wire with paint or gesso. Then draw ears, eyes, designs, mouth, and teeth with marker. Paint within these designs with several colors of acrylic paint. The paint allows the wearer to see out, but viewers cannot quite tell who is behind the mask.

4. After the mask is painted, use a stapler, glue, or a glue gun to attach decorations made of strips of cloth. Or make a cone or bishop's miter hat to attach to the top of the mask. Sometimes the hats match the mask and are covered with cloth or decorated with sequins, glitter, or feathers. Another possibility is to line the mask with plain cloth, sewing the cloth to the outside edges of the mask.

5. If the masks are only used for display and will be mounted on cardboard, it is not necessary to bind the edges. Use your imagination in mounting the mask on a cardboard background, painting the background and adding hair of paper, crinkly paper, cloth strips, steel wool, etc.

PAPIER MÂCHÉ

Something about truly messy projects has enormous appeal for young people. Papier mâché has so many positive qualities that far outweigh the negative ones that I strongly recommend this experience for all ages. New pastes, armature ideas, and adaptations developed through the years have made it far easier than it used to be. Working in papier mâché is inexpensive and allows students to recycle newspapers and brown paper bags. Paper towels are also perfect for this project and cover large areas at a time.

PREPARATION

Papier mâché always needs to be formed over an armature. The armature can simply be made of rolled or wadded paper held together with masking tape, aluminum foil, balloons, soft-drink bottles, milk cartons, boxes, or chicken wire. The more stable and better prepared the armature, the easier the whole process will be.

Large "pitchy patchy" puppets were made to be held aloft in an all-school parade. The papier mâché face was formed over a balloon. Shoulder, arms, and hands were cardboard, and the whole was covered with strips of rags. From the classes of Marla Mayer and apprentice teacher Jennifer Feise at Highcroft Ridge School, St. Louis County, Missouri.

The fish was formed over a newspaper armature.

This student papier mâché penguin was formed over a large container.

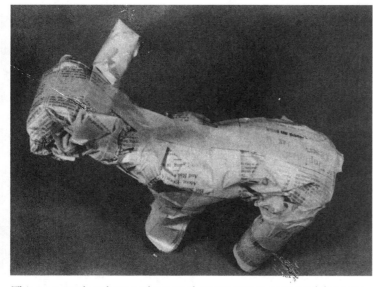

This wrapped and tapped "animal armature" is prepared for papier mâché.

PROJECT 6–12
PAPIER MÂCHÉ MASKS

FOR THE TEACHER   Before beginning this milk-jug mask project, consider having an overall theme so that when the masks are displayed together, they will appear unified. Suggested themes are Animals, Carnival, Native American (Northwestern, Kachina, Eastern Woodlands), African, Caribbean, Japanese, Chinese. While students could select any design they wish, once the basic mask is developed, many students will benefit from a specific assignment.

Vocabulary

form

emphasis

variety

pattern

Preparation   Have photocopies of masks available for students to observe as they develop their own designs. Particularly if headdresses will be part of the mask, examples help students to develop ideas. For younger students, you may cut the cartons or the students may bring in their milk cartons already cut in half at home. If using milk-carton armatures, simply leave the cartons inside. Making a mask on one side of a balloon offers an effective alternative to working on milk cartons. Advise students to especially reinforce the edges on a balloon-mask or it will curl in upon itself when painted.

Alternative Projects

PAPIER MÂCHÉ ANIMAL To form a newspaper armature (an animal or human, for example), loosely roll a long length of paper for the body and head, folding it in from each end to meet and be taped in the middle. Insert the legs and head (newspaper or foil) to go through the folded roll of newspaper. The body can be enclosed in foil and secured with tape before beginning so nothing will fall off. Make sure the sculpture will stand by itself before beginning to add the papier mâché. Paper tail and cardboard ears should also be taped on before beginning. Try this yourself before demonstrating it for your students. These animals could be unified through a general theme such as African Animals, Creatures of the Sea, Insects I have Known, Domestic Animals, etc.

PAINT THE JUG If you just do not have the time or inclination to apply papier mâché, you can cut the gallon milk jugs in half vertically, with the handle as a nose, and simply have students paint masks on the jugs with acrylic paint (or tempera mixed with liquid detergent or polymer medium to help it adhere to the plastic). These can be trimmed with almost anything.

Student Karen Brass's mask, formed on top of a half-gallon milk jug, shows the careful addition of cardboard features done before the mask was covered with papier mâché.

Student Julie Merz's playful lion mask was formed on the non-handle side of a half-gallon milk jug. Feathers are in the same color the mask was painted.

Student Ramona Roberts' mask, formed over a half-gallon milk jug, was painted in red and brown earth tones. The hair is composed of strips of kraft paper that have been painted using the same colors. Features were formed before the papier mâché was added.

PROJECT 6–12   PAPIER MÂCHÉ MASKS

Materials

plastic one-gallon milk jugs (clean)
utility knife
newspapers
balloons
cardboard
aluminum foil
masking tape
tempera paint
brushes
feathers, beads, raffia, jute
Pritt™ or Ross™ paste or wallpaper paste

Directions

1. Carefully cut the milk jug in half vertically on the corners so the handle is in the middle of one half. Select either half of the plastic milk jug as your base (the handle could be a nose). The neck of the carton can be placed up or down—your personal choice.

2. Before beginning the papier mâché, decide on the character of your mask. Add headdress, nose, horns, ears, or eye openings before beginning. These can be made of rolled or folded newspaper, cardboard, or aluminum foil. Tape these to the bottle.

3. Tear newspaper into strips and dip into the paste. Pull the strips up between two fingers to get rid of excess paste. Completely cover the mask with newspaper, folding it over the milk jug edges for a nice finish. For maximum strength, use four layers of paper, starting with a layer of newspaper and finishing with kraft paper torn into pieces approximately 1-1/2 inches square. If the carton–armature is left inside, one layer of newspaper and one layer of kraft paper will be adequate.

4. While the mask is drying, draw how you think it will look and consider how you will paint it. Use only a few colors. Patterns such as stripes, dots, diamonds, and checkerboard are especially effective. Small dots can be carefully applied using the wooden end of a brush. Use a paper punch to make holes in the side and insert string for hanging.

5. Some form of hair or headdress offers a finishing touch. One student cut thirty 25 × 2-inch strips of kraft paper and pulled it through the paste to give it "body." She then painted these to match the mask and applied them with Tacky™ glue all around the head and under the chin.

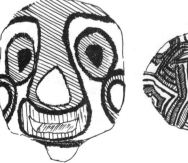

PROJECT 6–13 WALKING CANE

FOR THE TEACHER   A folk art from the American South, the decorated walking cane is based on African traditions. These normally are carved from sturdy branches that are cut to the proper length and sometimes painted to resemble "power" figures of snakes, lizards, and alligators. African tradition says that African holy men threw "conjuring canes" into the air to capture the attention of the gods. One modern carver, Luster Willis, carves most of his canes with figures of people at the top. Another explanation for the cane-making tradition is that they are based on the European walking stick used by gentlemen settlers of the South. Some Northeast Native American groups also have a cane-making tradition.

Vocabulary
form

variety

emphasis

folk art

carving

Preparation   If you have access to tree branches or can convince students to bring in their own, these would be ideal. You may be lucky enough to have a student who enjoys gathering them, or a parent who will help out. Reality, however, says that it is unlikely you will have enough sticks, so you could instead combine 1-inch dowels, PVC tubing, broomsticks, etc., with papier mâché to resemble these carved walking canes. For the students to do the modeling at the top prior to finishing in papier mâché, use whatever you have on hand that is malleable, such as paper towels and tape, clay, aluminum foil, papier mâché pulp, oil clay, or Model Magic®.

Adaptations for Younger Students
STICK SNAKES AND LIZARDS Find natural sticks of any size and simply use tempera to paint designs that resemble snakes or lizards. If the stick is thick enough, use a saw to cut a V-shape at one end for a mouth, and file the other end for a pointy tail. Show students how to make decorative designs with a small brush, a pencil eraser, or a cotton swab dipped in paint.

Interdisciplinary Connection
SOCIAL STUDIES

LEARN ABOUT FOLK ART Have students research the work of folk artists throughout the country to find out where some of these traditions might have originated. Help students to recognize the characteristics of work of naive sculptors and painters. Most self-taught artists use bright colors, are often inspired by nature, sometimes base their work on religion, show little sense of proportional scale, and try to make their work true-to-life. (Sounds like children's art, doesn't it?)

PROJECT 6–13 WALKING CANE

STUDENT PAGE

Materials

1-inch round sticks (dowels, broomsticks, branches)
aluminum foil, Model Magic™, oil clay, or clay
paper towels
paste (wallpaper, Pritt®, or Ross®)
containers for paste
masking tape
kraft paper torn into small pieces
pencil
brushes
acrylic or tempera paint
raffia, beads, jute

Directions   You will not be *carving* a wooden walking cane, as sculptors often did. Instead, you will be making your stick look like a wooden walking cane by adding "knots" onto it with tape as if it were real wood, and covering it with papier mâché.

1. Decide what the character of your cane will be. At the top of the handle you might mold the head of a snake, dog, lizard, alligator, human, or some other creature. If you choose to do a snake, lizard, or alligator, have the "body" wind around the handle from the head down to the tail at the bottom (paper towels might be useful for this step).

2. When the head is secure and you have placed all the knots or other character marks on the stick, it is time to add papier mâché. Some sticks appear twisted, and may have several creatures all the way from the top to the bottom.

3. Use small pieces of kraft paper to get greater detail on the head, although you may use larger pieces of paper on the rest of the cane. Dip the paper into the paste and pull it between two fingers to eliminate excess paste so it will dry faster and be less messy. Carefully place the paper, molding it on the modeled head and the remainder of the cane. Two layers of kraft paper should be enough.

4. When the cane is dry, use acrylic or tempera paint to cover it in bright colors. Many folk artists love using bright colors and patterns on their hand-carved work, while others prefer to make the wood beautiful just by polishing. If you prefer not to use bright colors, you could carefully paint yours to look like wood by using several shades of brown and a fine brush to make the grain of the wood.

5. It is also possible to make a decorative walking cane by adding things that hang down from string wrapped at the "neck" of the stick. These could be raffia, beads, bells, bones, shells, or coins.

PROJECT 6–14
GREEK VASE

FOR THE TEACHER   The Greek vase made from papier mâché can be formed over an armature of one- or two-quart soft-drink plastic jugs. This project, presented to a group of Parkway School District art teachers by Clare Richardson and Lauren Davis, has been used by many of the teachers' classes with great success. In addition to the potential for a variety of vase forms, consider other forms such as the chalice or victory cup that could be formed the same way. The Greek vase had specific color schemes based on the color of the clay. Early pottery was "black figure." It evolved to "red figure," and ultimately to "white ground." Each vase shape had a specific purpose ranging from storage jars to water carriers, oil jugs, perfume flasks, vessels for mixing water and wine, and even huge vases meant to be placed on graves. These were decorated with scenes of Greek mythology and daily life.

Vocabulary

myth

design

balance

Preparation   Read Greek myths and discuss figures that are sometimes seen on Greek vases. Show students examples of Greek vases and shapes. Students might not decide how to decorate the vases until after they are completed. The final coat could be brown paper towels or simply stained with brown, black, and white. Students of art teachers Mary Beth Wilson and Jan Cutlan of Parkway Northeast Middle School, St. Louis County, Missouri, used glue and string to apply decorative designs on shallow chalice shapes.

Interdisciplinary Connections
LANGUAGE ARTS

CREATE A MYTH If students illustrate a traditional Greek myth, have them write it in their own words and then tell the story to the class. They could also be challenged to write an original myth that would explain natural phenomena such as the phases of the moon, the seasons, the tides, or tornadoes.

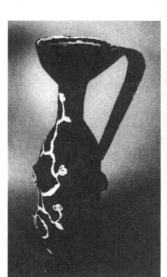

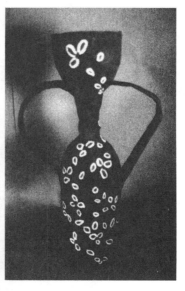

The "pitcher" and Greek vase were both formed or two soft-drink soda bottles.

321

The chalice made by a seventh grader in Jan Cutlan's class at Parkway Northeast Middle School combines wire, string, cardboard, and a soft-drink bottle.

These containers were created by Parkway art teachers, St. Louis County, Missouri at a workshop conducted by Clare Richardson and Lauren Davis.

PROJECT 6–14   GREEK VASE

STUDENT PAGE

Materials

2 plastic soft drink bottles (quart
   or half gallon)
utility knife
kraft paper (or paper bags)
masking tape
newspaper
Pritt® or Ross® paste
paper towels
gesso
brushes
tempera or acrylic paint
string and glue (*optional*)

Directions

1. Decide whether you want to make a short chalice, a victory cup, or a Greek vase. The necks of the two bottles will be taped together after you cut the bottles. Form newspaper to make the handles on either side. They can be in sharp folds or curved. Tape them in place on the bottle. Handles could also be formed of a wire base, then wrapped with papier mâché.

2. Begin applying newspaper strips on the bottles and handles, then add a layer of smaller pieces of brown kraft paper (or paper bags) to give it a smooth finish. The bottle will remain inside. Make sure you have covered everything. If you would like a raised decoration, string can be glued on in a design.

3. When the form is dry, brush on one or two coats of gesso. Decide how the vase will be finished. Most Greek vases had black figures on brick red, brick-red figures on black, or white with brick-red and black or purple figures. The scenes on Greek vases were based on Greek mythology, and often included fighting scenes, animals, or pictures of beautiful gods, heroes, and goddesses.

4. Draw your designs on the vase, then paint it. If you use tempera, it could be varnished when dry by putting a coat of polymer medium on top of it.

PROJECT 6–15
MEXICAN FOLK ART ANIMALS

FOR THE TEACHER Oaxaca (pronounced Wa-HAH-ka) is a state in Mexico that has become famous for its carved and painted folk art figures and masks. The ancient traditions have been brought alive in the last few years as Oaxacan carvings have been recognized as unique. Folk art collectors are buying them almost as fast as they can be produced. Subjects vary, and include peasants, mermaids, angels, animal–musicians, reptiles, and Nativity scenes.

This aluminum-foil armature can be covered with papier mâché prior to painting and decorating in the Oaxacan manner.

Vocabulary

emphasis

repetition

form

variety

movement

rhythm

Preparation Try this project yourself before you begin to teach it to the students. If you can demonstrate how to form the legs, head, and torso, it will be easier to persuade students how—with simple changes—they can give "movement" to their creatures. The book *Oaxacan Woodcarving, The Magic in the Trees* by Shepard Barbash has wonderful illustrations that could be shown to students before they begin the project.

Adaptation for Younger Students

PAPIER MÂCHÉ SNAKES Marla Mayer of Highcroft Ridge Elementary School in St. Louis County, Missouri had her first graders make papier mâché snakes simply by wrapping and taping newspaper for the bodies. Some were coiled and ready to strike, while others simply had interesting slithering bodies. The dots were painted with the wooden end of a brush or cotton swabs.

Alternative Project

BALSA FOAM® CARVINGS Although it is relatively more expensive than papier mâché, these animals can be carved from Balsa Foam® by carving with simple modeling tools and sandpaper. These would be small, but most of the wood-carved animals from Oaxaca *are* small but exquisite.

PROJECT 6–15   MEXICAN FOLK ART ANIMALS

Materials

masking tape

kraft paper or brown paper bags

tempera paint

large and small brushes

aluminum foil (approximately 1 yard per student)

Directions   Because you are making a piece of folk art, it will be relatively small and delicate. These directions are for creating an animal. Decide on the kind of animal you will make, and think about an "attitude." Instead of having the animal just standing, you could make it with the legs spread apart for balance and the head down to the ground as if it were grazing. Or the head, neck, and torso could be twisted to one side.

1. Cut two pieces of foil approximately 8 × 12 inches. Loosely roll these to make two 8 × 1-inch thick pieces to be folded in half for legs. For the head and body, use a piece that is approximately 15 × 12 inches. Loosely roll this long piece. Fold under at one end for the head and a longish neck. Place the legs underneath, then fold the piece under to enclose the legs and be taped at the neck.

2. Use one more piece of foil around the middle to form the torso of the figure. This will give you a sculpture about 5 × 7 inches in size. Use string, foil, or tape to form a tail. Form ears and other details from foil or cardboard. Before you begin to cover the foil with papier mâché, make sure it will stand by itself.

3. Tear the paper into small pieces (approximately 1-1/2 inches). These small pieces allow you to apply the paper smoothly and get detail. Completely cover the form with two layers of this paper. Allow it to dry. Mexican carvers sometimes added braided tails or manes of hair (if you have a source for real horsehair, it is a nice addition).

4. Apply a base coat of paint in bright colors, black, or white. The form of the animal tells us what it is, so it isn't necessary to have realistic colors. The details you will paint on afterwards will be what make this piece wonderful. The details in Oaxacan animals are painted very carefully, with repetitious designs such as flowers with petals, small white dots (applied with a toothpick or the end of a wooden brush), lines, and combinations of these designs. These designs are not haphazard, but are planned.

PROJECT 6–16
SCRAP-WOOD ASSEMBLAGE

FOR THE TEACHER   The students of several colleagues have made charming wooden sculptures using scrap wood. These include Sandra Nickeson's *Guardian Angels*, painted animals, faces, flowers, small cars and trucks (from the Guardian Angel Settlement Association), Toni Wilson's imaginary animals and people (North Kirkwood Middle School), Jan Cutlan's animals (Parkway Northeast Middle School), and Nora Olive's Celtic crosses (Remington Traditional School, Pattonville District, St. Louis County, Missouri). Young students accept that things don't have to be perfect and colors don't have to be real.

Vocabulary

pattern	repetition
variety	color
rhythm	emphasis
unity	

Preparation   Get the scrap wood! Get it from shop classes, parents who have home workshops, buy scraps by the box from a lumberyard, obtain leftovers from a factory, go to recycle shops. If you want it, you will find it. The less cutting you and the students do, the easier this will be.

You may need to use electric drills for screw holes or electric keyhole saws, but limit the use of *electrical* tools to yourself or another adult. Depending on the size of the pieces, some may have to be nailed together rather than glued, but avoid this when possible.

Although these can simply be abstract assemblages, middle school students react better to having a general theme such as living creatures (people or animals), houses, or cars. A theme will help unify the display and narrow the focus to have an overall idea before beginning. Many of the sculptures are better when they are painted in the Oaxacan manner as described in the preceding project (lots of pattern, unrealistic colors), but sometimes students prefer not to use the pattern all over.

Sandra Nickeson's students from the Guardian Angel Settlement in St. Louis, Missouri created these out-sized sculptures from saw horses, old stools, wooden boxes, and discarded lumber. Of their work, Sandra says, "they listen visually." Her students' work is done collectively, in a "call and response" method. "Someone expresses something visually, someone else looks at something and responds to it."

PROJECT 6–16 SCRAP-WOOD ASSEMBLAGE

STUDENT PAGE

This assemblage was created by a student of Jan Cutlan at Parkway Northeast Middle School, St. Louis County, Missouri.

Materials

scrap wood—all sizes and shapes

screws (to put pieces into a base for stability)

white glue

masking tape

hand saws

drill

Directions   You are limited only by your imagination on this project. If you can imagine it, chances are you can build it, too. Remember that it must balance and stand by itself or be attached to a base.

1. Look at various scraps of wood until you find pieces that "look like something" to you. If it is necessary to cut it or change its shape slightly, use a saw under the supervision of your teacher. Once you have your idea, make a small working sketch.

2. Put glue on each piece to be glued together and hold them in place (sometimes tape will work, or you can prop it against something until the glue sets). Sometimes you have to assemble several different sections, then glue them together to make the entire sculpture.

3. Test the piece for stability. If it does not stand, you will need to attach it to a base. This may involve drilling a hole in the bottom of the base and in the bottom of the sculpture, then putting the screw through both pieces. (The screw may need to be *recessed* into the base to avoid making the piece wobble.)

4. When you are satisfied that the sculpture is balanced, use tempera or acrylic paint to decorate it. This is where to really use your imagination. In general, you will know what the sculpture is by its shape. If it looks like an elephant, it really doesn't have to be painted all gray. Instead, paint it in bright colors and, when it is dry, paint it with an overall pattern. Designs can be dots, stripes, zigzags, using a combination of patterns.

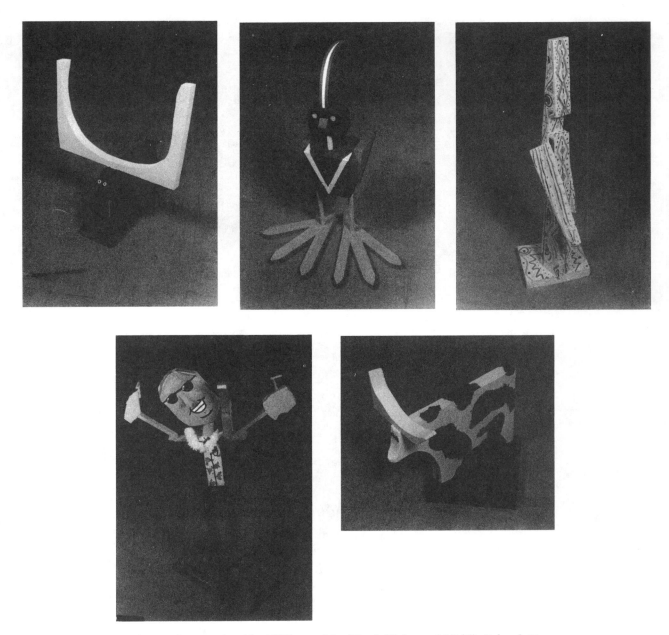

Students of art teacher Toni Wilson of the North Kirkwood Middle School, St. Louis County, Missouri created sculpture from scrap lumber. Some were painted in the Oaxacan manner, with pattern, while others were simply painted in plain colors.

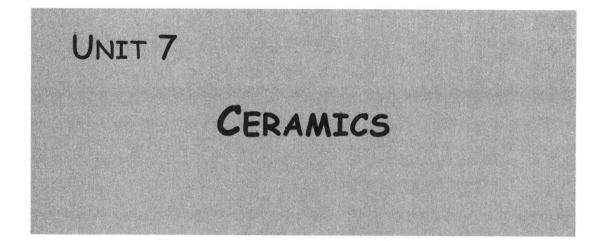

UNIT 7

CERAMICS

The tradition of handmade pottery has evolved all over the world as people felt the need for utensils, cooking and storage vessels, sculpture to represent spiritual needs, and decorative architectural elements. An *ancient* pot seen in a museum in China appears to be a scorched basket encased in clay. Perhaps it was an accidental discovery that clay would make a basket waterproof, and that if the clay-covered basket were put in a fire, it would last longer. Students may be fascinated about the long history of pottery, how archaeologists can tell a great deal about a civilization just from the pieces of broken pottery they dig up. Most knowledge of ancient Greek and Roman civilizations comes from paintings on pottery. One can deduce how people lived by their *artifacts*.

In this section, introductory projects are given that will expose students to several methods of working with clay. Because ceramics is a universal art form, any of these techniques could be adapted to fit almost any culture. Decorative designs on pots also appear to be universal, with identical motifs from nature, geometric designs, spirals, and curved lines found on pottery from cultures throughout the world.

These projects could easily complement a study unit in another subject such as Science or Social Studies. Take advantage of the units or themes being covered at a particular grade level, and you will find students eager, informed, and enthusiastic about what they are making. Because many schools do not have access to a kiln, you can adapt some of these projects to use self-hardening or plasticine clay.

If you ask students what their favorite activity is in art, many will answer that they love ceramics most. Perhaps it is because the opportunity to do ceramics is not offered so frequently as other media. With careful planning, even with a large student body, each student can do at least one ceramic project a year. As with other techniques, the more opportunities students have to work in a given medium, the more proficient they will become. Results will vary depending on the age and skill-level of the students. Some of these pieces will be found on tables in the students' homes long after the students are grown.

SOME CONSIDERATIONS FOR WORKING WITH CLAY

Hand-Building Methods include pinch pots, coil building, or slab building. Sculptural methods can be additive (built-up) or subtractive (taking portions away from a general form). Within these methods, an infinite number of possibilities is available for elementary and middle school teachers. Working in ceramics is a skill-building process. Some beginning students are first taught how to make a pinch-pot or simple small sculpture before moving on to coil or slab building. Any of these processes is entirely appropriate at any age level.

Distributing the Clay   Normally clay is purchased in large blocks. Pull a wire or piece of string through the clay to divide the block into the appropriate number of pieces. Collect plastic bags in advance to give each student so the unused portion of clay is kept damp while the student is working.

Wedging   Unless clay is straight from the box, it must be wedged before using to eliminate air bubbles. Air inside the finished artwork can cause the piece to explode in firing. If you are wedging larger quantities yourself, place the clay on canvas and use a kneading motion. Check for air bubbles by cutting apart with a string or wire. Students can wedge clay by forming a ball and firmly slapping between the hands for about ten minutes to force out bubbles.

Conditioning Clay   While you can buy powdered clay by the sack and add water, very few teachers choose to do this. Occasionally pre-mixed clay might already be too dry to use when it is delivered. To condition clay, use a wooden brush handle to punch deep holes and fill these with water. Store the clay overnight, and it will absorb the water. If clay is totally dry, it can be put into a barrel or bucket and covered with water until it becomes soft enough to work, then excess water poured off. The water-logged clay can be put on Masonite or plaster bats. (Bats are made by pouring plaster of Paris into aluminum pie tins.) Remember, clay is ancient soil. The only clay that can't be reconditioned is that which has been fired; however, small amounts of fired clay can be pulverized to make grog (clay stiffener). If you are using recycled clay, it is advised that you wedge the clay and form it into individual balls (stored in a plastic bag) for distribution.

Working Consistency   Test clay for elasticity by rolling a 1/2-inch thick coil. If this can easily be bent around a finger without cracking, it is ideal for work. It is far easier to have the clay at the correct consistency than to have students using bowls of water at their tables to smooth the outside. When water is used to smooth the surface, the outside dries more quickly and tends to crack. It should be used only if no further smoothing can be done with their fingers. A large sponge could be cut to make smaller sponges (1 × 1 × 1-inch) that could be dampened to smooth the surface.

Identifying the Artwork   Depending on the ages of your students, you will probably prefer to write the student's first and last names, grade, and teacher's initials on the bottom of the work upon collecting it. For very young children, it would be lovely to have a parent or older student–aide helping in this crucial step of identification.

Storing Clay Overnight or Longer   With primary classes in particular, make every effort to complete the project in one working period. To store unfinished work, dampen paper towels and loosely wrap them around the work-in-progress. Carefully wrap the work completely in plastic, then store. Use a piece of masking tape and permanent marker to identify the artwork within each plastic bag.

Safe Storage Is a Chronic Problem   Ideally you would have closed drying cabinets, but reality says you will be fortunate if you can set aside a section of a counter. You should have a place where the artwork can safely dry slowly, be easily identified by class name, and easily retrievable by each student. Work can be stored by class on large pieces of Masonite and moved.

Clay Throwing (Around the Room) Control the natural tendency of children to find out they can make small balls of clay to throw. At almost any age, one or two students per class will think of this. It may never become a problem if you explain that if you see *any* sign of it, that student's clay will be put away for the day. With older students, the child who throws clay is invited to stay with you at recess or after school and wipe down the entire room.

Working Surfaces Squares (approximately 12 inches) of linoleum tile or Masonite placed on newspaper make great individual work surfaces. When the students are finished, they can scrape excess clay into the paper and throw it away, wiping the surface with a paper towel and stacking the square for another class. Burlap, canvas squares, or wallpaper samples are also good work surfaces. If the clay is in good working condition, even newsprint can be used for a work surface. Formica® modeling boards with rubber feet can be purchased from art supply houses.

Tools Purchased tool sets are lovely, but rarely available in sufficient quantity for classroom use. Substitutes are Popsicle sticks (evenly trimmed flat with a knife), pencils, needles stuck in a cork (as a substitute for needle tools), sharpened 1/4-inch dowels, 1 × 12-inch dowel "rolling pins," garlic press in place of a Klay Gun® (for making hair), stainless steel or plastic spoons and knives, used dental tools, and wire or string tied between 2-inch sections of dowels for cutting through large quantities of clay.

Clean-up Start early enough to leave the surfaces as clean as possible. Have enough sponges so tables can be wiped down twice, then they should be dried with paper towels. Keep a bucket where students can reach it to rinse sponges and to avoid washing quantities of clay down the sink. The clay settles to the bottom of the bucket and can be recycled.

Firing Make sure the artwork is completely dry. If it feels cool when you hold it against your cheek, it may still be damp. In the first firing (bisque), pieces can touch. After glazes have been added, make sure the bottom of the piece is clean, or place it on stilts. Make sure glazed pieces do not touch. Leave the kiln lid propped slightly open for the first hour before closing and turning the temperature higher.

Repairing A certain percentage of student work will break. If it breaks before the piece is completely dry, soak the two broken edges in damp paper towels until they are approximately the same consistency, then put together with slip, or slip with vinegar added. If the piece breaks during the bisque firing, it might be put together with white glue and glaze might hold it together during the final firing. When a broken fired piece still has recognizable parts, it can be glued, filled in with plaster of Paris, and painted. Two different colors of spray paint can cover a multitude of mistakes.

Finishing

GLAZING Most elementary and middle school teachers use purchased glazes rather than mixing their own. Underglazes can be applied to greenware (before a first firing), then a clear glaze applied for a second firing. Purchased glazes can be combined by overpainting for some interesting effects. Before applying glaze to a bisque-fired pot, have students dampen it with a sponge. Caution students not to apply the glaze too thickly, and remind them that the bottoms of the pieces *must* be clean.

PAINTING After one firing (bisque ware), pots could be finished by wiping shoe polish on and off, spray painting, or painting with acrylic paints. Because of time limitations or aesthetic choices, some teachers prefer to paint ceramics with acrylic paint after firing rather than devote the time to glazing and refiring the work.

Definitions of Ceramic Terms

Armature. a support for clay while it is being constructed, such as newspaper or a drape mold

Bat. a flat plaster of Paris block for drying clay; sometimes made by pouring plaster into pie tins

Battens. two 1/2 × 1-1/2 × 12-inch boards for rolling out even slabs of clay or to use for paddling

Bisque. (sometimes called biscuit ware) a first firing of clay without glazes

Bone dry. unfired clay that is free of water and ready to fire

Burnish. to polish clay while it is in the greenware stage with the back of a spoon or a stone

Ceramics. clay products that have been fired for permanence

Clay. a moist earth of decomposed rock; for products such as pottery, bricks, tiles, and sculpture

Coiling. a method of creating pots by building up bottom and walls with even, rope-like coils

Cone. mixture of clay and glaze with a specific, established melting point; used in firing

Engobe. thinned clay used to make designs on a different colored clay body

Firing. making clay products permanent through baking at high temperatures in a kiln

Glaze. ground minerals in a solution that adhere to the clay body that when fired have the properties of glass

Greenware. clay in an unfired state

Grog. pulverized fired clay is sometimes combined with clay as a stiffener

Kiln. electric, gas, or wood-fired oven for firing greenware

Leather hard. unfired clay that isn't quite dry, yet firm enough to carve or burnish

Plaster of Paris. cilcined gypsum used in bats for drying clay and to make molds for casting

Potter's wheel. a wheel for making pots driven by hand, foot, or electric power

Raku. a low fire often done outdoors that produces dark areas and iridescence

Scoring. making marks on two pieces of clay before joining together with slip

Scraper. shaped piece of fine sheet steel for use in forming objects

Sgraffito. cutting through a surface layer of engobe (clay) to expose a different colored ground

Slab. clay evenly rolled flat and formed by draping or joining

Slip. clay diluted with water to the consistency of cream; used for joining or as an engobe

Throwing. creating vessels on a potter's wheel

Turning. completing a piece of ware by rotating on a wheel and trimming with tools

Underglaze. colors that can be painted on bisque or greenware that will show through a clear glaze

Wax resist. the application of melted wax to the foot or body of a clay object to resist the glaze

Wedging. kneading moist clay to eliminate air bubbles and produce a uniform texture

Note: These definitions are a partial list from *The Art Teacher's Book of Lists* by Helen Hume (Paramus, New Jersey: Prentice Hall, 1998).

Storage Jar, c. 1900, Acoma Pueblo, earthenware, paint, diameter, 35.2 cm., The Saint Louis Art Museum, Gift of A. L. Dyke

Map of Ceramics Around the World

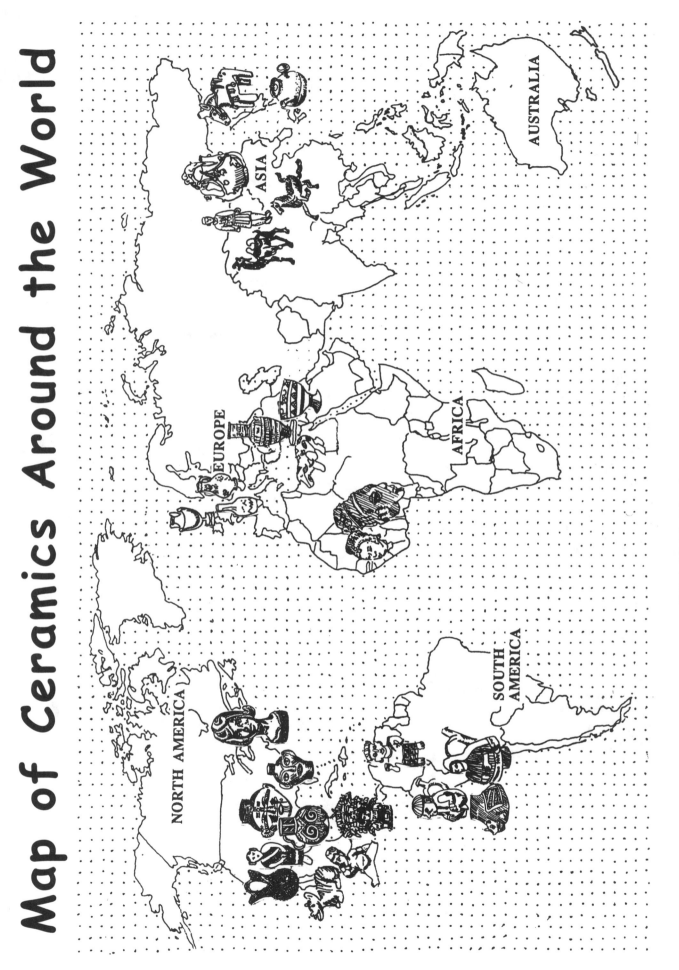

AUSTRALIA

ASIA

EUROPE

AFRICA

NORTH AMERICA

SOUTH AMERICA

TIPS ON PINCH POT, COIL BUILDING, SLAB BUILDING

PINCH POT

Materials Needed clay, plastic for covering work-in-progress, slip (thinned clay)
Pinch pots can be used singly, or combined to make various forms. The secret for a successful pinch pot is to have well-wedged clay of the right consistency.

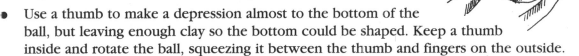

- These pots do not always have to remain round, but they usually begin with a round ball held in the palm of the hand.
- Use a thumb to make a depression almost to the bottom of the ball, but leaving enough clay so the bottom could be shaped. Keep a thumb inside and rotate the ball, squeezing it between the thumb and fingers on the outside.
- Make the walls of an even thickness from bottom to top. Coils of clay could be added if it needs to be made taller or you want to bring it inward at the top. The bottom could placed on a table to flatten, then placed on a "foot" made of a roll of clay.

COIL BUILDING

Materials Needed clay, pencils, paper, tagboard, plastic for covering work-in-progress, tile, Masonite, canvas or paper to work on, knives, paddle, scraper, slip (thinned clay)

- It is important to start with a drawing. A tagboard *template* (side-view cut-out pattern) will help in sticking to the original idea.
- A coiled pot can begin either with a coiled or slab bottom. Usually the larger the pot will be, the larger the size of the coils.

- Roll coils on a table, using the flat part of the palm. Roll from the center outward. The coils should be of uniform thickness.
- To join coils, use a pencil or knife to *score* the two surfaces that will touch. Coat these surfaces with slip (thinned clay).
- Cut the end of a coil at a slant, then score and use slip to join it to the slanted end of the finished coil.

- Apply three coils, then smooth them together on both the inside and outside.
- Carefully smooth the top. When the pot is leather hard (almost dry), it can be polished with the back of a spoon or a stone.
- Choice of surface:

  —Paddle the outside of the pot with a flat stick while a hand supports the inside.

  —Use a *scraper* to give a smooth finish.

  —Smooth only the inside, leaving coils showing on the outside.

  —Use a *pinch and twist* motion on the outside to join one coil with the one beneath it.

- *Glaze*: Painting one glaze on top of a closely color-related glaze sometimes gives a more interesting effect than a single glaze.

SLAB BUILDING

Materials Needed   clay, plastic, battens 1/2 × 1^1/$_2$ × 12 inches, rolling pins or dowels, knives, tagboard, masking tape, canvas or paper as a rolling surface

- Draw and cut out a pattern of tagboard. Loosely tape the pieces of the pattern together to make sure the pieces fit well. Remove the tape.
- Place a well-wedged ball of clay between two boards approximately 1/2 × 12 × 1^1/$_2$ inches placed on a table.
- Use a rolling pin or dowel to flatten the clay to an even thickness throughout.
- Place the pattern pieces on the flattened clay and use a knife to cut straight down around the edge of the pattern.
- Remove the cardboard and allow the pieces to harden slightly.
- To join pieces, score the edges to be joined and coat them with slip before placing them together. Smooth the joint inside and out. If this is to have corners, reinforce the corners with a coil of clay that is smoothed to both sides.

PROJECT 7–1
DOUBLE PINCH POT

FOR THE TEACHER   The pinch pot is excellent for introducing students to ceramics. They learn about the consistency of clay, sometimes that it has a "will" of its own, and doesn't quite do what the potter has in mind. Techniques such as wedging, incising, glazing, sgraffito (scratching a design through a different colored layer of slip [engobe]) can all be incorporated into this project. A pinch pot begins with a ball of clay held in the palm of the hand. The curved fingers of the *holding hand* give general shape to the pot. The pot is turned in the hand as it is developed with the *turning hand*. Larger, flat-bottomed pinch pots can be placed on a table and worked with both hands.

Vocabulary

planes	raku
wedge	form
organic	

Olla, Storage Jar, 1100–1250, Pre-Columbian, earthenware, pigment, Saint Louis Art Museum, Funds given by the Children's Art Festival

Preparation   Discuss *form* with students. This is a good time to talk about the names given to portions of a pot such as *foot, shoulders, belly, handle, neck*. Ask students why they think potters use those terms when they talk about pottery. Demonstrate how to open a pot, and suggest they leave some extra clay at the bottom in case they want to make the pot straight-sided.

Adaptations for Younger Students   Very young students will probably make a single pinch pot. By the time they decorate it by impressing grasses into the surface and put their names on the bottom, an entire period will be used.

Alternative Projects

MULTIPLE PINCH POTS   If you see the students several times a week, the pinch-pot project could incorporate several pots, with as many as five or six openings growing from one base. Challenge students to come up with imaginative forms.

PINCH-POT PEOPLE   If three consecutively smaller pots are used for this project, the inevitable resemblance to an abstract human form results. Encourage students to consider this, deliberately making small changes to create an abstraction. Discuss how shoulders could be created by gently pinching the pots near the top, or *planes* (flat areas) created by gently flattening.

Interdisciplinary Connection
SOCIAL STUDIES

JAPANESE TEA BOWLS   The Japanese Tea Ceremony is a longstanding tradition. Part of the ceremony involves handling and examining tea bowls (even the bottom). The pinch-pot method gives the tea bowls exceptional strength, allowing them to be *raku*-fired (low temperature wood firing). The resulting uneven finish is so greatly admired that some famous individual tea bowls have been given names. Tea bowls generally rest on a small rim, the "foot." Have students research and conduct a tea ceremony when their tea bowls are completed.

PROJECT 7-1   DOUBLE PINCH POT

Materials

slip (clay thinned and mixed with water to
  act as glue)

knives or Popsicle sticks

clay (approximately 2 pounds per student)

grasses (flat or with grain at the top)

plastic wrap

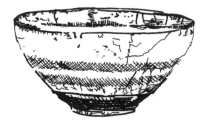

Tea Bowl, Muromachi Period, 16th
Century

Directions   The Japanese pinch pots shown at the bottom of the page show
a variety of shapes. This assignment is to make two pinch pots, then join them
together to make one pot.

1. Make two balls of *slightly* different sizes. Reserve the second ball inside plastic
    wrap while you are making the first pot. Select the larger ball. Using a thumb,
    push it into the ball, but not so deeply that you go through the bottom.

2. Turn the ball in your hand, gently squeezing the sides of the clay with the
    thumb and fingers of your *working* hand while you continually rotate the
    ball with the *holding* hand. The bowl should be about 1/2 inch thick.
    Smooth the inside and outside as you work. The top opening ideally would
    curve slightly inward making it smaller than the bottom. When it is finished,
    set it aside to dry slightly. The bottom should be flat-
    tened enough so the pot will be stable.

3. Work the second ball in the same method as the first,
    making sure it can be set on top of the first ball
    without falling inside. The balls can be in the
    same shape, or you could make one of them tall
    and thin rather than short and round.

4. Cut a hole in the bottom of the top ball and remove the clay. Use a knife to
    score (make rough marks) where both balls will be joined. Cover both
    scored surfaces with slip, then place one pot on top of the other. Use your
    fingers to smooth the two pots together inside and out. Use the knife to
    reach inside if your fingers aren't long enough.

5. To decorate the pot, scratch designs on the outside, or press leaves, grass, or
    stamps into the surface. These natural materials could even be left in the sur-
    face, as they would be burned out in the firing. Depending on the color of
    the clay when the pots have been bisque fired, you may prefer to glaze only
    the *inside* and the lip of the top pot, or rub on shoe polish, allowing the
    color of the clay to show through.

Tea Bowl, Edo Period, 17th
Century

Tea Bowl, Edo Period,
17th Century

Tea Bowl, Edo Period,
17th Century

Tea Bowl, named Hashihime,
Momoyama Period, 16th Century

PROJECT 7-2
COIL-BUILT FACE POTS,
A SOUTHERN TRADITION

FOR THE TEACHER The tradition of making face pots was brought to the American South by African slaves. The techniques were passed down through the generations and continue today. These "grotesque," "voodoo," or "ugly jugs " (as they were sometimes called) are avidly collected and appreciated today. Some families have continued a tradition of creating face pots for more than 50 years. Many contemporary artists use the face-jug forms.

Vocabulary
scoring

slip

exaggeration

function

utilitarian

Preparation These pots will be made using the method of coil building. Depending on the age of your students, you may prefer to have the clay already wedged and divided into individual portions and set aside in plastic. The directions call for enough clay to make a traditional large pot. Naturally you can control the size, depending on the age of the students. Read the introduction that covers preparation and clean-up. The rewards of working with clay more than compensate for the extra time involved.

Adaptations for Younger Students Although we tend to think younger children cannot do effective coil building, I recently saw 6-inch high coil pots made by kindergarten children—so with time, patience, and sufficient budget, there are no limitations. Introduce the youngsters to the technique of rolling and attaching coils through the use of plasticine clay. Or younger students could make face pots using the pinch-pot technique.

Alternative Projects
NATIVE AMERICAN COILED POTTERY Native Americans of the Southwestern Pueblos have developed unique decorations for their coil-formed ceramics. Many fine books are available that describe the differences in appearance among pots from Pueblos such as San Ildefonso, Acoma, Santa Clara, Jimez, and Taos (to name only a few). Individual families of potters from these pueblos have become internationally known, as they pass their traditions from generation to generation.

COILS FORMED IN A BOWL Coils can also be formed on the inside of a plastic container. While coils can be built up in the normal manner, this allows them to be rolled into a spiral, used in a wavy line or zigzags, made into balls, and to have open spaces. With variations in forms, such a pot can be quite interesting.

MEMORY JUGS Another Southern tradition is the *memory jug* that was created to commemorate the life of someone by covering a jug or bottle with a photo and the everyday items used by that person. Items that were embedded in plaster on the surface of a jug included buttons, safety pins, bits of broken ceramics, seashells, a thimble, a watch face, metal objects, numbers, doll parts, marbles. Students can make their own memory jugs by bringing in their own treasures. This project will have to be developed over a period of time. Cover a portion of the jug with plaster on one side, then inlay objects, allowing that side to dry before doing the next portion. If you choose to do memory jugs in ceramics, students could make small clay "bits and pieces" to put on the surface.

Interdisciplinary Connection
SOCIAL STUDIES

PERUVIAN PORTRAIT POTS Ancient South American cultures, in particular those of Peru, specialized in making *portrait pots*, with each face resembling a real person or animal. They sometimes made the pot's subject something like a bird or frog. A stirrup handle (a hollow, rounded handle that had a spout sticking up in the center) made the pots practical containers for liquid. The pots were polished and decorated with slip. By depicting all facets of daily life, these pots and sculpture told a great deal about the culture.

Jug, c. 1862, $9^3/_4$ inches tall, attr. to Thomas J. Davies Pottery in the Edgefield District of South Carolina, Philadelphia Museum of Art, Gift of Edward Russell Jones

PROJECT 7–2 COIL-BUILT FACE POTS, A SOUTHERN TRADITION

STUDENT PAGE

Materials

3 pounds of clay per student

canvas or paper working surfaces

slip (clay thinned in water to the consistency of cream)

knife (for scoring or cutting)

paddle (12-inch batten board or ruler)

scrapers (*optional*)

Directions The tradition of creating face pots was brought from Africa to the Southern United States, and continues today. These were functional objects, but simply made more interesting by the features that were used to decorate them.

1. Avoid air bubbles by wedging a ball of clay between your hands, turning and gently slapping it for approximately 10 minutes. To make the bottom, flatten a ball of clay, then begin building on it with coils. Make coils by rolling a small amount of clay on a surface until it is approximately 1/2-inch thick and 12 inches long. Roll with the flat part of your palm to make them smooth.

2. To attach coils, use a knife, making X's to *score* (roughen) the two surfaces of the coils where they will touch. Coat both roughened surfaces with slip (thinned, creamy clay). When you add a new coil, make a slanted cut on one end. Then make a slanted cut on the new coil, scoring and putting slip between them before continuing to build the sides upward.

3. Attach approximately three coils, then smooth the inside and outside of the pot using your fingers or a scraper. Paddle the pot on the outside with a flat stick while supporting the inside with your hand.

4. Add features when you get near the shoulders of the jug, making the nose from a wedge of clay. Roll thin coils to make the eyes, eyebrows, ears, and mouth. Score and attach these features with slip, smoothing them so they are firmly attached on one side. Sometimes eyeballs and teeth are formed of extra pieces of clay. To allow the pot to dry evenly, remove excess clay inside the pot underneath the nose.

5. The top and shoulders of the pot should be smoothly rounded. The pot should come inward at the top and have a coil around the edge in which you could stick a cork. It would be smoothly finished like a bottle opening.

6. Attach a handle to the neck of the jug and halfway down the back. Because face pots were used to hold liquid and were utilitarian, they were traditionally finished with a simple dark glaze (sometimes darkish green or brown). For contrast, teeth and eyes were sometimes glazed white. Some contemporary jugs have lighter colored faces, although the pots themselves are dark.

PROJECT 7–3
CERAMIC ARCHITECTURAL BIRDHOUSE

FOR THE TEACHER Discuss with the students the great interest in birdhouses as folk art rather than for actual use. (If these are intended to be functional, purchase flat corks 2-1/4 inches in diameter, and have students make a matching hole in the back of the birdhouse so the house could be emptied out after each season's nesting.)

Vocabulary
miniature

slab

folk art

Preparation This project simply teaches students how to roll slabs and assemble them into a box. Discuss different periods in architecture and different types of buildings with students. Photocopies of a variety of architecture, including Greek temples, lighthouses, barns, log cabins, colonial houses, Swiss chalets, even a skyscraper, would introduce students to the variety of forms used in architecture. They might even choose to bring in a photograph of their own house or apartment building to make into a birdhouse. A list of sizes for holes is given here for a few birds known to appreciate pre-built homes. Specific information about other types of birdhouses for specific birds of your region should be available from your state Conservation Commission or from stores that sell bird feed. This project will take more than one day, so have the students bring in plastic bags to keep their work moist until they can complete it.

Adaptations for Younger Students
BIRDHOUSE PICTURE TILE Young students can make a birdhouse tile. Encourage them to use their imaginations here. Talk with them about folk art country birdhouses, apartment houses, Swiss chalets, and gingerbread houses. They can make a slab in the traditional way, then cut around their own tagboard pattern. A small bottle cap could be used to lightly impress a hole shape. A small bird shape looking into a "hole" could be formed and adhered to the outside of the tile with slip. Have students use a pencil to make a hole at the top for hanging. Underglazes applied to greenware will give bright colors to these tiles.

Alternative Slab Projects
SLAB BOWLS A slab can be draped over the outside of a plaster bowl-form and a wedge removed to make it fit. Score both sides of the wedge and join with slip. When the bowl is leather-hard, shapes can be cut from it to make it a decorative work of art. The plaster is reusable and aids in rapid drying. You can make reusable plaster forms by pouring plaster of Paris into shallow bowls of various sizes and shapes. A parent might be recruited to make these for you at home.

HOUSE-BOX PLANTERS Make a 6- to 8-inch square ceramic house, complete except for the roof. To use this as a planter, put a circular hole in the bottom for drainage.

CORNER OF A ROOM Make a small *corner* of a favorite room by forming two intersecting walls and a floor. Furnish it with a bed or sofa, table, lamp, pictures on the wall. It could be any room in a house. Use underglazes while it is drying to add patterns in a rug or sofa. Glaze in a clear glaze.

SLAB SCULPTURE Many different projects can be created from the slab process, including quite large pieces of sculpture built from irregular slab shapes. A colleague, Libby Cravens, has her students make "people" by making a slab circle, then cutting out a wedge so the two sides can be joined, making a conical-shaped body. A ball for the head and coils for arms complete the form.

DRAPED SLABS OVER A FORM Drape a thin slab over almost any form such as a plastic bowl. By elevating the bowl on a can, the ends of the clay can be allowed to hang down like a handkerchief until the form dries and will support itself.

DRAPED SLABS INSIDE A FORM A V-shaped wedge can be removed from a slab draped over an inverted bowl. The edges would be scored and joined to make the clay "fit" the bowl. The same method of making *tucks* would allow you to fit a slab *inside* a bowl.

WALL-HUNG PLANTER Make a wall-hung planter from two slabs. Put a hole in the flat piece that will hang against the wall. Crumple newspaper, placing it on top to support the pocket-like second slab (attached on three sides and left open at the top). Use stamping objects such as screws or a fork to give interesting texture. Simply wipe with shoe polish after firing.

COIL-METHOD BIRDHOUSE A coil-built birdhouse can be made inside a paper towel-draped bowl (to keep a rounded bottom). It can be built up to a height of approximately 10 inches with a knob at the top that has a hole for a hanger. Slightly more than halfway up, a $2^1/_4$-inch hole is cut for a cork, which makes it easier to clean when the birds vacate it. A $1^1/_4$-inch opening is good for small birds.

Interdisciplinary Connections
SCIENCE
MIGRATORY PATTERNS This is a good opportunity for students to learn about migratory and territorial patterns of birds.

SOCIAL STUDIES
STATE BUILDINGS This is also an excellent opportunity for students to become familiar with well-known buildings throughout the state or country. Usually state tourist departments are more than happy to send brochures for students to use. Each student could make a ceramic birdhouse in the shape of a famous building.

Suggested Sizes for Birdhouse Openings

Bird Variety	Floor of Cavity	Depth of Cavity	Entrance above floor	Diameter of Opening	Height above Ground	Placement
Bluebird	5 × 5″	8″	6″	1-1/2″	5–10′	side of tree or fence post, open area
Chickadee	4 × 4″	8–10″	6–8″	1-1/8″	6–15′	hanging from a tree near wooded edge
House Finch	6 × 6″	6″	4″	2″	8–12′	side of tree or under eaves of house
Nuthatch	4 × 4″	8–10″	6–8″	1-1/4″	12–20′	attached to side of tree in wooded area
Purple Martin	6 × 6″	6″	1″	2-1/2″	14–20′	away from buildings, wires, trees
Wren	4 × 4″	6–8″	1-6″	1–1-1/4″	6–10′	hanging from a tree or wall

PROJECT 7–3 CERAMIC ARCHITECTURAL BIRDHOUSE

Materials

clay

plastic for keeping clay moist

1-inch dowels or rolling pins

canvas or burlap for rolling slabs

knives

pencils

newsprint

tagboard (for patterns)

masking tape

needle tools (a needle stuck in a cork will do)

battens (1/2 × $1^1/_2$ × 12-inch wooden strips)

slip (clay mixed with water to cream-like consistency)

bottle cap (to make the hole in the front of the house)

Directions The birdhouse will be in the form of a box. It will have a base, four sides, and a top (roof). Make a sketch that shows what it will look like from the front. The roof could be flat, come to a peak with three or four equal sides like a pyramid, or have two long sides and a triangle (pediment) at each end to give support.

1. Before beginning, draw a newsprint pattern of each piece. Transfer this to tagboard, writing the name of each piece on the pattern (roof, sides, front, back, bottom). Cut out the tagboard pieces and loosely tape them together to make sure they will fit. Take them apart to use as patterns.

2. Wedge a ball of clay by slapping between your hands for approximately ten minutes before you begin. Place the ball of clay between two wooden strips and use a rolling pin or dowel to roll an even slab. If you see bubbles, prick them with a needle tool to release air.

3. Cut out the pattern pieces and place them to make the best use of the flattened clay. Use a knife to cut straight down around the pattern. Make a perfectly round hole about halfway down the front of the birdhouse by tracing around a cardboard circle of the desired size. Set the pieces aside to slightly dry.

4. Join the four sides together by scoring the edges with the knife, then applying slip. Reinforce the corners as you work by adding a finger-sized coil of clay to the inside of each corner, smoothing it into place. When the sides are done, join them to the bottom, again scoring, using slip, and reinforcing with a coil all the way around the inside bottom.

5. When the pieces are joined, use a pencil to incise details such as bricks, stone, windows, shutters, tiles, or shingles on the pieces. Use slip (thinned clay) to attach details such as pilasters (flat, attached columns), doors, shutters, or other decorative details.

6. If the roof will be attached to the box, make pencil holes for hanging at the center, approximately 1 inch from the peak of the roof. If this will be used as a box with a removable lid, make strips all the way around the inside of the lid to hold it in place inside the box. Rather than having a removable lid, a hole could be placed in the rear for a large cork, to allow for ease of cleaning at the end of the season.

7. Details could be painted on with underglaze before firing, then the entire house could be glazed with a clear glaze for a second firing. Consider an overall color scheme that will resemble a real house. You would seldom use more than three or four colors whether you paint or glaze.

PROJECT 7–4
CERAMIC MURAL

FOR THE TEACHER   The tradition of glazed ceramic murals goes back before the *Ishtar Gate* in ancient Babylon in 575 B.C. This portion of the city wall had fantastic animals such as dragons, bulls, and lions. Byzantine and Roman mosaics remain as beautiful today as when they were created. It is exciting for students to realize that they might make something that will be permanent for 2,000 years!

Vocabulary

planes (levels)	mosaic
tile	glaze
theme	mastic
cartoon	incise

Preparation   Look around the school for a location for a ceramic mural (a big bare wall that cries out for a work of art). Likely locations are long halls, the cafeteria, library, gymnasium, a stair well, or a wall outdoors. Select an appropriate theme for the mural.

Before you begin the mural, figure how it will be hung (talk with someone in your district's facilities office). Have plywood cut to size and holes drilled in the wood backing for mounting. It can be framed with molding for a nice finished edge. Put the plywood on tables so the students will have someplace to keep their work while it is in process.

Because several different classes may be involved in this, the theme needs to be carried through in each class. Each student will be responsible for one piece of the mural. Dry the tiles slowly to avoid having them curl up. Tiles dry from the edges inward, so you may choose to keep the edges loosely wrapped with damp paper towels until the centers dry. Have students use a pencil to put two holes to give extra support to large pieces. If pieces are relatively small, you may not need to screw them to the back.

The mural seen in these photos is based on transportation by air, land, and sea. It was created by fifth graders to celebrate the anniversary of a nearby railroad station for which Barretts School (near Barretts Station Road) in St. Louis County, Missouri was named more than 100 years ago.

Alternative Projects

GLAZED TILES This project could be done in glazed tiles similar to those of the Ishtar Gate. Each tile could be individually designed, or an overall design could be developed, with each student responsible for one tile. A suggested subject would be fantasy animals such as dragons, chimeras, griffins, unicorns, or minotaurs.

MURAL ON PRE-FIRED PURCHASED TILES Students can do a mural on pre-fired purchased tiles. Glazes can be painted directly on the glazed or unglazed surface, and the tiles refired for permanence.

PROJECT 7–4   CERAMIC MURAL

Materials

newsprint

kraft paper

scissors

glazes

plywood

screws

mastic

pencil

clay (approximately 1 pound per student)

1/2 × 12 × 1$\frac{1}{2}$-inch wooden strips

canvas (or paper) for rolling out

Directions   Wall murals have a tradition that goes back almost 3,000 years. You will be making one for your school that could last as long as the school exists! The theme selected can be almost anything. Suggestions would be: people, sports, colonial days, circus, tropical rainforest, animals, flowers, kinds of ships, the evolution of the automobile, the zoo, a farm, city buildings, or whatever other subject might be appropriate to the area where you live.

1. Following a discussion about the subject of the mural and who will be responsible for what, draw your small portion of the mural on newsprint. Later this drawing may have to be made larger or smaller. When it is complete, cut it out.

2. Place it with drawings by other people in your class and arrange them on kraft paper that is cut slightly smaller than the wooden base to allow space between the pieces for mastic. Most likely not all drawings will be used, and some shapes may have to be redrawn larger or smaller. Some students might be selected to make the plain background or in-between areas.

3. Go over the back of your pattern with pencil and transfer your drawing to the large *cartoon* (master drawing). After the drawing is transferred, your teacher will make sure each student's name is on the area for which he or she is responsible. The original patterns will be used for tracing around on the clay.

4. After wedging, roll the clay to a thickness of approximately 1/2 inch and place your pattern on it. Use a knife to cut straight down, cutting exactly around the pattern. While the pattern is still in place, use a pencil to redraw the original design. This will transfer a light outline to the clay, and will be useful when you are completing your section of the mural.

5. Remove the pattern and redraw (incise) the design directly on the clay. Make very thin coils of clay to attach on top of some of the lines with slip. You could also make stamped patterns with *found* objects. While the clay is moist, use a pencil to make approximately 1/2-inch holes in two corners so the piece can be screwed to the plywood. Use a pencil to write your name and the number of the piece on the back before placing it on the plywood to dry. If you are not able to complete it in one period, wrap it in a damp paper towel and enclose it in plastic.

6. After firing, glaze your piece in colors that have already been decided on by you and the teacher or the entire class. When it is finished, each piece will be screwed into the plywood base. Mix mastic and fill in around the pieces, wiping the surfaces clean.

PROJECT 7-5
MURAL: CERAMIC, CEMENT, MARBLES, NOODLES, AND GLASS

FOR THE TEACHER A major all-school project such as the one described here obviously is an uncommon occurrence, and takes considerable involvement from parents, teachers, and students. It is an *event* and, as such, will take advance planning. This all-school, intensive project was under the supervision of visiting artist Pat Imming of Highland, Illinois, and is used with her permission. The project was done at Highcroft Ridge School, Chesterfield, Missouri, with the classes of art teachers Raizell Kalishman and Marla Mayer. As you can see by the accompanying photos, these individual panels are of the human figure in action. Each figure was cut into smaller sections, and each section had a number of names impressed into it with alphabet noodles. After firing, the figures and names were painted with acrylic paint. The figure was reassembled, cemented in place on a wooden board, and accentuated with textured cement. Pieces of glass and glass marbles were embedded for added interest. These impressive sculptures are mounted in the entry of the school.

Vocabulary

texture

variety

repetition

emphasis

background

Preparation To avoid having the pasta soften, make the slabs in one working day.

For each large panel, make a drawing of an entire figure on folded butcher paper. Cut through two layers of paper at the same time so one of the figures can be cut up for individual patterns, while retaining a master copy. Number the back of the individual patterns and write a corresponding number on the master pattern so later assembly will be easier.

Prepare the wood for hanging by drilling holes for supporting screws in all four corners. On the *big day*, have parents or other adult volunteers on hand to help. Arrange the painted ceramic pieces on the wood. Have trays with clear marbles and broken pieces of glass ready for students to select. Have parents mix the mortar and help apply it with a trowel or pieces of matboard. You have a short time for students to embed glass into the cement. Have parents make sure that glass edges are covered by the mortar. Kindergarten students could put the clear glass marbles in place. Allow the cement to set slightly before wiping excess cement from the ceramic slabs and the glass and marbles. **SAFETY NOTE: Obviously when you are working with broken glass around students, great care must be taken. The glass was broken at home in a sack, then pieces of usable size selected (wear gloves) and brought to school. Edges were carefully covered with cement.**

Adaptations for Younger Students

TILES WITH NOODLE NAMES Young students could simply roll out slabs to make small tiles and set their names in with alphabet noodles. Allow the slabs to dry slowly, or place under a piece of Masonite to keep flat while drying. These could be painted with acrylic paint after firing.

Alternative Project

OUTDOOR MURAL Two other murals within the Parkway District were done with the cooperation of visiting artist Pat Imming, using a similar technique, but involving greater variety in the ceramic inserts. The large outdoor mural done in art teacher Laurie Leleu's classes at Hanna Woods School in St. Louis County had an environmental theme that included a real birdhouse, ceramic leaf prints, and self portraits. It also included many words and names made with alphabet noodles, marbles, and found objects.

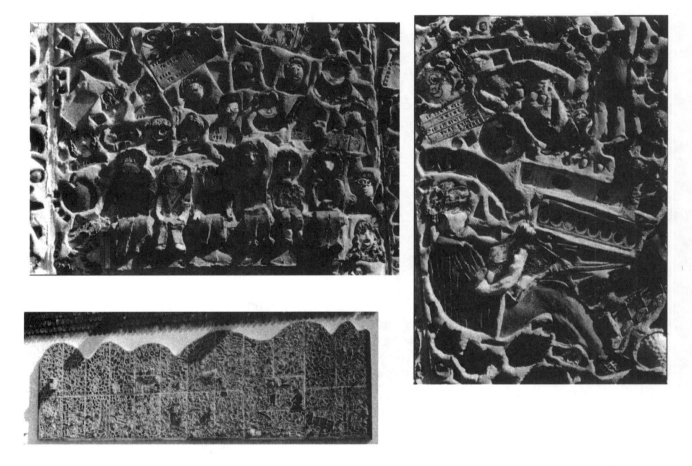

These details show a small portion of a large, colorful outdoor mural at Hanna Woods School, St. Louis County, Missouri. The work was done in art teacher Laurie Leleu's classes also under the direction of Highland, Illinois visiting artist Pat Imming, using the same general technique of adding letters, marbles, etc., described in Project 7–5.

PROJECT 7–5   MURAL: CERAMIC, CEMENT, MARBLES, NOODLES, AND GLASS

STUDENT PAGE

Materials

kraft paper	glass bottles broken into pieces
pencils	clear glass marbles
scissors	high-strength mortar mix, no aggregate
clay	plywood
alphabet noodles	screws
acrylic paint, colors and white	wooden molding
paper towels	

Directions

1. The theme for this project is figures in action. When we think about action, what do we mean? Throwing a ball? Jumping in the air? Running a race? Turning a somersault? Do a small drawing of yourself in action. Because this will be a group project, discuss with the friends in your group which of the action drawings you will actually use.

2. When you have decided on an action, one of the members must volunteer to lie down on the piece of butcher paper and allow the other members of the group to draw around him or her, holding that action. This drawing is unfinished, so now it needs to be redrawn and *refined*, putting details in the face, hands, shoes, and clothing.

3. Before cutting out the clay, select the alphabet noodle letters for the names of each student involved in the project. If you find that your first and last names share a letter with someone else in your group, the first name could be horizontal and the last name could be vertical (see photos). Carefully arrange the noodles on the table so when you have to work quickly, you know what you will be doing.

4. Place a pattern piece on a slab and carefully cut around it. Press the noodles that spell names into the clay slab. Leave the letters in place. The pasta will disappear in the firing process.

5. After firing, each piece will look somewhat like the others, so it is important to be able to identify which piece goes where. Number the piece on the back according to the pattern number. The surface can be painted with acrylic paint. Use white acrylic paint to repaint the letters of the names so they will be visible from a distance. Spray with varnish to make the surface shiny.

6. Assemble the figure pieces together on the board, then quickly spread the cement around the figures. Allow to dry in place, then clean the surface.

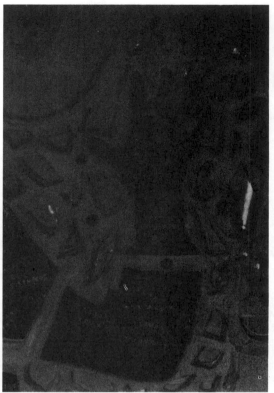

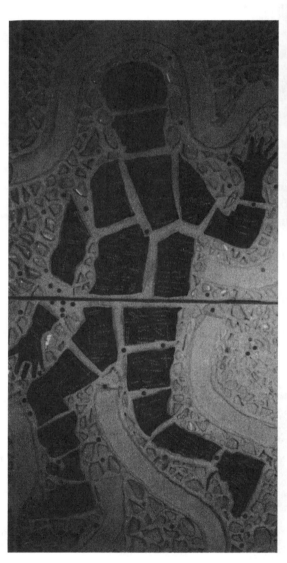

These are examples taken from six large ceramic/cement/broken glass panels made in the classes of Raizell Kalishman and Marla Mayer at the Highcroft Ridge Elementary School in St. Louis County under the direction of visiting artist Pat Imming.

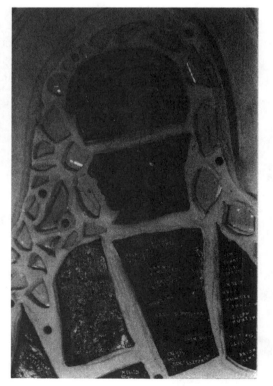

PROJECT 7–6
AQUAMANILE: SCULPTURED CLAY ANIMAL PITCHER

FOR THE TEACHER People in all cultures and all times have been fascinated by animals, often ascribing mystical powers to them, sometimes even worshipping them. In Medieval times animals were sometimes used as models for water vessels made of precious metals. These vessels were called *Aquamaniles*. Certain animals such as the lion, tiger, or bull were thought to have great power and were especially admired. The sculptures can be made by simply forming the creature, then cutting it apart and hollowing it out.

Vocabulary

aquamanile

spout

decoration

Preparation
This project is most appropriate for students who have had prior experience working with clay, because younger students sometimes have difficulty attaching legs.

An aquamanile must have a pouring spout (usually the animal's open mouth) and a handle for holding (often the animal's tail). I recommend that students first make the animal, making sure it is stable, then hollow it out.

Adaptations for Younger Students
PINCH-POT ANIMAL Younger students can create a seated animal in two parts by the pinch-pot method. Have students make two balls (of unequal size) for the body and head of the animal. Show them how to "pull" ears, noses, tails, and feet from the body of the clay to avoid the problem of features falling off. These creatures could also be made of plasticine clay.

SQUEEZE AND PULL Have younger students begin with a ball of clay. Ask them to roll it slightly between their hands to make a rounded "sausage" shape, then squeeze around one end to form a head and neck. They then can take a pencil and, on the underside of the body, make a line going from the neck to the tail and a second line across the middle. From the four "corners" formed, they can use thumb and fingers to "pull" legs. They can then pull ears and a nose in the same manner. The animal can be whatever they think it most closely resembles.

Alternative Project
PITCHER CREATURE Draw a design for a coil-built pot that will incorporate the head of an animal. Make a tagboard template that will assist you in adhering to your original design. When the pot is mostly complete, form an animal or human head to attach at the neck. Open it at the top and use the mouth as the pouring spout. Attach a handle.

Aquamanile, German sculpture, 1300–1499, bronze, 12$\frac{1}{2}$ × 12 inches, The Nelson–Atkins Museum of Art, Kansas City, Missouri (Purchase: Nelson Trust)

PROJECT 7–6   AQUAMANILE: SCULPTURED CLAY ANIMAL PITCHER

Materials

pencil

paper

2–3 pounds of clay per student

glazes

knife

slip

Lion Aquamanile, 13th century, lizard
on back of lion

Directions   In Medieval times, a water vessel with the features of an animal
was called an *aquamanile*. We see examples of these vessels in museums, because
they were very special and were given special care. A functional (useful) sculptural
vessel has three requirements:

- hollow inside

- has a handle (sometimes a long tail, attached to the back)

- has an opening in the mouth or top of the head, or a spout for pouring
  water

1. Draw a picture of your animal, thinking how you will attach a handle, and
   make an opening in the mouth or top of the head. Wedge the clay to get rid
   of air bubbles.

2. Legs, neck, tail, and head are less likely to break when they are *pulled* from
   the main body of the clay, rather than formed and added on later.
   Remember that the legs are usually in proportion to the body's weight
   (think how short and thick the legs are on a hippopotamus, elephant, or
   bear), and how much thinner and longer they are on a cheetah.

3. If you must add on legs afterwards, rather than pulling them out, use your
   finger to make an indentation on the body where the leg will be attached.
   Score the indentation and the top of the leg. Add slip to each surface. When
   you have put the leg in, smooth the surface where they are joined, making
   sure there are no trapped air bubbles.

4. When your animal is almost complete, use a knife or string to cut the body
   across the middle. Use a spoon to scoop out excess clay so the animal is no
   thicker than one inch anywhere. The legs will not need to be hollowed.
   Make an opening at the mouth that will allow the animal to dry.

5. To reattach the two halves of the animal, score both openings and put slip
   on each half. Reattach the two halves. You may be able to put a thin knife
   through the mouth opening to support the stomach while you smooth the
   two halves together.

6. When the two halves are back together, and you know you have a hollow animal, you can use a pencil or knife blade to texture the surface as if it were fur, helping to hide the area where the two halves are joined. Put on other details such as ears, eyes, and mouth, and give an interesting finish to the outside.

7. After the animal is fired, it can be painted in a solid color or spray-painted in bronze (to look like metal).

Drawn from an Islamic Aquamanile, Freer/Sackler Gallery, Washington, DC

Drawn from *Dragon* aquamanile, German, 13th century, The Metropolitan Museum of Art, New York City

Drawn from Lion aquamanile, Islamic Freer/Sackler Gallery, Washington, DC

Bull aquamanile, First Millennium B.C., Amlash potter

PROJECT 7–7 PORTRAIT HEADS

FOR THE TEACHER Portrait busts can be traced back to ancient times. Roman families commissioned wax death-masks and carved marble portrait heads of relatives. A special room was set aside in homes for these busts. Africans also created portrait busts in ceramic or bronze to honor their leaders. Students can probably think of some portrait busts they have seen, such as those of Abraham Lincoln or George Washington. Portraits in clay or stone continue to be commissioned today. Show students any reproductions you can find so you can point out hair treatments, expressions, and how features such as eyes have to be developed in order to be visible.

Vocabulary

portrait

bust

character

expression

attitude

variety

originality

humor

value

Preparation This project is most appropriate for students from fifth grade and up because they are able to follow directions well. Ideally it would follow a unit on portraiture, in which students have already become familiar with the proportions of the face. This process is excellent for right brain development, as it demands pre-visualization.

Stress to students that anytime they add something on, they must make sure they have scored the two surfaces and used slip. The most common firing accidents occur when students simply stick a chunk of clay on the back of a head, trapping a bubble between the two layers. If a head almost disintegrates in firing (a true disaster), I have found that it can be glued back together—missing pieces and cracks filled in with plaster—and the entire thing covered with gesso and painted.

Alternative Projects

CLAY PORTRAIT FOR A MAGAZINE COVER Sometimes artists are asked to make a "bust" of someone to be photographed as a magazine cover. Challenge your students to make a bas-relief portrait of someone famous. This could be carved and modeled from a flat slab of clay. It is not necessary to worry about wedging or firing because the finished product is a photograph of the work. When the portrait is complete, have students write the name of the person on the slab. Take photographs of the portraits.

PORTRAIT WITH ATTITUDE Have students make faces for each other showing anger, fright, surprise, happiness, sadness, surliness, disinterest, etc. Suggest they draw how the eyes, eyebrows, and mouth show that emotion. (There are books on cartooning that also have such expressions in them.) Students could then make portrait heads with an expression that appeals to them.

Joseph Froehlich, Court Jester of Augustus the Strong, 1730, Johann Gottlieb Kirchner, Meissen hard-paste porcelain, 20 inches, Gift of Mr. and Mrs. Henry Ford II, © The Detroit Institute of Arts.

PROJECT 7–7   PORTRAIT HEADS

Materials

clay (5 pounds per person)

plastic

paper towels

spoon

pencil

wire (for cutting the head in half to hollow it)

Directions

1. To make a portrait head, you must first make sure the clay is well wedged. Reserve a third of the clay for the neck and shoulders. Be aware that if you are looking down at the face, it will *look up* at you. You might prefer to put a stool on the tabletop and work on that surface so you could look at it straight on.

2. Before beginning, *feel* which features on your face stick out and which ones go inward. Notice how thick your neck is, how your head sits on it, how prominent your jawbones and cheekbones are. Your head is egg-shaped, larger at the top than the bottom. The eyes are halfway down the face, and the bottom of the nose is not quite halfway between the eye line and the chin. The mouth is one-third of the way between the bottom of the nose and the chin.

3. Form an egg shape for the head itself, then attach it to the neck by first *scoring* the base of the neck, then the egg shape. Apply slip to join these pieces together and smooth them carefully. If you decide to make a portion of the shoulders, attach these to the base of the neck in the same way.

4. With a pencil, make a light vertical line down the center of the egg shape. Now make a horizontal line halfway down the face for the eyes. The distance between the eyes will be one eye-width (almost as if you had three eyes). Realistic eyes can be formed by making two thin rolls of clay and smoothing one side of each roll in place. Make an eyeball with a small ball between the thin rolls and use a pencil to make an indentation in it.

5. Add features by pulling out and pushing in the clay with your fingers. Use a pencil to make the line in the center of the mouth (the outer edges are directly below the eyeballs), then pinch to form the lips or add two thin coils. Ears can be formed from a coil, smoothed, with one end of the coil touching the head just opposite the eyes, and the other end opposite the nose (ears are much bigger than we think). A ball placed in front of the coil and smoothed on one side will make the ears even more realistic.

6. To hollow the form, cut from the top of the head to under the chin, removing the face without disturbing the features. Use a spoon to hollow the entire bust to approximately 1-inch thick overall. The bust must have an opening at the base to allow it to dry. Score the edges of the pieces you

have hollowed. Put slip on them, and join them back together. A knife stuck in from the bottom may help support the clay from the inside while you smooth the outside.

7. Now examine the head. Even though you might have intended to have a young woman or boy, it may look more like an old man. Use the clay you have scooped out to make hair, beard, hat, glasses, or anything else that may give character to your portrait. Finish it completely, making sure your name and date are on the bottom. When it is fired, you may simply finish it with shoe polish, varnish, or spray paint.

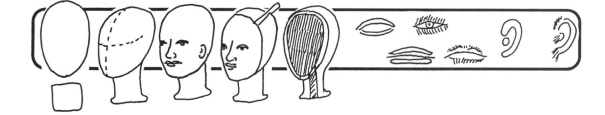

Black and White Head, 1966, Roy Lichtenstein, 15 × 8 × 8 inches, Ceramic, Eliza McMillan Fund and gift of Gerhard J. Petzall. Saint Louis Art Museum. This sculpture from the Pop Art era demonstrates that pattern can enhance a "generic," idealized portrait head.

PROJECT 7–8
BAS-RELIEF FAMILY SCULPTURE
WITH OIL CLAY

FOR THE TEACHER   Bas-relief sculpture has been done through the ages. Examples are medals or coins, Benin (African) bronze plaques, Assyrian architectural decorations, and Middle Eastern cylinder seals. You may not have access to regular ceramic clay, or decide that you would rather not use it for certain classes. This project was developed by Beth Scott of Ross School in St. Louis County, Missouri who has her students make oil-clay bas-reliefs of their families (on 6 × 6-inch pieces of matboard). Modeling clay of this type comes in a wide variety of colors, including a multicultural set (skin colors) and neon. If you are limited to one or two colors, simply explain to students that historically, sculptors creating bas-reliefs were limited to one color. They had to make the sculpture more interesting by the positive–negative use of clay and the textures they added.

Vocabulary

bas-relief

incising

line

texture

balance

overlap

Preparation   Oil clay can be used for modeling three-dimensional figures and animals, and is perfect for introducing young students to the use of clay without the mess.

Distribute oil clay portions for students to be holding between their hands to soften while you are giving directions. It takes approximately five to ten minutes of handling for oil clay to be brought to body temperature, then it is quite easy to use.

Of course, this project could be easily done in self-hardening clay or regular clay. If self-hardening clay is used, these can be painted afterwards with acrylic paint.

Alternative Projects

COMMEMORATIVE PRESENTATION MEDAL Students can be challenged to design and produce a *medal*. Have them draw around a circular lid, first drawing, then translating their drawing into clay. Such medals are given in the Olympics or for special events throughout the world. Among other uses, they were commissioned and presented to Native Americans to seal the signing of a treaty. These "medals" should be approximately 1/4-inch to 3/8-inch thick. If you wish, you could then have students make plaster molds of each medal, making more than one casting.

PAINT WITH MODELING CLAY Elizabeth Mitchell, formerly of Mason Ridge School in St. Louis County, Missouri, had her younger students *paint* animals on cardboard using oil clay. My students have used this method to make bas-relief landscapes. Students can paint with oil clay by making small balls and coils, then smearing one side of a ball onto the board, leaving part of it sticking up, making a bas-relief sculpture up to 1/2-inch thick (for this type of work, the cardboard support should be matboard or heavy cardboard). Designs can be incised into oil clay using a pencil. If you are using many different colors for a bas-relief painting, give a different color to each student at one table and they will be able to share the clay.

Interdisciplinary Projects
SOCIAL STUDIES
U.S. GOVERNMENT TREATIES WITH NATIVE AMERICANS Have students research treaties between the U.S. government and Native Americans. In most instances, a commemorative medal was struck. Have students follow through to see how many of those treaties have been honored.

COIN DESIGN Have students select a person to honor by having a new $1.00 coin made with that person's image on it. Traditionally in many countries, royalty or great leaders have been so honored. If a human were not chosen, what other kind of symbol could be placed to represent their country (not using ones that have already been used). Students could then make a small coin, removing clay with a small tool.

Pew Group, Aaron Wood, c. 1740–45, English ceramics, salt-glaze, $6^1/_2 \times 6^3/_4$ inches, The Nelson–Atkins Museum of Art, Kansas City, Missouri (Gift of Mr. and Mrs. F.P. Burnap)

PROJECT 7-8 BAS-RELIEF FAMILY SCULPTURE WITH OIL CLAY

Materials

pencils

paper, cut to the same size as the cardboard

oil clay in a variety of colors

6 X 6-inch pieces of matboard or railroad board

Directions   Painting with clay will produce a *bas-relief sculpture* (flat on one side, standing out from the background on the other).

1. Before you begin, draw a plan for your sculpture. If you belong to a small family, you might choose to make large portraits to use most of the space. If you have a large family, you may have to *overlap* to get in all the family members. Use a pencil to draw a 1/2-inch border all the way around the edges of your picture. As you work, try to stay within this border to keep the table clean.

2. Soften the clay between your hands by squeezing. It will soon be soft enough to use. To do a bas-relief painting of your family, you will mostly make balls and coils. You may not have realistic colors, and perhaps will have only one color of clay. Depending on the number of colors you have, think about which colors you will use for hair, faces and hands, and clothing.

3. Press the balls and coils firmly to the cardboard, using a finger to smooth the edges of the coils in place, or they will fall off. When you have put all the family members in place, look to see if any cardboard is showing through. Use a pencil to incise details such as eyes, mouths, hair, and patterns in clothing.

4. If you would like to have a "frame" around your picture of the family, use one color or combine two colors to make a frame. Decorate this also by incising with a pencil.

Drawn from the plasticine clay "paintings" of Beth Scott's fifth graders at Ross School, St. Louis County, Missouri.

ARCHITECTURE, THE BUILT ENVIRONMENT

We talk with students about painting, drawing, and printmaking, but we don't always let them know that artists also design useful things such as houses, furniture, and dishes. Students can become aware that almost everything that is manufactured or constructed was *designed* by someone. Architecture, one of the most enduring functional art forms, can become more meaningful to students if you can show them examples of buildings, mentioning specific architects such as Ictinus and Callicrates (the *Parthenon*), Frank Gehry (the architect of the *Bilbao Museum* in Spain), Louis Sullivan (skyscrapers), Frank Lloyd Wright (the Prairie School), or Gustave Eiffel (the *Eiffel Tower*).

The study of architecture is more than just learning about houses and buildings. It includes history, patronage, government, the natural and "built" environment, city planning, garden design, and the responsible use of resources. Talk with your students about career options that are open to architects. Many architects work for the government or large corporations. Others design monuments, playgrounds, or parks. Architects teach, write about, or make renderings of architecture. Some design furnishings for the interiors and exteriors of buildings. Many great architects (Frank Lloyd Wright, for example) design *everything* in their houses ranging from stained-glass windows, carpets, and chandeliers to every piece of furniture.

This is an opportunity to incorporate other subjects with the study of art. As students make models, it is imperative that they learn to measure correctly. They can learn that much of what we know of history is what we deduce from investigating ruins of buildings. They can learn about the government of many countries by studying government buildings and palaces.

RESEARCH ACTIVITIES IN ARCHITECTURE

Many activities that are already commonly incorporated into art programs are based on architecture. To help students become aware of their "built environment," any of the following activities could be all-classroom assignments. Or divide the class into groups, giving a different assignment to each group.

Historical Research "Why is your town where it is? Find out who founded your own city. Was it built near a railroad or a river? What were the first businesses in your town? Which was the first church? Where was the first jail? City Hall? Talk with older relatives or residents to find out what they can remember about old buildings. Where is the oldest part of your town? Are there any buildings on the historic register? Should some be registered? What could you do to help get a special building or district entered on the National Historic Register?" (This would be a great enrichment project.)

Government in the City/State/Nation   Students can learn about landmark buildings in their own city or the capital of the state or nation. "What are the important buildings? What functions are carried out there? Who makes the laws? How do the buildings function? Where is the jail? Where does the leader have an office?"

Archaeology   Archaeology is ongoing, with many "digs" happening in cities throughout the world. Perhaps your students can participate in an *actual* dig nearby. Or you can make an archaeology game by putting clues in a box of sand and letting the students find puzzle "shards" made of laminated tagboard, which they reassemble to make a pot when they have dug out all the pieces.

Architectural Timeline   "Make an architectural timeline for your community. Draw small outlines (silhouettes) of buildings on black paper and cut them out. On long white paper, make a timeline, pasting the buildings appropriately. Or, you and friends can make a photo record of the town using photos, postcards, or videos."

The Old Homeplace   "Look through family photographs for pictures of a house (the older the better). Try to find out who lived in it and what relationship they are to you. Try to find out more about where your family came from, making a family tree. Interview family members to see what they can remember about the houses in which they grew up."

Talk About Buildings   "Compare two buildings that serve the same function from two different time periods (such as places of worship or government buildings). Explain why they look so different, depending on their historical periods."

Then and Now   "How have houses changed in the last 100 years? What are some of the differences between homes built 'in the old days' and homes built now? How does climate or environment influence how homes are built?" (basements, stilts, need for air conditioning—how they were built before air conditioning.)

Cornerstone   When a special building is erected, it often includes a *cornerstone* with the date of the building. This cornerstone might contain a sealed box with mementos of the culture of that time, often including newspaper clippings, catalogue pages that show clothing or housing, popular music, the names of the people who made the cornerstone or anything else they considered important for people of the future to know about the past. Students could bury their own cornerstone to be found by a class just ten years later, or they could themselves agree to come back and dig it up near the time of high school graduation.

ART ACTIVITIES BASED ON ARCHITECTURE

Your Favorite Room   "Write about your favorite room in the place you live. What is it about that room that makes it special to you? colors? furnishings? the view out the window? a fireplace? high ceilings?"

Architectural Tour Field Trip   Take an architectural tour of an interesting town in your area. Perhaps a local architect would be willing to conduct the tour or at least give pointers on where to go. Students could either do small sketches of some buildings or several students could work together to make a photo-essay of historical buildings in the town, using a video, digital, Polaroid®, traditional, or simple throw-away camera.

Corner-lot Park   Many cities have empty corners that have been improved with the addition of shrubbery and trees, a mural on the side of a building, benches or "pocket-playgrounds." Students look at their own surroundings for such a vacant lot, designing improvements for it. It might actually be implemented, as it was for two twelve-year-old boys in San Luis Obispo, California. They designed a small park for their neighborhood that was actually constructed by the city and named after the boys (it had originally been called "dog-poop park").

This corner lot in Kirkwood, Missouri has been transformed into a mini-park through the addition of trees and sky painted on adjacent buildings. With a fountain and benches, it is an oasis in the middle of a busy intersection.

Tourist Map   Students make a *tourist* map of their city. (The degree of accuracy, of course, is dependent on the ages of the students.) Note major features such as railroads, highways, rivers, and major buildings. Include small drawings of the important features. Students could then make a tourist map of their state or the entire United States, including anything they can learn about important architecture in each state. Special features will naturally not be illustrated according to scale. Draw lightly in pencil, then go over with fine-line marker. Maps of Chicago and other large cities, for example, include places of special interest (including popular restaurants) rendered in a humorous style.

Sentimental Journey   Students write a poem or song about a building or city. Poets and song writers sometimes write about favorite cities. Such songs as "Chicago;" "New York, New York;" "I Left My Heart in San Francisco;" "A Foggy Day in London Town;" "I Love Paris in the Springtime;" and "Route 66" started about unlikely subjects. Students start by writing several words or sentences about what they know of a place. See if they can figure how to make the words or phrases into some sort of order. It isn't at all necessary for this to rhyme.

Architectural Roots   Students research architecture used in certain regions of the world (for example: Spain, France, Greece, The Netherlands, Germany, Sweden, Africa, The Caribbean, Southwestern Native American Pueblos, Alaska). They try to find out where in North America people from different countries originally immigrated. Did the availability of wood, stone, clay, or sand influence what material they used to build homes? Or did they select a certain part of the country because it had the same types of building materials as their former locations? Students design a brand new house using some of the characteristics in a particular culture's typical housing. They include design elements such as the exterior finish, roof style, arrangement of rooms, colors, building materials.

Reproduce a Foreign City   A project that involved considerable research about German buildings and daily life in Germany was jointly developed by art teacher Kathy McGinty and the Social Studies teachers of Parkway Central Middle School, St. Louis County. Students made tall, thin building façades on construction paper-wrapped cereal boxes. Balconies, window boxes, signs, awnings, roofs, and shop windows were added. In addition to the construction of the buildings, each student wrote a research paper about the particular shop he or she created.

Stained-Glass Window   Gothic stained-glass windows have retained their beauty for almost a thousand years. Cut an intricate design in black or gray construction paper and glue tissue paper behind the openings. Or photocopy pictures of stained-glass windows on 8-1/2 × 11-inch transparencies. After students have colored these in with permanent markers, they are beautiful to hang on a window.

Victorian House Doorstops or Bookends   On 2 × 4 × 8-inch blocks of wood or bricks, students paint brightly colored Victorian house fronts, sides, and backs. Use at least two values of one color, and a complementary color for an accent. Almost all houses of that vintage also had white accents around the windows.

Five-Story Building   On a 6 × 18-inch piece of paper, have students draw and color with marker, cut paper, or colored pencil a five-story building, with each story a different architectural period (for example, Victorian, Classical, Art Deco, Modern, Egyptian Revival, Baroque, etc.).

Rubbings   Depending on the age of your school or where you live, students can use copy paper and crayon to do rubbings of architectural details at home or school. This could include metal plates, carvings, or registers. To make this a classroom activity, try to find old metal registers, decorative iron ornaments, or even molded plastic. Use tape to hold the paper in place. Multi Color Chunk-O® crayons or rainbow crayons are perfect for this.

Architectural Stencils   Discuss the use of stenciling as an architectural tool to make room interiors more interesting. Louis Sullivan, the father of the skyscraper, was a master of this art form.

Students can make stencil designs on tagboard, combining several different designs that could be used in a room interior. Art Deco and Art Nouveau designs are especially appropriate for this. Students can trade and combine stencils to make a design on butcher paper or 18 × 24-inch drawing paper.

Architectural Stamps   Make designs from nature on large block erasers or Soft-kut® print blocks. On $8^1/_2$ × 11-inch copy paper, students can carefully combine stamps to create designs such as those Louis Sullivan used to make borders around the edges of rooms. Or you can have architectural stamps made from a photograph of almost any architectural detail such as those of Louis Sullivan's or Frank Lloyd Wright's.

A group of students produced this version of a famous temple with initial eraser stamps dipped in colored tempera. In addition to creating the artwork, students researched the building and presented a group report about the architecture.

The City Museum of St. Louis has a children's corner where students can do rubbings or stamp patterns based on designs by Louis Sullivan.

These are examples of stamps based on Sullivan's work.

ARCHITECTURAL DEFINITIONS

Adobe. sun-dried brick made from mud and straw; used to construct homes

Arch. a (usually) curved structural element that spans an opening and supports the weight above

Art Deco. architecture of the 1930s featuring flat roofs, geometric design, and simplified shapes

Beam. a support for a roof or floor, usually going from wall to wall

Blueprint. working drawings for construction

Brickwork. decorative arrangement of bricks; particularly popular in Victorian architecture

Buttress. an upright-attached column to help support a wall

Capital. the top of a column; seen in a variety of styles from various cultures

Column. a usually round or fluted post to support beams or a roof

Crenellation. battlements, a notched parapet for defense, usually found in a castle

Cupola. a small dome atop a roof, sometimes used for ventilation

Dome. a round or evenly curved vault on a base

Dormer. an attic window usually with a gable and roof

Eaves. the lower portion of a roof that projects beyond the wall

Elevation. drawing of one side of a building

Façade. the front view (elevation) of a building

Flying buttress. an upright pilaster attached, open at the top to resemble a wing, yet further away, allowing walls to be built higher

Formal balance. symmetrical arrangement of architectural elements on each side of a center axis

Fresco. decorative painting done on wet lime or gypsum plaster

Gable. the upper, pointed part of a wall underneath a pitched roof

Gambrel roof. barn-like roof imported to the United States from Holland

Gargoyle. a water spout of lead or carved stone that resembled a beast or monster

Half-timbering. exterior decorative timber allowed to show on top, contrasting with white walls

Hipped. a traditional gabled roof, but with the ends slanted and enclosed

Lintel. the horizontal beam at the top of two vertical supports to support the wall above it

Log cabin. home made by early settlers in the United States; originated by Northern European cultures

Machicolation. the opening behind battlements in a castle that allows oil or pitch to be poured

Molding. a decoratively carved ornamental strip mostly used in classical architecture

Mosaic. a decorative floor or wall mural made of pieces of stone or colored glass

Mud and wattle. woven vine or sticks chinked with mud to make an adobe-type finish

Pediment. the triangular decoration above a door or temple, often decoratively carved

Pilaster. a squared flat attached (engaged) column with capital and base

Post and lintel. a support system that consists of vertical uprights and a horizontal beam

Pyramid. a structure with a square base with triangular sides that slope upward to a point

Rendering. an architect's artistic interpretation of a structure in paint, pencil, or ink

Shot-gun house. house of African origin with each room directly behind the other so that if a shotgun were fired through the front door it would go straight out the back

Spire. the pointed top portion of a tower

Steeple. a spire and its supporting structure

Turret. a small tower attached to the top of a castle

Vault. an arched ceiling usually of brick, stone, or concrete

Note: This abbreviated list is taken from *The Art Teacher's Book of Lists* by Helen Hume (Paramus, New Jersey: Prentice Hall, 1998).

James Lick Mill, c. 1860, Santa Clara, California

Selma, Alabama, mid nineteenth century

PROJECT 8–1
CITY PLANNING

FOR THE TEACHER   An all-class project to create a city can help students become aware of their own surroundings, and of the need for a variety of buildings to accommodate people's needs. Begin with a chalkboard discussion of various buildings and districts in a city. Let students come up with (for example) center city, suburbs, monuments, schools, churches, banks, houses, court houses, streets, rivers, street lights, public restrooms, water supply, parking lots, waste treatment plant, parks, green space, transportation (circumferential highways, buses, underground transportation). Ask them why some buildings in a city look so old and different from what is being built today. Discuss planned cities such as Washington, D.C. or Paris, with their boulevards radiating from the circles.

Vocabulary
architecture

city planning

environment

infrastructure

suburb

inner city

proportion

classical

skyscraper

Preparation   Make a decision on a common scale so the buildings will complement each other. If you have little space, milk-carton size (3 X 3 inches) is adequate. Show slides or books of architecture as created by collage artist Red Grooms or as drawn by David McCauley (*Cathedral, Castle*). Demonstrate on the board how students can draw decorative detail on houses such as horizontal siding, a brick pattern, or irregular stones.

Adaptations for Younger Students
CITY PLANNING   Make 4 X 4-inch tagboard squares to represent the basements of individual buildings. These buildings will not necessarily be built. The flat squares will simply be labeled and arranged to help students consider how a city evolves.

CITY BUILDINGS   Younger students can make a tall, simple construction paper *skyscraper* on which they can draw windows, doors, signs, bricks, etc., with crayons or markers. Make a tab by folding 1 inch on the short edge of a piece of 12 X 18-inch light-colored construction paper. Bring the other end to the fold line and crease. Then fold in half and crease it again. Open the paper, making sharp creases all on the same side of the paper. Have students draw details such as windows, a door, stone or brick, roof, etc., before gluing together. The top could be shaped with scissors if they wish.

Alternative Project
SKYSCRAPERS; NIGHTTIME IN THE CITY   A frieze of three-dimensional skyscrapers goes all the way around the room, just below the ceiling in art teacher Cathy Williams's classes at Hageman

Elementary School in St. Louis County, Missouri. Make these by using black or dark blue 12 × 18-inch construction paper, folding the paper to make a $2^1/_2$ inch deep × 6-inch wide × 12-inch tall rectangle (open at the top and bottom). Students can vary the shape slightly by folding differently. Construction paper details might include a neon sign on top that is lit, small, mostly yellow or white windows that would indicate lights inside the building, awnings, silhouettes of people in windows. The top of the building might have an unusual shape. Street-level windows could be filled with displays.

Interdisciplinary Connections
SOCIAL STUDIES

NEIGHBORHOOD MAP Have students draw a map of their own neighborhood, including streets, houses, a school, parks, buildings, and sidewalks. This could be a bird's-eye view, a worm's-eye view, or a kid's-eye view (straight on).

IN THE FUTURE Students can draw a view of what they think a city will look like when they are old. Following a discussion of how transportation, homes, and cities have changed in the last century, discuss with students what they think homes will look like in the coming century. Students can draw their version of the "built environment" of the twenty-first century.

The City from Greenwich Village, 1922, John Sloan, oil on canvas, 26 × 33³/₄ inches, National Gallery of Art, Washington, DC, Gift of Helen Farr Sloan

PROJECT 8–1   CITY PLANNING

Materials

cardboard milk cartons	construction paper	acrylic or tempera paint
small cracker or cereal boxes	glue	masking tape
sheets of posterboard	scissors	

Directions   Working as a class, you will have to decide with your classmates what kind of buildings are needed in the town you will create. Plan the city by deciding on water supply, parks, transportation, schools, factories, city center, shops, malls. Decide whether it is okay to have two buildings that serve the same purpose (*Yes:* houses, banks, restaurants, churches, McDonald's, shops. *No:* city halls). Think about whether you want to build around a village square or would like to have a "Main Street."

1. Residences can be made from 3″ × 3″ milk cartons and covered or painted. To make a taller building such as an apartment building, department store, or city hall, use larger or taller milk cartons or stack and tape small cartons together and cover them with construction paper.

2. If you use an ordinary milk carton, the roof can simply be painted. Or fold a square of cardboard in half to make a peaked roof. These houses can be covered with construction paper or a layer of newsprint glued on with polymer medium or white glue.

3. If you choose to paint the cartons, use acrylic paint or add liquid detergent to tempera to help it stick to a slick surface. Add details such as windows, doors, and painted brick, clapboard or stone. When the individual houses are complete, work in small groups to complete a "neighborhood" on a square of cardboard or posterboard.

4. People who have made larger buildings would probably group these together as "downtown," while small houses might be a suburban neighborhood. You may decide to give individual yards to each house, or group them closely together as apartments. Draw streets, make playgrounds, and trees of found materials such as Popsicle sticks, sponges, and/or crumpled construction paper.

5. When each section is complete, join these small neighborhoods together to make a larger city. Talk about changes you would make if you had a chance to do this over again.

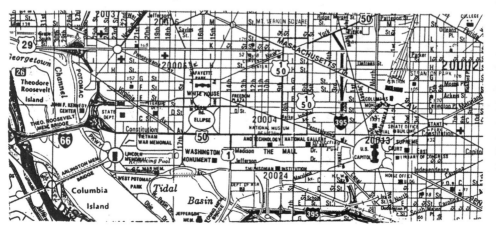

This section of a Washington, D.C. map shows city planning that includes the Capitol, Mall, White House, and presidential memorials.

PROJECT 8–2
EVERYONE IS AN ARCHITECT

FOR THE TEACHER Your students will need to consider the same information architects must have as they design their buildings. They need to decide what the purpose of the building is, how large it will be, what the materials are, what the "cost" will be, etc. The models they make will all start with approximately the same-size basic tagboard box, but their building's purpose will determine how it will be built. Ask students what building material they mostly see on houses in the area where they live (it might be aluminum siding!), but it could also be brick, stone, adobe, shingles. Show students some "typical" architectural styles from other countries such as half-timbered houses in England or thatched-roof homes in Denmark. Discuss structures such as a mill, country stores, theme-restaurants, churches.

Vocabulary

structure

adobe

stone

brick

shingles

shutters

exterior

pattern

repetition

Preparation This project will take several periods. It is useful to have photocopies of various structures available for students to see. Create an architectural file of small black-and-white photocopies of buildings. Mount them on index cards or construction paper and laminate to keep them from year to year.

Discuss *scale* with the students in order to have buildings approximately the same size. Make a plain sample tagboard box and roof to show students where they will begin. Talk with them about how they could transform their building before painting by adding shingles cut from tagboard, windows with small panes, and porches. The roof might be the most interesting part of the building.

Adaptation for Younger Students

LUNCH-BAG HOUSES Young students can cut out windows, doors, flowers, etc., from construction paper to glue on the fronts and sides of newspaper-stuffed paper lunch bags. A 6 × 9-inch piece of construction paper can be folded in half to form the two halves of a 6 × 4$\frac{1}{2}$-inch roof. Students can glue on a chimney and use marker to decorate the paper with shingles. Staple the roof onto the top of the bag/house across the fold. To add stability, glue these to a "lawn" made of 6 × 9-inch piece of green paper.

Alternative Project

PUEBLO Each student can make a portion of a Southwestern Pueblo, such as Taos, New Mexico, by constructing a simple brown cardboard box. If cardboard isn't obtainable, cover small boxes with brown kraft paper or paint with tan paint. The doors and window outlines can be painted turquoise. When each student has made a box, these can be grouped together, leaving some as single-story dwellings, but also stacking some together to make a two- to three-story high pueblo. Round vigas (logs used to support the roofs) can be painted near the flat tops, or actual twigs can be poked in holes.

Interdisciplinary Connections
LANGUAGE ARTS
DESIGN A DREAM HOME Students can write about what their dream house will contain. It could be a modern home or an old building in the country. Writing in advance of actually designing the home may help them to individualize it. Or, when the process is finished, have them write about changes they made as they went along, and how different it looks from their original idea.

SOCIAL STUDIES
HISTORIC VILLAGE Students can construct similar houses to produce historical, cultural, or regional architecture, such as 18th- and 19th-century row houses of many American cities, a town of the Old West, an Indian Village, Prehistoric village, African village, a small German town, Stratford-on-Avon, or a Greek Acropolis.

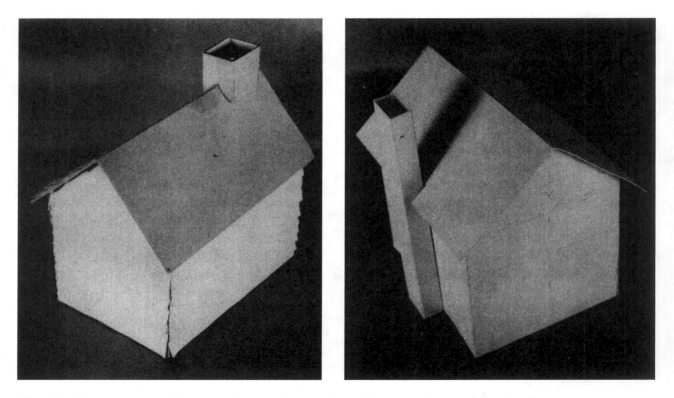

These buildings, constructed by Jan Cutlan's students at the Parkway Northeast Middle School in St. Louis County, Missouri, show basic tagboard and cardboard construction.

PROJECT 8-2   EVERYONE IS AN ARCHITECT

Materials

tagboard	rulers
alphabet noodles	gravel
scissors	tempera paint
sandpaper	Popsicle sticks
brushes	corrugated cardboard
toothpicks	

These buildings, constructed by Jan Cutlan's students at the Parkway Northeast Middle School in St. Louis County, Missouri, were constructed of a variety of materials. Students were limited only by their imaginations!

Directions   Consider what and where your building is going to be. If it is to be in the country, it might look entirely different than if it were in a city. The climate (wind, snow, scarce water), trees, location (urban or country) all help to determine how your building will be made. Because this is the exterior only, consider how it will look from the outside. How many windows will you have? How many doors? Will there be a front porch, dormer windows in the second story, shingles on the roof?

1. Do a rough drawing of your ideas, then when you have decided on a structure, carefully measure and cut the tagboard that will be used for your basic house. The two ends will be taller and come to a point to support a peaked roof. You can put two 2-story box-houses side by side, or make a 1-story ranch house with a front porch going all the way across.

2. The roof will be a simple peaked roof, with a chimney attached to the top or going up one side of the house. Dormers can be added. Finish the roof with individually cut pieces (shingles) of tagboard. Begin at the bottom of the roof and apply shingles horizontally, carefully overlapping and working toward the peak. To make them resemble European-style shingles, cut them round on the bottom.

3. Use a ruler to measure, carefully spacing and drawing windows and doors. Emphasize windows by outlining with tagboard strips. The exterior can be finished in a variety of ways. Long strips of tagboard can be overlapped to look like siding (start at the bottom and work up), or you can make a surface of small shingles (like the roof). Texture can be added with Popsicle sticks, washed gravel, or sandpaper. Toothpicks, wooden skewers, or small twigs could make a log cabin-style surface. A name or sign can be fashioned on matboard using glued-on alphabet noodles.

4. When the building is completed, place it on an irregular cardboard base slightly larger than the structure. The base is a plot of land. A small tree (twig) can be stuck into a block or Tinkertoy® and glued on. You could paint the base with a mixture of tempera, white glue, and sand to make grass or dirt. Or cover the base with sandpaper. Small pieces of sponge could be cut up to use as shrubbery.

PROJECT 8-3
VICTORIAN HOUSES

FOR THE TEACHER   The Victorian house offers unlimited opportunities for interpretation because there were so many one-of-a-kind Victorian house designs. There were very few subdivisions at that time, and most Victorian-era homes (nineteenth century) were designed by the owners and builders, who reveled in the unique characteristics they could put in their houses. Building materials were brick, shingles, stone, clapboard, and often combinations of more than one material. Wooden houses were often painted in several colors to highlight the turrets, cupolas, balconies, porches, dormers, and *gingerbread* of which Victorians were so fond.

Vocabulary

balcony	columns
symmetrical	cupolas
asymmetrical	gingerbread
turret	clapboard
tower	dormers
balustrade	ventilation
fish-scale shingles	balance
pilaster	lattice
bay window	widow's walk

Preparation   This project will be done with diluted bleach (1/3 water to 2/3 bleach), applied with cotton swabs on construction paper (appropriate for fourth graders and up). Test this yourself before you begin, as some construction paper works perfectly, while other brands do not. It is most effective on black paper, but also interesting on other dark colors, including red. Distribute and collect the unused bleach yourself to avoid spills. Approximately two tablespoons of bleach are needed per table. **SAFETY NOTE: Explain to students that bleach can ruin their clothes if they get it on their hands and wipe hands on the clothes. Have students wash hands with soap after this project.** Show students slides or black-and-white photocopies of actual Victorian houses to help them become aware of the extensive detailing in homes of this age. Discuss the uniqueness of most Victorian homes. Ideally you would have the opportunity for students to make sketches from real houses. To speed the design process, make sets of patterns by cutting old tagboard folders on the paper cutter. It is recommended that for this project the drawings should be a front view only, as pre-cut patterns do not work for perspective drawing.

Talk with students about total composition and use of the picture plane. Students tend to let houses float in the middle of the page, without giving any thought to foundation, landscape, steps, etc. It would be helpful to demonstrate how to make front steps on a piece of paper or the board, as this is always difficult. Point out how architects might have a symmetrical or asymmetrical design.

Adaptations for Younger Students
PUT YOURSELF IN THE PICTURE Young students can draw Victorian houses freehand with crayons or watercolor crayons on white paper. They can understand the concept of drawing with squares, rectangles, and triangles to make a building. When they have drawn the basic building, have them "put themselves into the picture" (looking out a window or playing on the porch). Encourage students to add details such as window panes, shingles, bricks and siding, shrubbery, possibly even lattice work around the foundation.

Interdisciplinary Connections
SOCIAL STUDIES

THE VICTORIAN ERA Victorian houses and Victorian times were all so "proper." Discuss with students some of the social practices of those times, comparing them with today's relaxed standards. They might find interesting explanations about such terms as "limbs" (legs), calling cards, bustles, spats, gloves, parlor, butler, tea, butler's pantry, and parlor maid. Some students who are fortunate enough to live in old homes might like to know what life was like when those homes were built. If students have old family photographs, they will get clues about differences in daily life in those times.

MATH

COMPASS, RULER, AND PROTRACTOR Students can design the houses with pencil, using rulers, compasses, and protractors. Although this will take longer, they will experience a sense of pride in learning to use these tools and measure carefully. This can simply be a pencil rendering or can be enhanced with fine-line markers or colored pencil.

Student work. Details such as steps and a front yard keep the house from "floating."

PROJECT 8–3 VICTORIAN HOUSES

Materials

photocopies of Victorian houses

tagboard patterns:

    squares (2 × 2-, 3 × 3-, 4 × 4-, 6 × 6-inch)

    rectangles (2 × 3-, 2 × 4-, 2 × 6-inch)

    triangles (2-, 3-, 4-, 6-inch hypotenuse)

    cone shapes (curved on bottom for turrets)

    strips (1, 2, 3 × 12-inch)

rulers

pencils

12 × 18 or 18 × 24-inch dark colored construction paper

cotton swabs

small plastic containers (or butter tubs) for bleach

bleach (diluted 1/3 water to 2/3 bleach) (can be collected and reused)

smocks

newspaper for covering tables

oil pastels

Directions   Decide in advance how many stories your house will be (two to three would have been normal for that time). If you will have an asymmetrical house, turn your paper vertically. For a symmetrical house, work horizontally. Victorian homes always had interesting roof lines. Many had turrets (towers), balconies, porches, dormer windows, and cupolas.

If you have seen San Francisco's Victorian "Painted Ladies" (as such fancy homes were sometimes called), most have color schemes that include white as an accent color (*examples:* yellow, blue, and white; white, olive green, and rust; violet, pink, and white; orange, yellow, and white).

1. Assemble tagboard patterns on your construction paper to get the general idea of how you want your house to look. Trace around them in pencil to make the "bare bones" of the house. Now become creative with the details.

2. Most Victorian homes had a basement, so you may see a foundation with lattice work or small windows at the base of the house. Steps could lead to a porch. Put in shrubbery or lattice work around the base of the house. A fence, grass, or flowers might show at the side or behind the house. If you have too much empty space at the top, use bleach to add clouds or sky.

3. Because air conditioning was not yet present and few homes had electricity, these homes often had bay windows or large windows that could be kept open for ventilation. The windows and doors were often surrounded with

carvings or pilasters. A cupola on top of the house might have been kept open in the summer to improve ventilation. Now give consideration to fireplaces, front porches, exterior trim (shingles, brick, stone, clapboard, or combinations of these). Lightly draw the details.

4. Use a cotton swab frequently dipped in bleach to go over your pencil lines. The paper will get lighter where the bleach touches. You may find you will want to simply lighten some entire areas (such as shingles) by going over them with bleach. After the outlines have all been done with bleach, color inside the lines with oil pastels. Firmly apply oil pastel to get brilliant colors that look good on dark paper. Avoid using dark colors that will not contrast with your paper; instead, work in lighter colors such as yellow, turquoise, light violet, magenta, light green, light blue, and white. If you use light-colored paper, then the darker pastels will be fine. It isn't necessary to completely color the house and background.

PROJECT 8–4
CASTLE

FOR THE TEACHER Many students may never have an opportunity to see an actual castle, but they love learning about the lives of the people who had them built and lived in them—the knights and their ladies. Most *real castles*, built between 1050 and 1350, offered refuge against warfare. Later *palaces*, often much larger than castles, were built primarily as the residences of royalty or wealthy landowners. Students may be familiar with the castle at Disneyland that is modeled on the 19th-century romantic "castle" of *Neuschwanstein* in the Bavarian Alps.

Most castles were not built all at once, but were added to as time allowed. Those that were high on hills could be easily reached from only one direction. If they were on lower ground, they were often surrounded by a moat, and at least one castle in Germany (the *Pfalz* near Kaub) is in the middle of the Rhine River. Students are interested to learn that slits or crenellation allowed archers to shoot at enemies, while being protected themselves; that the towers were to enable sentries to spot enemies from a distance; and that a moat and drawbridge were to keep unwelcome visitors out. *Machicolation* (just above the entrance) was to allow rocks or boiling liquid to be poured on raiders.

Castles often had two sets of walls: a low outer wall and a high inner wall with space between them (the *bastion*). They were mostly occupied by the nobility and servants unless townspeople needed to move there during a siege for protection. Castles are usually made of thick stone walls because they had to be very tall and sturdy to resist climbing, tunnels, catapulted stones, or blazing torches during a siege. The castles had an inside well and storage for food, and there was room within the walls for horses and soldiers. A "keep" where the owners lived usually was dominated by a great hall.

Your students would find it hard to imagine a world where the use of a *crossbow* was forbidden (by the second Lateran Council in 1139 and by King Conrad III of Germany) because it was considered such a lethal weapon.

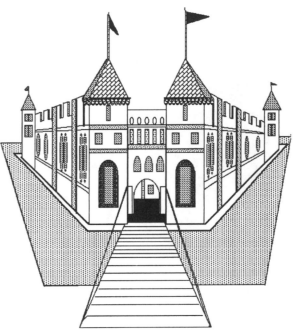

Vocabulary

bleed

watercolor wash

composition

pattern

castle

palace

crenellation

crossbow

garde-robe (bathroom)

gatehouse

siege

machicolation

moat

drawbridge

keep

murder holes (holes near the gate or walls through which boulders could be dropped
    on invaders)

Preparation Many fine books about life in castles are available for young people. These explain daily life in the castle, how they were built, who lived in them, and how they were organized and maintained. Some of the most famous castles are pictured in detail. Several books give information about medieval warfare, clothing, food, entertainment, and the relationship between the castle and the community. Read students a story about life in the Middle Ages, or a fairy tale about a princess in a castle.

Adaptation for Younger Students

PALACE Have students fold a piece of construction paper in half. They may then use chalk on one half to draw a curved or crenellated top with towers. They will then cut through both layers at once to shape the top and add details such as windows, a gatehouse, or slits for archers. The castle should be mounted on contrasting background paper and more details added with contrasting paper or marker. (This project was developed by apprentice teacher Kristina David in Beth Scott's classes at Ross School, St. Louis County, Missouri.

Alternative Project

CARDBOARD WALLED CITY Students can collect small boxes and cardboard tubes to create an all-class three-dimensional walled fortress/city. They can use tagboard to make "curtain walls" (undulating), outer walls, corner towers, a "keep" in the center, battlements, a moat and drawbridge. *Carcassonne* and *Mont-Saint-Michel* are two such city–fortresses in France.

Interdisciplinary Connections
SOCIAL STUDIES

MEDIEVAL PROFESSIONS Have students select a profession of the Middle Ages, researching how they would dress, what they would commonly do with their day, what their tools might be, and the duties they would be expected to perform. Suggestions would be the archer, blacksmith, cook, lord of the manner, lady of the manner, jester, knight, baker, butler, clerk, crossbowman, musician, taster, carver, cupbearer, mat weaver, spinner, groom, fencing instructor, armorer, stone mason, friar, seamstress, artist, squire, peasant, teacher, manuscript illuminator, merchant, miller, sailor, jeweler, cobbler, wattle and daub plasterer, doctor.

MATH

TWO-POINT PERSPECTIVE CASTLE DRAWING Post pictures of castles within the room, and demonstrate on the board how to use two-point perspective to draw a castle. Let it be seen from the front opening, which might include a gate, towers, a drawbridge, details such as rock walls or brick, and flags flying.

Debbie McConnell's fifth-grade students from the Barretts Elementary School in St. Louis County, Missouri created these castles using watercolor and marker. Details such as battlements, towers, drawbridges, and moats were included.

PROJECT 8–4   CASTLE

Materials

paper

pencils

fine-line black watercolor
marker

watercolors

brushes

Directions

1. Consider whether your castle will be high on a hill or on a plain near a river. Wherever it is, it will have at least one lookout tower so enemies can be seen in the distance. A flag often flies from the tower when the owner is "in-residence." Many people live and work in a castle. You might want to draw people inside or outside the walls.

2. Use pencil to lightly draw an outline of your castle. Think about what the top will look like and where you will place towers and the entrance gate. When the castle outline is complete, go over it with fine-line black watercolor marker. Add details such as slate shingles, stone walls, a drawbridge and gatehouse, turrets, flag, people. Depending on how much time you have, this drawing can be very detailed.

3. When you are satisfied that the marker drawing is complete, add a watercolor wash (thin watercolor). Fill in areas with several different colors of watercolor. The black marker will bleed (run), but this gives a very interesting effect. Or you may choose to paint the entire castle in bright watercolors.

4. Remember to not let the castle just "float" in the air. It may be high on a hill with rocks, or have a drawbridge and moat. It might even be surrounded by tiny houses that are "outside the wall." You can show clouds by leaving some areas white while you paint most of the sky blue.

PROJECT 8–5
FAÇADE, THE FRONT SIDE

FOR THE TEACHER   Some façades for buildings created in the 1890s were of textured cast-iron painted to look like stone. Even today, store fronts of buildings in many towns are often made of different materials from the sides. Students can appreciate that façades can change by noticing how store fronts in malls change from year to year. Only the façade, or front of a building, was often used in movie sets of old-time "Westerns."

Vocabulary

façade

cast-iron

elevation (drawing of one side of a building)

repoussé

texture

variety

shutters

stories

Preparation

Announce in advance that students will be doing drawings of the façades of their own homes. Help them avoid the elementary school "cliché" house by first drawing a "typical" child's house on the board as students describe it to you. Young children will tell you it is a square with a triangle roof, chimney with smoke coming out of it, path surrounded by flowers, one window with shutters and curtains and a flower box. Ask them if their own homes look like that, and if not, what they do look like.

Help students visualize their own homes by asking them to write answers to such questions as "What is the building material? Is the front door in the middle or off to one side? How many windows are there? Do the windows have shutters? Is it more than one story tall? How is the roof shaped? Is there a tree in the front yard? Are there bushes? What about steps—do you have to walk up steps to go in the front door? Does a garage show at the front of the house? Are trees and bushes near the house?

Perhaps a photo of the house will help students remember architectural details. If time allows, have them actually do a pencil drawing at home to bring to class.

As preparation, give students a small piece of tooling foil to make as many textures as they can think of.

Alternative Projects

ALUMINUM-FOIL FAÇADES Give students tagboard rectangles to make a collage of two- or three-story building façades. Tagboard can be cut and glued in layers for architectural details such as windows, trim, doors, awnings, bricks, or stone. Wrap with ordinary aluminum foil, encouraging students to emphasize details by drawing with a dull pencil or ballpoint pen. Wipe with brown or sienna paint, using paper towel or fine steel wool to shine the highlights.

BAS-RELIEF FOAM BUTCHER TRAY FAÇADES With older students, butcher meat trays could be cut up and layered to make façades. Windows and doors could be cut, and strips added for detail. It

would not be necessary to cover these with foil. **SAFETY NOTE: When students use X-acto®**
knives, remind them that the holding hand is always behind the knife.

CERAMIC FAÇADES Have students do a drawing of their own homes, working out details completely prior to making a clay plaque. On white clay these could be underpainted in realistic colors prior to covering with clear glaze. On red clay, emphasize texture. Fire once, then simply wipe with shoe polish or thinned brown acrylic paint (polishing highlights).

BLACK CONSTRUCTION PAPER STRIPS ON WHITE PAPER Use the paper cutter to cut black strips 1/2 X 12 inches. Challenge students to make building façades on 12 X 18-inch white paper by creative use of the strips. Talk about girders, beams, exterior supports, set-backs, interesting "crowns." Emphasize that gluing should be deferred until they have tried several different possibilities.

Edge of Town, 1921–41, Charles Ephraim Burchfield, watercolor with touches of gouache over graphite on paper, 26¹⁵/₁₆ X 39¹³/₁₆ inches, The Nelson–Atkins Museum of Art, Kansas City, Missouri (Gift of the Friends of Art)

PROJECT 8–5   FAÇADE, THE FRONT SIDE

STUDENT PAGE

Materials

masking tape

pencils

folded newspaper pads

paper cut to size of foil

6 × 8-inch pieces of copper
  or brass-colored tooling
  foil

10 × 12-inch black mount
  board

2 × 4-inch pieces of foil for practicing textures

gold, silver, or copper marking pens

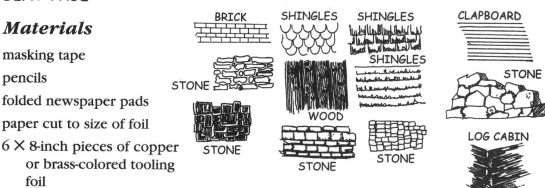

Directions

1. Do a pencil drawing of the front of your home, noticing details such as building materials, landscaping, and textures such as brick, clapboard, or shingles.

2. A texture experiment will help you get ideas for making details on your repoussé house façade. Work on a soft pad of newspaper to get greater depth. On a small *practice* piece of foil, make as many textures as you can think of. These can be a circle-within-a-circle, spirals, waves, dots, lines, criss-cross. Repeat textures more than once. Turn the foil over and "repush" (repoussé) from the back. Now go over the front again in some areas. These techniques may be used when you do a repoussé drawing of your house.

3. Tape your pencil drawing to the front of the tooling foil. Carefully draw over the outlines of the house to transfer your drawing. Remove the pencil drawing. You will need to go over the outlines again to create depth. Now look at the texture experiments on your small piece of foil. Could you use some of the same textures on the façade of your house?

4. When you have drawn on the front of the house, turn the foil over and draw from the back, as you did on your practice piece. Alternate working front and back to get the greatest depth. When you are satisfied that it cannot be improved, place it on a piece of black cardboard.

5. As a finishing touch, make similar textures to those in the "house" around the outside of the black mount board, using gold, silver, or copper marking pens to match the color of your foil. Or mount the repoussé on white paper and draw texture designs with a black fine-line marker.

PROJECT 8–6
IN YOUR OWN LITTLE CORNER IN YOUR OWN LITTLE ROOM

FOR THE TEACHER   While some students are involved in the decoration of their rooms, others are totally oblivious of their surroundings. Students may never have thought of their own rooms as being "architecture," or that the colors, decorations, and objects in it might be called "interior design." Many artists, including Vincent van Gogh, Edgar Degas, Henri Matisse, Pierre Bonnard, and Edouard Vuillard, chose room interiors for their paintings. Some interior designers have created watercolor renderings of rooms they have decorated.

Vocabulary

interior design	model
color coordination	swatches
theme	perspective
vanishing point	renderings

Preparation   Ask students to draw their own rooms in total detail, perhaps including an open closet door. A drawing could be just of one corner of the room. Students could make a floor plan before doing a drawing of one corner or wall. Talk with them about what is in their bedroom—what colors the walls are and what they have on their walls.

Introduce one-point perspective by drawing on the board or a piece of paper how to make and use a vanishing point in a simple drawing of a room. Particularly help students notice that all horizontal and vertical lines are exactly parallel to the sides of the paper, and that the diagonal lines all go to the vanishing point.

Adaptations for Younger Students

DRAW YOUR SURROUNDINGS Although younger students are not yet ready for perspective drawing, they are certainly ready to draw their surroundings. Let them draw themselves doing something in their rooms (reading, sleeping, dressing, drawing). This can be done with pencil, crayon, or marker.

Alternative Projects

INTERIOR DESIGN Fold a 12 X 12- or 18 X 18-inch square of drawing paper or tagboard in fourths. Cut one fold line to the center. The two bottom "flaps" will be overlapped and the upper portion folded to give a cut-away "corner" of a room. The overlapped flaps will be the floor, and the sides will be two walls. Have students glue the bottom when the drawing is all finished. They can draw their own rooms, including details such as windows, doors, shelves, and pictures. Boxes for dressers, bookshelves, and a bed can be glued in place.

STAGE SET Make a stage model of a room by cutting away the front of a cardboard box and slanting two sides. Use construction paper, cardboard, cloth, and other found materials to construct a "living room" that could be used by actors.

REDESIGN A CLOSET Make a list of all the things that are kept in a bedroom closet. Ask students if their own closets are in order. How could they change the closet so that they would have a "place for everything and everything in its place"? Do an *elevation* of the closet, considering how it could be improved. Sometimes by adding another pole, shelves, labeled boxes, or cubbyholes, the closet can be kept in better order. Do before-and-after drawings of the closet as it *really* is now, and as it *could* be with a little organization.

CITYSCAPE WITH ONE-POINT PERSPECTIVE Have students place a dot (vanishing point) in the center of the paper. Lightly draw lines from the corners of the paper to the dot (the lines in the center will be erased). The vertical sides of the buildings, windows, and doors will parallel the sides of the paper. Windows, sidewalks, cars, doors, and people can be drawn in perspective by keeping one end of the ruler on the dot and making lines from the edges of the paper. To make the picture more interesting, vary the building heights, window styles, and signs. Add details such as lightposts, cars, street markings.

COMPUTER GRAPHICS INTERIOR The use of one- or two-point perspective works well in computer graphics, and some students will enjoy the challenge of designing a room, transforming boxes into beds, dressers, pictures, sofas, chairs, doors, and windows. In place of perspective, a floor plan of a room or entire house could be done.

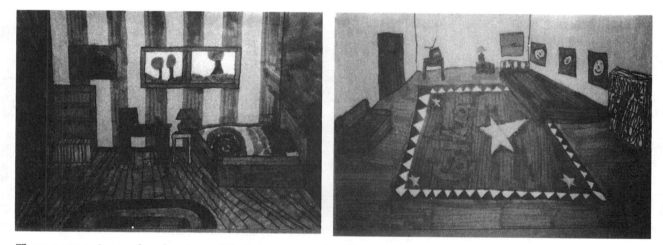

These perspective marker drawings of their own rooms, based on van Gogh's *Bedroom at Arles*, were by students of Nancy Raleigh at LaSalle Springs Middle School in the Rockwood District, St. Louis County, Missouri.

The Bedroom, 1888, Vincent van Gogh, oil on canvas, $28^3/_4 \times 36$ inches, Art Institute of Chicago, Helen Birch Bartlett Memorial Collection

PROJECT 8–6   IN YOUR OWN LITTLE CORNER IN YOUR OWN LITTLE ROOM

Materials

paper

pencil

crayon, marker, or watercolor

ruler

Directions   To draw a picture of your room, think about a point of view. You will be looking toward one end of the room. The headboard of the bed may be either on that wall or on a side wall.

1. Put a dot in the center of the paper. This is the vanishing point. Holding a ruler, lightly draw lines from the corners to the vanishing point. These lines represent the walls, floor, and ceiling. Draw a rectangle to represent the far wall from the diagonal lines, making sure the straight lines are exactly parallel to the top, bottom, and sides of the paper.

2. To make the bed, dresser, mirrors, windows, bookcases, doors, and rug, draw more diagonal lines. Then draw vertical or horizontal lines where needed.

3. When you have lightly drawn details, erase unnecessary lines. Use crayon or watercolor to add color and pattern.

PROJECT 8-7
INTERIOR DESIGN, MY APARTMENT

FOR THE TEACHER   Conscious choices are made about colors, scale, balance, and motif or the "feel" of an interior when it is *designed* by either a professional or an amateur. Before inviting students to select an artwork by an individual artist as inspiration for designing their "apartments," have them help as you write on the board selections that are made when decorating a room. Walls, rugs, curtains or draperies, and furniture colors all should be considered.

Vocabulary

interior design	theme
accent	color scheme
monochromatic	complementary
analogous	triadic
neutral	scale
eclectic	accessories
dominant	

Preparation   Send home an appeal for shoeboxes. Some students may be able to bring several, or you may be able to get your local shoe store to donate some. Each student will make an apartment from a shoebox. These can be subdivided into rooms by cutting cardboard to size and inserting it.

Collect postcards and art reproductions by several artists whose style is easily recognizable. Some whose work would be ideal for this project are: Vincent van Gogh, Geroges Seurat, Claude Monet, Fernand Leger, Pablo Picasso, Louise Nevelson, Frank Stella, Piet Mondrian, Jasper Johns, Frieda Kahlo, Chuck Close, Henri Rousseau, and Jean Dubuffet. For visual unity, you may prefer to have each student interpret different artworks from one artist. Reproductions of work by these artists are readily available.

Show students how they can make furniture by covering small boxes with cloth, construction paper, or wallpaper.

When the apartments are complete, use large paper clips to join the boxes together to make an apartment house. The outside of the stack could be covered with roll paper to unify the building and to offer stability.

Alternative Project

CULTURAL INFLUENCES   In designing their interiors, students could base their work on a culture or time period. During some decades, design has been influenced by world events. The discovery of King Tut's tomb, for example, spawned Egyptian-style furniture and Egyptian themes in movie theaters and restaurants. Asian, Turkish, and Middle Eastern influences have been commonplace since the beginning of trade with those regions. Art Deco, which was often based on Egyptian or Mayan designs, was introduced in the 1930s. The latter part of the twentieth century brought the Southwestern influence, based on colors, climate, and Native American artworks of that region. *Eclectic* design reflects the influence of diverse cultures and time periods, and has been popular for many years.

Note   The following three red, white, and blue works of art created by Dutch artists early in the twentieth century demonstrate how three totally different decorative items tie together when they are displayed together.

Composition of Red and White, 1938–1942, oil on canvas, Piet Mondrian, 39$\frac{1}{2}$ × 39 inches, Friends Fund, Saint Louis Art Museum.

Side Table, designed 1923, Gerrit Rietveld, made 1980 by Gerard van de Groenekan, Funds given by Richard Brumbaugh Trust, Saint Louis Art Museum.

Red and Blue Armchair, designed 1917–1918, Gerrit Rietveld, made 1980 by Gerard van de Groenekan, Funds given by Richard Brumbaugh Trust, Saint Louis Art Museum.

PROJECT 8–7 INTERIOR DESIGN, MY APARTMENT

STUDENT PAGE

Materials

shoeboxes

rulers

scissors

glue

pencils

newsprint

tagboard or posterboard

construction paper

wallpaper sample books

marker or tempera

large paper clips

Drawn from *Red and Blue Armchair*, Gerrit Rietveld; *Composition of Red and White*, Piet Mondrian; and *Side Table*, Gerrit Rietveld

Directions   Your shoebox will be displayed on its side, with the opening facing front. All the individual shoeboxes will be stacked one on top of another to make an apartment building. Your box (apartment) is approximately the same size as everyone else's, so the only way to make it uniquely yours is by your *interior design*.

1. Select the work of an artist whose work you like. Several of your friends might select the same artist, but if you choose different artworks, then each one of you will have an unique apartment. The room that you will decorate could be a family room, living room, or kitchen. To make two rooms, cut a piece of cardboard to fit vertically.

2. Examine the artwork that will provide your *theme*. What are the main colors? Would you like the walls to be that color, or is it so bright that you might prefer that color as an *accent*? Consider how you will cover the floor and furniture. One "rule of thumb" that has been used in decorating is "Something dark, something light, something dull, and something bright."

3. Think about your color scheme. What kind of color scheme does the painting you are working from have? It could be monochromatic (different variations of one color), complementary (colors opposite each other on the color wheel), analogous (colors next to each other on the color wheel), neutral (black, white, gray, brown, tan), or triadic (*examples:* red/blue/yellow or orange/green/violet).

4. Accessorize your room with small things you have made. These could include lamps, vases, pictures on the wall, clocks, flowers, books, rugs, magazines. For example, you may have a perfect small shell that could be used as a bowl, or you could make something from oil clay or dough. Cut small "paintings" from magazines.

PROJECT 8–8
DESIGN A CHAIR

FOR THE TEACHER   Many timeless chair designs have been created by famous architects. Talk with students about the requirements for a chair; then if available, show them pictures from books that show some cultural influences. Point out the "feet, knees, arms, backs" of chairs, then ask how they can design *their* chair to reflect the artwork of another culture or a specific artist.

Vocabulary

form	function
unity	variety
emphasis	line

Preparation   Preparation for this might include a visit to a museum to encourage children to notice details and do drawings of chairs. If this is not possible, ask students to look at the chairs in their own homes, bringing in drawings of details of seats, backs, and legs. Show pictures in books or slides of chairs. Or photocopy enough pages of a variety of designs for every student in the class to have one.

If you request it of your school's print room and the local copy center, it should not take long to get enough copy-paper cardboard boxes for an entire class.

Gather printed recycled paper or have students bring it from home for covering the chair. The printed materials can be interesting. If students use a computer at home, they may well come up with phrases or graphics that they would like to use to personalize their chairs.

Alternative Projects

MODELING CLAY CHAIRS   Have children use two sticks of oil clay (plasticine) to make their "dream" chair (possibly a throne, easy chair, or recliner). They will find out within a few days that "form follows function." If they have not carefully constructed it by pulling out extensions, or have carelessly stuck too many fancy "decorations" on it, the oil clay will fall apart. This leads to interesting discussions about how the material may dictate what you can do with it.

INDEX-CARD CHAIRS   Fold a 3 × 5-inch index card horizontally in thirds. Open it, then fold it in half lengthwise (a hot-dog fold). Use scissors to cut along the vertical center fold to the horizontal fold lines leaving the center third uncut. The two center sections are the seat and back. You will need to fold the resulting seat and back toward the center, folding one set of flaps the opposite way to be the legs, and folding the arms inward. For example, the back, arms, and legs may be shaped to make a "wing chair" or an "arm chair."

TAGBOARD CHAIRS   Simply use old file folders and cut chairs from them. Use the same directions as those of the index-card chairs, joining them with masking tape, and decorating with markers. (You could provide a pattern for younger students.)

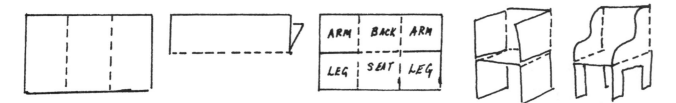

ETHNIC CULTURE CHAIRS Photocopy designs (possibly on colored paper) from chairs of various cultures such as Native American, African, or Asian. Chairs from various time periods would be another option. Dover Books have copyright-free illustrations such as these. These could also be done on card stock and small chairs could be cut directly from the colored sheets. Or the patterns can be used to decorate chairs.

RECYCLED WOODEN CHAIRS Teacher Toni Wilson of the North Kirkwood Middle School in St. Louis County, Missouri has her students paint wooden library chairs. Students first sand the chair to bare wood, then paint with acrylic paint. A theme is selected for each one, such as an African Safari Chair or a "Monet" or "Picasso" chair. This project is worked on in the students' spare time, so many students are involved in each chair. The chairs are finished with polymer medium. Classroom stools can also have "masterpieces" painted on them.

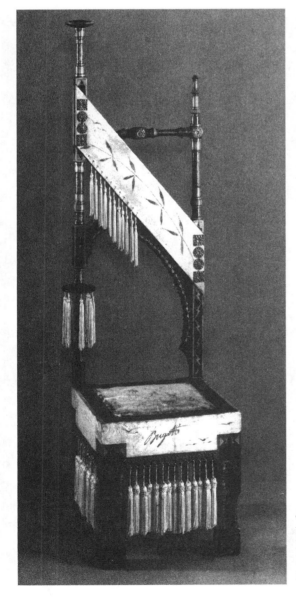

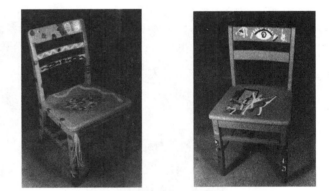

Toni Wilson's students at North Kirkwood Middle School in St. Louis County, Missouri transformed wooden chairs by sanding, repainting, and interpreting the work of an artist or a culture in their designs.

Side Chair, 1895–1904, Carlo Bugatti, wood, parchment, brass, pewter, and silk, Funds given in memory of Alfred Landesman and Museum Purchase, Saint Louis Art Museum

PROJECT 8–8   DESIGN A CHAIR

Materials

cardboard boxes, all sizes

brushes

masking tape

polymer medium or thinned white glue

wallpaper samples

recycled copy paper

5 × 7 cards or old tagboard file folders

pencils

scissors or utility knives

"found" objects

Directions

1. To make a chair of two cardboard boxes, cut off the top flaps so the box is open at the bottom (a copy-paper box will already be open). Cut away an opening on each side, leaving the corners of the box as the legs of the chair. This makes a bench or footstool. To complete a chair, glue a second box on top, cutting away the front and shaping the sides to resemble an arm chair.

2. The chair can be decorated many different ways.

   a. Paint color designs on it, using acrylic paint or tempera paint mixed with polymer medium.

   b. Cut up recycled copy paper and apply it with polymer medium, thinned white glue, or Ross® or Pritt® paste. When the glue has dried, decorate it with marker or paint. You can strengthen the box by putting paper even where it won't show. You can put personal messages or drawings underneath.

   c. Cover with wallpaper samples, applying it with paste.

3. Use "found" objects to make the chair more interesting. These could include shells, empty film containers, objects from the workbench, recycled aluminum containers, a few colored magazine pictures, fringe, yarn, bells, golf tees, etc.

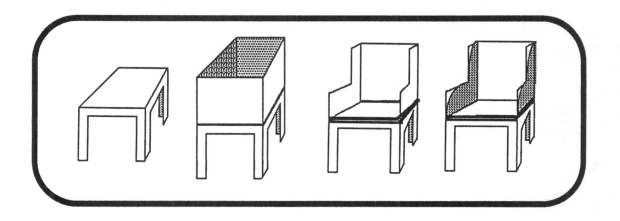

PROJECT 8–9
PAINT YOUR DREAM HOUSE

FOR THE TEACHER Architects are not the only people who have ideas. Some of the most interesting homes in the world—such as William Randolph Hearst's home *San Simeon* in San Luis Obispo, California, or "Mad" Ludwig's castle *Neuschwanstein* in Bavaria (the castle at Disneyland was modeled on it)—are the result of one person's dream.

Tell students about architect Frank Lloyd Wright's *Falling Water*, a dream house that is built right next to a waterfall and has balconies that overhang a creek. You can look down a staircase from the living room to see a pool, and the sound of rushing water is always present.

Vocabulary

form	function
adobe	variety
balance	creativity

Preparation Have a conversation about what a "Dream House" is. (When I was a child I wanted to live in the Lowe's Midland Theater because it was the most beautiful place I had ever seen. I was sure I could figure out how to adapt it to have bedrooms and living rooms.) Challenge your students to think about what they would like their house to be like. What are their favorite colors? Their favorite room in a house? Where might the house be located? How big a family would they hope to accommodate?

Depending on the ages of the students, you may wish to pre-mix colors with white to provide softer colors than those used straight from the bottle. Very few homes are painted dark purple or dark blue, for example. For this project, tempera paint gives a wonderful effect when it is mixed 50/50 with glue (it then closely resembles acrylic paint in its ability to be painted on any surface). With the younger students, you may later prefer to wash the ink off yourself, as the students are sometimes over-enthusiastic about removing the India ink!

Decorative effects have often been used by architects. Encourage students by showing photos of eclectic architecture such as St. Basil's Cathedral in Moscow.

Alternative Project

TAKE A CHANCE Geometric forms such as the spiral, pentagon, pyramid, cylinder, sphere, and arc have led to a variety of structures. Write these and other words such as circle, square, rectangle, etc., on individual pieces of paper and allow each student to pull a piece of paper "from a hat" as inspiration to design a structure based on that geometric form. Or photocopy a variety of shells and challenge them to design a home based on a shell.

St. Basil's Cathedral, Moscow

PROJECT 8–9   PAINT YOUR DREAM HOUSE

STUDENT PAGE

Materials

drawing paper	chalk
tempera paint	glue
containers with lids	brushes
paper	pencil
8 × 10-inch newsprint	India ink

Geodesic Dome—These buildings by famous architects might have been inspired by natural forms such as the sea shells shown next to them.

Directions   Many designs used by architects are based on geometric forms or forms found in nature. The location of the lot often determines whether a home is tall and narrow or low and sprawling. The climate is a factor as well. In the Southwest, where it is quite hot much of the year, adobe walls help a house remain cool. Where it is plentiful, wood may be the natural building material. Many homes combine a variety of materials.

1. In designing your dream home, begin by thinking where you would want it to be located. If it has a view in the distance, you may want to have large windows in the front. Consider materials you will use, then begin to think about the form. On a piece of newsprint, draw some ideas. You might make your home look like a shell or base it on circles or combine natural and geometric forms.

2. When you have your idea, use chalk to first draw an outline. Apply paint almost to the chalk outlines, but avoid touching them, in order to leave a place for black ink outlines. Anyplace on the paper that is not painted will be black when the India ink is applied. It is okay to have a "brushy" effect in some places.

3. Paint the background also, showing the "site" of your house, perhaps including trees and shrubs around it. If a lake or river is in front of it, you might even paint the house's upside-down reflection in the lake. (A reflection is painted the same size as the original, but with some interruptions where the water is shimmery.) It would be almost the same colors, but then loosely brush blue or green over it. The sky and water are often almost the same color.

4. When the painting is done, brush undiluted India ink over the entire painting. Allow the ink to dry, then hold the painting under running water, using a brush to help remove some of the ink. Allow the painting to dry. Then mat it for display.

The Great Mosque at Samarra, Iran, 847

The Solomon R. Guggenheim Museum, New York City

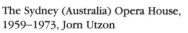

The Sydney (Australia) Opera House, 1959–1973, Jorn Utzon

PROJECT 8–10
THE ARCHITECTURAL COMPETITION: MAKING MODELS

FOR THE TEACHER   This project is to challenge your students to incorporate *found* materials into an architectural model, to think beyond the ordinary. Architect Frank Gehry has spent a lifetime in experimentation with materials. He even designed furniture that was manufactured from rolls of corrugated cardboard. His art museum in Bilbao, Spain is bold in its use of a stainless-steel exterior.

Since at least the Renaissance, it has been commonplace for cities or sponsors to conduct architectural competitions for special buildings, civic centers, monuments, bridges, and museums. Other works of art that have been chosen by competition are stadiums, urban park designs, and gates. Architects submit renderings, blueprints, and models for the competition. A model of cardboard, balsa wood, or plastic is constructed to scale according to the blueprints. Many museums have such models in their collections. The Royal Academy in London devotes an entire gallery to displaying such models in their annual summer show. Students might be interested to learn that making architectural models is a full-time career for many people.

Vocabulary

model

competition

blueprint

rendering

scale

Preparation
You can make this project as simple or as complex as you want. You might just have students do a pencil drawing or *blueprint* of a plan. *Renderings* can be done in watercolor, ink, or collage. Have students begin bringing in "quality junk." This can include plastic packaging, discarded displays from grocery stores, or plastic straws. If possible, send a note home to parents that students will begin making architectural models, and that almost any clean discards might be used in the process. This project could be worked on individually or in pairs.

Alternative Projects
FOAMBOARD OR CARDBOARD MODEL Older students could make a model by measuring and cutting a material such as posterboard or foam core with a cutting knife. **SAFETY NOTE: If you use cutting knives, count them before and after class, and caution students always to have the holding hand behind the knife—never to cut toward the holding hand.**

FOUND-OBJECT BLUEPRINT AND DESIGN Marcie Dairaghi, who teaches gifted students at Sappington Elementary School in St. Louis County, Missouri, assembled a grouping of found objects that she then challenged pairs of students to use. The problem assigned was to develop a model home for a specific use, such as one for seniors or a young family. The students then actually constructed a model from their blueprint.

ACCESSORIZING A BUILDING Some students might be more interested in creating a sculptural maquette (model) for outdoor sculpture for the front of the building. Some cities now have laws that the costs of new buildings include some money for monumental sculpture and landscaping. Other students might like to consider what kind of monumental artwork could go inside a lobby. Tapestries, sculpture, murals, fountains, and mosaics are all being used in one form or another in new buildings. Someone else might be interested in designing a façade or interesting top for a basic skyscraper. The 1950s plain black boxes have given way to buildings that are far more decorative.

THE DOOR COMPETITION Have students design new doors for their school or home. These can be made of layers of tagboard or construction paper, cut out and glued. Lorenzo Ghiberti was the winner of a famous competition in Florence, Italy, when he designed beautiful bronze doors for the Cathedral Baptistry, called by some *The Gates of Heaven*.

Model of Schroder House, Utrecht, The Netherlands, 1924, Gerrit Rietveld, plywood and glass, $18^1/_2 \times 30^1/_4 \times 21^1/_4$ inches, The Museum of Modern Art, New York. Gift of Mrs. Phyllis B. Lambert. Photograph © 1999 the Museum of Modern Art, New York.

PROJECT 8–10   THE ARCHITECTURAL COMPETITION: MAKING MODELS

Materials

graph paper or drawing paper

rulers

pencils

scissors

white glue or glue guns

brads

cutting knives (only for older students)

straight pins

cardboard

plastic

foamboard

paint or gesso

Model of Schroder House, Utrecht, The Netherlands, 1924, Gerrit Rietveld, plywood and glass, $18^1/_2 \times 30^1/_4 \times 21^1/_4$ inches, The Museum of Modern Art, New York. Gift of Mrs. Phyllis B. Lambert. Photograph © 1999 the Museum of Modern Art, New York.

Directions   This project is for you to think of a building type that has not been done before. Although you will be making just the exterior, interior considerations would include access for the disabled such as ramps and elevators, stairs, entrances, and exits. Think about the purpose of your building. What will it be used for? You could make a stadium, museum, restaurant, school, railroad station, or rapid transit station.

1. When you have decided what type of building you will make, look at some of the materials you have available for building it. Almost any shape is possible to build, so it is a matter of how you combine your materials. This is the time to let your imagination go. Doodle! Try various combinations of shapes.

2. After you have decided on a general idea, make a more complete drawing. This could be your rendering (a painting or drawing of what it will look like from the front). It can be done in pencil, ink, pasted paper, or watercolor.

3. If you choose not to do a rendering until after the model is complete, decide on the size of your structure, and do a pencil drawing to *scale*. On your drawing, 1/4 inch could be equal to 5 feet or 10 feet.

4. Now construct your model as close to your blueprint as you can. Select a base (cardboard, Masonite, or plastic). Don't make the model too large, or it will be difficult to find a place to store it. Combine materials, joining them together with white glue or a glue gun. If you use white glue, you may need to use straight pins to hold sections together until they dry. If you use foamboard, you can hold pieces together with small metal nails. The exterior finish could be left in its natural color, painted with gesso or tempera, or covered with paper.

UNIT 9

TECHNOLOGY: COMPUTERS, PHOTOGRAPHY, VIDEO

COMPUTER GRAPHICS

Computer technology in the classroom is a natural for the art teacher. Graphics components in most modern computers include line, shape, color, value, pattern—the elements and principles of design! Even the media include brushes of various sizes and shapes, the spray-can, and a "pencil point," the cursor. Although teaching computer skills is not a substitute for helping students enjoy the use of charcoal, paint, crayons, and clay, it may be used at times to speed up the design process.

Computers and software change at such a rapid rate that no attempt is made here to relate to specific programs. Rather, the main consideration is helping students learn to use the computer as a tool for creating and appreciating art. Helping students master graphics tools can serve to advance learning in other disciplines, and earn parent and teacher support.

As more and more museums make their collections available to viewers on the Internet, and as interactive video allows students to access historical images, familiarizing students with how to use the computer to their advantage will become as much a part of teaching art as using crayons on paper. New computer "games" and software for teaching art are constantly appearing on the market. As art teachers also work with students in developing language skills, students are writing, talking, and researching about art and artists. Many students are highly motivated to become computer literate, and will sit for hours improving their skills.

Many schools have digital cameras available for classroom use, which will allow students to expose and manipulate their own photos. The scanner also allows students to reproduce their own photographs, or to scan a historical work of art and transform it.

COMPUTER ART LESSONS

Having one or more computers in every elementary and middle school art classroom is still a dream in many districts, but a reality in many. To get the maximum use out of classroom computers, most elementary and middle school teachers introduce a project to the entire class, reviewing it from time to time as individual students progress through a lesson.

The teaching of a computer art lesson follows lesson design as in any other curriculum, with motivation, input, resources, practice, and evaluation. Recent innovations in art education include giving more emphasis to the history of art, as well as looking at and talking about art.

Suggestions from Experienced Computer Graphics Teachers

- Work out a schedule that ensures students can work singly or in groups to complete an assignment while other students are working on a different classroom project.

- Make a "tutorial" packet for introducing students to the computer. Have them show they know how to save their work and use the tools such as line, spray, mirrors, cut and paste.

- In a classroom where students are seen daily, each student could maintain computer projects, notes, etc., in a personal notebook/portfolio. A personal disk is also advised. Printed-out projects could be kept in clear plastic sleeves. For classes that are seen only weekly, an all-class portfolio would be sufficient for storing printed work.

- Post simple instructions for an assignment in the computer area.

- Print out successful interpretations of an assignment and post them to encourage those students just starting.

- Suggest that students make two prints of any completed assignment—one for themselves and one for your archives.

- For students to give a signal for help, glue a small red cup and small blue cup bottom-to-bottom and keep them on top of each computer. If students have a question, the red cup is turned up, and the student can get on with his or her work instead of sitting with a hand in the air waiting for you.

Uses for the Computer in the Art Classroom

- Write instructions for *any* classroom art project on the computer. Then use a document camera to transfer the continually repeating instructions to an overhead monitor.

- Make a slide show of the work of a particular artist or medium, having it continuously showing on an overhead monitor.

- Much of the new software includes wonderful interactive art history, discovery programs, and art games for students. Some of these appreciation programs can be used to introduce a project or at the end of the hour by a small group of students.

Computer Graphics Assignments

AFRICAN, HISPANIC, OR NATIVE AMERICAN MASK Have students make a mask based on images from a book. This introduces symmetry, proportion, shapes, texture, and color, and emphasizes the differences and similarities in cultures throughout the world.

SELF-PORTRAIT THREE WAYS Have students make a line-drawing self-portrait by looking in a mirror. A second version of the line portrait is filled in with totally wild colors. For a third portrait, realistic coloring will be used. Each of these could be mounted separately, then displayed together.

SWITCH MEDIA Work out a design in another medium before transferring it to the computer. Examples are watercolor/computer; torn paper/computer; fine-line marker/computer.

CD LABELS AND BOX COVER Have students design a label for a CD and do a mock-up of a box to contain it.

STILL-LIFE A still-life containing six to nine objects, some overlapping, could be effective. Students could relate this to Pablo Picasso's work, in which he tried to show several views of the same object in one composition.

VICTORIAN HOUSE The Victorian house lends itself very well to computer graphics because of its use of geometric shapes. Students could first draw it on paper, complete with all the details, then interpret their drawing onto the computer.

HEX DESIGN A hex design uses geometric shapes. Working within a circle, many different divisions can be made, then colored in brightly.

ARABESQUE The curved designs found in Persian arabesque allow total freedom of form, yet teach the use of symmetry and repetition. Such a design could be translated into a tile or rug.

ONE-POINT AND TWO-POINT PERSPECTIVE CUBES For one-point perspective, have students make a point at the center of the composition, then make a number of different-sized rectangles at random on the screen. Using lines from the vanishing point, they can come to the corners of the squares, then make horizontal and vertical marks to make boxes, going back to erase the lines drawn to the vanishing point.

For two-point perspective, make two dots at the side of the page, again making boxes and drawing lines to the vanishing point.

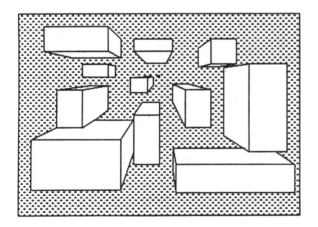 

One- and two-point perspective computer-generated drawings

METAMORPHOSIS The literal metamorphosis of a caterpillar to a butterfly is the basis of this project. In successive pictures, students could change, for example, an airplane to an eagle, or an automobile to a tiger. Toni Wilson's students of North Kirkwood Middle School in Kirkwood, Missouri begin by changing one letter to another.

NAME DESIGN Have students print out their first names, then fill the complete page using repetition of the name in many different fonts, overlapping and working out an interesting composition. If working in black and white, this could involve value changes; if working in color, it could be done using the entire color spectrum.

CAREERS IN COMPUTER GRAPHICS Middle school teacher Ronald Young of the Nipher Middle School in Kirkwood, Missouri has a continuously changing bulletin board as students take responsibility for investigating and submitting reports about various careers in the field of computer graphics.

QUILT Students can "piece" a traditional quilt square using geometric shapes. If students find that too simple, challenge advanced students to make a "crazy quilt," with the entire square filled with odd shapes, textures, animals, and decorative "embroidery."

ANIMALS IN THEIR ENVIRONMENTS Using resources such as *National Geographic* magazine, students can draw an animal or reptile on the screen, then

"Crazy Quilt"

create an environment for it. One version of this could include the animal "camouflaged" to blend in with the background. Another version could have the animal in either cool colors with a warm background or in warm colors with a cool background.

DESIGN IT ON THE COMPUTER Have students select five of the following elements, principles of art or compositional devices to include in their project. Each completed project should be labeled, and all could be mounted together. The pictures could be unified through the use of a cool or warm color scheme. A group of people could divide the assignment, with each one doing a portion. This ongoing individual or group project was developed by Timothy Smith of the Parkway School District, St. Louis County, Missouri.

symmetry

formal balance

informal balance

one-point perspective

foreground, middle-ground, background

movement

repetition

texture

picture combined with letters

TIPS FOR DISPLAYING COMPUTER ARTWORK

Ways to Exhibit Student Computer Artwork

- Save it on disk and show it directly on the computer or overhead monitor.
- Save images in a series for a "slide show" directly on the computer.

Hard Copy

- Print it on a color printer and mat it. It could be enlarged on a color copy machine.
- Photograph it directly from the screen using slide or print film.
- Have large laser-print enlargements made at a copy store.

To Photograph Directly from the Screen

- To eliminate reflections, photograph the screen in a darkened room, allowing the camera to select the exposure. It will be approximately 1/8 of a second. These prints can be enlarged by color laser print.
- Use a tripod and cable release or delayed timer function (to avoid camera shake).
- For a slide show, use Ektachrome, Fujichrome, or Agfachrome film.
- To make color prints, use Kodacolor, Fujicolor, or Agfacolor film.

Ways to Transform Black-and-White Computer Copies

- Print one image on several different colors of printer paper. Cut out portions of the image and make a collage in many colors. These layers could be fringed, folded, curled, and glued together to make a bas-relief print.

- Print on fadeless paper cut to size.

- Print on transparency film. Cut or tear fadeless paper to fit appropriately underneath a transparency film image. Glue the fadeless paper collage to a base, then tape the edges of the transparency over it, covering the edges with a mat. Supports for transparency film presentations, available at photocopy stores, make perfect mats.

- Cut up the print and combine it in a collage with fadeless paper, based on the geometric forms of Art Deco designs.

- Print it on white copy paper and hand color with colored pencil, markers, pastels, or paint. This image can be cut up, stretched, repeated, and combined with fadeless paper and black marker to make stunning Art Deco-style compositions.

To Manipulate Your Own Photographs on the Screen

- Use a scanner and appropriate software to scan an image to your computer.

- Use a digital camera and dispense with film altogether, working directly from disk. View from screen or print out.

- Have a print or negative transferred to disk at your local camera store.

Microsoft Word Sizes and Fonts

12 Bodoni MT Ultra Bold

24 Bodoni

48 Bodo

22, New Bertolina MT,

14 New Bertolina

36, Klang NT,

48 KLANG NT

12, Geneva

20 Geneva

26 Geneva

24 COOPER BLACK, ABCDE FGHIJKLMNOP QRSTUVWXYZ

72 Cooper

24 MESQUITE ABCDEFGHIJKLMNOPQRSTUVWXYZ

28 MESQUITE ABCDEF GHIJKLMNOPQRSTUVWXYZ

18 Hobo abcdefghijklmn

opqrstuvwxyz

24 HOBO ABCDEFGHIJKLMN OPQRSTUVWXYZ

24 CASLON OPEN FACE ABCDEFGHIJK LMNOPQRSTU VWXYZ

24 B. KAUFMANN ABCDEFGHIJKLMN OPQRSTUVWXYZ

24 ARIAL CONDENSED ABCDEFGHIJKLMNOPQR STUVWXYZ

24 CHICAGO Bold ABCDEFGHIJKLM NOPQRSTUVWXYZ

14 TIMES ABCDEFGHIJKLM NOPQRSTUVWXYZ

24 TIMES abcdefghi jklmnopqrstuvwxyz

Zapf Dingbats

PROJECT 9–1
ALPHABET SOUP

FOR THE TEACHER Because even young students may have had an opportunity to type words on the computer, this first project is based on letters using different typefaces and font sizes. Modernists such as Charles Demuth (*I Saw the Figure Five in Gold*, 1928) and the Pop artists of the 1950s and 1960s felt that the *subject* of an artwork was unimportant. Sometimes their compositions consisted of nothing but words, or words combined with other images. Stuart Davis, Robert Rauschenberg, James Rosenquist, Tom Wesselman, Andy Warhol, and Roy Lichtenstein combined words with shapes and color to make memorable compositions. Artist Barbara Kruger, who had been a magazine editor, became so fascinated with words that her artwork consists primarily of large lettering as commentary on modern life. Some of her titles are: *Untitled: Use Only as Directed; Untitled: Buy Me, I'll Change Your Life*; and *Untitled: Give Me All You've Got.*

Vocabulary

disk	save
rotate	flip
repeat	enlarge
font	serif
sans serif	bold
italic	center-of-interest
capitals	upper case
lower case	free-hand
cursor	overlapping
emphasis	repetition
texture	shape
proof	

Preparation Discuss the word *font* with students, explaining that it was a term primarily used by graphic designers in the past, but now is understood by most people who use a computer. Talk about font size and define terms such as *bold* and *italic*. Before the computer was available, some artists "drew" pictures on an ordinary typewriter, using only the letters X or O.

If your computer has a drawing program, have students combine larger letters and smaller letters. These can be overlapped, filled with texture, turned, flipped, repeated, and combined with geometric shapes. For letter forms that can be drawn freehand, use a lettering book as a reference.

Alternative Projects

NON-COMPUTER ALPHABET SOUP This project is easily adapted by having students draw one letter in different sizes and fonts on small pieces of tracing paper and arranging them in a pleasing composition. Students do not have to solve all their problems at once, but by experimenting with a movable arrangement of different fonts and shapes, they can make one larger composition. If you have access to a computer, you can make sheets of letters to be cut up or traced. They could also be projected on a screen or wall by printing on an overhead transparency. Libraries have many type specimen or calligraphic books.

STENCIL ALPHABET Have students select one or more letters from a 4- or 6-inch cardboard stencil alphabet (available at hardware stores) to trace around with changeable markers, crayons, or pastels. The letters may be overlapped or partially run off the page.

ONE-WORD COMPOSITION If students are intrigued with this project, suggest they use only one word to make a composition. The word could be sports- or action-related and could reflect a student's favorite pastime (art, poetry, food, hanging out at the mall). A drawing could be created to illustrate that one word.

Interdisciplinary Connection
LANGUAGE ARTS
ART HISTORY RESEARCH REPORT As students have more access to images from the Internet or can scan images into a report, each student can take responsibility for researching the life of a different artist. This might include a picture of the artist, a description of his or her life, and some images of artwork created by the artist.

PROJECT 9–1   ALPHABET SOUP

Materials

pencils

copy paper

computer

Directions   Create a composition using one letter in a variety of fonts (alphabets) and sizes (ranging from 8 to 72 or more; sizes in some drawing programs may go higher).

1. Select one letter of the alphabet, such as your own initial. Before beginning the actual project, find how large or how small you can make the letters. Experiment with other changes you can make such as *outlining, shadows, bold,* or *italic*. Try *upper-case* and *lower-case* letters. (These are old printing terms from the days when printers set type by hand from cases where the type was stored. The capital letters were kept in the upper case, while the small letters were in the lower case.) These experiments are helpful as you learn how to manipulate the cursor.

2. Many famous artists in the past have found that a combination of letters and shapes helps to unify a composition. Computers allow you to make circles, rectangles, spheres, and ovals of various sizes. Begin by overlapping and repeating some of these shapes. You may use a drawing tool to draw the letter *free-hand*.

3. Whether you are creating something realistic or nonrealistic, think about your *center-of-interest*. (It is seldom in the center.) This is the largest, darkest, or brightest area of the composition, and may be the first thing the viewer will see. You may have to add *texture* to one area to make it *dominate*. Sometimes in a composition that will hang on a wall, the larger areas may be nearer the bottom to keep it from looking as if it might topple over.

4. Consider *repetition*. You will want to fill most of the surface and might find that if you use a shape in one place, it needs to be repeated in another for *balance*. After you think you have filled in every place that needs to be filled and the composition is complete, do a trial *proof*. Look at it carefully to see if you have enough white space and if you have a dominant area. Did you use one font or font size in more than one area? If you are working in color, try to have one color dominate.

5. If your print is black and white, you might be able to make an entirely different version by adding color with colored pencils or paint. Again, select a dominant color just as you would when working in color on the computer.

PROJECT 9-2
GRAPHIC DESIGN: A PUBLIC SERVICE FLYER

FOR THE TEACHER   Students are accustomed to seeing advertisements wherever they look; billboards, television, magazines, the newspaper, and grocery stores. This is an opportunity to teach them that someone has a career in art *designing* and making decisions about what kind of lettering, color, and images they see. Graphic designers frequently rely on computers to do work that was formerly done by hand (such as lettering). Students need to understand that even with such tools to make the work easier, graphic artists continue to rely on such principles and elements of art as line, shape, space, color, emphasis, repetition, etc. Originality and creativity separate interesting and exciting ideas from the ordinary.

Show examples of posters by such artists as Alphonse Mucha, Peter Max, Toulouse-Lautrec, and Andy Warhol. Your local video-rental and grocery stores may be willing to save outdated posters and advertising for you to use as examples.

Vocabulary

space	asymmetry	image	rule of thirds
emphasis	balance	graphic design	

Preparation   This assignment is to make a public service advertisement for an event at school (real or imaginary). It could be an announcement for a Spring concert, open house, a play, Library Week, Bus Driver Appreciation Week, Nurse Appreciation Week, National Education Week, or an art exhibition. These events happen at all schools, so posters for each one of these occasions could be assigned to various students or groups of students in the class. These designs could be placed on a school's web site or sent home in newsletters. A friendly competition could be done to select the most effective design to be used on each of the flyers.

Ask students to look around their homes for examples of graphic designs that they could bring in to share. Suggest they look on the fronts of CDs, cereal boxes, and T-shirts. Have students analyze such examples, noticing how space or color is used for emphasis.

Alternative Graphics Projects

COMPUTER LETTERING ON OVERHEAD TRANSPARENCY If several identical *large* posters are needed, computer lettering can be photocopied onto an overhead transparency, then projected and traced with pencil onto posterboard. Students could use marker or watercolor to fill in the letters.

CREATE YOUR OWN WEB SITE Have students design a web page for themselves. They need to think about what is special about them, and how they would present themselves. Tell them that a web site should have basic information each time, but if they can't think about what would be appropriate to put on one for now, suggest they consider what they might be in the future, and how they might advertise themselves then.

DESIGN A BOOKPLATE This is another "real" assignment in that the bookplates can actually be printed and used. Suggest students make a border, then include enough lines in the bookplate for a name, date, and other information. They could make six bookplates to the sheet of paper. Perhaps the student's own favorite book would be an inspiration for a design.

DIRECTORY OR YEARBOOK COVER Students are really into school names and mascots. A friendly competition for something that would actually be published is usually a welcome assignment, especially meaningful, of course, for the students whose designs are chosen.

T-SHIRT DESIGNS Most commercial designs on T-shirts are a combination of words and images. Have students think about what they would like to see imprinted on a T-shirt of their own. They could advertise their school mascot, a special team, or a place they would love to visit. Photo stores will now transfer original designs onto T-shirts, so having a design printed is a reality.

COMPUTER-DESIGNED MAGAZINE COVER Have students bring in magazines from home, and notice how the typeface and cover images give a good idea of what is inside. Upscale, expensive magazines often use traditional type with serifs and have rather restrained, conservative covers. Gossip magazines frequently have the pictures of celebrities and screaming headlines on the front, to tempt one to read the inside while standing in the grocery line. While the entire page might not be done on the computer, the title, border and other writing could be computer-generated.

DESIGN A TRAVEL POSTER Almost all states and countries stage special events to attract tourists. Examples are the balloon races at Albuquerque, New Mexico; folk festivals and beauty pageants at Branson, Missouri; dance festivals in Europe; surfing in California or Hawaii; the Indian Market in Santa Fe, New Mexico; the Music Festival in Salzburg; and so on. Students can design a computer-generated travel poster. If a scanner is available, this will allow you to use travel pictures taken from magazines or personal photographs for images. If not, images can be drawn by hand.

DESIGN A CEREAL BOX ON TAGBOARD The front of a cereal box will use letters of different sizes (it could incorporate the student's name). A scanned (or pasted) photo of a sports hero or comic character would also be appropriate. Have students look at cereal boxes at home and bring in examples to get ideas. Design all four sides and the top of the box.

DESIGN A LOGO FOR A BUSINESS CARD OR STATIONERY Talk with students about logos. The business itself might suggest a shape in which letters could be placed (a trucking company might have the name contained within a truck shape). It might have a slogan or a visual image to complement the name (perhaps the student's own name).

DESIGN A BORDER Create a border for an award certificate or commemoration of a special occasion. Although a certificate is just a piece of paper, it represents a significant event in someone's life. Certificates are awarded for excellence in sports, academic subjects, or art. A certificate could be made for graduation from Kindergarten, elementary school, or middle school. Software programs already exist for making borders, but student-designed borders can be much more interesting because of using a variety of line widths, images in the corners, and shapes.

A FLAG DESIGN Most countries' flags contain simple geometric shapes and bold colors that can be seen from a distance. Challenge students to think about new countries being founded around the world. How would one go about designing a flag for a new country that would be different from other countries? Challenge students to make a personal or seasonal flag that can fly from their home or school.

Interdisciplinary Project
SOCIAL STUDIES
CAREERS IN GRAPHIC DESIGN Have students research various careers available to the person who can do graphic design either with or without a computer. Some suggestions are: designers in fashion; advertising; magazines; newspapers and catalogues; animators; cartoonists; commercial printers.

PROJECT 9–2 GRAPHIC DESIGN: A PUBLIC SERVICE FLYER

STUDENT PAGE

Materials

computer

pencil

copy paper

disk

Directions The purpose of a flyer is to give information: Who? What? Why? When? Where? If you are advertising an event, the primary information is What? The other information is secondary.

Certain principles in designing a computer-generated flyer should be remembered:

- Make the primary message the largest. Try to keep it on one or two lines, using as few words as possible.

- Secondary information (date, time, location) can be printed much smaller, perhaps set aside in boxes.

- Make reading easy. Avoid putting words diagonally or using a complex font.

- Try not to put too much information on the flyer. Empty space is a great eye-catcher around small bits of type or a small picture. A drawing that is used in addition to the lettering might be a large, simple outline (lettering could be inside the outline).

- Create a sense of motion by directing the viewer's eye. Most readers read across, starting at the top left.

- Balance can be symmetrical (*formal:* everything the same on both sides of an imaginary dividing line in the center) or asymmetrical (*informal:* often the main image is at one of the intersections of an imaginary tic-tac-toe division).

- Dividing the available background space might help in the design. These divisions might be diagonal, horizontal, vertical, circular, or a combination of more than one. A diagonal line creates a sense of motion. These dividing lines may not be visible in the finished product, but they help in organizing the components of the design.

- Limit your color somewhat. Black and white used in combination with three to five other colors should be more than enough for anything.

- If you plan to use color, do the lettering in a dark enough color so it can be easily seen from a distance. Even if you cannot print in color, hand-coloring could be done later with markers. For unity, use only one color for lettering.

1. Write all the information that will go on the flyer. Make thumbnail sketches on copy paper to consider where you will place the information.

2. Think about pictures that will go with the information. For example, a line drawing of a musical instrument might be suitable for the announcement of a concert. You may decide you would like to use a border. Try several ideas on this piece of paper before you select the design you intend to do on the computer.

3. You can begin working on the screen with either the lettering or an image. You may be able to move either one around, previewing it on screen until you find the best placement. It may be that you will have to print the drawing on the paper first, then print the lettering over the same piece of paper.

4. Check to see if your composition is balanced and if enough open space remains to make it interesting.

Drawn from MacMillan's Illustrated Stand
and Novels, 1896 A. A. Turbayne

PROJECT 9–3 COMPUTER CITY

FOR THE TEACHER   For as long as there have been cities, artists have loved to do paintings of them. Vermeer did a cityscape of Delft, Holland. Many Renaissance artists did detailed paintings of their cities, such as Lorenzetti's *Good Government in the City*. In the twentieth century Joseph Stella captured the frantic pace of the city with his impressions of traffic movement. Red Grooms did witty drawings and sculptures of the city such as his *Ruckus, New York* and *Chicago*. Other artists who loved to draw the city were John Marin, realists such as George Bellows and Richard Estes, and Robert Henri, a member of the "Ashcan School." You may be able to find drawings or photographs of cities near you.

Vocabulary

horizon

foreground

middle-ground

background

depth

overlap

texture

proportion

value

Preparation   If you live near a big city, ask students to close their eyes and think about what they see when they look at the city. Ask them to think about buildings they see on the horizon. Are all the details clear, or do they seem to mostly be boxes with tiny lines on them? Help students to think about foreground, middle-ground, and background when they are drawing a city.

Perhaps the city itself is far off in the distance, and hills and trees could be drawn in the foreground. Encourage students to make buildings facing frontwards. This first assignment is not the place to teach perspective.

Discuss the several ways to achieve depth:

Overlapping.   In this case, the tops of the buildings in the middle-ground and foreground will overlap the bottoms of the buildings behind them.

Placement on the page.   Things farther away are higher. Buildings in the middle ground might start almost halfway up the page. A tree in the foreground might be almost the height of the entire composition.

Size.   Make things farther away look smaller; closer things, larger.

Detail.   Closer things have much greater detail; farther away they might be hazy.

Do this project first yourself. Then demonstrate to students any tools available on your particular computer program that would allow them to make buildings of various sizes primarily composed of geometric shapes. Show them how to automatically add texture and color if they desire. Also demonstrate how they can move shapes around from one place to another, or erase them if necessary. Have students explore drawing tools that will allow them to make trees, automobiles, people, street lights, or any other details of the city.

Alternative Project

PERSPECTIVE DRAWING Older students could do a perspective drawing of a building on a street corner using two-point perspective. This is the principle of making a simple three-dimensional box, adding details such as shop windows, awnings, street lights, sidewalks, and people. Having lines (later erased) that go to the two vanishing points will keep everything in proportion.

Drawn after *Looking Along Broadway Toward Grace Church*, 1981, Red Grooms, Marlborough Gallery, New York City

PROJECT 9–3   COMPUTER CITY

STUDENT PAGE

Materials

pencil

paper

computer

Directions   When drawing buildings on the computer, think about special buildings in your town. You may have to bring in pictures you cut from the newspaper or magazines to help you with details. When you see a cityscape, you mostly see the tops of buildings. While you might make rectangles, usually the bottoms of the buildings have other buildings or trees in front of them.

1. The cityscape you draw on the computer will have greater depth if you think about *proportion*. If you have a chance to actually look at the city, you will notice that buildings in the *background* are quite small and you can see very little detail such as windows or even colors. Most of them are almost the same color. The background is placed near the top of the drawing. Even trees seen in the background all blur together and are somewhat hazy.

2. Buildings in the *middle-ground* (near the middle of the drawing) will have more detail. Details such as balconies and windows will be clearer. The tops of buildings might have boxes on the roof (to hide elevators and air conditioning). Trees will be larger. The tops of the middle-ground buildings might *overlap* the bottoms of buildings in the background.

3. Naturally you see much greater details in buildings in the *foreground*, which will be near the bottom of the composition. Because these are closest, you might see shop windows, cars in the streets, even people. The buildings are much larger and may overlap the buildings in the middle-ground. Sometimes you see the tops of trees peeking behind the buildings.

4. When you have drawn the buildings in the three levels, look at the overall composition to see if you can improve it by adding more detail such as trees (remember the closer they are, the larger they appear). Perhaps some of the buildings could have some *texture* added by using drawing tools. The use of *value* (areas of dark and light) and repetition will make the picture more interesting.

PROJECT 9–4
RADIAL DESIGN

FOR THE TEACHER   Students of all ages might be introduced to computer graphics through the use of a nonobjective design. Artists such as Wassily Kandinsky, Joan Miro´, and Helen Frankenthaler composed pictures that did not always have a recognizable subject, but were arrangements of line and color. However, even an abstract composition will be more effective if an effort is made to unify it through an idea.

Vocabulary

radiate

overlap

texture

balance

freehand

Preparation

Try this yourself first on the same software the students will use (it is fun). There are infinite variations on this project, and you may come up with unique subjects that could be made with radial designs (faces, animals, food). I usually do not believe in showing examples to students, as they tend to copy the example rather than develop their own unique solutions; but in this case, your examples may serve as springboards for their ideas.

Alternative Projects

NONOBJECTIVE DESIGN Suggest that students select one of the following ideas as a starting point for nonobjective compositions: symmetrical balance, asymmetrical balance, cool colors, warm colors, small shapes, large shapes, curving shapes, geometric shapes, lines, beginning at a corner, combinations of straight and curved lines. Suggest they hide something somewhere in the composition that will be difficult to see unless people look closely.

THREE-DIMENSIONAL FLOWER GARDEN If you are printing in black and white, this could be printed on several different colors of copy paper. To make a three-dimensional picture, cut out shapes from different colors and slit them on the edges, curling the edges slightly. Students can share leftover printed paper with their classmates. If this is printed in color, print several copies, leaving one paper whole and cutting details from other copies to layer. Glue these extra "flowers" directly on top of the bottom paper. Stems can be added with green fadeless paper strips.

SYMMETRY Most graphics programs allow for repetition of one design many times. An original design could be repeated once, four times, or twenty times.

KALEIDOSCOPE This is a slightly more controlled project than the radial design project, in that regular repetition is encouraged. Have students use line to divide the screen in half horizontally, then vertically, then diagonally from corner to corner, going both directions before using ovals and circles to complete the design.

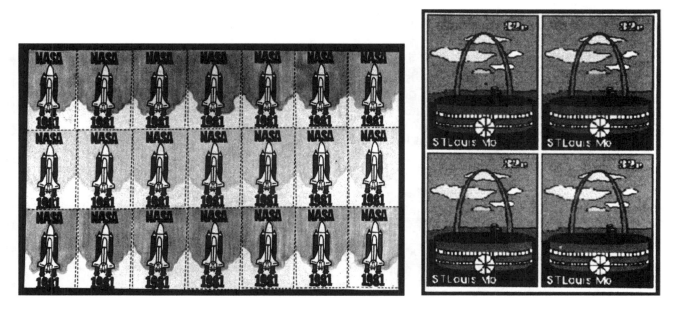

Computer graphics teacher Timothy Smith of the Parkway School District, St. Louis, Missouri, has his students design a postage stamp, which they then repeat to make a "sheet" of stamps.

PROJECT 9–4   RADIAL DESIGN

Materials

computer

computer paper

marker (if printing black and white)

Directions   You will make a design that will radiate (go out) from a center point. Your basic shape could be small ovals, circles, triangles, or rectangles. If you draw this freehand, you might begin with small flowers, making them gradually larger until they bump the edges of the screen.

1. Make a minimum of at least 16 shapes, radiating from the center and working all the way to the edge of the screen. Overlap at least four or more of the shapes. Begin with a tiny shape somewhere near the center of the paper. Make several similar, slightly larger shapes all the way around that point. Continue to make gradually larger shapes, working from the center outwards until they "run off" the screen.

2. Now examine the shapes you have made. Could you put texture in some of them? Could you make some of them very dark? Your center-of-interest is near the center of the paper. Can you work from dark to light? Or light to dark?

3. Where is the surprise? Could you put something in the picture that is different—an odd color or a shape that is different from all the rest? Maybe you could draw something (like a tiny person or car made of geometric shapes) that seems *alien*. It might even be your name or initials hidden someplace.

4. If this is printed in black and white, use marker to carefully color parts of it. Of course, you can color it entirely, but it could also be nice just to color some of it.

  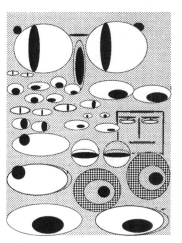

PHOTOGRAPHY AND FILM

Although photography is not often taught in elementary schools, middle schools frequently offer photo developing and printing in black and white. Having taught photography in both elementary and high schools, I know firsthand how exciting it is for students at all levels to see their mental visions translated to film. This section does not contain technical advice on teaching photography because of a limited need. If you are interested in teaching photography at your school, talk with a hobbyist or professional at your local camera store to find out which equipment and supplies would be necessary for beginning.

Scheduling is important because a small darkroom can accommodate only a few students at a time. You can convert an inside room, a large closet, or an entire classroom into a darkroom with the addition of a safelight. If you choose to do this, a table can be your developing area.

Many courses for students and adults involve simply taking photos to learn about the process of being a photographer. The film is professionally developed. Students do photo essays, explore their town, take portraits of themselves and friends, record a field trip, and in general learn to get beyond the "point and shoot" mentality.

Sometimes one camera (the school's or the teacher's) is the only one available. If a parent or older student is available to work closely with the students, each student can have the opportunity to expose two frames, which can then be professionally developed and exhibited.

RECESS PHOTOS

This involves taking one or two rolls of film on one camera (perhaps a throw-away) and having them developed. Work out a schedule that assigns each student to take two photos at recess of two other students (to make sure you have every single student featured in your display). Talk about some of the activities they could be doing, such as ball games, playing on equipment, or running. Students who no longer have "recess breaks" could take photos during art class, showing students and their artwork. Discuss getting in close enough to eliminate a distracting background.

PHOTOS BROUGHT FROM HOME

All About Me   On posterboard, have a student assemble photos of him- or herself from infancy to present age, including family and friends. This assignment challenges students to really look at composition in photos, noticing backgrounds, contrast, clarity, and emphasis. Ask them to write their own captions. Make sure names are on the backs of the photos, and do not permanently glue them in place.

Autobiography   A single snapshot for a school photo could be scanned into the computer (or pasted on a computer report) and be the basis for a written autobiography. Even young students could dictate a report to an older mentor (upper-level student).

PROJECT 9-5
LINE DRAWING WITH A FLASHLIGHT

FOR THE TEACHER   This project challenges students to draw in the air with light instead of on paper with a pencil. In a regular photography course, students' first experience with the camera might be to take "air pictures" with empty cameras. In this project, students must rehearse the "drawing" actions they will make while the camera lens is open in the dark.

Vocabulary

line

emphasis

Preparation   To actually expose the film, students will work in total darkness using penlights, flashlights, or strings of holiday lights. The one thing that will distinguish good from so-so composition is the full use of the picture plane. If this project is done with black-and-white film, the colored "gels" that could be used with colored film are not necessary. If using colored film, students can create some interesting compositions by moving to different places in the dark or by using strings of colored lights. Use tape to mark positions on the floor where students can stand to be sure they are in the picture.

The camera must be set on a tripod where it won't be tripped over. One person must take charge of keeping the camera's shutter open for at least one minute using a cable release or delayed timer. On most cameras this is done by depressing the shutter while the camera is set on B (B stands for *bulb*, a leftover term from the early days of photography when a camera's shutter was tripped by squeezing a bulb at the end of a tube). One- to two-minute exposures are normal with 200 ISO film.

PROJECT 9–5 LINE DRAWING WITH A FLASHLIGHT

STUDENT PAGE

Materials

flashlights (standard and penlight)

colored plastic report covers (red, yellow, green, blue, magenta) cut into 4 X 4-inch squares

clear tape

tripod

cable release (if it will fit your camera)

strands of colored or tiny white lights

completely dark room (an interior classroom or a long storage closet will work)

35mm camera with a B (bulb) setting

color or black-and-white film

Directions   Normally if the film in a camera is exposed for a long period of time, it simply turns white (overexposed). If there is not enough light, it may remain black (underexposed). Drawing with a pinpoint of light from a flashlight takes advantage of both of these qualities by exposing tiny amounts of film at a time. The developed picture will give a dark background with light lines. If you work with colored film, you can cover either the light of the flashlight or the camera lens with colored plastic to also give various colored lines.

1. Work with groups of two to four students to carefully *plan* your line drawing with light. You can do an outline drawing of a friend, remembering to keep the light pointed toward the camera. If two friends are seated on stools, two people could use flashlights to trace all around your friends *and* around the stools, making a composition to completely fill the space.

2. Fill the picture! If you just stand in place holding a flashlight pointed toward the camera, and move it back and forth across your body at the waist, you will end up with a photo that will look like a couple of scribble lines in the center of the picture. It is important to use the whole picture frame for your composition, just as you would use all of the paper in a painting or drawing.

Options

FOR COLORED FILM If several people have flashlights, each one can have a different colored plastic "gel" (colored plastic) in front of the light. For example, each can stand in a different place and do an air drawing for five seconds of a subject such as their own hand or a flower, then turn out their lights. They can rotate to a different location, then do another lighted hand drawing at a different level (squatting or holding it high). This could be done many times in total darkness, and the only thing that might be seen on the film is hands or flowers drawn in many different colors of light.

GEOMETRIC DESIGNS Your composition could be completely abstract. For example, two people could make circles, squares, or triangles of different sizes all over the picture plane—high, low, in the center. Or perhaps you could write something in the air (remembering it will be backwards).

STRINGS OF HOLIDAY LIGHTS If three students pose themselves in different positions and stand perfectly still, they can be silhouetted by holding strings of lights behind them, first high, then taken to the floor, back up high, and back down again, or zigzagged at different heights.

PROJECT 9–6
THE BLUEPRINT PHOTOGRAM

FOR THE TEACHER   One of the earliest photographic processes that did not require a darkroom was that of cyanotype. A modern-day version of this process is the *blueprint*. The blueprint process was used in Victorian times to make what Victorians called *Sun Gardens*. Although professionals were using cameras by that time, this process was used to make scientific photographic records of plant life. Objects such as ferns or leaves were laid on light-sensitized paper and held in place with glass.

Your students can make photograms by using opaque objects—such as photographic negatives, lace, shells, leaves, sticks, feathers, raffia, or designs cut from black construction paper—that will block out the light. They could also draw pictures on overhead plastic with black permanent marker and place that on top of the blueprint paper. When the paper is exposed to sunlight, images are made, then developed in the fumes of ammonia. An alternative blueprint process that is more expensive but allows developing in water is Nature Print® paper available through art supply catalogues. Light-sensitized cloth squares for the cyanotype process are also available through these catalogues.

Vocabulary

photogram	blueprint
light sensitized	composition
variety	space

Preparation   In dim light, cut the paper into usable sheets (it comes in large sheets or rolls). Keep inside a black plastic bag until needed. Look in the Yellow Pages under "Blueprints" for sources where you may purchase paper by the roll or cut sheet. Household ammonia is adequate for this project (it needs to be changed at least daily). If you are doing the developing, industrial-strength ammonia is available at industrial cleaning or blueprint suppliers. (I have used it safely with students, but it has a very strong odor.) **SAFETY NOTE: Caution students to take a deep breath and hold it before inserting their paper, and to keep the developing jars with the open side *down* to avoid taking a big whiff of ammonia.** Large prints can be developed overnight inside an upside-down cardboard box (the ammonia dissipates by morning).

Alternative Projects

NATURE PRINTS   Using the same blueprint process described, select a subject such as butterflies, insects, fish, mammals, flowers, trees, etc., and photocopy a "class set" on overhead transparencies from an encyclopedia. This would give you enough reusable individual copies for each student to have an individual transparency. They could draw a "scientific image" with a transparency marker and write a few sentences directly on the reproduction transparencies (which could be cleaned for reuse later). Any of these diverse subjects could also be combined with natural objects and placed on blueprint paper for exposure. For older students, this blueprint could be the cover for a research project on such a subject.

PHOTOGRAPHIC SELF-PORTRAIT PHOTOGRAMS (NON-DARKROOM)   Take black-and-white close-up photos of each student and have them developed for high contrast; then enlarge on an overhead transparency to approximately 8 × 10 inches. An alternative is to enlarge students' largest black-and-white or color school photos on transparency film.

PROJECT 9–6   THE BLUEPRINT PHOTOGRAM

STUDENT PAGE

Materials

Diazo black-line positive dry reproduction paper (available by the roll or cut
    paper at blueprint supply houses)

ammonia (household or industrial-strength)

several 1-gallon plastic mayonnaise jars

small plastic bottle caps

11 × 14-inch plexiglass or plate glass
    (tape edges)

$8^1/_2$ × 11-inch copy paper

black construction paper

scissors

cutting knives for older students

overhead transparencies

transparency markers

colored pencils (*optional*)

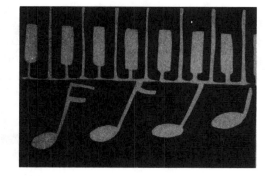

Directions

1. Plan your arrangement before removing the copy paper from the bag
   because it will quickly change color (be exposed). For practice, arrange the
   images you will use to block out light on newsprint or copy paper of the
   same size. Black construction paper can be cut into almost any shape and
   combined with objects you have brought from home. (CAUTION: If using a
   cutting knife, always remember to keep the non-cutting hand behind the
   cutting edge.)

2. Remove the blueprint paper from the bag and work very quickly on your
   arrangement. The actual exposure time may be from 10 seconds to 3 minutes, depending on the time of the year and how close the sun is to the
   Earth where you live. Cover the design with a piece of plexiglass or glass to
   hold everything flat and place it in sunlight (perhaps on the floor near a window) or under a photoflood lamp. The surface will turn from yellow to
   white when the exposure is complete.

3. The blueprint may be developed in large upside-down plastic jars filled with
   ammonia fumes. These inverted (open side down) jars will be on a work surface, and fresh ammonia will be in small bottle caps sitting right at the center of the opening. Keep the jar upside down (to prevent the fumes from
   escaping), and quickly put your blueprint paper inside, with the exposed
   (yellow) side facing inwards. Quickly replace the gallon jug over the bottle
   cap to allow the ammonia fumes to develop the blueprint.

4. The blueprint may be matted (put in a frame), or you can use colored pencil to further enhance it.

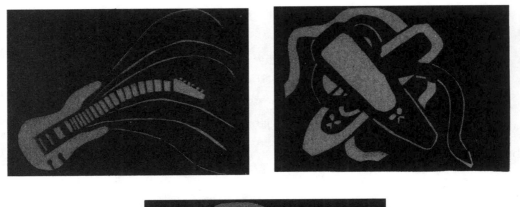

Student work. These 5 × 7-inch blueprints were made by cutting stencil designs in black construction paper. The guitar picture was combined with a texture screen made by printing computer texture on an overhead transparency. They were exposed and developed as described in this project.

PROJECT 9-7
VIDEO PRODUCTION

FOR THE TEACHER Most schools have a video camcorder available for a special purpose, or perhaps a parent would bring one from home, assisting students in a video production.

Vocabulary

camcorder

script

storyboard

zoom

pan

fade

transition

title cards

tripod

editing

Preparation Students need to prepare a script and "storyboard," which would have a story line and rough sketches of what the camera would see. If costumes are necessary, these should be brought in and a "dress rehearsal" conducted with the camera person doing everything he or she would do if film were being used.

Things to Remember

- Have a plan. Students should make a storyboard.
- Make title cards in advance.
- If the camera is on a tripod, you will avoid camera shake. It can scan vertically, pan horizontally, or be fixed to view an entire scene.
- Rather than moving a camera unnecessarily, have the people in front of it move. Avoid zooming, tilting, or widening the lens, unless you have a good reason for it.
- If using a panning motion (side to side), do it slowly enough so the viewer has time to see detail.
- For best results, have the light source behind the camera.
- If you will be editing later, allow an extra five seconds before and after each scene.

Suggestions for a Production

REENACTMENT OF HISTORY Students reenact a moment in the history of the community, state, or country.

SURVEY OF ART Students make a report on the life of a particular artist by showing reproductions of work taken from a book, stopping the filming until the picture has been focused, then telling the name of the artist and the name of the artwork.

BE AN ARTIST Individual students dress up to portray a particular famous artist. This could include pictures of the work and discussion of daily life. Or a group of students research a group of artists such as the Impressionists, Hudson River School, Ashcan painters, or Artists in a "Happening."

BE A WORK OF ART Students work in groups to produce living works of art. Help them select paintings or sculpture that they can reenact for the camcorder. Costumes and background would be a nice option to include.

ARCHITECTURAL REPORT If they have access to a camcorder and a parent willing to go with them, students make an architectural tour of the city or the neighborhood.

ADVERTISING Students write a television "ad" selling a product of their choice. This almost certainly would involve wearing costumes and props.

PERSONAL INTERVIEW This can be a personal interview of each person in the class. Have students pretend they are doing a video interview for a job or for a news program. They will need to write a personal biography before going on camera. These could be two-personal dialogues, with one person being the interviewer and one the interviewee. Students could also team up to interview various school personnel.

Storyboard

Title _____   Page _____ of _____
Date _____

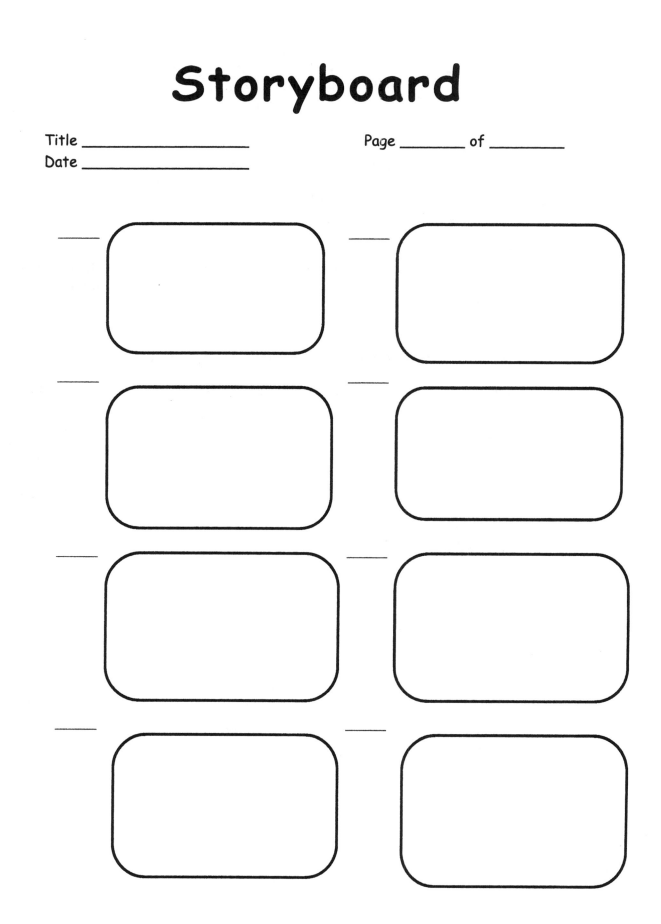

PROJECT 9-7   VIDEO PRODUCTION

Materials

video camera
film
cardboard
markers
storyboard
costumes

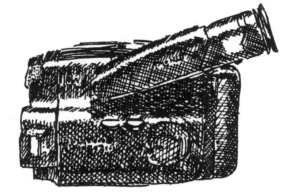

Directions

1. Plan ahead! Decide what it is that you want to "say" with the film you are making. Things to consider:
   - scenery
   - script: title, story line, length of production
   - ending
   - dressing the "set"
   - costuming
   - sound
   - transitions
   - title cards
   - credits

2. When everyone knows what he or she is supposed to do, have a dress rehearsal before actually filming. A producer/director could keep everyone on track. Perhaps you need a narrator to provide dialogue between scenes.

3. If editing equipment is available in your library or district, it is a good idea to take advantage of it in order to edit out awkward transitions and "tighten up" the video.